Foundations of Health Psychology

Foundations of Health Psychology

Ron Roberts, Tony Towell, John F. Golding

with contributions from Antje Mueller and Dawn Baker Towell

palgrave
macmillan

First published 2001 by
PALGRAVE
Houndmills, Basingstoke, Hampshire RG21 6XS and
175 Fifth Avenue, New York, N.Y. 10010
Companies and representatives throughout the world

PALGRAVE is the new global academic imprint of St. Martin's Press LLC
Scholarly and Reference Division and Palgrave Publishers Ltd (formerly
Macmillan Press Ltd).

ISBN-13: 978-0-333-73858-0
ISBN-10: 0-333-73858-6

This book is printed on paper suitable for recycling and
made from fully managed and sustained forest sources.
Logging, pulping and manufacturing processes are
expected to conform to the environmental regulations
of the country of origin.

A catalogue record for this book is available
from the British Library.

Typeset by Footnote Graphics, Warminster, Wilts

Printed and bound in Great Britain by
CPI Antony Rowe, Chippenham and Eastbourne

Contents

part 6 — Deconstructing Health Psychology

249

List of Tables

List of Figures

List of Psychometric Tests

Preface

We have organised this text around a series of six themes, all of which bring an openly critical stance to the emergence and development of health psychology. We have chosen this in part because of what we feel to be the largely uncritical way in which health psychology has usually been presented to audiences. To present material uncritically can often exclude the audience from the cut and thrust of debate which is essential to any discipline and obscures the means by which knowledge is realised in science. This is a young discipline and needs the stimulus provided by an open questioning of its motives and methods. We hope, therefore, that the text gives some refreshing angles on some of the perennial debates in psychology. The issue of what are appropriate levels of intervention for changing problematic behaviours features strongly, as does the emerging question of what are the most suitable methods for studying human beings in the health context. With so many rapid developments in many fields of science – many of which affect psychology – we have devoted no small consideration to the relationship between health psychology and other related disciplines.

The text opens with an introduction to the history, main concepts and research methods. This reviews the development of health psychology in recent years examining the various reasons – philosophical, social, political and academic – for the growth of the discipline. The core ideas behind the emergence of health psychology are examined, including the changing nature of disease and concepts of health (both physical and mental), and a critical review of methods for assessing health status and quality of life. There is an emphasis on health psychology as a research-based discipline, together with a critical assessment of the most popular methodologies employed. This is followed by a broad overview of the basic physiological systems of the body, with a view to reviewing the main biological pathways through which psychological experience is translated into physiological and medical outcomes. New research in stress and psychoneuroimmunology (PNI) forms the background to this. The third part reviews data on what is usually considered to be the core foundation of health psychology – examining a range of behaviours which either compromise or enhance health, with a critical look at health promotion – emphasising the weaknesses of attempts to change behaviour at a purely individual level. This forms a logical link to Part 4, which focuses upon different forms of social organisation and their impact on health. Much of this research has not previously been presented to a psychological audience although the effects are mediated primarily through psychological means. Research examining relationships between physical and mental health and social class, gender, ethnicity and disability are extensively reviewed. Relationships between smaller-scale forms of social organisation (community, group, social supports and so forth) are also explored here.

Whilst the previous parts deal predominantly with the issue of disease causation and prevention, Part 5 considers how psychological knowledge is useful in the treatment and management of a range of disabling and chronic conditions. Finally, Part 6 returns to the themes introduced in the opening chapter and poses some questions regarding the nature of the discipline, its aims and methods and who stands to gain from its practise. Throughout the text we have included details of a range of popular psychometric instruments used in health research which should enable the reader to proceed to practical engagement in the field.

Acknowledgements

We would, of course, like to thank many people who have helped and influenced our thinking in preparing this book, and everyone whose encouragement and helpful advice has made it possible. We would also like to thank the many students who have engaged with us in developing the ideas expressed here. Our thanks go to our editor, Frances Arnold, whose friendly approach has made the process of producing the book easier than it might otherwise have been. Additional thanks to Frank Hucklebridge and Angela Clow for their helpful comments, and to Merry Cross, Rosalie Ferner, Dawn Baker Towell and, last but not least, Antje Mueller who have all managed to make us laugh and supported us well in the course of producing the finished article.

The authors and publisher wish to thank the following for their help in obtaining images and their permission to use these:

Box 2.2, The Physical Functioning Scale of the SF-36™ is reproduced with permission of QualityMetric Inc. The SF-36 is a trademark of the Medical Outcomes Trust, John E. Ware, Jr. All Rights Reserved.

Figure 2.1 is reproduced with permission of the BMJ Publishing Group from Hickey, A. M., Bury, G., O'Boyle, C. A., Bradley, F., O'Kelly, F. D. and Shannon, W. (1996) 'A New Short Form Individual Quality of Life Measure (SEIQoL-DW): Application in a Cohort of Individuals with HIV/AIDS', *British Medical Journal*, **313**: 29–33.

Figure 3.2 is adapted with permission of Thompson Learning Global Rights Group from Howell, D. C. (1992) *Statistical Methods for Psychology*, 3rd edn, Duxbury Press (Wadsworth Publishing Co.) Belmont, California.

Table 3.4 is reproduced with permission of the BMJ Publishing Group from Campbell, M. J., Julious, S. A. and Altman, D. G. (1995) 'Estimating Sample Sizes for Binary, Ordered Categorical, and Continuous Outcomes in Two Group Comparisons', *British Medical Journal*, **311**: 1145–8.

Figures 4.1 and 4.2 are reproduced with permission from Rosenzweig, M. R., Leiman, A. L. and Breedlove, S. M. (1995) *Biological Psychology*, 2nd edn, Sinauer Associates. MA.

Table 4.2 is adapted with permission of Thompson Learning Global Rights Group from Kalat, J.W. (1995) *Biological Psychology*, Brookes/Cole Publishing Co. California.

Figure 9.1 is adapted from Holman, C.D.J. and English, D.R. (1996) Ought Low Alcohol Intake to be Promoted for Health Reasons?' *Journal of the Royal Society of Medicine*, **89**: 123–9. Reproduced with permission of the Royal Society of Medicine.

Figure 13.3 is reproduced with permission of the BMJ Publishing Group from Sacker, A., Firth, D., Fitzpatrick, R., Lynch, K. and Bartley, M. (2000) 'Comparing Health Inequality in Men and Women: Prospective Study of Mortality 1986–1996', *British Medical Journal*, **320**: 1303–7.

Figure 13.2 and Tables 14.1 and 16.1 are adapted from *Health Inequalities*, Office for National Statistics, Crown Copyright 2000.

Figure 14.1 is reprinted from Arber, S. Copyright (1997) Comparing inequalities in women's and men's health: Britain in the 1990's. *Social Science and Medicine*, **44(b)**, pp. 773–87. With permission from Elsevier Science.

Table 14.2 is reproduced from *Social Science and Medicine*, **42**(4): 617–24, McIntyre, S., Hunt, K. and Sweeting, H. (1996) 'Gender Differences in Health. Are Things Really as Simple as they Seem?', Copyright (1996), with permission from Elsevier Science.

Figure 15.1 is adapted from Johnston, M. (1995) 'Models of Disability. British Psychological Society, Presidents' Award Lecture'. *The Psychologist*, **9**(5): 205–10. Reproduced with permission.

Figure 19.1 is reproduced with permission of the BMJ Publishing Group, adapted from Grønbæk, M., Becker, U., Johansen, D., Tønneson, H., Jensen, G. and Sørensen, T. I. A. (1998) 'Population Based Cohort Study of the Association between Alcohol Intake and Cancer of the Upper Digestive Tract', *British Medical Journal*, **317**: 844–8.

Every effort has been made to trace all the copyright-holders, but if any have been inadvertently overlooked the publishers will be pleased to make the necessary arrangements at the first opportunity.

Box 2.1 General Health Questionnaire (GHQ-12) © David Goldberg, 1978. Reproduced by permission of the Publishers, NFER-NELSON, Darville House, 2 Oxford Road East, Windsor, Berkshire SL4 1DF, England. All rights reserved.

The good life is one inspired by love and guided by knowledge
Bertrand Russell

Part 1
History, Concepts and Methods

Health Psychology is a new discipline. This means that its boundaries are still in the process of being forged, and consequently have not been fully grasped even by many psychologists. If one is to comprehend the potential of the discipline, then an appreciation of its scientific roots is essential. However, such a stance, common in most textbook treatments of health psychology still fails to tell us the whole story of why health psychology emerged in the late 20th century. To this must be added knowledge of the social context which has driven the scientific problems that the new discipline sets out to address. A major theme of this book therefore is to set the unfolding 'drama' of health psychology against a backdrop of social concerns; rising health care costs, social and economic inequality, ageing populations and AIDS.

The story begins with the changing conceptions of health which have fuelled demands for an approach to understanding health and well-being which is centred less on the precepts of biological medicine and more on identifying dimensions of human need and responding to them. The study of quality of life is now rightly seen as a cornerstone of both health psychology and modern medicine. Knowledge of the practical and ethical dilemmas contained within it is therefore essential for anyone hoping to participate in health psychology or indeed in other branches of health science. Similarly a broad overview of the range of tools and methodologies which can inform one's thinking and practice when conducting research is a necessary prerequisite to understanding how researchers present their findings and evaluating what they mean.

Historical and Conceptual Basis of Health Psychology

'The transition from a paradigm in crisis to a new one from which a new tradition of normal science can emerge is far from a cumulative process . . . Rather it is a reconstruction of the field from new fundamentals, a reconstruction that changes some of the field's most elementary theoretical generalizations.'

Thomas Kuhn (*The Structure of Scientific Revolutions*, 1970)

INTRODUCTION

In order to comprehend the emergence of health psychology in the 1980s and 1990s we need first to look at the model of health – the biomedical model which was then preeminent and which still informs much of the practise of modern medicine. In it a number of key assumptions can be identified regarding the *determinants of health, how ill-health should be treated* and *who should treat it.* The medical model regards the human body as if it were a very complicated mechanism, and the overwhelming majority of today's scientists likewise subscribe to a materialist philosophy which holds all life to be the manifestation of an evolving order of biological (read physico-chemical) complexity (Dennett, 1995). However, even if human beings are purely physical entities, this does not mean that it makes sense to treat them as if they exist only at the physical level of complexity and nothing more. In modern philosophical parlance, human beings are intentional agents – beings whose behaviour can at least sometimes be better predicted and explained by reference to their beliefs, goals and desires than by reference to their inner workings or design (Dennett, 1978).

The biomedical model holds that disease originates from purely physical causes, whether these be external agents such as bacteria and viruses or else precipitated internally by genetic factors or physiological changes in the body. Implicit in this formulation is the idea that deviations from optimal functioning (however defined) beyond some arbitrary point are to be considered an indication of ill-health. Health and illness are seen as irreconcilable opposites – and therefore to be healthy excludes the possibility of being ill. The idea that one's health may benefit or indeed may depend upon bodily challenges and illnesses is not a logical consequence of this way of construing health. It follows from this that the inevitable consequences of ageing are also to be regarded as unhealthy. Within this framework it is difficult to envisage human beings able to make peace with the realities of their physical and temporal existence. It seems only in isolation from these that one can hope to attain the nirvana of everlasting health enshrined in the ideology of medicine. This is not to deny the advantages inherent in medical practice, merely to point out part of what one perhaps unwittingly subscribes to in adhering to a strict biomedical model.

Responses to ill-health which seek to identify malfunctioning parts of the body and either restore them to their presumed normative functioning state or remove them, are entirely consistent with this philosophy of the body as machine. However, to be treated as a passive malfunctioning machine is not the sum total of what people want when they seek treatment from health professionals, and the notion that 'doctor knows best' is being increasingly called into question. The result has been less than total satisfaction with medical treatment and complaints of depersonalisation from some patients. A high proportion of patient complaints refer to poor attitudes, conduct and communication skills of attending staff (Lim, Tan, Goh and Ling, 1998; Yarnold, Michelson, Thompson and Adams, 1998), whilst analysis of physician consulting styles by Roter *et al.* (1999) has found that a narrow biomedical pattern of communication characterised by close-ended medical questions and biomedical talk accounted for almost one third of patient–physician encounters.

HEALTH AND ILLNESS

Given the aforementioned rationale for diagnosis and treatment, it follows that ill-health is best treated by medical practitioners, that is, those who subscribe to the medical model of ill-health. Whilst it may seem obvious today, it has not always been apparent that such states and processes as pregnancy, physical disability, behavioural problems or psychological disorder easily fall within its remit. That it now does so, and in fact appears to do so naturally (except perhaps for members of the above categories who are treated accordingly), is merely an indication of the psychological strength the medical model holds in the minds of people, following the undoubted political might with which the medical profession colonised these areas for itself (see, Foucault, 1965; Oakley, 1980; Szasz, 1991; Oliver and Barnes, 1998 for extended consideration of these issues).

Paradoxically, the expansionary zeal of medicine (Illich, 1977) has both directly and indirectly brought pressure to bear on traditional notions of health and illness. Directly, as we have seen above, as alternative modes of care have been brought within its boundaries, so they too have become subject to the metaphors of health and illness, which in turn has had to expand to accommodate them. Indirectly, growing awareness of the limitations of technological medicine (revealed most strongly in those areas where it is conceptually ill-equipped to deal with particular phenomena – usually those it has most recently expropriated) has brought demands to develop new means of evaluating health care and health interventions as the traditional health indicators based on physical morbidity and mortality do not accurately predict health-service usage (see Chapter 2). The development of these new health indicators has led in turn to new ideas on what constitutes health and illness (McDowell and Newell, 1987). Thus, notions of what constitutes health and illness, far from being static, have always been subject to reevaluation – perhaps more so than ever during the last one hundred years. A major transition occurred after the end of the Second World War. In the optimistic spirit of reconstruction which ensued, the World Health Organisation (WHO) set out to create a new agenda for understanding health and illness. Their oft-quoted definition states simply that,

Health is a state of complete physical, mental and social well-being, and not merely the absence of disease or infirmity. (WHO, 1946)

Accordingly, in the absence of ideal social, political or economic conditions people cannot be healthy. In the state of the world as it exists today it is therefore difficult to imagine how, given the remit of the WHO definition, anyone at all can be considered healthy. The WHO offered a more recent definition in the 1980s by emphasising the ability to function normally in one's own society – though the reference to normal standards opens up an entirely new set of problems. Seedhouse (1995) offers a radical perspective on definitions in changing the emphasis from the state of health to the process of attaining it. This is seen as requiring the removal of obstacles and the provision of the basic means by which individual goals can be achieved. This perspective poses challenging questions, though in its basic form it presupposes no inherent conflict between the pursuit of individual and social goals or indeed supposes they can be neatly separated.

HEALTH PSYCHOLOGY: WHY NOW?

A precondition for the emergence of health psychology has been this concern to reconstrue the nature of health and illness. As well as the political manoeuvres of organised medicine and the proclamations of the WHO, developments within scientific medicine itself have also played a part – developments which have a direct bearing on the subject matter which health psychology lays claim to. Both psychosomatic medicine and epidemiology have laid the conceptual foundations for studying the interaction between psychosocial and biological factors in health and illness. The idea of psychosomatic illnesses originates from the psychodynamic approach to the mind and has gained credence primarily within clinical practice. This contends that states of pain and ill-health are sometimes the body's best available means for expressing psychological distress. This does not mean, though it has sometimes been interpreted as such, that these illnesses are somehow less 'real'. Rather, it alludes to a person at some level of awareness as somehow choosing or allowing themselves to become ill in order to try and solve a particular difficulty – with on occasion the overt expression of physical symptoms able to be interpreted as an attempt to fulfill an unconscious wish. From this perspective, improved health could result from appropriate psychotherapy which addresses the underlying issues.

More concrete scientific evidence of the influence of psychosocial factors has emerged from the science of epidemiology (see Box 1.1). The problems which have been encountered here contain important lessons for psychologists seeking to establish relationships between cognitive and behavioural variables and specific health outcomes. The failure of epidemiology to successfully deal with people's experiences provides psychologists with an opportunity to bridge the gap between work which identifies risks to health and the desire to have people take appropriate action to bring about desired health outcomes. At the same time there is a danger that, like epidemiology, individuals will be conceptually removed from their social context in trying to understand how they respond to the challenges of health. In addition, as much of the evidence linking psychological and psychosocial variables to health are also associational in nature, the successes of the risk-factor approach to health and illness must not blind psychological researchers into thinking that it is unnecessary for them to establish why these associations are present and whether the psychological or psychosocial events occupy a primary position in the causal chain of events.

A further incentive for enquiring into psychological issues in health and health

Risk factor A variable with a statistically significant association with some specified (health) outcome. A causal relationship is not assumed.

BOX 1.1   What is epidemiology?

Epidemiology evolved as a branch of medical science over the last two centuries with the expressed purpose of studying the distribution of disease in human populations through the use of quantitative methods in the hope that the knowledge accrued will help in the prevention of ill-health. Two early influences were paramount. One was the introduction of statistical methodology to medicine (the growth of statistics and epidemiology are in fact closely interwoven); the other was that of campaigning movements whose efforts sought to highlight the importance of social and economic factors in causing disease (Beaglehole and Bonita, 1997).

As western societies in the twentieth century have undergone a change in the predominant causes of mortality, shifting from communicable to non-communicable diseases, the same analytic methods responsible for investigating infectious diseases have been brought to bear on the modern epidemics of cancer and heart disease. Epidemiology has thus been in the forefront of providing evidence of the damaging effects on health of specific patterns of behaviour (e.g. smoking) as well as exploring the role of psychosocial stress on health. Interpreting epidemiological evidence is far from straightforward, however, as studies tend primarily to be non-experimental (i.e observational). However a number of core concepts exist for guiding researchers in trying to establish whether an obtained association between risk 'exposures' and disease outcome represents a causal relationship and not merely a statistical artefact. These include the following (Hill, 1965):

1. Has the association been repeatedly observed at different times, in different places, by different persons and in different circumstances?
2. Does a dose–response relationship exist?
3. Is the putative relationship confined to specific groups of people?
4. Is the relationship biologically plausible?

Despite these, several criticisms have been aired. One is that because epidemiology is not concerned with people's experiences and their attempts to make sense of the events in their lives it is likely to be less than fully effective when it comes to disease control. A more frequently voiced complaint concerns the emphasis on identifying risk factors for ill-health in the absence of any specific knowledge of biological mechanisms. Where contrary findings have been reported, it seems far from difficult to produce equally plausible biological mechanisms for each (Davey Smith, Phillips and Neaton, 1992). Furthermore Mann (1995) finds that opinion amongst epidemiologists is divided on the levels of relative risk and the degree of replication which must ensue before an association is regarded as robust. Weaker relative risks, even if representing real relationships, may be particularly difficult to accept. Of considerable importance are the technical difficulties in measuring variables with precision and ensuring that the effects of potential confounding variables on relationships of interest have been taken into account (Phillips and Davey Smith, 1991; Davey Smith and Phillips, 1992). These difficulties are likely to be the greater where studies have not been planned for the specific purpose of exploring a given topic. None of these matters are helped by the pressures on researchers to publish results early and the eagerness of the press to put these in the public domain prematurely. The risk-factor approach has been further criticised on the basis that it too easily leads to individuals being removed from their social context (Krieger, 1994).

care comes from the fact that society is becoming ever more burdened by the demands imposed by 'undesirable' behaviours, whether directly health-related or in the interpersonal domain. It is precisely in the arena of behaviour that the medical model has found itself least able to cope – both theoretically and from the perspective of managing the consequences (Orford, 1985; Boyle, 1990) (see Box 1.2). Smoking, excessive drinking, drug taking (both prescribed and illicit), gambling, sexual behaviour, all carry potentially serious consequences for health and well-being, as well as posing severe social, financial and legal problems (see for example Garcia, 1997).

BOX 1.2   Has the biomedical model failed?

Ideally, ascertaining the success or otherwise of a model should entail a comparison of its current achievements against some clear criterion. Unfortunately, explicit criteria for evaluating the biomedical model have not been clearly stated. In part this is because its function is not so much that of a potentially falsifiable theory, but more a framework for guiding and interpreting medical interventions. As such it is more akin to an ideological stance towards human health. Whilst there can be no doubting the considerable technological achievements of new surgical and pharmacological interventions and immunisation techniques, in combatting and treating a whole array of conditions, there are other counts on which the model of the person as a machine can be said to have failed. These lie predominantly in the ethical and psychological domains and include how people respond cognitively, emotionally and behaviourally to ill-health and to health interventions, as well as how these in turn affect health outcomes. The biomedical model has also had difficulty in addressing a range of recalcitrant problematic behaviours including violent antisocial behaviour and some forms of drug use. Undoubtedly, these failures to adequately address the human concerns of health and illness have contributed on occasion to undesirable levels of patient dissatisfaction.

The health consequences are well-illustrated by findings from the Alameda County Study involving almost 7000 individuals. A number of good health habits were identified by the researchers: sleeping 7–8 hours a day, being less than 10 per cent overweight, eating breakfast every day, not eating between meals, getting regular exercise, not smoking and no more than two alcoholic drinks every day. It was found that the fewer the number of these health practices reported initially, the greater the risk of mortality on follow up almost 10 years later (Belloc and Breslow, 1972). The importance of behavioural factors to health are usually summarised in stating that they are now implicated in 7 out of the 10 leading causes of death in the USA (Sheridan and Radmacher, 1992). This startling figure certainly seems to underline the importance of behaviour for health, but what does the statistic really tell us? One could be forgiven for reading into this the claim that successful psychological prevention will alter the leading causes of death – but to what? Certainly not a return to infectious diseases. It must be remembered that eventually we do have to die of something. Given the very definite limits on the human lifespan, perhaps it would be clearer for the detrimental effects of certain behaviours to be expressed in terms of their effects in reducing life expectancy.

Unhealthy behaviours carry burdens far beyond the toll they take on the physical and mental health of individuals who engage in them or those in their immediate vicinity. The financial costs of drug and alcohol use to health services and industry for example are considerable. In the UK, around one in four people over 16 years of age are now estimated to have used an illegal drug. The costs for health services stemming from drug use have been put at over $100 million in 1997, with the costs of drug and alcohol-related absenteeism calculated to cost British industry over US$1 billion every year (White, 1997). To this can be added the considerable costs incurred through drug-related crime, and the United States provides a disturbing illustration of the proportions this can reach. In 1996, 16 per cent of convicted jail inmates said they had committed their offence in order to raise money for drugs (Dorsey and Dawitz, 1997). The total costs of drug and alcohol abuse in the USA are now thought to be in the region of US$246 billion (National Institutes of Health, 1998). Additional problems arise from behaviours associated with mental disorder, as well as child abuse and violent conduct. The awareness of the effects of these behaviours on health has led to an emphasis on 'pathological' lifestyles, personalities and even genetic constitutions, and rather less on the circumstances which promote these behaviours. As we shall see throughout this book, this has led to a tension between social and situational theories/models of behaviour and ones based within the domain of individual differences. This struggle is one which is not unique to health psychology.

With this plethora of factors coalescing in the latter part of the twentieth century, it should not be considered surprising that our understanding of health, well-being and illness is undergoing a radical shift, nor that profound questions are being raised about what are the best ways to respond to illness. Having set out some of the broad strands which have led to the emergence of health psychology, it remains to determine whether health psychological reasoning really does mark a transition between old and new ways of thinking about health and to what extent the problems leading to the conceptual shake-up in health are being addressed by the new discipline. It would be unfair to attempt to answer these questions just yet. Given the spirit of the present book perhaps these are better left for the reader to consider as they read through and digest the material in the pages which follow.

AIMS OF THE BOOK

The emergence of health psychology as a separate branch of psychology is generally agreed to have occurred in the late 1970s and early 1980s. Workers such as Matarazzo (1980) emphasised the importance of psychological factors such as beliefs and behaviour in the aetiology and prevention of ill-health. This has led to claims that the model of health which it upholds – the biopsychosocial model – is a direct challenge to the biomedical model. At the end of the day these claims must be evaluated on the basis of evidence produced. At present the boundaries of the discipline are ill-defined, and rather than attempt to describe them in this opening chapter, we hope that the nature of the activities which are undertaken by health psychologists will emerge in a more coherent fashion in those that follow. We therefore have several aims:

1. To survey those areas of health-care research and practice in which psychologists have contributed.
2. Provide a guide to a range of commonly used research tools and methodologies in health psychology and the contexts in which they have been used.
3. Encourage an evidence-based approach to the evaluation of health care and theories of health and illness.

4. To situate health psychological research within the broader health and social sciences.

5. To critically examine the assumptions present in a range of psychological models applied to health and illness.

6. To critically examine the achievements and claims of the discipline.

Discussion points

A To what extent has the development of health psychology stemmed from theoretical developments within psychology itself?

B What do you think should be the aims for a psychology of health and health care?

Suggested reading

Belloc, N.B. and Breslow, L. (1972) 'Relationship between Physical Health Status and Health Practices', *Preventive Medicine*, **1**: 409–21.

Davey Smith, G. and Phillips, A.N. (1992) 'Confounding in Epidemiological Studies: Why "Independent" Effects may Not be All They Seem', *British Medical Journal*, **305**: 757–59.

Dennett, D.C. (1995) *Darwin's Dangerous Idea: Evolution and the Meanings of Life*. (Harmondsworth: Penguin).

Mann, C. C. (1995) 'Epidemiology Faces its Limits', *Science*, **269**: 164–9.

Matarazzo, J.D. (1980) 'Behavioural Health and Behavioural Medicine: Frontiers for a New Health Psychology', *American Psychologist*, **35**: 807–17.

Assessing Health and Quality-of-life

'How should I not be grateful to my whole life?'

Friedrich Nietzsche (*Ecce Homo*, 1908)

INTRODUCTION

The last few years have witnessed an explosion in the development of methods for assessing various aspects of quality-of-life (McDowell and Newell, 1987; Bowling, 1991, 1995). In part this has been a response to demands to improve the audit and assessment of medical procedures (both physical and psychological) as well as economic pressures to limit health-care interventions, which some see as spiralling out of control owing to increased numbers of people surviving to old age and making ever greater demands on medical services.

Until fairly recently, most existing indicators reflected a 'disease' model of health (Bowling, 1991). As such, ill-health was indicated by feelings of pain and discomfort or perceptions of change in a patient's usual functioning and feeling. The crudest such indicator of quality-of-life and the longest is provided by mortality data, and despite its crudeness remains a useful source of information. On the global stage, few standardised measures of life quality exist, and mortality data is at least routinely collected in a large number of countries and provides some basis for making comparisons between countries (Beaglehole and Bonita, 1997).

Other indicators which have traditionally informed medical practitioners of quality-of-life, albeit in a very general sense, include routine biochemical tests, symptom rates and measures of role performance such as sickness absence and return to work. The latter have been favoured by those with an interest in occupational health, though their value outside this arena is tempered by the limits imposed by economic and social influences in determining opportunities for work irrespective of health state. Less direct information can be gleaned from service utilisation, readmission rates to hospitals and length of stay whilst in hospital. None of these, however, adequately address the issue of the impact of care on patients' lives. High service utilisation, for example, may be a function of knowledge of service provision rather than need, whilst successive readmission may indicate either continuing risk and exposure to the determinants of ill-health, genuine relapse or unsuccessful prior treatment. Self-report data such as that on individual alcohol or tobacco consumption was long confined to community surveys, and self-reported perceived health was frequently viewed as poor data compared to the 'hard' evidence provided by biochemical and physiological tests. It has gradually been recognised that this traditional view, which assumes health to be a continuum with death at one end and perfect health at the other, contains a number of serious problems, perhaps foremost of these being the simple fact that ill-health may be present long before disease is manifest.

CONCEPTUAL ISSUES IN QUALITY-OF-LIFE MEASUREMENT

With the growth in health assessment there now exist a plethora of measures concerning both specific (Meenan, 1982; Tursky *et al.*, 1982; Duncan and Sander, 1991) and more general facets of health (Hunt, McEwen and McKenna, 1985a; Krupinski, 1980; Patrick and Deyo, 1989). The instruments used encompass the assessment of both psychological and physical function. In the psychological and social domains these cover cognitive impairments (Copeland, 1990; Wechsler, 1986), mood states such as depression or anxiety (Beck *et al.*, 1974; Zigmond and Snaith, 1983; McNair *et al.*, 1992), social support and role performance (Corney *et al.*, 1985) or general mental health (Goldberg and Williams, 1988: see Box 2.1). In the physical domain a host of instruments exist for assessing the physical functioning of patients with particular diseases, physical problems or disabilities (Schag *et al.*, 1992; Ferrans and Powers, 1985). In addition, many tools recognise the inseparable nature of physical and psychological morbidity and assess functioning from a multidimensional perspective (Nouri and Lincoln, 1987).

Instruments which address physical functioning or limitations in physical functioning are usually concerned with addressing the ability to perform routine tasks of daily living – walking to the shops, climbing stairs, carrying shopping and so on. The consequences of particular physical conditions may mean that these tasks cannot be performed, or are achievable only with the help of others. Such a measurement strategy, however, is not without problems. Physical limitation as a consequence of impairment need carry no inherent implications for quality of living – hence a low score on a measure of physical functioning (e.g. the SF-36, see Box 2.2) does not necessarily inform us about an objectively measurable quality-of-life. The view that it does, ignores constraints imposed on mobility and well-being not just by the designed physical environment but also by the reactions of other people towards the person whose physical functioning is currently limited. Thus the outcome of a complex interaction between environment and person becomes reified as the definable state of an individual. To equate poor physical functioning which may necessitate additional physical care from others with poor quality-of-life is to assume that dependence on others is undesirable or abnormal. This, as Beail and Beail (1982) noted, suggests dependence has become devalued – associated with helplessness and indecision. Such a view is a relatively recent historical phenomenon – and is more likely a reflection of western cultural values associated with late twentieth-century capitalism than any abiding scientific truth. It is not surprising, therefore, that such thinking has come under fire not least from disabled people (Sobsey, 1994; Westcott and Cross, 1996). Much of this confusion Muldoon *et al.*, (1998) argue, is because quality-of-life measurements have frequently confused types of information which in reality are quite distinct – those pertaining to objective capacities on the one hand, and on the other subjective information regarding how someone feels. Whilst objective information may pertain to either behavioural or psychological functioning, subjective information can refer to the affective stance someone has about their current physical health status, or how they appraise their own psychological well-being.

A number of additional, more general criticisms have also been levelled at quality-

BOX 2.1   The General Health Questionnaire (12-item version)

Have you recently

1. Been able to concentrate on whatever you're doing?

1	2	3	4
Better than usual	Same as usual	Worse than usual	Much worse than usual
[ ]	[ ]	[ ]	[ ]

2. Lost much sleep over worry?

1	2	3	4
Not at all	No more than usual	Rather more than usual	Much worse than usual
[ ]	[ ]	[ ]	[ ]

3. Felt that you are playing a useful part in things?

1	2	3	4
More so than usual	Same as usual	Less useful than usual	Much less useful
[ ]	[ ]	[ ]	[ ]

4. Felt capable of making decisions about things?

1	2	3	4
More so than usual	Same as usual	Less so than usual	Much less capable
[ ]	[ ]	[ ]	[ ]

5. Felt constantly under strain?

1	2	3	4
Not at all	No more than usual	Rather more than usual	Much more than usual
[ ]	[ ]	[ ]	[ ]

6. Felt you couldn't overcome your difficulties?

1	2	3	4
Not at all	No more than usual	Rather more than usual	Much more than usual
[ ]	[ ]	[ ]	[ ]

7. Been able to enjoy your normal day to day activities?

1	2	3	4
More so than usual	Same as usual	Less so than usual	Much less than usual
[ ]	[ ]	[ ]	[ ]

8. Been able to face up to your problems?

1	2	3	4
More so than usual	Same as usual	Less able than usual	Much less able
[ ]	[ ]	[ ]	[ ]

9. Been feeling unhappy and depressed?

1	2	3	4
Not at all	No more than usual	Rather more than usual	Much more than usual
[ ]	[ ]	[ ]	[ ]

10. Been losing confidence in yourself?

1	2	3	4
Not at all	No more than usual	Rather more than usual	Much more than usual
[ ]	[ ]	[ ]	[ ]

11. Been thinking of yourself as a worthless person?

1	2	3	4
Not at all	No more than usual	Rather more than usual	Much more than usual
[ ]	[ ]	[ ]	[ ]

12. Been feeling reasonably happy, all things considered?

1	2	3	4
More so than usual	About same as usual	Less so than usual	Much less than usual
[ ]	[ ]	[ ]	[ ]

Scoring: Each item endorsed with either a '3' or '4' is scored as one point. When used as a screening test for probable psychological disorder, a cut-off point of 2–3 has been suggested (Banks, 1982).

Source: © David Goldberg, 1978. Reproduced by permission of the Publishers, NFER-NELSON, Darville House, 2 Oxford Street, Windsor, Berkshire SL4 1DF, England. All rights reserved.

BOX 2.2 Measuring physical functioning: the Physical Functioning Scale of the SF-36

The following items are about activities you might do during a typical day. Does your health now limit you in these activities? If so, how much?

	Yes limited a lot	Yes limited a little	No, not limited at all
1. Vigorous activities, such as running, lifting heavy objects, participating in strenuous sports	[ ]	[ ]	[ ]
2. Moderate activities, such as moving a table, pushing a vacuum cleaner, bowling or playing golf	[ ]	[ ]	[ ]
3. Lifting or carrying groceries	[ ]	[ ]	[ ]
4. Climbing several flights of stairs	[ ]	[ ]	[ ]
5. Climbing one flight of stairs	[ ]	[ ]	[ ]
6. Bending, kneeling or stooping	[ ]	[ ]	[ ]
7. Walking more than one mile	[ ]	[ ]	[ ]
8. Walking half a mile	[ ]	[ ]	[ ]
9. Walking one hundred yards	[ ]	[ ]	[ ]
10. Bathing and dressing yourself	[ ]	[ ]	[ ]

Scoring: Scores are summed across all 10 items. Respondents receive 1 for each item endorsed Yes limited a lot, 2 for each item endorsed Yes limited a little and 3 for each item endorsed No, not limited at all. A final Physical Function Score is then derived by subtracting 10 from this total, dividing this by 20 and multiplying the resultant score by 100. This yields a scale with a possible minimum of 0 and a possible maximum of 100. Higher scores denote better health (Ware, Snow, Kosinski and Gandek, 1993). The scale has high internal consistency (alpha = 0.85, though test–retest reliability over one month is only 0.60 (Roberts, Hemingway and Marmot, 1997).
Source: Reproduced with permission of QualityMetric Inc. The SF-36™ is a trademark of the Medical Outcomes Trust, © 1994–2000, John E. Ware Jr., all rights reserved.

of-life measures which apply to both physical and mental health. One complaint concerns the question of who actually performs the ratings of psychological and behavioural function, and carries important implications for the practice of medicine (see Box 2.3). It has been further argued that item contents and scales of various instruments have failed to reflect the diversity of people's impressions as to what constitutes being 'well', and instead have displayed an over-concern with morbidity and other negative aspects of health (WHO, 1987). With an estimated 15 per cent of the general population having chronic physical limitation and 10–20 per cent substantial 'psychiatric' impairment, these negative definitions of health may say little or nothing about the well-being of a substantial proportion of the population.

In one effort to counter this, Hunt and Macleod (1987) have emphasised the varying natures of what they loosely term health, fitness and well-being – an approach more in keeping with the WHO definition of health as a state of complete social, physical and psychological well-being. Lamb *et al.* (1988) include both physical fitness and physical health amongst their dimensions of positive health, which also encompass the ability to cope with **stressful** situations, the maintenance of strong social supports, social integration into the community, high morale and life satisfaction and psychological well-being. In turn, the dimensions of social health can be more fully specified by reference to levels of family support, friendship and

Stress is where the demands of a situation exceed the personal resources to cope with it.

BOX 2.3   Who should assess quality-of-life?

When assessing patients' subjective states the judgement of physicians has for a long time been considered sacrosanct. Discrepancies between physicians' and patients' assessments have, however, been found in a wide variety of circumstances. Turkington and Drummond (1988) found doctors were likely to rate drug users' withdrawal from opiates as more severe than the drug users themselves, while Da Silva *et al.* (1996) concluded that physicians' ratings may not accurately reflect the functional health and symptom experience of their patients with prostate cancer. Quality-of-life judgements made by patients after treatment for hypertension show similar differences (Jachuk *et al.*, 1982), while in a revealing piece of work, Pearlman and Uhlmann (1988) found chronically-ill elderly patients rated their own quality-of-life significantly higher than did their physicians who were more likely to emphasise medical criteria in making their judgements. The patients themselves emphasised psychological and socioeconomic factors. Such discrepancies between carers and cared for are not, however, confined to the role relationship existing between medical practitioners and their patients. Brown, McGee and O'Boyle (1997) point out that low agreement is in fact regularly observed when comparing quality-of-life judgements made by disabled and chronically-ill people and those entrusted with their care.

   The implications of these findings are worrying – both for the theoretical development of quality-of-life measurement, but more disturbingly for the quality of care various groups receive on the basis of carer judgements. These include potentially inappropriate levels of medication used to combat opiate withdrawal or pain – particularly in elderly patients – an area where concordance between carers and cared for has been especially low (Magaziner, Hebel and Warren, 1987). Neither can it be ignored that judgements of insufficient quality-of-life can lead to actions that result in termination of life, whether directly or indirectly. Gross *et al.* (1983), for example, compared outcomes for 24 babies with spina bifida given supportive care compared to 36 given vigorous care. Within 6 months, all 24 in the first group had died and all in the second group had survived. Duff and Campbell (1973) reviewed 299 consecutive neonatal deaths and found 14 per cent had died because treatment was withheld on the grounds of their impairment. This can only be understood on the basis that judgements were made about the presumed quality-of-life of the infant. Yet as Hauerwas (1986) reminds us, no evidence exists that people with developmental disabilities enjoy their lives less than any of the rest of us, except that they may be badly treated by others. Because of the potentially serious nature of the consequences of quality-of-life judgements made by proxy raters, O'Boyle, (1997) comments that research to determine the influences upon them is now urgently needed. And of course measurement problems aside, even if someone's quality-of-life were extremely low it is a truism (frequently overlooked) that this quality-of-life cannot be improved by their death. The argument for terminating severely impaired children's lives is often couched in the language of their presumed quality-of-life, but as we have seen this is a view without evidence or logic to support it – rather the use of the language of quality-of-life in this context often masks the real issues of resource allocation for health and social care and the negative attitudes towards people with disabilities which are prevalent in society.

personal confidences, social activity, sexual satisfaction, work achievement, financial adequacy and personal achievement (Kaplan, 1975). A full list of the attributes which comprise quality-of-life, however, is inadequate without some system for weighting its various components. Should social well-being be considered more important than, say, financial security, or what about personal achievement relative to physical health? Even if we are capable of deciding answers to these questions, is there any reason to suppose that the weightings will remain constant over time for a given individual, or group of people? A number of instruments attempt to deal with the issue of relative importance by assigning standard weightings derived by averaging responses over all groups of people – the developers of the Nottingham Health Profile (Hunt, McEwen and McKenna, 1985a), for example, used this strategy. The alternative course of action, to allow subjects themselves to weight the various components is, however, now emerging as a viable alternative.

MEASURING QUALITY-OF-LIFE

We have seen that conceptualising quality-of-life raises a number of ethical, practical and philosophical problems. Given the existence of these, a number of quite distinct approaches have been adopted to measuring its various aspects. In this section we will consider two contrasting approaches to assessing general quality-of-life – the SEIQoL and the SF-36. They sit alongside a number of other generic instruments such as the Nottingham Health Profile and Sickness Impact Profile. These differ in the assumptions they make and the problems which they tackle. As minimal criteria for meeting requirements of validity, such health indicators need to be sufficiently broad that they capture the diversity of health experience, and sufficiently comprehensive that they are able to distinguish between respondents whose quality-of-life differs with respect to positive as well as negative health states (Ware, 1990). In addition, it is usually considered necessary that what is purported to be measured is measured consistently – that is, that the measurements are reliable. Questions of validity and reliability occur repeatedly in the literature on deciding the utility of quality-of-life measures and rely heavily on psychometric analyses applied in a variety of contexts.

The SEIQoL

The Schedule for the Evaluation of Individual Quality-of-Life (SEIQoL) developed by O'Boyle and colleagues (O'Boyle, 1994; Brown, McGee and O'Boyle, 1997) approaches validity at the level of the individual's own conceptions and perceptions rather than from aggregated group data. This avoids problems resulting from the use of standardised fixed measures which may not be relevant to an individual's present life situation or which may vary in importance for different people (Hickey *et al.*, 1996). Accordingly, the SEIQoL seeks to evaluate each person on the basis of the areas of life they consider to be the most important, quantifying current functioning in these areas and weighing their relative importance. The process begins with cue elicitation – with individuals asked to name the five areas of life which are most important to their overall quality-of-life (in the event of any difficulty a standard list of prompts are used). In the second stage, subjects are asked to rate themselves on each of the nominated areas on a scale from the worst possible (as bad as could possibly be) to the best possible (as good as could possibly be). Whereas the original SEIQoL uses a complex decision-analysis technique to assign weights to the five areas nominated by the individual, the short form of the instrument (SEIQoL-DW) uses a set of five interlocking disks, each manipulable to allow the person to produce a pie-chart where each area represents the weight attached to each domain – with weights

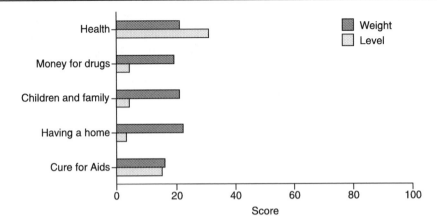

Figure 2.1   **Quality-of-life profile of 31-year-old man who formerly injected drugs**

Source: Adapted from A.M. Hickey *et al.* (1996), *British Medical Journal,* **313**: 29–33, with permission from the BMJ Publishing Group.

summing to 100. As well as being reliable and comparable to the longer version, the procedure is simpler to understand and quicker to administer. Global quality-of-life is operationally defined in terms of an overall SEIQoL computed by multiplying the weights and individual ratings for each domain and summing the products (O'Boyle, 1994) – possible scores range from 0 to 100. This global score can then be used to collate scores from individuals and may be used to compare groups. The approach appears promising and has been used as a research instrument with AIDS patients (see Figure 2.1; Hickey *et al.*, 1996), healthy elders (Brown *et al.*, 1994), people with mild cognitive impairment (Coen, O'Mahoney, O'Boyle and Joyce, 1993), patients suffering from gastrointestinal disorders (McGee *et al.*, 1991), people with multiple sclerosis (Murrell, Kenealy, Beaumont and Lintern, 1999) and carers of people with severe head injury (Hickey *et al.*, 1997).

The SF-36

The SF-36 (Ware and Sherbourne, 1992) is probably the most widely used of current quality-of-life instruments, both as a research tool in epidemiological work and for monitoring health in patient populations (Bowling, 1995). It emerged, after several earlier incarnations (Stewart *et al.*, 1992), from the Rand Health Insurance battery of tests used in the Medical Outcomes Studies (Tarlov *et al.*, 1989; Anderson *et al.*, 1990; McHorney *et al.*, 1992). Currently the form comprises 36 questions and yields scores on eight dimensions; four in the domain of physical health (Physical Functioning, Role Limitations due to Physical Problems, Bodily Pain, and General Health Perceptions) and four in the domain of mental health (General Mental Health, Social Functioning, Role Limitations due to Emotional Problems, and Vitality). Composite scores for physical and mental health may be derived from these. The extensive use of the SF-36 stems in part from its apparent superiority over other measures. For example in comparison to the Nottingham Health Profile, the SF-36 has demonstrated greater sensitivity to variations in health status within both clinical and normal populations. Though they appear to measure a range of similar health constructs, the overlap is not complete – for example the pain scales in each appear to be measuring different aspects, the SF-36 providing a measure of severity rather than frequency of pain (Stansfeld, Roberts and Foot, 1997). Though heated debate has ensued over their relative merits (Hunt and McKenna, 1992; Brazier *et al.*, 1992a) it seems likely that the trend towards greater use of the SF-36 will accelerate now that it has been chosen as the instrument of choice in the international quality-of-life assessment (IQOLA) project (Aaronson *et al.*, 1992). This was a four-year project set up to adapt a health-related quality-of-life instrument for use in up to 15 countries, making comparisons in diverse medical, social and cultural settings feasible. The intentions behind this project were to establish population norms within each country for the SF-36, which in turn may assist in evaluating the impact of medical care in multinational clinical trials (Tarlov *et al.*, 1989), the prediction of future demand for health care (Fitzpatrick *et al.*, 1992), and enable valid cross-cultural health comparisons to be made (Ware and Gandek, 1994). Though it lies outside the main scope of this discussion, developing valid cross-cultural standards for quality-of-life concepts is itself a major undertaking – not least of which is the comparability of concepts and linguistic terms used to communicate these concepts. Readers are directed to Bullinger (1997) for a detailed consideration of these.

PSYCHOMETRIC ANALYSIS

Reliability refers to the consistency of findings and is usually measured by means of a correlation coefficient.

To fulfill the aims of the IQOLA project, the SF-36 like any health measurement scale must fulfill psychometric criteria of *reliability* and validity. For reliability it is usually considered desirable for items within a scale to be internally consistent (that is to be homogenous with respect to the measured attribute, and to possess good test–retest reliability (McDowell and Newell, 1996). Though there is no hard and fast cut-off, acceptable magnitudes of reliability generally fall in the region of 0.80 and are best evaluated with the use of appropriate confidence intervals. Validity may take many forms. In addition to face and content validity which was touched upon earlier, tests of item-scale discriminant validity, for example, will ascertain whether single items from within a particular scale correlate more highly with their own total scale score than with scores which purport to measure other unrelated attributes. Where the aim is one of distinguishing between different respondents, which may be vital in demonstrating the clinical validity of a measure (see Figure 2.2), situations may arise where a scale possesses good discriminatory power yet is not internally consistent. In fact an increase in one of these attributes can often be at the expense of the other (Streiner and Norman, 1991). Thus the conflict between item-homogeneity and scale-utility is a perennial difficulty when constructing suitable measurement scales, particularly where one is trying to ensure that the contents of the items are sufficiently broad to capture the health construct in question. Once health-related measures have been deemed to overcome the formidable range of psychometric hurdles, then they may be considered suitable for use as outcome measures in their own right. As far as the SF-36 is concerned, work to date suggests it possesses acceptable psychometric properties (Brazier *et al.*, 1992b; Ware *et al.*, 1993; Roberts, Hemingway and Marmot, 1997), though it is not without problems.

COMPARISON OF SEIQoL WITH THE SF-36

Though the settings in which the SF-36 have been used vary considerably – it has for instance been used in primary care settings (Brazier *et al.*, 1992b), and community

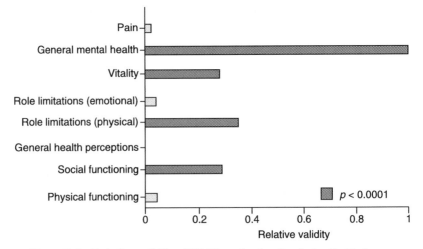

Figure 2.2   Relative validity of SF-36 scales for discriminating between respondents with angina and those meeting GHQ criteria for possible psychiatric disorder

Source: Adapted from R. Roberts *et al.* (1997).

postal surveys in the UK (Garrat *et al.*, 1993) as well as rural communities in the US (Hill and Harries, 1994) – doubts have been expressed about the properties of some of the scales when used with particular clinical groups (Jenkinson *et al.*, 1996). Because of its later development, this issue is yet to surface with the SEIQoL. Furthermore, the apparent sensitivity of the SF-36 to changes in health states may in certain contexts lead to difficulties of interpretation. In the Whitehall II study of Civil Servants, for example, Roberts *et al.* (1997) found four-week test–retest reliability for one of the scales (*Role Limitations due to Physical Problems*) to be very low ($r = 0.38$) – in contrast with Brazier's work (1992b) where test–retest reliability over a two-week period was considerably higher. These differences may reflect acute sensitivity of the scale to short-term physical health problems impinging on social role performance, or alternatively that the reliability of the scale itself in a population of healthy workers is low. Future work is necessary to resolve this matter. A comparison of the SEIQoL with the SF-36 in a sample of people with MS, however, found the SEIQoL to be more sensitive to reports of life changes between assessments (Murrell *et al.*, 1999). Another concern is the breadth of the health concepts assessed; there being an absence of indicators for determining cognitive functioning (Hays and Shapiro, 1992), sleep or sexual health. The absence of suitable indicators of mental state in particular limit its application in populations of patients where this might be a real concern (for example the elderly or HIV/AIDS patients). In comparison, the manner in which the SEIQoL has been devised make this kind of criticism less applicable, although it may be necessary in appropriate contexts for it to be supplemented with tests of cognitive impairment.

Both these general instruments possess the common advantage of being brief to administer (approximately 10 minutes in both cases); however, the job of comparing them is made harder by the very different assumptions which they embody. The SEIQoL construes quality-of-life in terms of a person's own constructions about what matters – in that sense it is less health-centred. The SF-36, in contrast, sees the dimensions of health-related quality-of-life as somehow existing outside of the person, so that although the person may decide where they may be placed along-side these, it is a tool which does not fully resolve the contradictions of who should assess quality-of-life. From a conceptual and theoretical standpoint, therefore, it might be argued that the SEIQoL is a less-problematic instrument. However, by virtue of reaching the quality-of-life assessment marketplace ahead of its rival, the SF-36 does possess a distinct advantage and may prove difficult to shift, not least because of its proven value in standardising health-related quality-of-life and making cross-cultural work in this area tenable.

However, there are lessons to be drawn. The debate concerning 'evidence-based medicine' and the proper assessment of outcomes is largely predicated upon the assumption of suitable evaluation technology being available. As Muldoon *et al.*, (1998) point out, however, with few exceptions measures of physical functioning in quality-of-life indices have not been validated against objective assessments of physical abilities. It also remains true that the question of who decides what is most suitable is one made by clinicians and academics – and not the patients and subjects whose efforts they are dependent upon. It is not necessary that flawless instruments be developed – a long wait would ensue – but what surely is necessary is that the limits residing in any one instrument are clearly known and the range of domains in which it can be legitimately applied well-understood. Both these tools provide composite indices of health – a global index in the case of the SEIQoL, and summary scores of mental and physical functioning in the case of the SF-36. Use of these should be exercised with extreme caution as they seem to contradict one of the principal underlying messages of all current generic measures, that quality-of-life is inherently multidimensional. Other than the desire for simplicity there seems no logical reason why composite indices should be employed.

Finally, the nature of both the tools we have reviewed permits the possibility that in future they could be used beyond their original remit to provide objective measures of quality-of-life and be of further value in systematically exploring differences in interpersonal perceptions of health and disability. The nature of any putative differences might vary both with the type of chronic illness or disability under consideration and the nature of the relationship which another person has with the disabled or ill-person. Such use could tell us more than just how quality-of-life affects health outcomes, but how our own conceptions of others' quality-of-life, may in large part determine it for them.

DISEASE-SPECIFIC QUALITY OF-LIFE MEASUREMENT

In clinical settings it is well-recognised that all relevant aspects of quality-of-life as it is currently envisaged (whether solely in health-related terms or more broadly) cannot be captured within the realm of a single instrument – or that generic instruments are not always sufficiently sensitive to detect small but significant changes in health status domains (O'Boyle, 1997). It is customary, therefore, that disease or domain-specific measures are used alongside generic ones. For example, if one is interested in evaluating physical and psychological outcomes for people following a heart attack, specific measures of cardiac and respiratory function, current symptoms and satisfaction with treatment will accompany measures of sleep, pain, emotional status, sexual and social life and economic status. To get a more complete picture of the range and scale of disease-specific tests in a particular area, however, it will be instructive to briefly consider their use in oncology (cancer care), the area of medicine which has been at the forefront of quality-of-life research (Fallowfield, 1995a). Quality-of-life assessment is particularly important in cancer because appropriate measures – and there are many to choose from (Bowling, 1995, for example reviews over 35 different scales which have been used with cancer patients) – can assist medical practitioners and patients to choose between treatment options where there is no clear survival advantage but where there may be significant pay-offs in greater quality-of-life by following one course rather than another.

When using quality-of-life measures with cancer patients it is usual for several domains of functioning to be examined – notably physical, social and psychological well being. Aspects of physical well-being may include symptoms, pain, fatigue, nausea and physical functioning. With the psychosocial consequences of diagnosis and treatment becoming increasingly recognised – around one-quarter of patients experience anxiety or depression at levels serious enough to warrant psychological interventions (Fallowfield 1995b) – a number of facets of psychological (e.g. anxiety, depression, anger, satisfaction with life and self-esteem) and social well-being (effects on social activities, social supports and sexual relationships) may be assessed. Because of the multidimensional nature of the psychosocial domain, simple mental health scores such as are provided by the SF-36 general mental-health scale are probably too crude for the more subtle investigations of psychological state which are becoming increasingly favoured. Fallowfield (1995a) considers use of the Profile of Mood States, which measures tension, depression, anger, vigour, fatigue and confusion, and the GHQ-28, which provides scores on depression, anxiety, social functioning and physical functioning, as suitable instruments. These psychological tests can of course also be used in a number of different medical contexts. Cancer-specific tests which may be considered include the Cancer Rehabilitation Evaluation System (CARES) – which includes nine questions specifically relating to chemotherapy – the widely used Functional Living Index – Cancer (FLIC), The Rotterdam symptom checklist and the EORTC-30 (European Organisation for Research and Treatment of Cancer) which utilises a modular approach – currently there are five functional scales (physical, role, cognitive, emotional and social), three symptom scales (fatigue, pain, nausea and vomiting) a general quality-of-life scale and six single items.

Quality-of-life measures used within a specific domain of health have utility beyond the obvious purpose of evaluating the benefits of treatment in clinical trials. As well as identifying people potentially at risk of developing psychological problems, there is as mentioned the possibility of choosing one treatment option over another. This latter possibility has associated with it important commercial ramifications as drug manufacturers seek evidence of benefits associated with their products compared to rival pharmaceuticals. As much as any other considerations it is likely that this factor will continue to fuel the search for better and more sensitive measures of quality-of-life.

Finally, whilst contemplating the influence of economic factors in the quality-of-life arena a few words of caution should be said regarding what have come to be called Quality Adjusted Life Years (QALYs). In contrast to what has been emphasised in this chapter – that is the multidimensional nature of life and all its potential benefits and pitfalls – QALYs seek to condense this complexity into a composite index which purports to provide measures of life expectancy or length of life adjusted for the presumed reduced quality-of-life resulting from physical distress. Quite apart from the question of measuring quality-of-life in a single dimension, the assumption that quality-of-life runs parallel with physical functioning is one which we have already seen rests on shaky foundations. QALYs, therefore, cannot be considered to be accepted or validated measures of quality-of-life (Carr-Hill, 1989), but rather a means for making decisions about rationing health care (Bowling, 1995) – the preferred treatment (or most cost effective) options are held to be those where the patients have the greater number of QALYs after treatment. It is obvious that such a system of measurement puts the elderly and the disabled at a serious disadvantage in the queue for health care. As QALYs gain a stronger foothold in medical discourse there is the possibility of considerable confusion and error as ethical decisions about the allocation of medical resources (that is, the provision or withdrawal of treatment in certain contexts) which can affect life expectancy become increasingly based on economic criteria, whilst they are presented as being based on medical or scientific criteria.

In closing it is important to note that despite the increased recognition of the importance of patients' experiences and preferences, quality-of-life measures are still infrequently used in randomised controlled trials. Sanders *et al.* (1998), for example, found that less than 5 per cent of all randomised control trials between 1980 and 1997 reported on quality-of-life, reaching only 8.2 per cent even in cancer trials. Reasons for these low figures are complex; the threats posed by evidence-based medicine to established practice, dominance of the biomedical over the psychosocial or biopsychosocial models of health, difficulties in switching from an expert-centred to a patient-centred perspective, and difficulties in developing suitable evaluation technology.

Summary and conclusions

Recent years have witnessed an explosion in the development of methods for assessing quality-of-life. These encompass various general and disease-specific measures which cover both physical and psychological well-being; a number of issues remain problematic. These include what is meant by quality-of-life (e.g. what are its components and how should these be weighted in any overall assessment), an undue emphasis on negative as opposed to positive well-being, the not so small matters of who should assess quality-of-life (self-rated vs other) and how should it be assessed (e.g. standard or user-specified domains). This last issue includes the question of whether objective or subjective capabilities should be considered (e.g. what is the relationship between physical functioning and self-perceived quality-of-life?). However assessed, it is generally agreed that the measures used should be user-friendly, of high quality and possess demonstrable reliability and validity. This will enable their greater use in evaluating the influence of numerous factors which influence health as well as in determining the impact of medical interventions, and by so doing contribute to improved health care.

Discussion points

A   Is it desirable for quality-of-life measures to be stable over time? Is real quality of life like this? What additional difficulties does this create for deciding on the validity of a measure?

B   Are the conceptual issues surrounding quality-of-life measurement relevant to the question of euthanasia?

Suggested reading

Bowling, A. (1995) *Measuring Disease. A review of Disease Specific Quality of Life Measurement Scales.* (Buckingham: Open University Press).

Brown, J.P., McGee, H.M. and O'Boyle, C. (1997) 'Conceptual Approaches to the Assessment of Quality of Life', *Psychology and Health*, **12**(6): 737–51.

McDowell, I. and Newell, C. (1996) *Measuring Health*: A Guide to Rating Scales and Questionnaires, 2nd edn (Oxford University Press).

Muldoon, M.F., Barger, S.D., Flory, J.D. and Manuck, S.B. (1998) 'What are Quality of Life Measurements Measuring?', *British Medical Journal*, **316**: 542–5.

O'Boyle, C. (1997) 'Quality of Life Assessment: A Paradigm Shift', *The Irish Journal of Psychology*, **18**(1), 51–66.

chapter 3

Doing Research: Questions and Methods

'Imagination is more important than knowledge.'

Albert Einstein ('What Life Means to Einstein: An Interview by
George Sylvester Viereck', from *The Saturday Evening
Post*, 26 October, 1929)

INTRODUCTION

Einstein's oft-quoted remark celebrates the triumph of imagination and reason, and
in opening this chapter with it we do not wish to assert that the considerable knowledge base required to conduct and evaluate research is not important. But against
this backdrop of knowledge, what is crucial is the nature of the questions one formu-
lates, how these are situated amongst the crop of recognised problems in a field, and
what interpretations one dares to place upon the answers one's questions incite.
These all require acts of imagination and ultimately determine the progress or lack of
it in a given field of knowledge. Imagination does not, however, mean unstructured
chaos, and to this end we intend to provide some perspectives, tools and guidelines
which we hope will be useful for organising our path through the research process.

Whilst these pages are not the place to repeat a course in research methods, a few
words about why people do research in the first place are appropriate. Identifying
from published work why particular people have undertaken a piece of work at a
given time in their lives is not easy, though it may sometimes provide a useful starting point for understanding them as well as the work done. The personal rationale
guiding a given project may at times only be gleaned from biographical analysis, at
others, such an understanding may arise as part of a larger discourse about the place
certain ideas and ways of working occupy within a culture. At a fundamental level,
one reason for carrying out research arises from our natural human propensity for
curiosity, our desire to know the world we live in better and thereby negotiate our
way through with greater wisdom. Kelly (1955) constructed an influential body of
work from the premise that human beings can be looked upon as scientists, check-
ing out and testing their hypotheses. Asking questions of the world enables us to
challenge our assumptions and so leads to new ways to see the world; new ways not
just for other people, but for those doing the research too. As we seek to improve
our picture of the world – sometimes by changing it – we correspondingly reduce
uncertainty that alternative ideas are equally adept at explaining things.

All science is grounded in observations – in the human sciences these are usually
informal and may comprise part of what is called common sense. From these we
proceed to check out more closely and more systematically the patterns noticed and

try to understand why they have occurred. Because people are all different, with unique histories (even identical twins), we can't judge how anyone else will act in a particular situation on the basis of how we would. Consequently, the general principles behind the observations are sought through developing and testing theories and this requires gathering data on repeated occasions. This may come from the same person repeatedly, or from different people or different groups of people. From such repeated sampling we can begin to distinguish patterns with greater ease against the background noise of fluctuating influences. Research is of course not driven by simple curiosity alone – often the force of circumstances demands rapid solutions, and in health psychology a good deal of impetus has come from the needs for behavioural change in areas where large numbers of peoples' lives are at risk.

Research is often painted as an activity best carried out in the absence of human feeling – and with utmost seriousness. It is important to remember that the process of asking challenging questions, carrying out studies, being involved with participants, examining and interpreting data can be immensely enjoyable and that such enjoyment may actually enhance one's thinking. Good, rigorous and logical thinking is not incompatible with empathy and passion. The ideal state of mind for a researcher is not that of Mr Spock! Just as every long march must begin with a single step, the process of becoming a competent investigator is one requiring patience and persistence – and the necessary knowledge before one can make full use of one's flights of fancy is sometimes hard won. It is important to remember that the work can be enjoyed. Before we proceed to review and explicate some of the conceptual tools which lie at the heart of contemporary research practice it must be admitted that in health and in other areas of social science, work has often been carried out for the wrong reasons – perhaps the worst of all being to stave off action somewhere else. The repeated chorus of 'more research is needed' wheeled out by policy-makers is frequently intended to prolong inactivity, delay implementation of what would be costly but effective preventive actions or simply to promote public image. Moore, Beazley and Maelzer (1998) provide a candid account of the pressures which worked against their own research producing positive change for young deaf pre-school children and their families. Science is a powerful tool for abuse as well as use!

METHODOLOGY IN HEALTH PSYCHOLOGY

The process of framing questions and evaluating data is similar across many disciplines, though each tends to favour a set of methods and techniques that have been developed for answering questions in a particular domain. This is also true in the health sciences. The use of multiple research methods can partially overcome deficiencies that flow from any one investigative approach and when considered together may provide a more compelling picture. We can, for example, supplement quantitative methods with qualitative methods to check accuracy, content, validity and the possible nature and direction of causal pathways. This multiple cross-checking of the outcomes of different approaches is what is meant by triangulation. It serves the valuable function of ensuring consistency in the interpretation of findings. What methodology is employed will be heavily influenced by the source of the data – where the information to be 'worked on' originates. These can be broadly organised along a continuum from qualitative to quantitative methods (see Figure 3.1). Which approach is taken will depend on the question asked, and the intended use to which the data will be put. At one extreme along this continuum we have real-

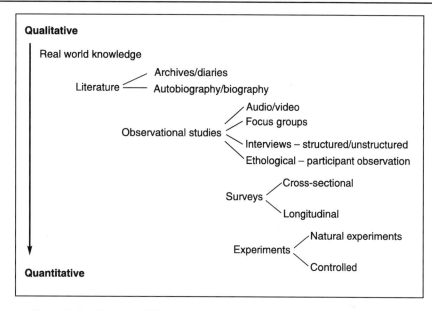

Figure 3.1 Sources of Knowledge/Spectrum of Research Methodologies

world experience – from introspection on one's mental processes to direct social interaction with others. Both are vital sources of information which can inform the process of hypothesis formation and serve as a reference point for the evaluation of existing hypotheses. At the other end of the spectrum there lies the randomised controlled trial (within-subjects, between-subjects, mixed designs). In principle this is the only method which is capable of rigorously demonstrating causal relationships between variables.

What constitutes scientific method is frequently misunderstood. It is not necessarily the exclusive use of any one of these methods nor the use of statistical techniques *per se*, but the gathering of data for the purpose of generating and testing theories about what is observed, the repeated use of which leads to a more accurate and useful model. This makes the scientific method an iterative process. In principle all data sources can be used in this way, but by far the most powerful for providing definite information on cause and effect relationships is the randomised controlled trial. The most powerful, though, does not necessarily mean the most appropriate for every situation. Having decided upon one's question and with it one's chosen method of research, a number of additional aspects of the research process warrant our attention. We will review some of these below for both quantitative and qualitative methods.

QUANTITATIVE METHODS

Power Analysis and Sample-Size Calculations

Many studies are unable to answer the question for which they were designed because they fail to take account of the concept of statistical power. Put simply, the effects hoping to be found cannot be detected because of an inadequate sample size. Larger samples enable one to detect experimental effects which are quite weak. On the other hand to detect very large effects, small samples should suffice. Most of the statistics that we perform involve rejecting the null hypothesis, and the major concern is to avoid a Type I error (falsely rejecting the null hypothesis when it is in fact true). The probability of making a Type I error is determined by the significance level (alpha) chosen – which is usually set at 5%, 1 chance in 20 ($p = 0.05$). However, we can also make a Type II error when the null hypothesis is false but we fail to reject it. The probability of a Type II error is denoted as beta, and the probability of correctly rejecting the null hypothesis is termed the Power and is defined as 1-beta. So if alpha is 5%, beta is therefore 95%. Performing what is called a power calculation enables one to calculate the minimum sample size necessary to achieve the required power and therefore detect an effect one thinks is there (see Box 3.1). Typically, power is set at 80% for a two-tailed alpha of 5%. This means that one would have an 80% chance of detecting a given effect which was capable of meeting statistical significance at the 5% level. Performing power calculations is often left to statisticians (see Box 3.2), but a useful strategy is to have access to tables which enable one to look up the desired number of participants needed to detect a variety of different effect sizes. Below we provide abbreviated tables for some commonly occurring research designs; correlation, independent groups (between subjects), paired samples (within subjects) and chi-square (2×2) designs to give the reader some flavour of what is involved.

Table 3.1 shows the numbers required at each of three effect sizes (given by the correlation coefficient) to have an 80% chance of detecting a significant correlation of this magnitude at the 5% level (based on Wright, 1997: effect sizes suggested after Cohen, 1992).

BOX 3.1   Concept of effect size

Effect size is an indication of the strength of relationship between independent and dependent variables. The effect size may be described as small, medium or large.

Power analysis is conducted prior to running a study and is concerned with determining appropriate sample sizes so that there is a reasonably good chance that the effects of interest will be detected when the appropriate statistical analysis is performed.

Power calculations require that we estimate the **Effect Size** which we expect to occur or which would be the minimum that we would consider important. The effect size may be described as small, medium or large and gives an indication of how strong a particular relationship is. When comparing two groups and where the level of measurement is approximately interval, the effect size is the difference in the magnitude of the scores in each condition (d) divided by the standard deviation (SD). In other words it is the standardised difference between groups (compare this to the notion of standardised or z-score differences):

$$\text{Effect size} = d/SD \qquad (3.1)$$

For categorical data the effect size is the difference in proportions expected. For example, where Pa is the proportion in group a and Pb is the proportion in group b, the effect size is just the difference between them,

$$\text{Effect size} = Pa - Pb \qquad (3.2)$$

If a large effect is at work then the numbers required to detect this can be small. If we are looking for a small effect then, unsurprisingly, we will need large sample sizes.

Power analysis is therefore concerned with determining appropriate sample sizes so that there is a reasonably good chance that the effects of interest for the investigator(s) can be detected with the appropriate statistical analysis. This entails that hypotheses will not be needlessly rejected and that the vast amount of time and resources in recruiting participants, collecting and analysing data, is not wasted.

Table 3.1   Effect size and power in correlation

Effect size	r	Required sample size for 80% power at $p = 0.05$
Small	0.10	783
Medium	0.30	85
Large	0.50	28

Table 3.2   Effect size and power in between-subjects designs (independent t-test)

Effect size	$D = d/SD$ (z-score)	Required sample size in each condition for 80% power, $p = 0.05$
	0.10	1571
Small	0.20	392
	0.30	176
	0.40	100
Medium	0.50	64
	0.60	45
	0.70	33
Large	0.80	26

Source: Adapted from D.C. Howell (1992).

As can be seen, there is an enormous difference between the numbers required to detect medium-size relationships as compared to small ones. Larger sample sizes thus give greater sensitivity to detect these weaker effects, and this is essentially the reason epidemiological studies are conducted on such a large scale. They enable investigators to detect effects that might be very small. This is also evident in Table 3.2 which shows the sample sizes required when analysing data with an Independent t-test. From this it can be seen that in order to have an 80% chance of detecting a significant difference (at the 5% level) between two conditions, equal to an effect size of 0.40, 100 subjects in each condition are needed.

For within-subjects designs, such as in a paired t-test, the situation is more complicated and computation of power involves knowledge of the test–retest reliability of the measure. In Table 3.3 we have computed the required sample sizes for different effect sizes (calculated as though for independent samples) against a range of test–retest reliabilities. This shows the sample size required for a paired t-test to have an 80% chance of detecting a significant difference (at the 5% level) between two conditions, for three different effect sizes – against different levels of reliability of the underlying measure.

Table 3.3   Effect size and power (80%) in within subjects designs

Effect size	$D = d/SD$ (z-score)	Test–retest reliability					
		0.9	0.8	0.7	0.6	0.5	0
Small	0.20	39	78	118	157	196	392
Medium	0.50	6	13	19	25	32	63
Large	0.80	3	5	7	10	12	25

Note that as test–retest reliability tends to zero, then the power calculation indicates that the paired t-test reduces to the efficiency of an independent t-test in power and sample size requirements.

When a researcher wishes to determine sample sizes for data which are clearly non-parametric (for example if the data is ordered or ranked), the difficulties multiply. Three options can be considered where this is the case. First of all specialist commercial software is available, often developed for clinical trials and the drug research industry (see suggested reading and notes on software at the end of this chapter). Secondly Campbell, Julius and Altman (1995) provide a set of equations which can be used for the purpose, and as a final option an approximation can be made whereby the ranked data is treated as if it was interval and estimations derived as though for independent or paired t-tests. This last option is likely to produce underestimates of the sample sizes required as non-parametric tests typically have less power. As a final example of power analysis, when using categorical data which one wishes to analyse by means of a 2×2 chi-square test, the sample sizes required to achieve 80% power at the 5% level in detecting a difference in two proportions (given as Pa and Pb: see equation (3.2) in Box 3.1) can be estimated from Table 3.4. An example use of the table is provided in Box 3.2b, where it is assumed that equal

---

BOX 3.2A. Example power calculation, between subjects

The 12-item General Health Questionnaire (GHQ-12) is well normalised having a mean score (SD) of 22.8 ($SD = 4.93$) with relatively small age and sex differences.

Question: What are the sample sizes necessary to demonstrate (at 80% power for $p = 0.05$, 2-tail) a 3-point difference in GHQ-12 score between a group of people with multiple sclerosis and a control group of people with non-neurological disease?

Answer: The effect size is equal to $3/4.93 = 0.60$. From Table 3.2 it can be seen that for an effect size of this magnitude, 45 subjects are required in each condition, making 90 in all. It is always worth allowing for attrition and some non-respondents and therefore if we increase this figure by 50% (making around 67 in each sample) the sample size should be sufficient.

BOX 3.2B. Example power calculation, binary data (chi-square)

The combined risk of anticipatory, concurrent and 48-hours-plus delayed vomiting in patients undergoing chemotherapy is around 70%. With conventional $5HT_3$ receptor antagonist antiemetics this is reduced to 30% vomiting. It is hoped that the new neurokinin receptor antagonist antiemetic will reduce this to 20% vomiting.

Question: What sample sizes are necessary to demonstrate the conventional therapy effect at 80% power for $p = 0.05$, 2-tail?

Answer: $Pa = 0.70$, $Pb = 0.30$. Therefore 24 patients per group, that is total $n = 48$.

Question: What sample sizes are necessary to demonstrate that the new therapy is more effective than the conventional therapy at 80% power for $p = .05$, 2-tail?

Answer: $Pa = 0.30$, $Pb = 0.20$. Therefore 294 patients per group that is total $n = 588$.

Table 3.4   Sample sizes to detect difference in two proportions, *Pa* and *Pb* (5% level with 80% power)

Pa	Pb									
	0.00	0.05	0.10	0.15	0.20	0.25	0.30	0.35	0.40	0.45
0.05	152									
0.10	74	435								
0.15	48	141	686							
0.20	35	76	199	906						
0.25	27	49	100	250	1094					
0.30	22	36	62	121	294	1251				
0.35	18	27	43	73	138	329	1377			
0.40	15	22	32	49	82	152	356	1471		
0.45	13	18	25	36	54	89	163	376	1534	
0.50	11	15	20	27	39	58	93	170	388	1565
0.55	10	12	16	22	29	41	61	96	173	392
0.60	8	11	14	17	23	31	42	62	97	173
0.65	7	9	11	14	18	24	31	43	62	96
0.70	6	8	10	12	15	19	24	31	42	61
0.75	6	7	8	10	12	15	19	24	31	41
0.80	5	6	7	8	10	12	15	18	23	29
0.85	4	5	6	7	8	10	12	14	17	22
0.90	4	4	5	6	7	8	10	11	14	16
0.95	3	4	4	5	6	7	8	9	11	12
1.0	(2)	3	4	4	5	6	6	7	8	10

Source: Adapted from M.J. Campbell *et al.* (1995), *British Medical Journal*, **311**: 1445–8, with permission from the BMJ Publishing Group.

sample sizes are used and the table gives the size of each sample (that is, the number to give the total experimental sample size must be doubled).

Other Designs

Where large data sets have been gathered and the researcher hypothesises relationships between several variables – that is, multivariate analyses are required to test the hypotheses – the process of determining the exact sample sizes for different size effects is extremely complex. In the absence of this, a working rule of thumb frequently adopted when performing analyses such as multiple *regression* or factor analysis is that to detect anything of statistical significance one should use at least 10 subjects for every variable to be used in the analysis (Tabachnik and Fidell, 1997).

Regression is a statistical technique which enables the simultaneous effect of several variables on a dependent variable to be estimated. The magnitude of the effects of individual variables are given by beta values (which can vary between zero and 1). The combined effects of all the variables are expressed in terms of the total percentage variation in the dependent variable which they (statistically) explain.

Questionnaire Construction

Prior to designing it, it is worthwhile spending time thinking about what the main aims of a questionnaire are. On occasions, aims may only be stated in quite general terms – for example when an area of investigation is poorly understood, or when there is a lack of basic information about who is doing what, and how often, and so on. More often, however, it is worth its weight in gold to have an explicitly formulated hypothesis or set of hypotheses before constructing the questionnaire. Once this is done, thought needs to be directed to how the questionnaire will meet the desired goals. This may be attained through the use of a series of existing reliable and well-validated scales, or instead may consist of a number of questions specifically constructed to gather relevant information.

Where scales exist to measure an attribute of interest, then it is certainly better to use these than set about reinventing new ones. Away from the use of validated scales it will usually be necessary to gather some information by means of a series of specially constructed questions. There are advantages and disadvantages to be weighed up regarding the form in which these questions are set. *Open-ended*, sometimes called free-response questions offer greater flexibility and allow respondents more opportunity to say what they wish. Greater meaning may be present in these and they will usually provide a rich source of data. However, on the downside they may be very difficult to score or interpret reliably. *Closed* questions on the other hand may be answered quickly and the answers can be readily compared across individuals. The downside with these is that they may reduce respondents' expressiveness and fail to capture their views accurately. A variety of closed question types can be employed. These include simple *categorical* questions (e.g. requiring Yes/No answers); *checklists* where respondents are given the option to tick a number of possible responses (e.g. whether different types of recreational drugs have been used in the preceding month); *multiple-choice* questions; and *Likert* scales in which respondents choose from amongst a series of ordered possibilities (e.g. 'all of the time', 'most of the time', 'some of the time', 'a little of the time', none of the time'). Visual analogue scales (VAS) have also been successfully used in a variety of contexts (e.g. measuring current levels of happiness or perceived pain). With these a straight line may be used to represent the continuum of the quality to be assessed, with each end of the scale marked with labels to indicate the range being considered (McDowell and Newell, 1996). Pictorial scales may be particularly useful with children, whose ability to rate their own well-being has often been underestimated (Fallowfield, 1995c).

Having chosen one's questions, the next step is to decide the ordering of the questions and the overall structure of the questionnaire – where best to place sensitive questions, how long to keep the questionnaire, what balance of open-ended and closed questions there should be. A first draft should be thoroughly edited and scrutinised from the perspective of a prospective respondent. Only after this has been done will it be the time right to pilot the questionnaire. Between 5–10 people may be thought of as providing a reasonable number for ironing out obvious flaws.

The process of revising the questionnaire should culminate in decisions about how it will be presented and delivered to prospective respondents. The instructions for its completion, for example, must be unambiguous, and it is important to remember that providing respondents with anonymity is more likely to produce truthful responding and a higher response rate. This should be considered essential where questionnaires are enquiring about illegal or potentially socially undesirable attitudes or activities (for example alcohol consumption, drug taking, criminal activities and so on). As a matter of courtesy and ethics the background or purpose of the questionnaire should be clearly explained, who it is that is carrying it out, and who to contact in the event of any queries. Remember always to thank the respondent too. These steps are summarised in Figure 3.2. The steps prior to piloting can be thought of as forming an iterative cycle and not something to be rushed through

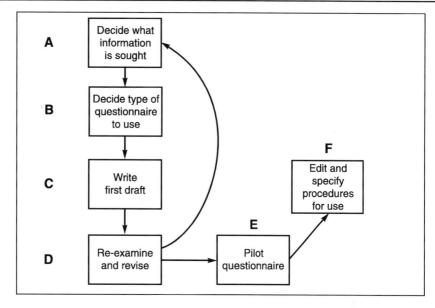

Figure 3.2   Steps in questionnaire design

Source: Adapted from *Statistical Methods for Psychology (with InfoTrac)*, 3rd edn, by
D.C. Howell, © 1997. Reprinted with permission of Brooks/Cole, a division of Thomson
Learning.

as quickly as possible. Time well spent in the earlier stages will save time later, and
enable more useful analyses to be performed. Indeed, the planning of the questions
should proceed hand in hand with deciding how data will be analysed. Finally, of
course, the questionnaire has to get from the researcher to the potential respondents. This can take place by a variety of means; mail (postal surveys), in large or
small groups, by personal interviews, by telephone, or by means of the Internet.

QUALITATIVE RESEARCH METHODS

Positivism A branch of
philosophy which holds that
only knowledge which can be
empirically verified is of
value.

The re-emergence of interest in qualitative methods of investigation in psychology
has arisen as a backlash against what some now see as the extreme positivism inherent
in scientific psychology and its shortcomings in understanding questions of meaning in human affairs (Harre and Gillet, 1994). Important questions have been posed
regarding the consequences of measurement, the view of human nature enshrined
within the measuring process (for example flexibility versus inflexibility) and to
what degree given instruments capture the history of interaction between person
and environment. In critiquing the politics and methods of positivist work, qualitative
researchers have provided an important reminder that the focus of all our enquiries
ultimately concerns ourselves, and that how we as human beings are constructed
within the research process has important personal and social consequences. The
search for and construction of meaning within our lives is inextricably interwoven
into the fabric of a continuously changing socially constructed landscape (Denzin
and Lincoln, 1994). This apparent lack of ground for anchoring conceptions of
human nature is what has led some to reject scientific method altogether simply
because of its assumption of a knowable real world.

It is inescapably true, as Foucault argues, that the forms of our knowledge are socially constructed, and that this knowledge is sought and expressed under the determining effects of social and historical forces (Rabinow, 1984). However there are constraints on how such forces can shape received wisdom, and the positioning of qualitative methodology as wholly antagonistic to the pursuit of science through quantitative means is we believe mistaken. These limits pertain to the type and range of cause and effect relationships which can be 'discovered' in any historical epoch. The prevailing *zeitgeist* may obscure certain relationships and promote others into view – however, it can be argued that certain cause and effect relationships cannot be 'discovered' unless some analogue of these perceived relationships actually exists in the real world. In using the scientific method it is extremely difficult if not impossible (a dangerous word!) to produce publicly verifiable knowledge of cause and effect relationships where the only evidence publicly available and disseminable is people's belief in such relationships. Social class may be socially constructed, for example, but its effects are not – people of lower social status are more likely to suffer all manner of physical and mental ill-health (see Chapter 12). This is detectable and verifiable whether politicians find it comfortable or not. This is not to deny that scientists (and others) are capable of getting the public to believe in the existence or non-existence of certain relationships, but that is a different matter. Science aspires to survive the nightmare of postmodernist assault through the continual public reproducibility under widely differing social conditions of the forms of knowledge it produces (the application of method and the results of that application). Without this, perhaps nothing would stand in the way of the continual re-invention of reality under some Orwellian subterfuge.

Thus we take the view that in the ground between entrenched unreconstructed positivism and the rejection of any absolute standards for knowledge lies a fruitful middle path, where there is a significant scientific role for qualitative methods in psychology (Burt and Oaksford, 1999). Here the emphasis is on the appropriateness of qualitative methodology to generate hypotheses, to investigate sensitive situations that are not initially amenable to quantitative enquiry, and to adopt critical realist perspectives on the assumptions underlying and guiding scientific practise. Notions of validity and reliability are not incompatible with such pursuits. In addition where research questions might require participants to monitor or sample their own cognitive processes or to reflect on major narrative currents in aspects of their lives no other methods can be considered as valid (see Box 3.3). Unfortunately, the current dominance of the biomedical model in health research means that these have so far had little impact in Health Psychology (Chamberlain, Stephens and Lyons, 1997). Because of this it will be useful to provide a brief background on two of the major forms of qualitative enquiry, **discourse analysis** and **grounded theory**. Though quite different, both follow the same path of attempting to reduce the complexity inherent in the raw data, displaying what are considered its key aspects and analysing/drawing conclusions from it. These quite broad features are shared with forms of quantitative analyses.

Discourse analysis Analysis of the systematic and coherent nature of images, language and metaphors which embody a particular way of seeing the world.

Grounded theory is a method of qualitative research in which theory is generated on the ground from the repeated inspection and collection of raw data.

Discourse analysis

To understand discourse analysis it helps to understand discourse. Discourse can refer to a systematic, coherent set of images and metaphors – a way of seeing the world from a particular vantage point. Additionally it can also refer to the actual spoken interchanges between people that reveal these vantage points. Discourse analysis of a piece of text is undertaken in order to reveal either the discourse operating within it or the linguistic and rhetorical devices that are used in its construction. Discourse analysts have rejected the traditional cognitive explanations of social interaction and rather than trying to explain actions as a consequence of mental processes, their interest is in how mentalist notions are constructed and used within interactions. Discourse analysts emphasise the way in which language not only serves to construct or reproduce existing power structures in society but how its very transparency allows for the multiplication of meanings by interpreters in varying contexts (Chamberlain *et al.*, 1997; Stainton-Rogers, 1999). This distinguishes it from say cognitive analysis of speech acts, in so far as the meanings inherent in texts and utterances are not seen as fixed. Because of this fluidity there is no one right way to conduct discourse analysis. Potter and Wetherell (1987), however, posit a number of criteria for validating its results. The first of these is that the analysis should bring coherence to the discourse. Secondly, participants should have the same orientation to the data as do the analysts – agreeing for example on the presence of inconsistency and contradiction in the discourse. Thirdly, the discourses identified and drawn on may produce both problems and solutions. Last of all the results should be fruitful, allowing others to follow the reasoning processes from data to conclusions and to apply the results to other novel settings – in other words it must be generalisable. The second of these criteria is certainly contentious as it is difficult to pinpoint where orientation to the data and interpretation of it diverge. Without a doubt where researchers are undertaking action research or participant observation, the local actors and the researchers may very well fail to agree on what is or is not there in the data (Miles and Huberman, 1994).

In health, discourse analysis has been used to examine the social and political consequences of the medical model of health for the health 'consumer' in general, as well as for discrete patient groups. Yardley (1999), for example, has examined the consequences and treatment possibilities for people with impairments of balance as one moves from a medical discourse to one where symbolic and cultural aspects of differences in physical functioning are recognised. Discourse analysis may also look at how notions of responsibility and blame arise from the notions of risk in traditional research work and lay perceptions of risk behaviour. Additional interest has concerned the discourse of the body as a battleground between competing war-like factions. This 'military'-style discourse is routinely employed in depicting death, disability and disease as the enemy with the medical profession fighting the good fight. Further moral discourses abound; cancer, AIDS, euthanasia, mental ill-health. Throughout this book we examine a variety of these in the field of health psychology itself; notions of health, individual responsibility, the relation between the individual and the social, professional power and status, and finally the future of the discipline (see particularly Chapter 24).

Grounded Theory

Grounded theory was first described by Glaser and Strauss (1967) in order to express the idea of theory that is generated by or grounded in an iterative process, which begins from inspection of the raw data. This would involve the continual sampling and analysis of qualitative data from either a single source or numerous sources such as interviews, participant observation and archival research. Great emphasis is placed on the participants' own accounts of social and psychological

BOX 3.3 Validity

Validity is, broadly speaking, concerned with the ability of a model (or construct) to represent reality. Various types of validity exist; discriminant validity refers to the extent to which a scale discriminates between people who differ in their degree of a particular attribute; construct validity refers to the degree to which a new measure agrees with existing measures of the same construct.

Postmodernism is a critical cultural movement contending that we have gone beyond the world view of modernism (associated with increasing certainty of knowledge, social progress, and progression towards truth in science). Post-modern critiques contend that no set of values, morals and judgements can lay claim to special status compared to others. In relation to the practice of science this has led to arguments that no system of knowledge has a privileged position for describing and characterising the world.

In quantitative research, **validity** is usually taken to indicate the extent to which the characteristics of a construct are well represented in a scale which purports to measure it (content validity), the extent to which the scale discriminates between people who differ in their degree of the attribute in question (discriminant validity) or the degree to which it agrees with existing measures of the same construct (construct validity). Where mathematical/statistical models are used to represent more complex processes assumed to be occurring in the natural/social world, validity refers to the ability (usually quantifiable) of a model to represent reality; i.e. it must incorporate sufficiently analogous features to those assumed to occur in the real world (Barrow, 1992; Cohen and Stewart, 1994). Given the conventional view of science expounded by Popper (1972), that a theory be considered valid to the extent that it enjoys repeated success in prediction despite attempts to demonstrate its unworkability, the validity of any model is bound up with its ability to yield repeatable findings under different conditions. Less-stringent philosophies, which assert that scientific activity defines the limitations within which theories or models are applicable to the real world, still emphasise repeatable testing (Dunbar, 1995). In the majority of instances in which statistical modelling has been employed in health psychology, however, the models have not been tested on new data and therefore, impressive as they sometimes appear to be, the information which they actually impart about reality is questionable. With repeatability, it is not clear nor universally accepted what kind of results should constitute an acceptance that what is important in a previous model has been replicated. The reproducibility of the effect size is one candidate in quantitative modelling, though is by no means the end of the story.

The above criteria are also applicable to ideas generated from qualitative analyses with reproducibility denoting the tendency for the same themes to emerge with some similarity in their salience and organisation. There is evidence that where focus groups are concerned this is questionable (Weinberger, *et al.*, 1998). More importantly, the extent to which the schemas generated in such research represent analogous features which can be said to exist independently of the coder must be addressed. Thus as a basic requirement, a level of consensus must be reached about what the data actually are and how to obtain them, before any theoretical claims based upon them can proceed. The danger is that various interpretative schemes – perhaps held by those with competing material, political or ideological interests – may lay equal claim to be 'true' and be equally capable of fitting the agreed data and mapping out future research programmes. This problem recurs throughout the history and philosophy of science (e.g. Feyerabend) and is not easily resolvable. In essence this constitutes the **post-modern** dilemma – for if competing claims to the truth cannot be distinguished by any means other than the social power wielded by the protagonists of one view over another, where does that leave claims to knowledge and what does knowledge then mean? Certainly science cannot lay claim to absolute truths, nor even to possess the best possible truths within the limits of the human condition. What it can do is provide a set of tests to be overcome if a conjecture is to prove its worth as the most fruitful means to further in good faith the human enterprise to know. This does not mean that this rationale is always predominant. For example, ideas exist in health which we believe have long exhausted their scientific merit but which survive in pockets of the academic community by means of the social power wielded. We contend only that in the long run such ideas will tend not to survive.

events and of their associated local phenomenal and social worlds. The interpretation of data and production of theory thus co-evolve in a kind of bootstrapping process in which each feeds into and shapes the other.

Analysis involves three stages; open coding in which general relevant categories are first outlined; axial or core coding in which these are refined and related to one another; and selective coding where core categories are formulated which structure and bind all the categories together into a coherent theory. Following such coding schemes, however, is no guarantor that a good theory will ensue. To address this Strauss and Corbin (1990) cite a number of criteria that a good grounded theory should meet. These include that the theory fits the data well, that it provides understanding, is comprehensible, generalisable and clarifies the conditions under which it applies. These criteria could be said to be equally applicable to any theory, however derived. What needs to be asked of any method (quantitative or qualitative) is whether its use is likely to lead to conclusions which are valid and reproducible (see Box 3.3).

RESEARCH PROTOCOLS

Research protocols or proposals or grant proposals have come to dominate the life of aspiring health psychologists (and indeed others) who need to obtain funding to carry out research. Whilst the numerous grant-giving bodies have their own in-house formats there are a number of important questions that are asked of all applications for funding. Does the proposal address a well-formulated problem? Is it a research problem or a routine application of known techniques? Will the outcome of the research have useful applications? Do the proposers have a good idea on which to base their work? Does the proposal explain clearly what work will be done? Is there evidence that the proposers know about the work that others have done on the problem? Do the proposers have a good track record, both of doing good research and of publishing it? Is the work cost-effective and value-added? Have ethical considerations been taken into account?

Some common shortcomings in grant applications concern the clarity with which a proposal is formulated. For example it may not be clear what question is being addressed by the proposal, or the question being addressed may not be well formed, so that it is not clear why it is worth addressing. Other difficulties may arise where the proposal is just a routine application of known techniques or when the research being proposed would be better carried out by industry. Insufficient details may be given of how the goals of the research are to be attained, although the ideas themselves are good. The proposers may be attempting too much for the time scale of funding requested. More concrete problems are where the proposers are unaware of related research or where the work is unethical. A more intangible problem may arise where the funding bodies are not convinced the researchers will succeed in addressing a problem area where others have failed. The best practice for first time applicants is to get feedback from colleagues experienced in getting grants or to include them on the application.

Summary and conclusions ●

Carrying out research effectively involves using methods appropriate to the questions being posed. Scientific method is not dependent on the application of statistical techniques *per se*, but is the gathering of data for the purpose of generating and testing theories about what is observed. In this chapter we have set out to provide some useful perspectives, practical tools and guidelines for conducting effective research in health psychology. These include an introduction to the principles and practise of power analysis, a review of the principal stages in questionnaire design, and a description of some pitfalls commonly found in funding applications. An understanding of these should mean less energy and effort is expended in designing research protocols or in actually conducting research which is not capable of actually answering the questions asked.

In addition we have also examined the issue of validity as it applies to both quantitative and qualitative research and attempted to describe both the common ground underlying both types of research, as well as some of the problems unique to each. We have also endeavoured to provide a brief introduction to some of the more well-known methodologies used in qualitative research which are increasingly being employed in health and social science research, and which students of health psychology should become acquainted with.

Discussion points

A Given that much qualitative research goes on in the so-called 'hard sciences', and has not required a new theory or approach, why is this deemed necessary in the human sciences?

B Do theories in health psychology tend to fall into disuse or are they disproved?

Suggested reading

Cohen, J. (1992) 'A Power Primer', *Psychological Bulletin*, **112**: 155–9.

Campbell, M.J., Julious, S.A. and Altman, D.G. (1995) 'Estimating Sample Sizes for Binary, ordered categorical, and continuous outcomes in two group comparisons. *British Medical Journal*, **311**, 1145-1148.

Day, S.J. and Graham, D.F. (1989) 'Sample Size and Power for Comparing Two or More Treatment Groups in Clinical Trials', *British Medical Journal*, **299**: 663–5.

Howell, D.C. (1992) *Statistical Methods for Psychology*, 3rd edn (Belmont, Cal.: Duxbury Press (Wadsworth Publ. Co.).

Software

For Power Analysis

Cytel Stats Software UK/USA.
Tel 0044 (0)1227 823 922
E-mail asru-cytel@ukc.ac.uk
IDV Munich Germany, Tel. 0049 89 8508001

Arcus Pro Stat contains options for computing sample sizes for a limited number of designs.

Medical Computing, Pine Crest, 83 Turnpike Road, Aughton, West Lancs, L39 3LD. United Kingdom. Tel 0044 (0)1695 424 645

For Qualitative Analysis

The Nudist program can be obtained from Qualitative Solutions and Research Pty Ltd., 2 Research Drive, La Trobe University, Melbourne, Vic, 3083, Australia. E-mail Nudist@latcs1.lat.oz.au

Part 2
Psychobiology of Health

It is customary in any comprehensive health psychology text to present an introduction to the basic systems of the body. This section begins with such a review, which includes discussion of the complexities of pain perception. This should enable the reader to gain an appreciation of the biological dimensions which are susceptible to disturbance from psychological and social forces and serves as a primer to the subsequent examination of what many consider comprises the core of health psychology – psychoneuroimmunology. Though this material is necessarily technical in nature, it does not escape critical examination of the methods and key assumptions employed, principally whether sufficient evidence exists to demonstrate causal links between psychological and biological processes.

Surprisingly health psychology has had little application in the area of mental health. As advances in the neurosciences lead to ever greater claims about the biological basis of mental ill-health, health psychologists have tended to remain silent. We believe this is unnecessary.

Some of the important contributions made by health psychologists concerning the measurement and validation of concepts of health have considerable relevance when employed in debates regarding the legitimacy of psychiatric diagnostic categories. To rectify this, the middle chapter of this part considers three controversial psychological disorders, now widely believed to have their origins in an underlying biological dysfunction and subjects them to scrutiny from a health psychology perspective. Further issues for health psychologists interested in mental health are also introduced in this section.

4

Biomedical Science and Health Psychology

'Not only our pleasure our joy and our laughter but also our sorrow, pain, grief, and tears rise from the brain, and the brain alone.'

Hippocrates, 400 BC

INTRODUCTION

Some knowledge of basic human physiology is necessary to understand health problems. In the context of a health psychology textbook there is insufficient space to cover such topics in depth, and the aim here is to provide some pointers for those readers with limited background in biological studies. The approach taken is to cover some of the basic systems of the body giving preferential weight to the nervous system, endocrine system and immune system, which arguably are of central importance to health psychology. Other major systems including cardiovascular, respiratory, digestive, reproductive (including genetics) and musculoskeletal systems are not detailed except indirectly, and the reader is referred to the many available basic human physiology textbooks or dictionaries of biology or medicine.

NERVOUS SYSTEM

The general function of the nervous system is to speed, integrate, and coordinate response to changes in the environment. As such the nervous system confers survival advantage to the animal. Evolutionary pressures resulted ultimately in the most advanced nervous system, that of the human. The building block of any nervous system is the nerve cell or neurone. The neurone is electrically active and can receive information from sensory cells or other neurones via fine branches (dendrites). Such diverse information is integrated and the neurone comes to a 'decision' which is represented by electrical firing (the 'all or nothing' action potential) which is transmitted along the output arm (axon) communicating with many other neurones. Each neurone may receive information through its dendrites from many thousands of connections and in turn its axon may branch to give perhaps on average up to one thousand connections (Kandel *et al.*, 1995, p. 181). An analogy might be made in which, rather than considering the brain as a computer, every neurone can be seen to have many of the properties of a hybrid analogue and digital computer.

The specialised junction of the axonal terminal with another cell is termed the synapse. Information passed across the synapse may either activate or by contrast

Neurotransmitters are the chemical messengers released from the pre-synaptic terminal of a nerve cell to convey excitatory or inhibitory information to another. Examples include acetylcholine, serotonin and dopamine.

inhibit effectors such as muscles or glands or other nerve cells in turn. Most synapses are chemical, in which **neurotransmitter** molecules are released from the (so-called presynaptic) terminal to convey excitatory or inhibitory information by diffusing across the synaptic cleft and binding very selectively to specialised receptors on the surface of another (so-called postsynaptic) neurone. Only a small minority of synapses ($<10\%$) are of the very fast electrical type where information is passed by ionic currents across a very narrow synapse called a gap junction. It is noteworthy that the mechanism of action of psychoactive drugs is to alter chemical neurotransmission in various ways, for example nicotine from smoking mimics many of the actions of the neurotransmitter acetylcholine.

Primitive animals may have only tens or hundreds of neurones, arranged in simple circuits or neural nets, more complex organisms may have thousands to millions organised in chains of concentrations (ganglia) whereas advanced animals will have billions of neurones organised into spinal cord and brain. The nervous system is conventionally divided on anatomical grounds into the central nervous system

Table 4.1   Structural and functional organisation of the nervous system

Peripheral Nervous System (PNS): peripheral nerves and ganglia

Somatic	Voluntary motor efferents to muscles and sensory afferents
Autonomic	Involuntary nervous system: controls heart, gut etc. Sympathetic/parasympathetic: are in balance and oppose each other, e.g. sympathetic activity produces heart rate increase versus parasympathetic activity which produces decrease. Sympathetic – through 2 chains of ganglia, controlled by hypothalamus Parasympathetic – mainly by cranial nerves from medulla

Central Nervous System (CNS): brain and spinal cord

Spinal cord	Inner core grey matter – cell bodies of neurones; outer white matter – axons; segmental levels each innervating sets of muscles and dermatomes
Ventricles	Cerebrospinal fluid (CSF) buffers against shock, buoyancy, nutritive and hormonal reservoir
Hindbrain	Brainstem: pons and medulla – vital reflexes such as breathing, heart rate, vomiting, coughing, sneezing, salivation; arousal controlled by ascending reticular activating system (ARAS)
	Cerebellum – control of movement coordination, balance, etc.
Midbrain	Tectum, tegmentum, superior/inferior colliculus – important routes of sensory information and controls orienting reflex
	Substantia nigra – contains dopaminergic neurons, cf. Parkinson's disease
Forebrain	Thalamus – main source of sensory information for cortex, does some processing Hypothalamus – controls feeding, drinking, temperature, sex, partly via control of the pituitary gland; suprachiasmatic nucleus provides 'biological clock' Limbic system – involved with emotions and also memory Basal ganglia – indirectly controls movement, cf. damaged in Parkinson's disease Corpus callosum – information transfer between the two hemispheres Cerebral cortex – sensory, associative, motor (see below)

Major Divisions of the Cerebral Cortex: simplified functions

Occipital	Vision
Parietal	Somatosensory, spatial awareness
Temporal	Auditory, language (Wernicke's area), advanced visual processing, face recognition, emotions
Frontal	Motor, speech production (Broca's area), all sensory modalities, planning and control (prefrontal)

(CNS: brain and spinal cord) and peripheral nervous system PNS (all nerves outside of the CNS). Some of the major subdivisions, together with their major functional roles are summarised in Table 4.1. In addition, Figures 4.1 and 4.2 show in a simplified fashion the major structures of the brain and autonomic nervous system.

One simplified method of considering the brain is to view it as approximately organised in an evolutionary manner, where those parts at the base and centre (brainstem) evolved earlier and those parts at the top and outside (cortex) evolved much more recently. In general, those 'older' parts of the brain such as the brainstem are involved in very basic functions absolutely essential to survival such as respiratory pattern generators, sleep–wakefulness, and so on, whereas 'newer' cortical areas provide more complex sensory analysis and motor outputs, as well as 'cognitive' functions. The cerebellum, an outgrowth of the brainstem which looks somewhat like a little brain itself, is concerned with muscle tone, balance and coordination of movements.

Surrounding the brainstem is the limbic system which includes the hippocampus, olfactory bulbs, septum, amygdala, mamillary bodies and cingulate gyrus (a primitive part of the cerebral cortex). The hypothalamus is also usually regarded as part of the limbic system, and it is through the hypothalamus that strong emotions provoke autonomic responses such as increased heart rate and sweating (see below 'Autonomic Nervous System'). The limbic system is greatly involved in the whole range of emotions; pleasure, fear, pain, sexual enjoyment, aggression, and so on. Electrical stimulation of some limbic areas can cause intense pleasure whereas stimulation of other limbic areas can be extremely aversive. It has recently been demonstrated using non-invasive brain imaging including PET and functional MRI (see Box 4.1) that the subjective experience of pain is associated with activation of

BOX 4.1   Functional Imaging

Positron Emission Tomography (PET) provides one means for measuring brain activity. In the procedure a substance used by the brain – usually glucose or oxygen – is labelled with a radioactive isotope and injected into the bloodstream. The radioactive molecules are incorporated into neurons in proportion to their metabolic rate. Collisions between positrons (positively charged electrons) emitted by the labelled substance and electrons lead to emission of high energy photons which are then converted by computer analysis into a pictorial representation of the metabolic rate, thereby denoting the level of activity in different regions of the functioning brain (Rosenhan and Seligman 1989).

Magnetic Resonance Imaging (MRI) is another non-invasive imaging technique. It is based on the principles of nuclear magnetic resonance (NMR). Computerised images of internal body tissues are produced based on the resonance of hydrogen atoms within the body induced by the application of a powerful magnetic field and radio energy of a specific frequency. Images are monitored by an MRI computer, which processes them and displays them on a video monitor for interpretation or photographing for later interpretation. Its greatest advantage is that it can see through bone and delineate fluid-filled soft tissue in clear detail. Contrast agents in MRI work by altering the local magnetic field in the tissue being examined. Normal and abnormal tissue will respond differently to this slight alteration, giving different signals. These varied signals will be transferred to the images, allowing the visualisation of many different types of tissue abnormalities and disease processes.

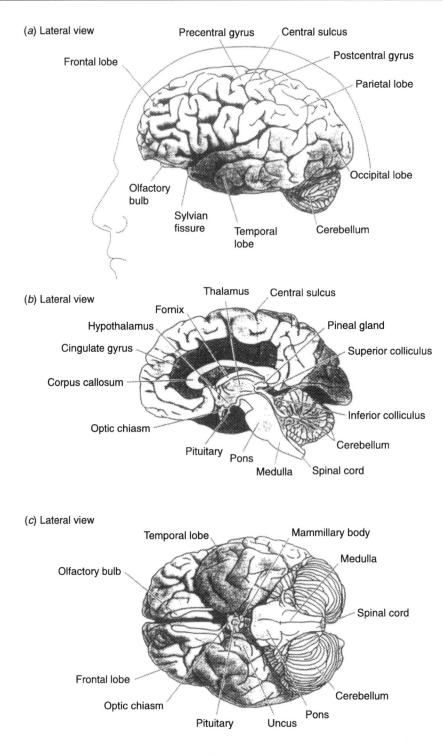

Figure 4.1 Main structures of the brain

Source: Rosenzweig, M.-R., Leiman, A.L. and Breedlove, S.M. (1995), *Biological Psychology*, 2nd edn, reproduced with permission from Sinauer Associates, MA.

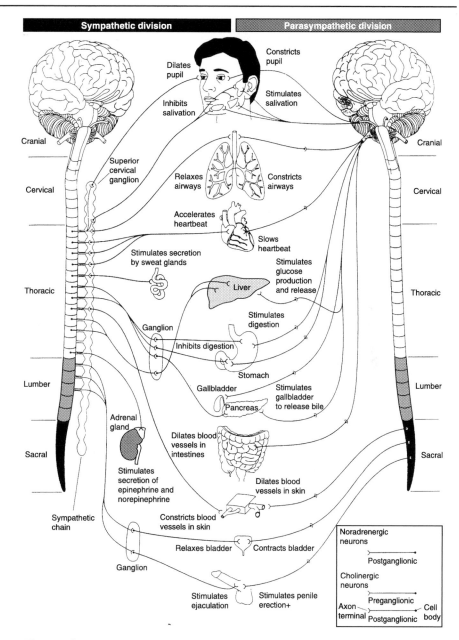

Figure 4.2 Schematic diagram of the sympathetic and parasympathetic branches of the autonomic nervous system

Source: Rosenzweig, M.-R., Leiman, A.L. and Breedlove, S.M. (1995), *Biological Psychology*, 2nd edn, reproduced with permission from Sinauer Associates, MA.

the cingulate gyrus of the limbic system and not simply the somatosensory processing areas of the parietal cortex. The limbic system forms the core of the reward/ punishment system of the brain in guiding behaviour. A related function of the limbic system is to relate value (reward/punishment) to external stimuli and consequent behavioural responses, that is learning and memory. For example, damage to the mamillary bodies of the limbic system can be caused by alcoholism, leading to the pattern of memory impairment denoted by Korsakoff's syndrome. The cerebral cortex encloses the limbic system and also the basal ganglia which are motor output regulatory nuclei. The main input gateway to the cerebral cortex is the thalamus, through which passes all sensory traffic to the cortex apart from smell. The cortex consists of the occipital, parietal, temporal and frontal lobes, which have sensory, motor and associative areas. It is here in the most recently evolved parts of the brain that the most complicated information processing is performed (see Table 4.1).

The autonomic nervous system (ANS) (see Figure 4.2) is a set of peripheral nerves and ganglia that control and receive information from smooth muscle (involuntary muscle such as heart, gut, bronchi of lungs, etc.) and glands (for example salivary, sweat, digestive, endocrine etc.). As the name implies, the ANS is self-regulating and not under direct voluntary control. The ANS is frequently defined simply as being part of the PNS (the other part of the PNS being the somatic motor efferents and sensory afferents). However, in terms of the overall system the ANS also includes the medulla of the brainstem and the hypothalamus which is closely linked with the limbic system and also controls the pituitary gland. The two main divisions of the ANS are the sympathetic and parasympathetic nervous systems which tend to work antagonistically, and generally on the same organs. The overall functions of the two might be described as 'fight or flight' when sympathetic activity predominates, *versus* 'rest and digest' when parasympathetic activity is dominant.

ENDOCRINE SYSTEM

The endocrine system is largely hormonal in nature and functions in a slower fashion than the nervous system, to which it serves a complementary role in regulating many bodily functions. It is usually characterised by negative feedback control where the production of a particular hormone will tend to inhibit further over-production. A summary of the endocrine system including the major organs, hormones and functions is given in Table 4.2.

Some aspects of the endocrine system are subject to direct influence by the nervous system, for example the release of adrenaline from the adrenal medulla of the kidney under the influence of sympathetic nerves during general activation of the sympathetic nervous system, the so-called 'fight–flight' pattern of widespread acti-vation. The released adrenaline passes into the general blood circulation and binds to specific receptors on various organs, for example it stimulates the heart to greater activity. This is a slower action than the direct (nerve) sympathetic stimulation of the heart. Other major branches of the endocrine system are subject to nervous system control through the pituitary gland situated just below the hypothalamus in the brain. One such is the hypothalamic–pituitary–adrenal (HPA) axis which con-trols the release of corticosteroids from the adrenal cortex of the kidneys via the release and systemic circulation of the intermediate hormone adrenocorticotrophic hormone (ACTH). The corticosteroids play a major role in regulating metabolic activity of the body (glucocorticoids, cortisol for glucose, etc.; mineralocorticoids for electrolyte balance). In addition, corticosteroids are involved in the control of inflammatory responses and immune system activity. The activation of the HPA is often caused by stress. Other aspects of the endocrine system are also under pituit-ary control and thus involve influence from the CNS. These include the regulatory hormones involved in the reproductive systems (e.g. gonadotropin), growth and repair (growth hormone), and water balance and blood pressure (vasopressin).

Table 4.2 Summary of the endocrine system: major organs, hormones and functions

Organ	Hormone	Function
Hypothalamus	Releasing hormones	Controls anterior pituitary
Anterior pituitary	Growth hormone (somatotrophin)	Promotes bodily growth
	Thyroid stimulating hormone	Stimulates thyroid gland
	Luteinizing hormone	Stimulates progesterone, ovulation (female) testosterone (male)
	Follicle stimulating hormone	Stimulates oestrogen, ovum maturation (female), sperm production (male)
	ACTH (adrenocorticotrophic h.)	Stimulates steroid release by adrenals
	Prolactin	Increases milk production
Posterior pituitary	Oxytocin	Uterine contractions, milk release
	Vasopressin (or 'ADH')	Water retention by kidneys, constricts blood vessels, raises blood pressure
Pineal	Melatonin	Inhibits gonadal development, modulates sleep–wake cycles
Thyroid	Thyroxine, triiodothyronine	Increases metabolic rate, growth
Parathyroid	Parathyroid hormone	Increase blood calcium, decrease potassium
Adrenal cortex	Aldosterone	Reduces salt secretion by kidneys
	Cortisol, corticosterone	Promotes synthesis and storage of sugars, fat and proteins, suppresses inflammation
Adrenal Medulla	Adrenaline (Epinephrine) Noradrenalin etc.	Wide ranging effects to prepare for fight or flight– heart rate increase, see sympathetic
Pancreas	Insulin	Increases glucose entry into cells and storage as fat
Ovary	Oestrogen's	Promote female sex characteristics
	Progesterone	Maintains pregnancy
Testis	Androgens (testosterone)	Promotes sperm, male characteristics
Liver	Somatomedins	Stimulates growth
Kidney	Renin	Converts blood angiotensin to regulate blood pressure and thirst
Thymus	Thymosin	Supports immune responses

Source: Adapted from *Biological Psychology*, 5th edn, by J. W. Kalat, © 1995. Reprinted with permission of Wadsworth, a division of Thomson Learning. Fax 800 730-2215.

IMMUNE SYSTEM

The immune system may be likened to the internal police force of the body. It is responsible for identifying and nullifying foreign agents such as pathogens including bacteria and viruses, allergens such as pollen and other particles, transplanted tissue and abnormal cells including infected and cancer cells. Central to the immune system is the ability to recognise 'self' from 'non-self' by means of recognising the shapes and binding properties of cells and pathogens. This is usually referred to as recognition of an antigen. Once recognised, an immune response can be mounted against the offending cell or pathogen in order to neutralise, destroy and remove it. Immunity depends on the presence in the blood of antibodies and white blood cells (lymphocytes) which produce an immune response. Although every individual is born with inherited (natural) immunity, the immune system can learn to recognise and attack novel antigens, so-called acquired immunity which can be promoted deliberately by medical immunisation. Immune functions may broadly be classified as 'cell-mediated' through the action of T-lymphocytes or 'humoral' through the action of antibodies produced by B-lymphocytes.

The immune system is complicated and still imperfectly understood. Immune cells (white blood cells or leukocytes) originate in the bone marrow and some also originate from the thymus located in the chest (to where they have previously migrated). Many leukocytes are not in general circulation all the time and reside in the spleen or lymph nodes located throughout the body. When the immune system is activated these cells can then be released to travel through the circulation to the site of action.

Some leukocytes (lymphocyte B-cells) produce antibodies whose function is to bind with specific antigens, thus neutralising and coating it, both disabling it and increasing its visibility to other parts of the immune system. This in turn will promote attack by other leukocytes. The antibody–antigen reaction is highly specific. Antibodies are classified into five types of immunoglobulin (Ig). IgA is found in fluids such as saliva and acts as a first line of defence against viral and other antigens at the skin/mucosal surfaces. IgG is the most common in the body and covers antigens to facilitate destruction by other immune cells; IgM is primarily effective against bacteria, and IgE and IgD have signalling and control functions in the immune system. Other types of lymphocytes include subvarieties of T-cells which variously have control (immune response activation and suppression) and killing functions, and natural killer cells whose function is as the name implies destruction of viruses and cancer cells. Other white blood cell arms of the immune system include monocytes (macrophages with scavenging and bacterial destruction roles) and granulocytes, subvarieties of which have scavenging, bacterial destruction, parasite destruction and allergic response roles.

Both underactivity and overactivity of the immune system can produce disease. Overactivity of the immune system, or autoimmunity may produce disorders or disease by the immune system compromising or actually attacking its own body, examples include allergic reactions, asthma, rheumatoid arthritis and multiple sclerosis (destruction of myelin sheaths of the nerve axons). Rejection of transplanted tissue by the immune system recognising this as foreign may lead ultimately to transplant failure, a process which can be prevented by drugs. By contrast, underactivity will result in the failure to eliminate pathogens and infection. An unwanted side-effect of immunosuppressive therapy following tissue transplantation may be reduced resistance to infection. AIDS is caused by the HIV virus which attacks T-cells, reducing immune function and leaving the individual vulnerable to opportunistic infections.

PHYSIOLOGICAL ASPECTS OF PAIN

Pain may be defined as an unpleasant sensory and emotional experience associated with actual or potential tissue damage, or described in terms of such damage. As such, pain has evolutionary survival advantages in terms of warning to avoid harm or to escape further injury, or to rest to promote healing. It becomes disadvantageous when pain prevents treatment, for example in dental or other surgery, and causes unnecessary suffering when inescapable in various chronic or terminal illnesses. Pain has three main dimensions – sensory, emotive and cognitive. In addition pain may be divided broadly into acute versus chronic, acute pain resolving within months or quicker, whereas chronic pain may continue for years without relief.

The term nociceptor has been coined to replace the older term pain receptor in order to highlight the fact that these sensory units contribute to the pain experience rather than produce it in a strictly sensory fashion (Kalat, 1995, Rosenzweig *et al.*, 1995). Nociceptors are peripheral nerve endings in the skin, muscle, viscera and deep tissues which are specialised to respond to intense or damaging thermal, mechanical or chemical stimulation including those released by tissue damage such as prostaglandin, histamine and serotonin. Two main classes of peripheral nerve fibres, A-delta and C, transmit information from nociceptors to the central nervous system (CNS). A-delta fibres are small myelinated fibres which are fairly slow in nerve conduction compared with the fast non-nociceptive Beta somatosensory afferents. If you prick your finger the almost immediate sharp well-localised pain felt within a fraction of a second is mediated by A-delta fibres whereas the less well-localised dull throbbing pain which follows after a second or so is mediated by the much slower C-fibres. These peripheral fibres enter the spinal cord through the dorsal horn and make multiple synaptic connections to pathways, especially the contralateral spinothalamic tract which transmits nociceptive information upwards to the brain stem. Substance P is an important neurotransmitter in this process.

Inhibitory 'gating' of this information may occur by interneurones in the spinal cord and periaqueductal gray matter in the midbrain and brainstem. This gating may be produced by (non-painful) somatosensory information carried along fast Beta myelinated fibres and/or descending inhibitory information from higher levels within the CNS. For example, the relief that is produced by rubbing a painful spot of skin is probably occurring by stimulation of mechanical somatosensory receptors in the skin along fast somatosensory Beta afferents. This somatosensory information then inhibits (gates) pain information arriving from the A-delta and C-fibres, the gating occurring by means of inhibitory interneurones in such areas as the dorsal spinal horn. Some types of electrical analgesia and acupuncture pain relief may operate by similar mechanisms.

Other more general and less physically localised types of inhibitory mechanisms occur. An example of this is stress-related analgesia (that is, the relative lack of pain sometimes observed during battlefield or sports injuries) which probably involves the inhibitory actions on the transmission of nociceptive information by a class of neurotransmitters called endogenous opioid peptides. These include enkephalins, endorphins, and dynorphins which are released by stress. Opiate-based analgesia using morphine etc. artificially mimics these endogenous pain-control neurotransmitters. A drug called naloxone which blocks opiate analgesia (and for that matter will provoke extreme withdrawal symptoms in heroin or opiate addicts) can block stress-induced analgesia and block some acupuncture analgesia. This suggests that opioid release and opioid receptors are an important mechanism in these types of intrinsic analgesic actions. However, this is not to deny that other higher order cognitive or attentional mechanisms may also be important in pain perception and pain inhibition.

Recent progress in understanding how the brain processes pain has been facilitated by the use of non-invasive imaging techniques. From anatomical and functional studies it would appear that sensory, affective and cognitive dimensions of pain are processed in parallel by different parts of the nociceptive system (Treede *et al.*, 1999). Our knowledge of the physiological basis of the cognitive-evaluative component of pain is limited to date, but more progress has been made concerning sensory-discriminative and affective-motivational components of pain.

There appear to be two major systems, the so called lateral and medial systems named after the lateral and medial thalamic nuclei involved in transmitting nociceptive information from the spinothalamic pathways to the cortex and limbic system.

In the lateral system, nociceptive information from the spinal cord is projected via the lateral thalamic nuclei onto primary parietal (SI) and the secondary (SII) somatosensory cortex. This lateral system appears to process the sensory-discriminative component of pain; for example the perception involved in determining where something hurts and how much. This includes stimulus localisation, intensity and quality discrimination which may be processed in parallel by separate pathways. The medial system has a nociceptive pathway from the spinal cord via the medial thalamic nuclei onto the anterior cingulate cortex of the limbic system and the insula cortex which in turn projects to the amygdala of the limbic system. The limbic system is known to have a general role in emotional behaviour. Further cortico–cortical connections then go to the prefrontal cortex. This medial system is thought to process the affective-motivational components of pain (involved in assessing how much one is bothered by the pain) as well as subserving the motivational drive to escape the pain. Finally it should be remembered that clinical pain states may in addition reflect plastic changes within the CNS, especially with chronic pain.

Summary and conclusions

A basic understanding of the systems of the body and how they function is important for a proper appreciation of how psychological and social influences can influence health. In this chapter the basic functions of the nervous system, endocrine system and immune system have been reviewed. The nervous system functions to speed, integrate, and coordinate response to environmental changes. In general, the evolutionary older parts of the brain are involved in functions essential to survival such as respiratory pattern generators, and sleep–wakefulness, whilst newer cortical areas provide complex sensory analysis, motor outputs and cognitive functions. Major branches of the endocrine system are subject to nervous system control, an important example being the hypothalamic-pituitary-adrenal (HPA) axis. Activation of this sub-system is often precipitated by stress, and involves the controlled release of corticosteroids from the adrenal cortex of the kidneys. These play a key role in regulating metabolic activity and are also involved in controlling inflammatory responses and immune system activity. The immune system is responsible for identifying and nullifying foreign agents such as pathogens. Its functions may broadly be classified as cell-mediated or humoral. Both underactivity and overactivity of the immune system can produce disease. Pain has been described as an unpleasant sensory and emotional experience associated with actual or potential tissue damage. Nociceptors are somatosensory units which contribute to the pain experience rather than producing it in a strictly sensory fashion. Two main classes of peripheral nerve fibres, A-delta and C, transmit information from nociceptors to the CNS. Inhibitory gating of this information may be produced by non-painful somatosensory information carried along fast Beta-myelinated fibres or by descending inhibitory information from higher levels within the CNS. Other less-localised types of inhibitory mechanisms also occur including stress-induced analgesia involving inhibitory actions by endogenous opioid peptides such as enkephalins and endorphins. Sensory, affective and cognitive dimensions of pain are processed in parallel by different parts of the nociceptive system.

Discussion points

A   This is a 'thought question' relating structure to function. Read the statement below, comment on possible faults, then consider how it might sharpen thinking in current debates relating mind to brain in a health psychology context. N.B., consider the possibility that any researcher can be right for the wrong reasons.

'The Spider and the Fly' An elderly professor of physiology claimed that the spider can 'hear' vibrations through its legs. As a demonstration to her students, she conditioned each spider to scuttle out to its web by ringing a bell to vibrate the web and then she rewarded the spider with a fly. The professor then ablated the legs of the spider. As predicted, now the spider ignored the bell, no longer responding to the conditioned stimulus, thus demonstrating that the arachnid vibration detectors are located in the legs.

B How might stress affect immune response and by what possible mechanisms? (see also Chapter 6 'Psychoneuroimmunology' for additional information).

C Draw up a list of symptoms which might match DSM-III criteria for generalised anxiety to typical measures of sympathetic arousal (see background information given below). Do they all match? Discuss why you think there may be divergences.

Background Information for C: synopsis of diagnostic criteria for DSM-III Generalised Anxiety–heart pounding; dry mouth; upset stomach; increased respiration; scanning and vigilance; jumpiness – startle; frequent urination; diarrhoea; fidgeting; apprehensiveness.

Suggested reading

Kalat, J.W. (1995) *Biological Psychology*. (Brookes/Cole Publishing Co., Cal.).

Rosenweig. M.R., Leiman, A.L. and Breedlove, S.M. (1995) *Biological Psychology*, 2nd edn. (Sinauer Associates, MA).

5

Mental Health

'Diagnostic validity is a neglected issue.'

R.E. Kendell (1975)

INTRODUCTION

In an earlier part of this book we examined the issues of reliability and validity of health constructs relating to quality of life. In considering mental health the purpose here is not to usurp the territory occupied by our colleagues in clinical psychology, rather, the intentions are twofold. Firstly we believe that by subjecting many of the principal concepts in psychological medicine to the same critical scientific scrutiny routinely applied to other measurement problems in psychology, important lessons can be learnt. Thus we hope to show that the dividends which derive from the proper application of scientific method to the study of health can yield new insights in areas which have previously been considered settled. This journey begins by questioning several hypothetical entities whose existence in the systems of classification adopted by medical practitioners is assumed to point to real psychological and psychiatric phenomenon. One of our intentions here is to argue for the application of the kinds of reasoning which health psychologists adopt when they seek to establish the validity of a measuring system (see Chapter 2) rather than the uncritical use of medical diagnostic categories. A further aim of this chapter is to underscore the contribution which health psychology can make to understanding the views of mental health system users – an area of mental health care which has to date received insufficient attention.

CONCEPTS OF MENTAL HEALTH

Arguments against the existence and conceptualisation of certain psychiatric disorders are not new. The 'anti-psychiatry' movement which arose in the early 1960s and 1970s spearheaded by Ronnie Laing, David Cooper, Aaron Esterson, Morton Schatzman and Jo Berke (see Laing and Esterson, 1964; Schatzman, 1973; Cooper, 1974; Berke, 1979; Crossley, 1998) is well known if perhaps less well understood. Although the corpus of these ideas have been flatly rejected by the overwhelming majority of the medical profession, social scientists are showing renewed interest in the questions raised by these earlier analyses (Burston 1996, Crossley 1998). In this section we will examine the modern variants of arguments directed against the concept of schizophrenia with the critical spotlight in turn directed upon some of the more recently named psychiatric disorders; these being post-traumatic stress disorder (PTSD) and attention deficit hyperactivity disorder (ADHD). However, to challenge the epistemological basis of these diagnostic entities most effectively it will be beneficial to first ask what exactly is meant by the term mental illness? Thomas Szasz has waged a long if unsuccessful campaign against what he believes is the mythological status of the concept. Clare (1976) went to some lengths to refute these arguments and, as his own words indicate, he sees the battle as won.

> I once debated with Szasz over the existence or otherwise of mental illness... I enquired as to the conceptual status of diseases before their biological features are known. What was epilepsy before the EEG? What was tuberculosis before the discovery of the bacillus? What was amphetamine psychosis before the association between the mental symptoms and the drug were noted? What was the correct classification of the psychological symptoms of pellagra before the underlying vitamin deficiency was identified? Have all diseases been discovered? ... Szasz maintained a steadfast silence. (Clare 1976, p.62)

If the above comments are examined more closely it can be seen that they rest on accepting the rationale that mental illness is best construed as disease because (1) there are diseases yet to be discovered, (2) that currently recognised diseases once lacked the firm evidence we now have that they are best construed as diseases, and therefore (3) what we now believe to be diseases are diseases because we may one day find the evidence to support this. This can be summarised as what the medical profession believes to be diseases will turn out to be diseases – because they have been right in the past. This argument is clearly not a scientific one. Contrary to Clare, we must argue that until evidence justifies it there are no logical reasons for labelling anything as a disease no matter how unpleasant or distressing are the phenomena at the centre of attention – for to believe otherwise is a recipe for labelling anything as a disease. Though Clare's rebuttal of Szasz's critique is untenable on scientific grounds, it may well be that the more technical definition of mental illness residing within the Diagnostic and Statistical Manual of Mental Disorders is soundly based on empirical grounds – as is frequently claimed (Reid and Wise, 1989). In the latest revision (DSM IV) mental disorders are conceptualised as:

> a clinically significant behavioural or psychological syndrome or pattern that occurs in an individual and that is associated with present distress (e.g., a painful symptom) or disability (i.e. impairment in one or more areas of functioning either has caused the individual distress or disabled the individual in one or more important areas of functioning) or with a significantly increased risk of suffering death, pain disability, or an important loss of freedom. In addition, this syndrome or pattern must not merely be an expectable response to a particular event, for example the death of a loved one. Neither deviant behaviour (e.g., political, religious, or sexual) nor conflicts that are primarily between the individual and society are mental disorders unless the deviance or conflict is a symptom of a dysfunction in the individual as described above. (American Psychiatric Association, 1994, p. xxi)

No doubt by this technical sleight of hand it is hoped that the problem of validity disappears. However, on further examination this definition is no more satisfactory than the many previous attempts which have sought to cloak culturally-based value judgements as objective medical reality. An important qualification embodied in this definition is that the manifest behaviour or response(s) must not be an 'expectable response to a particular event' – thus there is the implicit assumption that knowledge is available to make informed judgements in all cases as to what kind of responses should be expected.

At best such judgements could be normative, though if maladaptive behaviour in the same circumstance(s) is characteristic of a species then it properly belongs in the domain of 'normal' rather than abnormal psychology or psychiatry. However, the fact is the information simply does not exist. If we ask how people 'ought' to respond given the infinite variety of ways in which it is possible to undergo distress and trauma, then we must confess ignorance. For example, do we know what the 'expected' way of responding is to being shut up in a cupboard for 20 years, being repeatedly threatened with violence throughout childhood, being sexually and physically abused, or subject to routine humiliation? The depth of our ignorance can only increase when we consider any combination of such factors and how they might interact with other demographic, psychological and cultural variables. These may encompass gender, ethnicity, social class, age, family position, family size, educational and occupational attainment, early social environment, self esteem, as well as beliefs and fears about mental health to name but a few. In addition to these problems we have barely begun the task of understanding other cultures' 'ways of seeing' (see, for example Littlewood and Lipsedge, 1989), and how the effects of such misunderstanding contributes to and interacts with existing psychological distress. Particularly problematic in this latter respect is that western psychiatry appears only to recognise the existence of culture in ethnic minorities and acts as if the dominant ethnic culture was homogenous in all important respects that have a bearing on mental health. Health psychologists, however, are particularly well-placed to investigate the relationships between these different 'ways of seeing', and how people present their physical and psychological distress to health professionals, and the task should certainly not be left in the hands of cultural anthropologists.

In the absence of the kind of knowledge alluded to above which would be necessary simply to form normative judgements, the question then becomes who decides what is a normal response to distressing psychological phenomena? And on what grounds do they decide if these are not empirical? Szasz (1991) outlines five reasons medical diagnoses in general may be made. These comprise scientific (e.g. to identify organs and issues affected by illness), professional (e.g. to enlarge the scope power and prestige of medical monopoly), legal (e.g. to justify state sanctioned interventions outside the criminal justice system), political (e.g. to justify enhancing and enforcing measures aimed at promoting public health) and personal grounds (e.g. to enlist the support of public opinion, the media and the legal system for bestowing privileges). Szasz argues that psychiatric diagnoses are always driven by non-medical (economic, personal, legal, political and social) factors. In this connection a useful and as yet underexplored avenue for health psychologists to take would be to examine the relationship between the attitudes, beliefs and opinions of particular groups of health professionals (e.g. including health psychologists themselves) and how these inform their practice, as well as how their client groups perceive the situation. Although clinical psychology has dominated psychologists' contribution to the field of mental health, if health psychologists are concerned with health in toto, there is no reason why the area of mental health should be considered out of bounds.

In defence of the current orthodoxy it might be argued that decisions about mental ill-health are decided on scientific grounds. A precondition for this to be true would be for the concepts used to have demonstrable validity. We have already seen, however, that the general concept of mental ill-health does not reside on an empirical basis. If one adheres to Popper's (1972) view that the hallmark of a scientific discipline is for its theories and postulates to be open to potential refutation on the basis of experiment or systematically gathered empirical evidence and not opinion, mental illness appears to be an unfalsifiable concept. There can be no doubting that psychiatrists can (though not always) reliably diagnose different states of mental ill-health, but such reliability without the support of independent corroborating evidence can give no indication of validity. In short, without validity, reliability denotes nothing but shared opinion. Given the common curricula and *weltanschauung* promulgated within the western, indeed now global, practise of psychological medicine, that practitioners use the same categories to label behaviour and experience and are capable of broad agreement in allocating patient cases to these categories can hardly be considered surprising. A key issue then is whether corroborating evidence for diagnostic categories which delineate types of mental ill-health does exist, and if it does not, should psychologists be using these categories (Pilgrim, 2000)?

Evidence to validate the conceptual categorisation of varieties of mental ill-health could in principle be obtained in two ways. Firstly by demonstrating satisfactory rules of correspondence for inferring the existence of the hypothetical construct from other independent (usually biological) criteria. Alternatively the concept may be considered valid if its component parts – the symptoms which denote the hypothesised construct – can be shown to exhibit sufficient statistical regularity with one another. The weakest such type of symptom cluster where knowledge of antecedents is poor and no known causal sequence exists between the symptoms is labelled a syndrome. Within such a schema it is not necessary for the full symptom cluster to be reliably found in any individual deemed to be suffering from a disorder. At this level it is only necessary for the symptom cluster to be observed in populations – this is the basis for the statement in **DSM** IV (p. xxii) that 'A common misconception is that a classification of mental disorders classifies people, when actually what are being classified are disorders that individuals have'.

DSM or the Diagnostic and Statistical Manual of mental disorders. The guide to categorising and diagnosing mental disorders produced by the American Psychiatric Association.

SCHIZOPHRENIA

In a systematic review of the history and current practice of identifying schizophrenia as an identifiable disorder, Boyle (1990a, 1990b) has shown that there is no empirical evidence to support the DSM (or any other) classification of schizophrenia and that no satisfactory correspondence rules (read independent evidence) exist for inferring the validity of the concept. Without such evidence the concept of schizophrenia – like mental illness – is unfalsifiable. Boyle argues that the process of making a diagnosis here implicitly assumes the validity of the concept which is being inferred. This process is akin to conferring disease status on any behaviour simply because people trained to spot the behaviour can agree that it is occurring. For example, one could obtain 100% agreement between a group of people that another person was reading. That of course could never in itself make reading a mental illness or a disease. Some other independent criteria other than the categorisation of behaviour alone would be necessary in order to change its status. Categorisation alone can never logically entail the existence of other phenomena (that is, a hypothetical disease process) which have not been observed. What then is the status of schizophrenia as a syndrome?

Slade and Cooper (1979) set out to test the proposition that the correlations between schizophrenic symptoms found by Trouton and Maxwell (1956) – which provide some of the best evidence for the syndromal nature of schizophrenia – could in fact result from selection factors acting on a set of random independent abnormalities which exist in the general population. These selection factors could be of two types: patient self-selection could occur through those individuals having more than one symptom being less able to cope and therefore more likely to seek or be referred for psychiatric help; in addition diagnostic selection may operate through the comparison of people with 'clear-cut' schizophrenia against those lacking in symptomology. This latter type of selection would act to reduce the fuzzy nature of the diagnostic criteria. Slade and Cooper compared the observed correlations between five symptoms (mood disturbance, delusions, motor disturbance, hallucinations and thought disorder) in a hospital population of 700 people of whom 185 were diagnosed as having schizophrenia, with those obtained from random data constructed from Monte Carlo simulations. The randomly produced data was subject to two constraints; that the proportion of schizophrenic to non-schizophrenic cases and the frequency of each symptom were both proportional to that in the original study. Trouton and Maxwell's data suggested a mean correlation of 0.67 between any pair of symptoms. Three sets of randomised data produced correlations of 0.66, 0.70 and 0.71 and a mathematical model based on diagnostic selection generated exact agreement. The authors concluded that a random symptom model fitted the data equally as well as the disease-entity model.

It can be no surprise to learn then that the conceptual malaise and lack of rigour underlying the notion of schizophrenia has been transferred into the quest for treatment. In a comprehensive survey of the content and quality of interventions relevant to the treatment of schizophrenia, Thornley and Adams (1998) found a considerable proportion of clinical trials were inadequate; poorly designed, of limited duration, with little agreement on what outcome measures should be used and with biased conclusions drawn regarding the efficacy of pharmacological agents. Over three decades ago, Laing and Esterson (1964) opened their controversial study *Sanity, Madness and the Family* by remarking

> In our view it is an assumption, a theory, a hypothesis, but not a fact that anyone suffers from a condition called 'schizophrenia' . . . We do not accept 'schizophrenia' as being a biochemical, neurophysiological, psychological fact, and we regard it as palpable error, in the present state of the evidence to take it to be a fact. (1964, pp. 11–12)

It is perhaps somewhat ironic then, that though Laing's name has been virtually expunged from the historical record of scientific psychiatry, as the new millennium dawns there appears considerable scientific justification to support his view.

POST-TRAUMATIC STRESS DISORDER

We have highlighted schizophrenia as a specific example to underline the point that medical diagnostic constructs should not be uncritically interpreted as references to real medical entities. This is equally true of a number of other hypothetical entities which inhabit psychological medicine – for many of them there being no independent criteria to substantiate their existence other than the symptoms which are held to be the *prima facie* evidence of the presence of a disease process in the first place. For example, despite widely held beliefs to the contrary there is little or no direct evidence to causally link any specific psychiatric diagnosis with a neurotransmitter or other biological change (Charlton, 1990).

Like schizophrenia, post-traumatic stress disorder (PTSD) is a diagnosis with a controversial history. First recognised as a specific category of disorder in 1980, the essential feature of PTSD is held to be the development of a set of characteristic symptoms following a psychologically distressing event that is outside the usual range of human experience (for example war, transport accidents, physical assault or natural disaster) and that would be markedly distressing to almost anyone. The predominant symptoms include persistent re-experiencing of the traumatic event, avoidance of stimuli associated with the trauma, increased arousal and diminished general responsiveness – both socially and affectively.

Validation of the concept of PTSD requires that these combinations of symptoms tend to cluster together and only in circumstances associated with trauma and subsequent functional disability. This has been a subject of some debate. If the constellation of symptoms characteristic of PTSD are considered understandable responses to severe stressors however, it seems fair to ask what this implies for the concept of mental illness – which of course rests on the notion that mental disorders should not be the expected responses to particular events. Several authors (for example Forster, 1992; O'Brien, 1998) have argued that traumatic responses to stress are themselves not normal, whilst conceding the lack of any operational definition of what does constitute a normal response to trauma. Should there be one? In the final analysis these attempts flounder on the circularity of distinguishing between normal from abnormal responses on the basis of whether the person has recovered! This paradox can find a suitable resolution if it is accepted that the study of anticipated or understandable psychological responses to trauma properly belongs in the realm of normal psychology.

The existence of PTSD as a specific diagnosis within the field of mental disorders serves to legitimise the view of other psychiatric entities as biologically determined conditions without providing any empirical demonstration of this. For if all other 'psychiatric' events – disturbed experiences and behaviours – are not themselves the result of traumatic experiences, then what else can they be but the products of abnormally functioning brains. If we enquire into the conceptual status of all the experiences now labelled as PTSD before its defining features were understood, then the answer is discomforting. Presumably they were believed to be other mental illnesses and treated accordingly, that is as the product of an abnormal constitution. Ellenson (1986), for example, records that disturbances of perception in female adult incest survivors are frequently observed and that features of hallucinations can reliably be used to detect a history of incest. He writes,

> The fear of being crazy was unwarranted. The fear of (false) confirmation of this was warranted. Survivors who had revealed such symptoms (perceptual disturbances) in the past had been given a diagnosis of psychosis or severe character pathology. (Ellenson, 1986, p. 158)

Comorbidity is the prevalence of a given (medical) condition with other conditions.

It is evident then that the diagnostic entity of PTSD serves additional roles to that of identifying a specific disturbed response to severe trauma. But what of the actual evidence that it does delineate a common symptomology? Estimates of **comorbidity** between PTSD and other disorders have ranged from between 50 to 95 per cent (Yehuda and McFarlane, 1995; Bleich, Koslowsky, Dolev and Lerer, 1997). Chief amongst the associated complaints has been major depression, followed by anxiety, minor affective disorders, alcoholism and drug abuse. Discussion has therefore focused on whether there are sequelae to major trauma which are uniquely and accurately specified by this categorisation. If so, then PTSD should be clearly distinguishable from other forms of disordered behaviour and experience which can occur in response to broadly similar levels of trauma. A considerable difficulty in this task is how to equate similar levels of trauma. PTSD has been reported in high frequencies (47–50%) in both concentration camp victims and Vietnam veterans (lifetime prevalence 30%) (Yehuda and McFarlane, 1995). On face value the figures would seem to indicate that the concentration camp experience is the more severe. However, what is required in the field is an unambiguous measure for grading events which is not simply reliant on any subsequent epidemiological study. But herein lies a further problem – there is good reason for believing a key variable in the development of PTSD is how people actually appraise the situation they are in, and of course they will do this at least in part on the basis of their own personal histories. There is indeed good evidence that prior history plays an important role in the etiology of PTSD. Shalev *et al.*, (1998), for example found that those who had undergone trauma and who subsequently went on to develop major depression rather than PTSD already had a history of previous depression. Resnick, Kilpatrick, Best and Kramer (1992) found women with a prior history of rape were more likely to exhibit PTSD than those raped for the first time, while Yehuda *et al.*, (1997) found cumulative lifetime stress was a positive predictor of avoidance symptoms in holocaust survivors. In addition, evidence seems to indicate that disasters of human making lead to more distressing consequences than natural catastrophes (Green, Lindy and Grace, 1985). Is it possible to explain this without reference to how and why people interpret events in particular ways? Primo Levi's harrowing pleas for understanding of how survivors of the death camps emerged from their ordeal imbued with guilt and shame makes this clear:

> Coming out of the darkness, one suffered because of the required consciousness of having being diminished . . . We had not only forgotten our country and our culture, but also our family, our past, the future we had imagined for ourselves, because . . . we were confined to the present moment. Only at rare intervals, did we come out of this condition of levelling . . . but these were painful moments, precisely because they gave us the opportunity to measure our diminishment from the outside. (Primo Levi, 1989, pp. 56–7)

Given the conceptual difficulties suggested above, it is not surprising to find a degree of confusion is also present in the measurement of PTSD. For example, Lauterbach, Vrana, King and King (1997) found stronger relationships between the Civilian Mississippi PTSD scale and measures of depression and anxiety than with other measures of PTSD. Work supporting the differentiation of PTSD from depression is currently gathering momentum and argues that despite the large shared comorbidity, they should be seen as independent sequelae to psychological trauma (Bleich *et al.*, 1997; Shalev *et al.*, 1998). However, the grounds for making these distinctions appear to rely more on the number and intensity of reported symptoms than their actual type (Kean, Taylor and Penk, 1997; Blanchard, Buckley, Hickling and Taylor, 1998). Rather than suggesting fundamentally different psychobiological responses to trauma, the key variables in distinguishing the responses may well lie with antecedent events – particularly the appraisal of events, the prior history of distressing life events and levels of social support (Madakasira and O'Brien, 1987). Other factors may include something akin to resilience or 'hardiness' which itself may in part be a function of prior success in dealing with physical and psychological stresses. This is certainly consistent with the observations made after the First World War in which shell-shock was a more frequent response in officers (7–10%) than soldiers in the ranks (3–4%), though other factors are also likely to have contributed to this difference. In addition to the not inconsiderable overlap between the symptoms of PTSD and other affective disorders such as depression, Butler *et al.* (1996) have also argued that a diagnosis of PTSD should sometimes be considered with patients who exhibit positive symptoms of psychosis (hallucinations, delusions and bizarre behaviour) in the absence of thought disorder: a suggestion entirely in keeping with the observations of hallucinations in sexually-abused women referred to earlier (Ellenson, 1986). With such arguments continuing it is evident that no final consensus has been reached in specifying the nature of a post-traumatic stress syndrome.

The role of prior risk factors and the problems surrounding definition and measurement of PTSD have led Yehuda and McFarlane (1995) to question whether the circumstantial evidence for PTSD is not in fact suggestive of a general predisposition to mental illness that is triggered by adversity. The literature on the relationship between life events and mental health can tell us something of this relationship – although it is important to remember that life event research frequently asks questions only about events occurring in relatively recent periods of time and is therefore unlikely to shed light on the (cumulative) influence of earlier life events and how these and their interpretation may influence subsequent vulnerability to stressors (Norman and Malla, 1993a,b). Yehuda and McFarlane (1995) in their discussion of PTSD remark that available evidence does suggest a progressive sensitisation of biological systems occurs prior to the behavioural expression of disorder. Consequently, where examination of life events prior to onset of a disorder shows no particular relationship, it would be erroneous to conclude as some have (for example Birchwood, Hallettand Preston, 1988) that the disorder is not a specific response to stress.

A further difficulty facing researchers is that current methodology tends to prescribe the possible type of life events which subjects are merely asked to endorse. There is certainly a need for more broad-based measures of stressors, which include not just major events but daily stressors and hassles. Only recently, for example, has it been recognised that racism may constitute an enduring chronic source of stress which may mediate its effects by a host of different stressors such as overcrowding, poor accommodation, insecurity of tenure, poverty, long working days, personal abuse and social isolation (Littlewood and Lipsedge, 1989). A further complication is that the meanings of events themselves may vary with ethnic or cultural group. With a model based on progressive sensitisation there is even no particular reason to suppose that an individual should be consciously aware of the current events which (added to the cumulative increase of vulnerability) push them over the threshold into a dysfunctional state. Too frequently medical models of mental disorder have assumed the necessity for a catastrophic relationship between life events and functioning rather than a continuous one.

Despite such shortcomings some important relationships have been discerned. Prior negative life events have been shown to have a strong relationship with depression (Brown and Harris, 1978). In addressing specific kinds of events, Angermeyer (1982) and Leff et al. (1982) found a strong association between expressed familial hostility and anxiety (somewhat misleadingly referred to in the literature as expressed emotion) and subsequent relapse in people previously diagnosed as schizophrenic (to what extent should previous diagnosis itself be considered a stressful life event?) with more recent prospective studies (Pallanti, Quercioli and Pazzagli, 1997) confirming that relapsing 'schizophrenic' patients have a significantly higher number of life events (independent of the illness) in the month preceding relapse. Where research has concentrated on symptoms rather than hypothetical disease entities fruitful lines of research have opened up linking specific environmental events to specific symptoms. Hallucinations, for example, have been linked to stress-induced arousal (Cooklin, 1983), relative sensory deprivation, sensory loss (in elderly people) (Bentall,

1990), sexual assault (Ellenson, 1986) and military combat (Butler *et al.*, 1996) to name but a few. Given the greater propensity for psychoses to be diagnosed in certain ethnic and social class groupings, it is also tempting to add racism and class discrimination to the list of environmental stressors that may give rise to psychotic symptomology.

What is evident from the discussion so far is that the present system for organising concepts of abnormal behaviour and experience is flawed. Because psychologists have not been so heavily indoctrinated with these systems of thought as their peers in medicine (Roberts, 1990) they may be in a stronger position to evaluate them critically and therefore come up with alternative viable models of psychological well-being. Health psychologists could in this context form a useful alliance with their cognitive colleagues to investigate the reasoning processes whereby medical practitioners arrive at medical diagnoses and infer hypothetical biological entities following their interactions with psychiatric patients.

Given the dearth of evidence for a primary causal role of biological events in poor well-being, it could be argued that the concept of post-traumatic stress response offers a more fruitful organising framework for studying the impact of environmental events on mental health and for studying the biological consequences of acute and chronic stressors. Implicit in such a framework would be the assumption that a more useful starting place for research would be to view disordered psychological and social functioning as indicators of problems in living (Szasz, 1961) rather than as expressions of illnesses of the body (Rosenhan and Seligman, 1989). We will explore this idea further in the next section where attention deficit hyperactivity disorder is discussed.

ATTENTION DEFICIT HYPERACTIVITY DISORDER

In recent years a widespread belief has appeared that large numbers of children with behavioural problems are exhibiting symptoms of a biological disorder referred to as attention deficit hyperactivity disorder (ADHD). Since its first appearance in 1966, the volume of literature and studies on this topic would certainly support this belief (Figure 5.1). During the last few years, popularity for the concept has reached new heights. In 1996 the British Psychological Society produced its working party report (BPS, 1996) and in 1997 the first European ADHD conference was held. Training courses in identifying and managing ADHD are flourishing. However, of the 4609 studies between 1966 and 1997 produced by a Medline search on the topic, only a minute proportion of these, less than a half of 1 per cent ($N = 27$), have in a single paper addressed issues of reliability and validity.

Such a small proportion would not be surprising if the validity of ADHD had been established beyond doubt. However, argument about its merits as a diagnostic entity continue unabated, and arguments have raged about whether ADHD is under-diagnosed and undertreated (Kewley 1998) or whether in fact the opposite is true (Orford, 1998). Thambirajah (1998) criticises both the overzealous diagnoses of ADHD and the uncritical acceptance of data using functional brain imaging techniques – which have largely used small samples and are difficult to interpret. Several recent studies which have examined informants' reports against impairment criteria have failed to produce evidence of acceptable reliability (Hart, Lahey, Loeber and Hanson, 1994; Boyle, 1997). The latter authors comment that although estimates of the prevalence of childhood psychiatric disorders and particularly ADHD have fre-

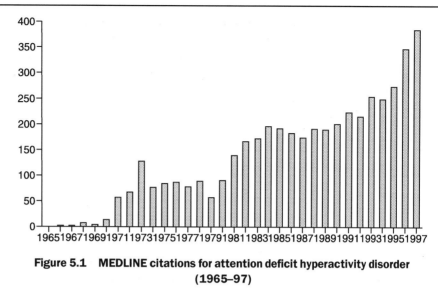

Figure 5.1 MEDLINE citations for attention deficit hyperactivity disorder (1965–97)

quently been based on such self-report measures, the advantages and disadvantages of lay-administered structured interviews and self-administered problem checklists have attracted little comment. Informants' reports are of crucial importance, because without referral from such sources, medical practitioners would have no evidence of disorder to work with.

Some of the difficulty in establishing satisfactory evidence that there is an identifiable disorder to be detected stems from the crude system of categorisation used in DSM IV which simply provides an unweighted list of symptoms of inattention and hyperactivity – six of either of which are sufficient for the diagnosis (Kewley and Orford, 1998). These include for inattention: failing to give close attention to details or making careless mistakes in school work, difficulty sustaining attention in tasks or play, often does not seem to listen when spoken to directly, often forgetful in daily activities and often losing things necessary for tasks or activities. For hyperactivity the list includes often fidgeting with hands or feet, often running or climbing about excessively in situations deemed not to be appropriate, difficulty playing or engaging in leisure activities quietly, and often talking excessively. Whether these itemised behaviours are even logically distinct let alone statistically related has not been adequately addressed. And we could ask why are six sufficient for the diagnosis and not five or eight? In the absence of hard biological markers this kind of arbitrariness is typical of functional psychiatric diagnoses (Pilgrim, 2000). Thus the current diagnostic system merely demands concordance between raters that the listed behaviours are occurring. As with schizophrenia no independent validating criteria have been satisfactorily demonstrated which might suggest that these behavioural problems are manifestations of an underlying neurological problem.

In common with many other psychiatric entities, ADHD is hypothesised to be genetic in origin – largely on the basis of twin studies. Yet data showing greater concordance rates between monozygotic twins has failed to satisfy some researchers (Minchin, 1998) and ignores evidence which conflicts with the basic assumptions on which this research this based. One such assumption is that the foetal and early postnatal environments of monozygotic twins do not differ substantially. However, differences in foetal growth affecting birth weight and congenital malformation have been found between monozygotic and dizygotic twins as well as differences in perinatal

Heritability The proportion of the variance in a dependent variable within a population which is accounted for by environmental or genetic factors. Is estimated from a regression equation.

mortality (Phillips, 1993) and the likelihood of breast or bottle feeding after birth (Minchin, 1998). This is impossible to explain if one is maintaining that identical twins share an identical genetic make-up and a qualitatively similar environment. Schwartz and Schwartz (1974, 1975) likewise point to the inadequate specification in many of the statistical models used to estimate the heritability of the environmental components which could plausibly explain the degree of similarity between mono-zygotic twins compared to dizygotic twins. The emphasis on genetic factors sadly has led to a neglect of current psychosocial circumstances and past experiences which might underlie problem behaviour (Thambirajah, 1998).

The trends in Figure 5.1 are also of relevance in considering the evidence favouring genetic causation. Why is this? It is important to ask what lies behind this trend, and several possibilities present themselves. First of all such a trend could plausibly reflect increasing scientific knowledge of an already recognised disorder. However, given the recency of ADHD as a diagnostic entity, the continuing debates about its validity, and the small number of published articles pertaining to validity and reliability this seems unlikely. A second candidate for explanation is that the increased interest in ADHD reflects the increasing prevalence of antisocial and problem behaviour in society. If this is the case then the multiplication of behavioural problems which underlie ADHD has occurred in such a short period of time that any genetic explanation for this increase is simply untenable. Data from Wall (1997) examining referrals to a child and adolescent mental health service in a London Borough over a 20-year period (1977–97), however, found that between 1977 and 1991, referrals for behaviour problems actually dropped by almost 50 per cent, a period during which Medline citations increased almost three-fold. Wall also notes that referrals of children under four years of age increased from 2 per cent of all referrals in 1977 to 25 per cent in 1997. In conjunction with this, referrals of over 12s decreased from 64 per cent of all referrals in 1977 to 33 per cent in 1997. Furthermore, 53 per cent of referrals for hyperactivity were in the under-fours – this despite evidence which suggests it is five and a half years before parents felt certain of the onset of ADHD (Sullivan, Kelso and Stewart, 1990). Wall's data, then, do not provide ready support for this second possibility, although recent data from the UK show exclusions from schools for unacceptable behaviour have risen dramatically, from under 3000 in 1990–91 to just under 14000 in 1996–97 (Social Exclusion Unit, 1998). With the majority of excluded school students being over 12 years of age, this might suggest that behavioural misconduct in older children is dealt with by social exclusion from school, but in younger children by referral to mental health agencies. Thus the possibility cannot be discounted that the increase in attention to ADHD reflects one response to increasing behavioural problems in children – one which the medical profession has been keen to seek explanations for in terms of a genetic predisposition to minimal brain dysfunction.

A final conjecture for what lies behind the pattern of scientific work on ADHD is that this neither reflects growing knowledge of a valid disorder, nor a medical response to increasing behavioural misconduct in society, but rather provides a further example of the medical profession's attempts, ultimately on behalf of the pharmaceutical industry to market social problems as medical problems (Illich, 1977; Breggin, 1993). Neurobiological work by Perry et al. (1995) provides grounds for linking patterns of hyperactivity to trauma in children and suggests that pharmacological interventions will be insufficient. While such findings are supportive of our proposal to place PTSD at the core of psychiatric and psychological models of disturbed behaviour and experience the idea and the evidence is hardly new. Most if not all of the commonly diagnosed disorders of childhood, including ADHD, depression, anxiety and learning disorders, can be linked to abuse and neglect (Green, 1989). For us, the question for those wishing to understand the behaviour and experience of those diagnosed with ADHD, as with schizophrenia and PTSD, is to ask whether it is more fruitful to view these actions primarily as the product of a disease process or the consequences of motivated human actions? Either way, without establishing the prior validity of these constructs any attempts to develop successful humane interventions are likely to be misleading and unworkable.

ATTITUDES AND ATTRIBUTIONS: MENTAL HEALTH SYSTEM USERS

So dominant has the biomedical model been that the existence of alternative discourses on mental health has often been overlooked, certainly amongst mental health professionals. The question of how users of mental health services construe their experiences and their treatment, for example, is highly relevant yet has received little attention (Molvaer, Hanzi and Papadatos, 1992; for a notable exception see Read and Reynolds, 1996). Lay perceptions and attitudes have been similarly neglected. Whilst health psychologists have been at the forefront in emphasising the importance of patients' perspectives and in describing the role played by psychological and psychosocial factors in the development and management of acute and chronic physical illness, they have, with few exceptions, remained curiously detached from such issues in the field of mental health, where they could surely make a significant contribution.

A number of reasons may underpin this. A reticence to become embroiled in issues of power and control characterises both the desire to avoid treading on the toes of clinical psychologists in the rush to establish health psychology as a distinct speciality and the somewhat remote position which psychologists have taken in response to demands for patients' rights in mental health. A more benign interpretation might be that the construct of health care itself does not travel well from physical to 'psychological' medicine, and that the realities of service provision in these areas is radically different. In response to such a contention, however, it could be pointed out that both psychiatric patients and recipients of physical healthcare (particularly those who are chronically ill) have to grapple with the limitations of the patient role assigned to them. This decrees changes in their capacity to act as a social agent or to make decisions for themselves thus allowing them to be subject to physical interventions decided by medical practitioners. Concomitant with this the 'medical facts' are ascribed a greater importance than people's own knowledge of their disorder and its location within their historical, social and personal circumstances (doctor knows best!).

In recent years, however, the marketisation of health care services has opened up the possibility of alternative roles to that of the patient. Health service users can now consume health service resources, their lives may unfold in areas embodying varying degrees of 'social capital' (Kawachi et al., 1997) and in the event of damaging interventions survive or succumb to them. These new roles of consumer and survivor permit new avenues of protest for disgruntled health service users, and with them pose a threat to established protocols of care delivery. Pilgrim and Rodgers (1993) note that funding evaluation of services to psychiatric patients is accorded a low priority by the Medical Research Council and that user-evaluation of services is entirely absent from their considerations. It is hardly surprising, then, that exclusion from decision-making remains the norm for the overwhelming majority of psychiatric service users (Maza, 1996). It is regrettable that service providers and researchers have so far failed to make connections between this exclusion and the continued social isolation of ex-patients. Thus a major failing of the biomedical model of mental illness whatever other merits it may possess is the persistent failure to reflect upon the social context or consequences of treatment. One unfortunate result (or perhaps cause) is that user's views (on all matters) are presumed to be irrational. Non-compliance with psychiatric medication, for instance, is understood (if at all) as an irrational response which hinders patient well-being, rather than an action which can sometimes arise as a reasoned response to reducing unpleasant symptoms of medication which interfere with important aspects of daily living (Barham and Hayward 1991). The general public appear to be more acquainted with this aspect of treatment – being more likely to perceive psychiatric medication as harmful than helpful (Jorm et al., 1997; Britten, 1998). It should not be forgotten that psychiatric services do in fact pose a number of risks to users – ranging from denial of liberty and loss of employment, through memory loss (from ECT) and tardive dyskinesia to death (cardiac toxicity of anti-psychotic medication). In addition, minor tranquillisers may exacerbate the risk of accidents through their sedative effects. If hospitalised, institutional life may carry its own risks ranging from staff mistreatment to depersonalisation (Pilgrim and Rogers, 1996).

A continuing challenge to the emerging movement of users/survivors is to clarify whether their primary goals relate to the improvement of mental health services within the constraints imposed by current definitions of mental health or to transform the meaning of mental health and with it the place of psychologically disturbed individuals in society (Campbell, 1996). Some of the possibilities afforded by the more radical of these positions is illustrated by the work of the Dutch psychiatrist Marius Romme (Romme and Escher, 1994) with people who hear voices. Rather than simply regarding these as pathological phenomenon and trying to drug them out of existence, people are encouraged to develop dialogues with their voices, to structure their relationships with them, to accept them as part of themselves and to share their experiences with others. One of the findings to emerge from this work is that voices frequently begin after intense emotional experiences accompanying such things as divorce, death, falling in love or becoming pregnant, and may occasionally actually assist in coping (Baker, 1990; Bentall, 2000). That hearing voices may point towards a process for helping people come to terms with powerful experiences or represent the byproducts of failed attempts to process emotionally charged information is certainly of interest. Whatever their origins in the thought processes of those who have them, the strategy of constructing a relationship with them and subsuming this within a broader supportive social environment without medication warrants further consideration.

A substantial obstacle to users of mental health services reclaiming control, order and self-esteem and with these the chances of successful rehabilitation into the community is the media portrayal of sufferers of mental illness. Evidence suggests the current influence of the media upon attitudes and knowledge about mental disorder is extremely negative (Borinstein, 1992; Wahl, 1992; Wahl and Kaye, 1991, 1992) with the topic of mental illness frequently presented in the context of violent behaviour. Appleby and Wessely (1988), for example, questioned representative samples before and after the Hungerford massacre of August 1987 in which Michael Ryan killed 15 people. After the event there was a significant increase in the number believing those who commit horrific crimes are likely to be mentally ill, even though Ryan himself was not. In another study, Wahl and Lefkowits (1989) showed one group a prime-time television film portraying a mentally-ill killer, whilst another group viewed the same film juxtaposed with a trailer-film intended to remind viewers that violence is not characteristic of the mentally ill. A control group viewed a film unrelated to mental disorder. Post-film attitudes toward mental disorder and community care of the mentally ill were significantly less favourable in those who had seen the target film, whether or not they had also viewed the trailer. Socall and Holtgraves (1992), using vignettes, demonstrated that those described as having a mental disorder were rejected significantly more than identically behaving physically-ill persons. It is hardly surprising, then, that a substantial proportion of the public see those with mental disorder as unpredictable, different and dangerous (Levey and Howells, 1994, 1995).

A number of researchers have demonstrated that differences in attitudes towards mental disorder also correspond to differences in the characteristics of the respondent – respondents from lower socioeconomic groups, those with less education and those who are older are consistently more rejecting (Hollingshead and Redlich, 1958; Nunnally, 1961; Rabkin, 1974; Ojanen, 1992), while evidence suggests female respondents, those who are more likely to have encountered the mentally ill themselves and those who have personal acquaintance of mental disorder (such as having a friend or relative affected) harbour more accepting attitudes (Norman and Malla, 1983; Brockington, Hall, Levings and Murphy, 1993; Arens, 1993; Wahl, 1993).

If attitudes towards the mentally disordered have received a measure of critical scrutiny, the same cannot be said for patients' attributions for their own disorder. One of the few studies in this area, conducted by Molvaer, Hantzi and Papadatos (1992) found that psychiatric out-patients placed more emphasis on non-physical factors such as family relations, chance and personal inadequacy in explaining the causes of their troubles. Studies of lay beliefs likewise affirm that psychosocial factors rather than physical factors are more likely to be cited as probable causes of psychotic behaviour (Furnham and Rees, 1988; Hall *et al.*, 1993). Wahl (1987) compared the public's (psychology students, community members and police officers) conceptions of common causes of and treatments for schizophrenia with mental health professionals' conceptions. A moderate bias on the part of the public in favour of stressing psychosocial over physical causes, and a moderate bias in favour of psychosocial interventions (e.g. psychotherapy) was found. Mental health professionals exhibited the opposite bias in favour of stressing physical causes (e.g. brain dysfunction) and physical treatments (e.g. drugs). Similarly, Shoham-Salomon (1985) found that medically-oriented hospital therapists were significantly more likely than psychosocially-oriented hospital therapists to explain schizophrenics' behaviour in terms of an underlying illness, rather than as responses to specific situational factors. The implication of this work is that as a person enters the mental health system and finds themselves faced not with psychotherapy but a regimen of physical treatments, they are likely to be dissatisfied. As indicated above, such dissatisfaction is likely to go unrecorded, and in extreme cases may even be considered as demonstrating delusional ideation or lack of insight.

The research reviewed in this chapter suggests that the traditional view of mental illness as a disorder rooted in biological dysfunction is lacking in conceptual rigour, with the philosophical and scientific underpinnings of the professional belief system far from secure. This belief system and the practice based upon it is also at variance with the attitudes and wishes of a good many of the people the mental health system is intended to serve. This gap between service users and professionals can be reduced either through users adopting a more biological model of experiential and behavioural disorders or by mental health professionals adopting a more psychosocial and experiential approach. The system of care which ultimately prevails will depend as much on the empowerment of users as on the research activities of the present custodians.

Summary and conclusions

This chapter has reviewed evidence on the diagnostic validity of three specific psychiatric disorders; schizophrenia, PTSD and ADHD. These have been chosen as examples because their diagnostic validity is more contentious than other disorders such as depression and anxiety. As the opening quote to this chapter indicates issues of validity in psychiatry have been taken for granted and as Boyle (1990a) and others have argued it would be a mistake to assume the validity of the diagnostic entities in the Diagnostic and Statistical Manual. Several lessons from this are of paramount importance to health psychologists. Firstly, though many health psychologists work with medical practitioners, they should not automatically accept the legitimacy of the constructs used to describe problems which present themselves as psychological problems. If the process of diagnosis is viewed as simply another measurement system, then the insights and procedures which psychometrically-oriented psychologists have contributed to the study of health and medicine in general are available for application. It is also possible that this same critical attitude applied to physical medicine will yield useful insights.

Cognitively-oriented health psychologists could also usefully investigate the processes by which mental health professionals make inferences about the causes of psychological disorder and arrive at diagnoses. There are no a priori reasons why the field of mental health should be left to clinical psychologists and regarded as separate from other avenues of health care. In addition to the application of psychometrics to classification and cognitive psychology to medical reasoning, one of the other neglected areas in mental health research has been the evaluation of service provision and the experience of 'illness' from the perspective of the user. Such audit can be useful in contextualising the behaviour of mental health system users as well as arguing for the relevance of other models of care which are based on broader principles than a narrowly defined biomedical one. If it is relevant and useful to examine such things as quality of life, coping behaviours, social support, professional belief systems, lay perceptions and attitudes to health and illness and doctor–patient relationships where physical illness is concerned, then surely the same must also be true when we are addressing issues of mental health care.

Discussion points

A What difference would it make to the mental health system if measurement and treatment were entirely evidence based?

B Does diagnostic reasoning in psychological medicine differ in any way from that used in physical medicine.

C How could quality-of-life assessment be useful in evaluating health care for psychiatric patients?

D Is the concept of mental health fundamentally different to that of physical health?

Suggested reading

Boyle, M. (1990a) *Schizophrenia: A Scientific Delusion*. (London: Routledge).

Heller, T., Reynolds, J., Gomm, R., Mustom, R. and Pattison, S. (eds) (1996) *Mental Health Matters: A Reader*. (London: Macmillan and Open University Press).

Pilgrim, D. and Rogers, A. (1993) *A Sociology of Mental Health and Illness.* (Buckingham: Open University Press).

Slade, P.D. and Cooper, R. (1979) 'Some Conceptual Difficulties with the Term Schizophrenia: An Alternative Model', *British Journal of Social and Clinical Psychology,* **18**: 309–17.

Wahl, O.F. (1992) 'Mass Media Images of Mental Illness: A Review of the Literature', *Journal of Community Psychology,* **20**: 343–52.

Psychoneuroimmunology

'Our love of the things of the mind does not make us soft.'

Funeral Oration, Athens, 430 BC in Thucydides,
History of the Peloponnesian War. Bk2, ch4, sect 1,
(translated by Rex Warner)

INTRODUCTION

Psychoneuroimmunology is the field of study focusing on relationships between psychological events such as stress and nervous, endocrine and immune functioning responses.

Immunocompetence is the extent to which the immune system is functioning effectively. Thus immunosuppression refers to reduced functionality in some or all of the immune system. May be caused by many factors, for example HIV infection or stress.

One of the principal tenets of psychosomatic medicine is that states of mind have the potential to affect the healthy functioning of the body. This idea is rooted in the belief that the motivational concerns (conscious or unconscious) of the individual are crucial to translating psychological stress to symptoms of physical distress. The burgeoning field of **psychoneuroimmunology** (PNI), does not concern itself with unverifiable psychodynamic influences and offers to put the age-old dilemma of the relationship between mind and body on a firmer footing. Although not in itself conclusive, the triggering of reduced **immunocompetence** by psychological events has been strongly suggested by findings which show a greater variety of illnesses in people undergoing stressful life events (Brown and Harris, 1989; Herbert and Cohen, 1993; Evans, Bristow, Hucklebridge, Clow and Walters, 1993). Within the new theoretical framework offered by PNI, however, the immune system has been shown to be responsive to psychological events and may play a key moderating influence between the impact of stress and adverse health outcomes.

In addition to a variety of general indicators of stress, research has examined several specific sources of stress to assess whether these have marked effects on immune function. These can be broadly categorised under the headings of interpersonal relationships, daily hassles and academic stress. Several populations have been the focus of this research – students because of their ready accessibility, members of the general public exposed to long-term stressors, people with HIV infection, and a number of diverse patient groups. As well as diversity in stressors and populations exposed to stress, a number of different markers of immune functioning have been investigated. In this chapter we will review some of the principal findings from this work and consider their implications for treatment interventions as well as looking at some of the methodological difficulties which researchers face.

In exploring the links between psychological stress, immune responsiveness and ill-health difficulties can arise from trying to quantify and measure stress (Box 6.1). Further difficulties exist regarding what is meant by immune responsiveness, and it is tempting to think that changes in the immune system can be described as indicating either enhanced or suppressed functioning. These terms, however, presuppose both the absence of inherent variability in the immune system and that any distinct changes which do occur can be consistently related to changes in existing states of health. Unfortunately neither of these is true. Overactivity of the immune system, for example, can lead to auto-immune diseases, whilst underactivity is likely to render the organism open to infection (Sarafino, 1998). At the same time certain aspects of down-regulation – for example of neutrophil production may offer protective effects by limiting chronic inflammation (MacKinnon, 1998), an effect which has been observed in high-level athletes. Thus the body must be geared towards maintaining a continuous balance in the levels of immune system activity in the face of hugely varying demands and environments. Because of this, the terms up and down-regulation are favoured over immune enhancement or suppression – but to what do these terms refer? Indicators of down-regulation include reduced lymphocyte pro-liferation following mitogen challenge, fewer lymphocytes in circulation, reductions in natural killer cell (NKC) activity and lower concentrations of antibodies, but higher antibody titres for some specific latent viruses (Evans, Clow and Huckle-bridge, 1997).

BOX 6.1 Measuring stress

In his original formulation, Selye (1956) envisaged stress as a physiological process of responding adaptively to environmental challenge. Further attempts have sought variously to define it in terms of the demands upon a person (e.g. the number and type of life events), the available resources to meet these demands (e.g. the level of social supports) or the person's responses to them – whether these be cognitive (e.g. appraisal processes) or behavioural (e.g. avoidance coping) (Cox, 1995). Current models are transactional in nature in that they involve an interaction between all these factors.

However practical assessment of all these in any given study can be problematic. In such situations one solution adopted by researchers has been to consider circumstances which the undoubted majority of any population would consider stressful – bereavement, relationship disharmony, financial difficulties or job loss for example. Successful as this strategy has been, because of variation in the meaning and appraisal of events it will not be suited for answering all research questions. When investigating links between stress and health, an area where particular vigilance is required is the avoidance of any overlap between the measures of stress and the measures of ill-health (Marmot and Madge, 1987) as this will inflate any estimate of the true relationship between them. An example would be including elements of the same measure of ill-health in the operational definition of stress (e.g. cancer diagnosis as a life event) and as the studied outcome (e.g. some measure of immune function).

STRESS, AFFECT AND IMMUNE FUNCTION

In studies of the effects of interpersonal relationships on health, marital relationships have predominated; many of these purport to show greater benefits for men than for women (see Chapter 13). However, how and why marriage should show such differ-ential effects is far from understood. One potentially important data source could come from studies of immune function in married couples. In this context, Kiecolt-Glaser *et al.* (1993) found decreased immune function (as measured by antibody titres to Epstein-Barr virus and mitogenic response of peripheral blood lymphocytes to phytohemagluttanin) in newly-weds following conflict-focused discussions, with the observed decrements being greater in women. In a further study of older couples by Kiecolt-Glaser *et al*. (1997), differential effects with gender were again reported; amongst females, escalations of negative behaviour were strongly correlated with endocrine changes (ACTH, nor-adrenalin and cortisol). Amongst both males and females, those showing poorer immunological responsiveness displayed greater negative behaviour at times of conflict. In a sample of couples seeking marital therapy and subjected to experimentally-induced conflict, Mayne, O'Leary, McGrady, Contrada and Labouvie (1997) found decreased lymphocyte proliferation in women accompanied increased levels of depression and hostility, while, interestingly, an increased proliferation of lymphocytes in males was observed following the conflict.

The suggestion that the above responses in women were mediated through the expression of negative affect has received support from elsewhere. Valdimarsdottir and Bovbjerg (1997) reported lower levels of NKC activity in a sample of women reporting at least some negative mood in comparison to women who reported none. In addition levels of NKC activity were found to rise in conjunction with positive mood, although again this was true only for those who reported some negative mood during the day. These authors proposed that positive mood may serve to buffer the depressing effects of negative mood on immune function. The view that stress by itself does not directly lead to immune depression, but indirectly through its effects on appraisal and coping mechanisms which influence mood is consistent with these results. This not only further serves to highlight the difficulties in defining stress purely in terms of objectively defined events, but also raises questions regarding how these relationships between mood and immune activity become distinguished by gender.

Besides interpersonal stressors, negative affective states precipitated in other situations have produced evidence of connections between environmental events and immune activity. The stress of different types of academic examination (written and oral) have been shown to have a variety of effects on immunological response. These include lymphocyte proliferation to mitogen challenge, percentage of plasma monocytes (Van Rood *et al*., 1995), increased neutrophil production of superoxide – a toxic oxygen radical (Kihara, Teshima, Sogawa and Nakagawa, 1992), increases in numbers of T and NK-cells (Shea, Clover and Burton, 1991) and decreased salivary immunoglobulin A (S-IgA) (Deinzer and Schueller, 1998).

Whilst relationships between mood and immune function have now been found in several studies, it is still uncertain whether mood itself always plays a primary role or is a correlate of a more fundamental variable involved in regulating immune function. Other candidates for this role which could preempt mood changes are certainly available. In a review of the role of psychological factors in immune system activity, Cohen and Herbert (1996) found strong evidence for the influence of social supports. They have, for example, been linked with both enhanced mood (Cohen and Willis, 1985) and greater NKC activity (Baron *et al*., 1990), with data even showing that the mere arousal of affiliative trust can lead to increases in S-IgA levels. In turn, poor or absent social relationships may lead to depression and reduced lymphocyte activation (Boccia *et al*., 1997). Yet another candidate for regulating mood is humour. Martin and Lefcourt (1983) reported that higher scores on a coping humour questionnaire were related to higher baseline levels of S-IgA. McClelland and Cheriff (1997) also found sense of humour (humour appreciation and humour production) was positively related to baseline S-IgA levels and that a good sense of humour (specifically humour appreciation, rather than humour production) was related both to a lesser incidence of colds and to less severity in the colds they had in the three months following assessment. There are indications, too, that the immune up-regulation associated with humour is independent of whether overt laughter is involved (Labott, Ahleman, Wolever and Martin, 1990).

This research, then, strongly suggests that it is how situations and events are appraised that is key to whether the neuroendocrinological changes behind regulation of the immune system are called into play. Such appraisal is likely to be heavily influenced by past experiences. A study by Pike *et al.* (1997) also suggests this. When two groups – one reporting chronic life stress, the other a control – were subjected to a psychological stressor (mental arithmetic) it was only in the already chronically stressed group that decreases in NKC activity were observed. Of course it is possible that the influence of past experience on immune responsiveness could make itself felt in two quite different ways. It could bias appraisal so that a threat in the face of some stimulus is more likely to be perceived, with immune changes flowing from this. Alternatively, the immune response itself may be subject to conditioning processes.

Much of the early work on the classical conditioning of immune responses has come from animal studies. A notable study by Ader and Cohen (1985), for example, demonstrated classical conditioning of antibody-mediated and cell-mediated immune responses in rats. There is now ample reason to believe that the immunological responses of humans may also be mutable in this way (Smith and McDaniels, 1983) and that this extends to both the suppression and enhancement of immune activity (Solvason, Ghanta and Hiramoto, 1988). There is growing interest in the potential applications of these findings to clinical settings (see Box 6.2).

BOX 6.2 Clinical applications of conditioned immune responsiveness

Work by Ader and Cohen (1982) established that a neutral stimulus (saccharine-flavoured water) when paired with cyclophosphamide (a drug used to suppress lupus-like symptoms in genetically prone mice) could be used to delay the onset of an autoimmune disorder. It was argued that such classically conditioned responses could have enormous benefits where the original treatment agents are physiologically toxic, such as when chemotherapeutic agents are used to treat cancers.

There is evidence, too, that conditioned immune responses may unwittingly be part and parcel of some routine treatment regimes. Bovjberg *et al.* (1990) found conditioned immunosuppression in women treated for ovarian cancer was triggered simply by being brought to the hospital where they received chemotherapy. This suggests a number of future treatment possibilities which could include varying the environmental settings in which treatments are administered and/or the repeated pairing of the treatment agents with neutral stimuli which could subsequently mimic their properties (Maier, Watkins and Fleshner, 1994). It is not just the treatment of autoimmune disorders and cancers which could benefit from the application of these principles; conditioned immunosuppression, it has also been suggested, might delay rejection of tissue transplants (Grochowitz *et al.*, 1991).

Whatever is ultimately proven to occupy a fundamental place in the causal sequence linking mood to immune system activity, the search is now on for hormonal agents which are activated by psychological states and which subsequently lead to enhancement of immune activity such as IgA levels or NKC activity. Candidates for this role include a variety of steroid hormones (Goldblum, 1990) and more recently a group of proteins known as cytokines such as interleukin-1 (IL-1). These are released by immune cells and have been proposed as the missing link to explain communication between the central nervous system and the immune system. A number have been postulated to play a role in a range of psychological disorders; IL-1 in sleep and sickness behaviour, IL-2 in disturbances of memory, cognitive impairment and schizophrenia, and IL-6 in depression (Mueller and Ackenheil, 1998). Indeed, striking parallels between organisms' responses to stress and to infection, both behaviourally and physiologically, have been noted – perhaps involving activation of the same brain-immune system circuitry that is involved in mediating innate (non-specific) rather than acquired immunity (Maier and Watkins, 1999). There are indications, too, that these influences may be bidirectional. Mood may influence activity of the immune system, which in turn is capable of affecting motivational and mood states. Low mood, for example, may not only instigate down-regulation of the immune system through reduced NKC activity, but has also been shown to occur following infection.

THEORETICAL PROBLEMS

One of the important challenges addressed by PNI researchers has been the issue of whether all indicators of immune activity respond to psychological events in the same direction. Here it has been useful to draw a distinction between acute and chronic stressors. Where short-term stressors such as public speaking, role conflict, anticipatory threat or mental arithmetic, for example, are concerned there are indications of up-regulation in the form of increases in circulating lymphocyte populations and natural killer cells and rises in levels of S-IgA. This is in contrast to situations of chronic stress where the opposite pattern has been observed (Evans et al., 1997; Dhabhar, 1998; Deinzer and Schueller, 1998). This pattern has been interpreted in terms of the responses of both the sympathetic adrenal medullary (SAM) system and the hypothalamic pituitary adrenal (HPA) axis. These systems underlie the normal fight/flight response. The HPA, for example, triggers the release of ACTH (adrenocorticotrophic hormone) which in turn stimulates the release of corticosteroids such as cortisol which over the longer term are known to depress certain aspects of immune function. In the short term, cortisol acts in a negative feedback loop to limit production of ACTH and is involved in responses to acute stressors. Kirschbaum, Wust and Hellhammer's (1992) study provides a succinct demonstration of a short-term cortisol response to the anticipatory stress of making a five-minute speech to a selection panel. Levels were elevated for approximately one hour before returning to baseline levels. The SAM system is also thought to modulate the activity of the HPA axis, and although it has been proposed that it underlies up-regulation of the immune system, firm evidence regarding the mechanisms through which it may do so is still awaited.

However, not all the data favours this straightforward picture. Natural killer cell activity has not always been found to change in response to the presence of a psychological stressor (Pike et al., 1997). Other inconsistent responses to psychosocial factors have also been noted; contrary to expectation, Kamei, Kumano and Masumura (1997) found that exposure to a comedy video actually led to reduced levels of NKC, and in one study of HIV positive men, lower levels of baseline loneliness predicted more rapid declines in CD4 T-cell levels over the follow-up period (Miller *et al.*, 1997). Further theoretical problems arise from the fact that the same stressor may have quite different effects on different markers of immune system activity. Robertson *et al.* (1993) found increased psychological distress (measured via the Profile of Mood States, Diagnostic Interview Schedule and Brief Symptom Inventory) correlated with increased titres of antibody to herpes simplex virus (HSV), but not to cytomegalovirus or Epstein-Barr virus. Benschop *et al.* (1998) also failed to find significant differences in Epstein Barr virus antibody titres between those scoring high or low on daily hassles, and a psychoneurotic symptom checklist. Some of these anomalies (e.g. comedy exposure, loneliness) may be consequent upon the different meanings of particular stressors to individuals, though it is likely that further understanding of the links between the central nervous system and immune system will be required before all of them are resolved.

While much of the previous discussion has centred on the problems of establishing causal links between psychological and social events and the activities of the immune system, the unstated assumption is that these relationships are important because variations in immune system activity have direct consequences on health and well-being. The major concern of psychological research is to show that variation in immune system activity which is directly attributable to psychological and psychosocial events affects health. This topic will be explored in the final section of this chapter.

PSYCHONEUROIMMUNOLOGY AND ILL-HEALTH

The major areas of health in which psychological factors have been postulated to cause ill-health through their action on the immune system are the progression of HIV infection to AIDS and the development of cancer. As yet little hard evidence exists that the progression to AIDS is hastened by stress (see Chapter 11), and in the case of cancer the evidence is inconclusive (see Chapter 19). By far the greater weight of material connecting psychological factors to ill-health through the intermediary activity of the immune system is correlational. The breadth and consistency of this evidence does, however, provide grounds for believing that causal relationships do exist, but gathering sufficiently good evidence is no easy matter. It is methodologically easier to link the variety of markers of immune system activity to actual ill-health than it is to establish psychological factors as sufficient to kick start the process (see Box 6.3).

Shah and Button (1998), following a review of literature examining the relationship between psychological factors and recurrent genital herpes simplex virus (HSV), argued that the evidence did not warrant the conclusion that psychological stressors are sufficient to trigger reactivation of the virus. They admitted the possibility that depression, stress and low social support may make people more susceptible to recurrences, but alternative explanations fit the data equally well. For example socioeconomic status, poor physical health or illness vulnerability (genetic or behavioural) are all capable of accounting for the relationship between greater risk of stress, negative mood and HSV recurrence. The cross-sectional nature of many of the studies, coupled with the absence of measures of socioeconomic status, makes any firmer conclusions impossible.

Where the evidence connecting psychological variables to ill-health is on firmer ground, the states of health in question tend not to be considered serious. For

BOX 6.3   Where is the psyche in psychoneuroimmunology?

One of the criticisms voiced over the current wave of PNI research is the overemphasis placed on molecular communication pathways (Schubert, 1998). Given the penchant for reductionism in much medical research and the relatively early days of this new field, this is understandable. More work, however, is now needed on categorising and standardising (in terms of degree/severity) the various forms of psychological inputs to enable robust psychophysiological links to be discovered.

This is more than simply a measurement problem. For example, it is not currently known if threshold levels exist for some classes of psychological or psychosocial stimuli to provoke altered immune activity, nor, given a particular psychoimmunological relationship, at what level of response and under what conditions (genetic, psychological, social and health) variations in immune responses will translate to specific disease outcomes. In trying to isolate specific sources of stressors as potential modifiers of immunity, some of the difficulties in controlling for the array of behavioural factors known to affect immune function (e.g. diet, alcohol consumption, social supports, sexual behaviour, life events) may be reduced by using single-case designs as well as the traditional group research and cross-sectional designs. Some of the ambiguities in the literature at present probably arise from the use of group sampling techniques and the brute force definitions of stress employed. By returning to individuals' own assessment of what they find difficult to cope with, and their subjective reports of how they feel, a more complete understanding of the relationships between mind and health may arise.

example, a range of chronic stressors are now well-established as causative factors in lowering levels of S-IgA, which in turn have been associated with a variety of mild infections – including the upper respiratory tract and ear (Deinzer and Schueller, 1998) – and are implicated in the development of the common cold (Evans, Clow and Hucklebridge, 1997). The demonstration that psychological factors may alter immune system activity (e.g. the association of anticipatory threat with increased NKC activity; Breznitz et al., 1998), however, cannot by itself be considered adequate evidence that ill-health will ensue. Several criteria are necessary. First of all, it must be conclusively shown that the level of change in immune system activity is of a sufficient magnitude to induce clinically significant effects on the health of the organism; secondly, such changes in health must actually be shown to occur following psychological input; and, finally, suggestive as animal models are, these relationships must be demonstrated in human beings. The presence of simple correlation only, without any further substantiation as to what it means, even if the relationships follow the correct temporal sequence of events for causality to be inferred, may simply be indicative of an orienting response on the part of the organism without specific functional significance for health.

Summary and conclusions

Research showing greater illness in people following stressful life events supports the view that reduced immunocompetence can be triggered by psychological events. Work investigating effects of specific sources of stress (e.g. relationships, daily hassles and academic stress) on immune system functioning has been undertaken. A number of distinct groups have formed the subject base for this (students, people exposed to chronic stress and people with HIV infection) and a number of different markers of immune system activity have been examined (e.g. lymphocyte proliferation following mitogen challenge, natural killer cell activity and S-IgA). Relationships between mood and immune functioning have been found in several studies though the nature of the pathways linking them are still unclear. Some general findings in the field of psychoneuroimmunology have emerged. Short-term stressors have been correlated with up-regulation of some immune system markers, whilst long-term stress appears correlated with down-regulation. However, at the present time conclusive evidence to causally link psychological factors to impaired health is lacking.

Discussion points

A What opportunities for positive interventions to improve health are offered by psychoneuroimmunological research findings?

B How might studies be undertaken to investigate how relationships between mood and immune activity become distinguished by gender?

Suggested reading

Cohen, S. and Herbert, T.B. (1996) 'Health Psychology: Psychological Factors and Physical Disease from the Perspective of Human Psychoneuroimmunology', *Annual Review of Psychology*, **47**: 113–42.

Maier, S.F. and Watkins, L.R. (1999) 'Bidirectional Communication between the Brain and the Immune System: Implications for Behaviour', *Animal behaviour*, **S7**: 741–51.

Solvason, H.B., Ghanta, V.K. and Hiramoto, R.N. (1988) 'Conditioned Augmentation of Natural Killer Cell Activity: Independence from Nociceptive Effects and Dependence on Interferon-beta', *Journal of Immunology*, **140**: 661–5.

PART 3
Health and Behaviour Change

The presentation of information to the general public about risks to health which arise from people's own behaviour has become so commonplace that in response many have adopted a fatalistic air and simply resigned themselves to a view which holds that everything is now somehow dangerous and therefore unworthy of serious attention (Beaglehole and Bonita, 1997). While this scepticism is of interest in its own right and may occasionally even be warranted (Davison, Frankel and Davey-Smith, 1992), there can be no doubting that there are a number of behaviours which people undertake which clearly have adverse consequences not only for their own but often also for others' health. Whilst much of the research which forms the basis for public health information has been generated by epidemiologists and other medical scientists, through an understanding of the meaning and context of the behaviour in question, health psychologists are well-placed to understand why these associations between particular behavioural practices and health outcomes may exist. In addition, by virtue of possessing a theoretical paradigm for understanding behavioural change they are in a position to develop and implement programmes which may lead individuals to change the patterns of behaviour which impact negatively upon their health.

In the next few chapters we will address five main areas of behaviour which as well as being widespread in western industrialised societies, are generally understood by members of those societies to carry strong implications for health and well-being. These concern (1) exercise, (2) eating behaviour, (3) alcohol use, (4) smoking, and (5) sexual behaviour. Many of these have been subsumed by Orford (1985) under the framework of appetitive behaviours. As a prelude to this task and to assist us in the evaluation we will begin by reviewing some key models which have been advanced by health psychologists to explain health-related behaviours, and which focus on the role of cognitions.

7

Modelling Change in Health Behaviour

> 'The Principle of Unripe Time is that people should not do at the present moment what they think right at that moment, because the moment at which they think it right has not yet arrived.'
>
> Francis M. Cornford (*Microcosmographia Academica*, 1908)

SOCIAL COGNITION MODELS

To date, psychologists have adopted several theoretical models which examine the cognitive determinants of health-related behaviour occurring in a variety of contexts. Though several have been proposed, paramount amongst these have been the Health Belief Model (Rosenstock, 1974), and the Theory of Planned Behaviour – derived from the earlier Theory of Reasoned Action (Fishbein and Ajzen, 1975). Were it to be acknowledged that interventions at the level of cognitions are unlikely to have major effects, then the practical significance of these models would be quite low and the effort, expense and attention devoted to them difficult to justify. Thus all the models must be said to embody the implicit assumption that cognitive processes are not only the final stage in causal chains leading from the biological and social determinants of behaviour, but must also constitute effective sites for interventions intended to bring about behaviour change. These it is hoped will be sufficient to break ingrained and well-established patterns of human behaviour and to instigate new behavioural routines to preserve and enhance well-being. In this chapter we will critically review and present the main features of three of these models; as well as the above two we will also discuss a third, Protection Motivation Theory. Together these do not by any means exhaust the number and variety of social cognition models as they have come to be called, but by virtue of their having exerted such a huge influence on the field a review of them will provide the reader with a sufficient basis for evaluating how well models of this genre can be applied to understanding and predicting health-relevant behaviours. Finally, we briefly consider some facets of the Transtheoretical Model of Change (Prochaska and DiClemente, 1984) as this has frequently been employed in conjunction with one of the social cognition models.

The health belief model (HBM)

This model has probably been the most widely used of the social cognition models – so-called because they incorporate subjects' representations of the social world. It identifies five key variables intervening between the social and personal character-

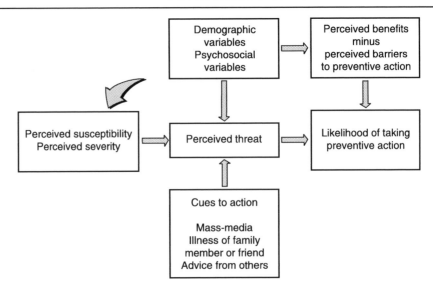

Figure 7.1   The health belief model

istics of the individual, and health-oriented action. These are *perceived susceptibility to a health threat, perceived severity of threat, general health motivation*, as well as the *perceived costs and benefits* to any proposed preventive action (See Figure 7.1). Later contextual constructs added to the model include self-esteem, interpersonal skills, peer norms, relationship status, knowledge and previous experience (Lowe and Radius, 1982). The model has been employed in a variety of health settings which include smoking, drinking, sexual behaviour and eating. Unfortunately, results have been disappointing (see for example Chapter 11), and where statistically significant relationships indicative of a causal role for health beliefs have been reported, the overall effect sizes have been small, rarely explaining more than a small percentage of the total variation in the outcomes studied (Sheeran and Abraham, 1995).

Though one undoubted difficulty affecting the predictive utility of the health belief model has been the absence of consensus regarding how to operationalise the constructs in the model (Sheeran and Abraham, 1995; Conner and Norman, 1995), a number of more fundamental reasons exist for its failure to adequately predict behaviour (Abraham and Sheeran, 1994). It can be argued that the 'rationalist' nature of the theory fails to pay adequate attention to the emotional or social nature of the situations in which these actions are embedded. An adequate account of human behaviour must give due weight to situational factors, and in this respect once again the health belief model is deficient. Furthermore, if they are to be maximally effective, health-related behaviours frequently require long-term maintenance. Consequently, in taking account of the continuous making and remaking of decisions, a proper theoretical account ought also to contain some developmental perspective. Finally, for all the emphasis placed on the cognitive structures underlying behaviour, the health belief model does not clearly specify how different attitudes relate to one another nor how cognitive systems translate into actual behaviour in the world.

The theory of planned behaviour (TBP)

In this theory (Figure 7.2) *attitudes* and *subjectively perceived social norms* are held to precede the formation of *intentions*, which fill the void between beliefs and

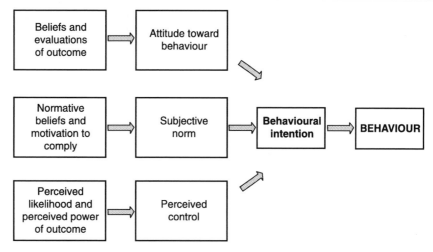

Figure 7.2   The theory of planned behaviour

behaviour evident in the health belief model. The greater specificity of this model in comparison to the health belief model has resulted in generally stronger relationships being found between its various components. The utility of this approach has been strengthened by the addition of *perceived behavioural control*. Ajzen (1991) has argued that this construct and the notion of perceived self-efficacy which some researchers have used within the TBP are synonymous. Some evidence exists to support the distinction; Terry and O'Leary (1995), for example, found self-efficacy to be a significant predictor of behavioural intentions, while perceived control was not. However conflicting results have been reported (Povey *et al.*, 2000) and it must be remembered that so long as no agreed standards exist for measuring these constructs, the results in any one instance could reflect differences in the precision with which each was measured rather than a true underlying difference in predictive power. It would be mistaken, however, to regard control or self-efficacy as characteristics which can be firmly located within individuals. Bandura (1998), for example, points out that the concept of collective efficacy has been almost totally ignored. The existence of the cognitive components specified in both the HBM and TPB, however, should be seen as relevant only in relation to those other people and situations with which a person is engaged. Though we are more likely to enact behaviours we feel competent to carry out and which we deem to be under our own control, these too are a function of context, whether interpersonal or ecological.

Protection motivation theory (PMT)

Elements of the health belief model and the theory of reasoned action are found in Rogers' (1975, 1983) protection motivation theory. In this scheme behavioural intentions receive inputs from four sources; two of which relate to threat appraisal (perceived severity and perceived vulnerability), and two to coping appraisal (self-efficacy and effectiveness of likely response). Together these determine the motivation to take self-protective action (Bennett and Murphy, 1997). Thus, in contrast to the earlier models, the application of PMT is specific to contexts which arouse fear for one's health. In principle the model permits the prediction of maladaptive responses which arise when coping appraisal is low but threat is high. Hodgkins and Orbell (1998) conducted one of the few longitudinal tests of the theory in asking whether PMT could explain motivation to enact breast self-examination. Unfortunately for the model, PMT variables were unable to discriminate between those who developed an intention for breast self-examination and those who did not, nor to account for future behaviour. In a further test applied to uptake of a cervical screening test within a one-year period of completing measures derived from PMT, Orbell and Sheeran (1998) found that although results suggest PMT provides a useful account of choice motivation, it does not address the psychological processes by which intention is translated into action.

EVALUATION OF SOCIAL COGNITION MODELS

The manner in which all the three above models describe the processes governing behaviour must be regarded as fundamentally misleading. All depict behavioural outcomes as essentially linear functions (of beliefs, motivations, costs and benefits in the health belief model; of perceived norms, behavioural intentions, efficacy and control in the theory of planned behaviour; and of coping appraisal and threat appraisal in protection motivation theory; Conner and Sparks, 1995). Neither do they give due consideration to the habitual nature of many behaviours in the health domain and this is certainly true of the behaviours which form the principal topics of this and the following chapters (Stroebe and Stroebe, 1995). Time and again past behaviour has been found to be the major predictor of current and future behaviours (see for example Sheeran and Abraham, 1994). Abraham, Sheeran and Johnston (1998) rightly point out that more work is now required on the processes involved in action initiation and goal achievement, and these must clearly involve some means of specifying the context within which decisions and actions unfold. However, to capture complex context dependent behaviour within a linear individual centred framework is doomed to failure. Any example of social interaction (and it is difficult to imagine the origin of any health-related behaviours outside of a social context) is also dynamic – subject to the interplay of person and context upon a canvas of fluctuating cognitions, actions and reactions (Dean, 1996). The choices people make cannot be extricated from the choices that others make, nor from the power relations between them nor the wider social milieu which dictates the availability of choice and sets limits to personal efficacy and control. Arguments, therefore, which propose improvements to social cognition models in the form of yet more cognitive constructs (for example perceived need; Paisley and Sparks, 1998), though perhaps not without some merit, must therefore be seen as missing the point. More sophisticated modelling techniques, perhaps of a kind that permit real-time simulation of behaviour in context, may need to be developed before significant practical headway can be made.

A further practical problem arising from these models is that relatively little work has utilised them as a basis for planning interventions, and where it has they do not seem to suggest that cognitions are an optimal intervention point. Povey et al. (2000), for example, found TPB variables could account for less than 20 per cent of the variation in actual fat intake. As a further example, if we take the observation that most people simply don't perceive themselves to be at risk of ill-health (this is certainly true for young people smoking and drinking to excess as well as engaging in unplanned and unprotected sexual behaviour), then logically one might consider means to alter perceived susceptibility. However, although when questioned respondents may acknowledge the potentially severe consequences of their actions (such as lung cancer, liver damage or HIV infection), the long delay between the action and its potentially adverse consequences constitutes a strong barrier to effective learning. The key question must be, do these models lead to viable effective intervention strategies or to the likelihood of developing them? In perusing the material which follows it will be instructive for the reader to compare the scope and efficacy of these models against others which have been posited at different levels of abstraction, be they biological or social.

STAGES OF CHANGE

Stages of change is a model of behavioural change which describes five stages: precontemplation, contemplation, preparation, action and maintenance.

Originally referred to as the Transtheoretical Model of Change, the **stages of change** proposed by Prochaska and DiClemente (1984) has been influential in attempts to understand how successful behaviour change occurs in a wide variety of settings including condom use (Harlow *et al.*, 1999), exercise (Courneya, Nigg and Estabrooks, 1998) and smoking (Prochaska and DiClemente, 1983). It was originally developed to explain the natural history of remission and relapse in the addictive disorders (DiClemente, 1993). Five stages are described; pre-contemplation, contemplation, preparation, action and maintenance. Strictly speaking this is not a true stage model as the three basic assumptions of stage theories – qualitative transformation across stages, invariant sequence of change and non-reversibility – are all violated (Bandura, 1998). The stages are in fact better considered as a continuum of degrees of duration of the behaviour to be adopted.

In this respect, this scheme is neither a theory nor a model, but a tautological description of what must logically occur. One cannot quit smoking, for example, without first contemplating it – but this does not mean that contemplation acts a *theoretical* construct to explain why someone quit. In short, there is nothing here as to why anyone either does or does not move from one stage to the next. There is no meaning. In short it is as Bandura (1998) argues *atheoretical* rather than transtheoretical. That social cognitive variables can be used to distinguish who actually passes from one stage to the next is merely a testament to the fact that social cognitive models, whatever their deficiencies, are genuine theories trying to explain observable behaviour.

Summary and conclusions

Three broad weaknesses exist in social cognitive models (that is, the Health Belief Model, the Theory of Planned Behaviour, and Protection Motivation). These can be summarised as follows:

A   No agreed standards exist for how to operationalise measurement of the constructs in any of the models.

B   Where relationships are successfully predicted between model constructs and health behaviours, these are usually too weak to provide a practical basis for health promotion or clinical intervention.

C   Theoretical proposals to date have tended to concentrate too heavily on individual factors. The role of emotional, situational and social influences in shaping behaviour have proved difficult to satisfactorily incorporate into existing models – even where their influence has been recognised. Allied to this is the assumption that relationships can be captured within a linear analytic framework. This is probably far too simple.

Stages of change models, though they have frequently been employed with social cognitive models, have been heavily criticised as lacking any theoretical basis for explaining and predicting change, as well as simply being tautological descriptions of the processes of change without adding any theoretical insights into why people's health-related behaviour may or may not change.

Discussion points

A   What future do social cognition models have in health psychology?

B   What place do individual meanings have in modelling change?

Suggested reading

Abraham, C., Sheeran, P. and Johnston, M. (1998) 'From Health Beliefs to Self-Regulation: Theoretical Advances in the Psychology of Action Control', *Psychology and Health*, **13**(4): 569–91.

Bandura, A. (1998) 'Health Promotion from the Perspective of Social Cognition Theory', *Psychology and Health*, **13**(4): 623–50.

Conner, M. and Norman, P. (eds) (1986) *Predicting Health Behaviour*. (Buckingham: Open University Press).

Exercise, Health and Eating

(with Dawn Baker Towell)

'The meaning and purpose of dancing is the dance.'

Alan Watts (*The Way of Zen*, 1957)

EXERCISE

The benefits of exercise are well-recognised and there is good evidence to suggest that physical activity protects against coronary heart disease (CHD) and can help protect against weight gain and obesity, hypertension, osteoporosis, stroke, diabetes and cancer of the colon. There is also considerable evidence that exercise can help people cope with anxiety and depression and suggestions that benefits in self-esteem and self-confidence may also ensue (Ogden, 1996). A major problem in western industrialised countries is, however, that a large number of people are at risk of developing CHD which in part is fuelled by the sedentary lifestyles that many children and adults now have. A major initiative of health policy is action to 'activate' the population and to encourage people to take regular exercise as outlined in the UK's *Health of the Nation* document (Department of Health). From this, programmes such as 'Active for Life ' have been implemented by the Health Education Authority which have specific targets and outcomes aimed at making exercise more frequent and more fun. Adults are encouraged to build up to half an hour of activity a day, involving sustained brisk activity for at least five days. Recommendations for young people aged 5–16 years are that they should participate in physical activity of at least moderate intensity for one hour a day!

Who exercises?

There is a clear gender difference in sport participation and recreational physical activity and some have claimed that few women are active enough to benefit their health (Vertinsky, 1998). Currently 59 per cent of men and 68 per cent of women take little or no exercise and only 14 per cent and 4 per cent respectively take enough to gain maximum cardiac benefit (HEA, 1999). There appear to be a number of negative stereotypes associated with women and sport participation, particularly so in the younger age range. Only 32 per cent of 16–24 year old women are active enough to benefit their health compared with 56 per cent of men of the same age but eight out of ten women in this age group would like to take more exercise. Young women appear to be more interested in the benefits of exercise such as weight loss, appearance, feeling good and fitness, some of which take considerable time and effort to achieve (Health Education Authority, 1999).

Like many areas in health, there appears to be a social gradient in sport participation. In a study of 1984 adolescents, subjects in lower socioeconomic groups engaged in sport less frequently than subjects in the higher SES groups (Tuinstra *et al.*, 1998). There are also clear differences in exercise behaviour and the effects of exercise across the lifespan and clear cultural differences. Among African-Caribbeans between 16 and 74 years of age, 62 per cent of men and 75 per cent of women do not participate in enough physical activity to benefit their health – nearly a third are sedentary compared with about a quarter in the general population (Health Education Authority, 1999). Similar statistics are true of South Asians in the same age groups (16–74 years). Activity levels in women vary: 83 per cent of Indians, 86 per cent of Pakistanis and 82 per cent of Bangladeshis do not take enough exercise to benefit their health, whilst the figures for men are 67 per cent, 72 per cent and 75 per cent respectively. About half of all South Asian women are sedentary comparing with about 45 per cent of South Asian men. Given the relative inactivity of black and ethnic minority groups compared to the general population and the increased risks of stroke, CHD and diabetes in these populations, it is important that exercise participation programmes are targeted here.

To date, it is unclear exactly what components of exercise provide maximum benefit to physical and psychological health. For instance, what is the role of relaxation in exercise? And is exercise obtained through participation in team sport better than exercise alone? Clearly there is a component of relaxation in both sport and exercising alone but one can ask the question of whether other forms of relaxation are also of similar benefit. Fellows and Jones (1994) investigated this issue in 364 subjects. They found 14 activities highly reported – in order of increasing popularity these were tea or coffee (at home), doing nothing, knitting or sewing, playing a musical instrument or singing, gardening, smoking!, playing indoors games, driving, cooking, sunbathing, cinema or theatre, sex, playing with children and eating at home. These data would merit further investigation especially determining the role of activities involving a physical component such as gardening. In fact in a more detailed analysis of their data they isolated five categories which were defined as providing relaxation, passive activities, sensory experiences, mental activities, social activities and physical activities. From this model it would be predicted that a combination of these categories would provide maximal relaxation and therefore have greater impact on health. However, there is a paucity of research comparing individual exercise and sporting activities. There is however some evidence showing greater adherence in unsupervised home-based programmes compared with supervised programmes at a local community centre, although only older subjects were recruited into this controlled trial (King *et al.*, 1991). In the UK the emphasis has now shifted to the young with programmes such as 'Action for Life' specifically targeting these age groups.

Benefits of exercise?

The physical benefits of exercise are widespread and apply across the whole of the lifespan. However, the main impact on health appears to be a reduction of cardiovascular problems, reduction in weight and obesity, reduction in diabetes, and reduction in some forms of cancer. Regular exercise has also been shown to improve insulin sensitivity cholesterol and fibrinogen levels (Morris and Hardman, 1997).

Participation in strength and weight-bearing activities is positively associated with bone mineral density and is believed to be related to protection against osteoporosis especially in older women. For a detailed review see Blair *et al.* (1992).

By far the biggest research initiative has focussed on exercise and coronary heart disease. Many studies have demonstrated that individuals who engage in regular physical activity are less likely to develop and die from CHD than those who do not and lead sedentary lives. However, implementing such health interventions has proved difficult despite the known benefits. In a general practitioner referral programme on modifiable CHD risk factors in 142 adults identified as smokers, hypertensive or overweight subjects were randomly allocated to an exercise group or control group. Although there were clearly short-term benefits in physical activity and reductions in the sum of skinfolds and blood pressure, the most notable changes were dependent on adherence to the programme with a significant reduction in systolic blood pressure after six months for high adherers only (Taylor *et al.*, 1998). So whilst exercise may provide protection from CHD by decreasing blood pressure, modifying cholesterol and increasing muscular activity which supports the functioning of the heart, there are other factors which are also important in affecting adherence such as social support, socioeconomic status and personality types.

The psychological benefits of exercise have only recently been examined in a systematic and controlled fashion. The evidence points to a beneficial role of exercise in depression, anxiety, coping with stress and building self-esteem and self-confidence (for a review see Ogden, 1996). For instance, Steptoe and Butler (1996) in a study of adolescents (2223 males and 2838 females) with a mean age of 16.3 years showed that sport and vigorous recreational activity was positively associated with well-being even when controlling for sex, social class, health status and use of hospital services. Similar positive effects of exercise have been found in older subjects (62–91 years old) where after six months on a public health model intervention, improvements in anxiety, depression, self-esteem and psychological well-being were seen compared to a no physical activity group (Stewart *et al.*, 1997). It has also been shown that sport/exercise results in increased happiness when compared to other leisure activities such as music, church and watching TV soaps (Hills and Argyle, 1998).

Exercise has also been proposed as an adjunct therapy for schizophrenia. In three patients a 10-week exercise programme of twice-weekly sessions indicated reductions in participants' perceptions of auditory hallucinations, increase in self-esteem and improvement in sleep patterns and general behaviour. The authors do acknowledge that the process of exercise, via the provision of distraction and social interaction rather than the exercise itself, was influential in providing benefits (Faulkner and Sparkes, 1999). Similarly, the Joint Working Group of the Royal Colleges of Physicians, Psychiatrists and General Practitioners has recommended graded exercise for patients with chronic fatigue syndrome. In a study to test this, a six-month prospective randomised placebo and therapist-contact time trial was instigated to compare exercise with no exercise. Exercise significantly improved health perception and fatigue at 28 weeks. Graded exercise produced improvements in functional work capacity and fatigue, while the antidepressant drug fluoxetine improved depression only (Wearden *et al.*, 1998).

Costs of exercise?

Paradoxically, there is literature investigating whether college athletes are at greater risk for maladaptive lifestyle and heath-risk behaviours than their non-athletic peers. A study comparing 2298 athletes with 683 randomised non-athlete controls showed that athletes were less likely to use seatbelts, and to use helmets with motorcycles and bicycles. Athletes drank more alcohol, had greater numbers of sexual partners with less contraceptive use, and were more likely to engage in physical fights. Female athletes reported a higher prevalence of irregular menses, amenorrhea and stress fractures compared with female non-athletes. Athlete subgroups at highest risk were those participating in contact sports (Nattiv *et al.*, 1997) which may reveal more about the motives of the participants engaging in high-risk activities. Exercise can have harmful effects in terms of exacerbating physical injuries and having negative effects on interpersonal relationships and mood (Morgan *et al.*, 1988; Pierce *et al.*, 1997). There is also the suggestion that some individuals who engage in high levels of sporting activity (in particular long-distance running) might themselves have a disorder that is in some way analogous to anorexia nervosa as there are many descriptive similarities between patients with anorexia and individuals who exercise to excess (Le Grange and Eisler, 1993).

Predicting exercise uptake and maintenance

In terms of health promotion strategies it is important to identify factors that will predict exercise behaviour especially in vulnerable groups where the benefits of exercise participation would be most evident. For instance, in a sample of early retirement older adults (65–70 years old) it was found that attitudinal, social norm and perceived behavioural control variables were strongly associated with intent to exercise. When habit was added to the model (based on the theory of planned behaviour) the associations were strengthened (Michels and Kugler, 1998). A more fruitful approach has been to combine the stages-of-change model and the theory of planned behaviour to identify factors in specific subgroups that will inform health promotion programmes. In a cross-sectional postal survey in Canada, Nguyen *et al.* (1997) targeted a sample of men (2269) with a view to planning more effective programmes in heart disease prevention. Nearly a quarter of the sample was physically inactive of whom 10.5 per cent were in precontemplation and 12.8 per cent in the contemplation stages. Of those who exercised less than twice a week (42.1%) 22.4 per cent were in preparation I and 19.7 per cent in the preparation II stages. Just over a third (34.6%) of the sample were in the action stage exercising for at least 20 minutes twice a week or more with the intention of continuation. Perceived behavioural control was associated in all stages, whereas attitude was related with stages in which individuals have intention of exercising (contemplation and preparation II). In contrast, subjective norm was associated with stages in which individuals have no intention of exercising (precontemplation and preparation I). Other studies have focused more on the perceived barriers to increasing physical activity in inactive subjects. From a randomly selected Australian sample of 2298 people, Booth *et al.* (1997) identified 35 per cent who were insufficiently physically active. Data were analysed according to age (young and old) and sex. The most preferred activity was walking (38% and 68% of the young and old groups respectively). The most frequently cited barriers to more regular participation in the young were insufficient time, lack of motivation and childcare responsibilities, whilst in the old they were injury or poor health. The preferred source of advice for older subjects would be from a health professional, whereas the opportunity to exercise in a group was the preferred source of support from the younger subjects.

Mechanisms

Although the relationship between exercise and health is well-established, attempts to explain factors which mediate the link have proved less fruitful. One possibility was that exercise increases levels of noradrenalin in the brain and promotes the release of endorphins, which are the brain's natural opiods, although a number of studies have failed to support this hypothesis (Kraemer *et al.*, 1990). Others have shown that appropriate exercise may enhance immune function and lessen acute upper and lower respiratory infection symptoms in older adults (Karper and Hopewell, 1998). Although the exact mechanism is unknown there is the possibility that the positive effect of exercise on mood modulates immune functions and increases the body's defence against disease (see Chapter 6). Additional conjectures as to why exercise is beneficial concern the social context in which exercise occurs – perhaps team activities or activities undertaken in the company of others provides social support. Exercise may also enhance psychological well-being via the effects of diverting attention from daily hassles and worries in addition to the effects of physical relaxation.

ANOREXIA AND BULIMIA NERVOSA

The desire for thinness and body awareness is a relatively modern phenomenon that has prevailed over the last half of the twentieth century. Prior to the Second World War a fullness of body had been associated with wealth, and emotional and physical well-being. During the 1960s and 1970s a general awareness of health and health promotion emerged, fat was considered not only as being bad for your health, but as aesthetically undesirable. The general population was encouraged to lose weight, and subsequently the diet and health industry boomed – thinness became equated with health and fitness of both mind and body. Within westernised society dieting as a facet of eating behaviour has now been normalised. Over 80 per cent of women will attempt to lose weight at some stage of their lives, and dieting is the only factor consistently identified as a precursor of an eating disorder (Szmukler and Patton, 1995). A prospective study of mid-adolescent schoolgirls found an eight-fold increase in the incidence of eating disorders 12 months following the onset of dieting behaviours (Patton *et al.*, 1990). However, the causal role between eating behaviours and eating disorders remains disputed, as associations are shared from many antecedents.

Anorexia nervosa is a disorder of eating characterised by a drive for thinness, a refusal to maintain a normal body weight and loss of menses.

Bulimia nervosa is a disorder of eating characterised by a cycle of bingeing or purging, the latter often including laxative and diuretic abuse, self-induced vomiting, voluntary starvation and excessive exercise.

Background, diagnosis and classification

Eating disorders are behavioural disorders, and for the purpose of this chapter the two main disorders of ***anorexia nervosa*** (AN) and ***bulimia nervosa*** (BN) will be discussed. Anorexia, first medically described by Sir William Gull in 1874, means a 'nervous loss of appetite' and is characterised by a drive for thinness and a refusal to maintain a normal body weight and loss of menses. Bulimia, described first by Russell in 1979, is characterised by a cycle of bingeing or purging, the latter often including laxative and diuretic abuse, self-induced vomiting, voluntary starvation and excessive exercise. Both AN and BN share common features such as disturbance in body shape and weight perception, with frequent co-morbidity of depression, substance abuse, obsessive compulsive disorders and secrecy.

Most UK centres adopt the criteria laid down in either the Diagnostic and Statistical Manual of Mental Disorders (DSM-IV) or the International Classification of Diseases handbook (ICD-10), a combination of both or have evolved their own diagnostic system, particularly in the case of early onset AN (Lask and Bryant-Waugh, 1992). For AN, both classifications include weight loss, body image distortion, amenorrhoea and weight phobia as key features, but only ICD-10 provides an algorithm to calculate weight loss that takes into account the build of the patient. ICD-10 includes widespread endocrine disorder whereas DSM-IV only refers to amenorrhea. Atypical cases are considered in both classifications although only DSM-IV includes subtypes of 'restriction' (where weight loss is achieved through starvation and excessive exercise) and 'binge eating/purging' (binge followed by inappropriate compensatory behaviour). DSM-IV fails to specifically define diagnostic criteria for eating disorders in males but defines lower prevalence rates. ICD-10 has incorporated Russell's 1970 criteria of reduced sexual interest and potency in males, to be equivalent to loss of menses in females, in order for diagnosis to occur. For a diagnosis of BN, both classification systems include binge eating and recurrent use of inappropriate compensatory behaviour to prevent weight gain, but DSM-IV specifies a minimum average of two episodes of binge eating and purging per week for 3 months and emphasises the body shape and weight preoccupation and also includes purging and non-purging subtypes. ICD-10 emphasises the morbid fear of fatness and an earlier history of AN. Both systems include a category of atypical BN in the absence of one or more key features.

Epidemiology

Although there have been numerous studies on the incidence and prevalence of disordered eating it is difficult to draw any firm conclusions because of the methodological differences in survey instruments, samples and analysis. However, the general trend appears to show a prevalence of 1 per cent for anorexia in the adolescent population and between 1–8 per cent for bulimia, although some recent studies show a higher prevalence in student populations and especially in female athletes. This has led to the description of anorexia athletica and female athletic triad to describe the presence of menstrual dysfunction, eating disorders and osteoporosis in young female athletes and dancers. It is generally believed that most studies underestimate prevalence rates, especially in the case of BN where it is possible to conceal the disorder not least because there is no apparent weight loss. However, the rate of occurrence of AN in males is approximately one-tenth of that in females, and 0.5–20 per cent of the total BN population (Olivardia et al., 1995), although there is some recent evidence that this gap is closing. The mortality rate for AN is between 5–10 per cent with death resulting from starvation, suicide or electrolyte imbalance (Neumarker, 1997). Whereas anorexia was once considered a disorder predominately of the higher social classes, it is presently becoming represented among all socioeconomic groups. Cultural factors are important, with reports of little or no eating disorders in non-westernised societies and increases in societies adopting western values. Immigrants from cultures in which an eating disorder is rare who emigrate to westernised societies are likely to increase their risk of developing one.

Clinical Presentation

The disorder of AN tends to begin in early adolescence although it may occur in the pre-pubertal period, where in girls it may retard growth and development with delays in puberty of up to three years. The adolescent with AN typically is a high achiever, often involved heavily in sports such as gymnastics, swimming or ballet dancing. They tend to be perfectionists, very competitive and to have developed marked obsessional personality features. They believe that they are subjected to high parental expectations of academic and social ability. The onset of dieting can begin following a chance remark by someone who is important to them suggesting that they are getting fat, big or clumsy and their performance is suffering. Other patients cite as precipitating causes media influences, wanting to look like a favourite film star or model. In other cases these girls articulate a fear of growing up and becoming adult. Discomfort towards sexuality has been found among both male and female anorexics (Schmidt *et al.*, 1997).

The anorexic behaviour typically begins a with pattern of dieting or particular food choices usually avoiding foods that are perceived as fattening, particularly carbohydrates. The anorexic becomes quite resourceful in hiding the eating anomalies and may avoid eating with the family or will change to a vegetarian or vegan diet to further avoid specific foods. Further attempts to reduce weight might include compulsive exercising, vomiting and/or the use of laxatives. The anorexic may wear multiple levels of loose clothing not only to hide thinness, but to compensate for inadequate temperature control. Loose clothing also provides an excellent opportunity to hide food. The condition may be far advanced before parents recognise what is happening. In extreme cases the diagnosis is only made during clinic visits for physical problems including physical weakness, lack of energy, excessive sleepiness and failure at school. Chronic starvation caused by anorexia has also been seen to induce seizure activity or fainting attacks.

At the time of first presentation the adolescent often looks pale, tired and wasted, bradycardia may be present, and the skin is cold to the touch. Characteristically a fine downy hair (lanugo) may be present on the arms and torso. The adolescent is in total denial about their condition and may insist that they are fat. Particular distortion in body image lies around the hips, thighs and stomach with the individual often describing themselves as feeling and appearing heavily pregnant. Laboratory investigations may reveal quite bizarre values and in particular there may be dehydration and severe electrolyte disturbances that can be life threatening. In postmenarchal girls there is cessation of the menstrual cycle which has probably not been present for some time and occurs when more than 20 per cent of expected body weight has been lost.

Clinical presentation of BN can vary greatly, ranging from a similar description as above for AN through to a picture of a 'normal' weight individual that appears physically and psychologically healthy. Only upon a detailed and systematic interview will a full description of inappropriate eating behaviours emerge. Again body shape and weight are of great significance and clear distortions in the individuals self perception and self esteem are evident. A binge episode may range from ten minutes to two hours. The binge episode is not confined to one particular environment but is surrounded in secrecy; it may be frenzied or dissociative in its nature. It is often 'triggered' by a specific food, hunger, mood or event. Caloric consumption at one sitting tends to be obtained through high calorie, mainly sweet foods, which are not necessarily just carbohydrates and may total tens of thousands in calorific value. The binge episode is then characteristically followed by a period of self-loathing and disgust. Feelings of contentment and satisfaction are short-lived and give way to depression and self-hatred for loss of control. To compensate for the large ingestion of weight-gaining food, inappropriate behaviours are used. Self-induced vomiting provides immediate relief. The individual may only use the binge to achieve the ultimate goal of vomiting. After some practice the BN sufferer is able to induce vomiting at will. Each individual may use a variety of methods such as laxatives, exercise and fasting, to a greater or lesser extent, to prevent weight gain. Over 50 per cent of bulimic people are actively engaged in stealing/shoplifting to provide the food/money necessary for the binge to occur (Mitchell *et al.*, 1992).

ETIOLOGY OF EATING DISORDERS

The etiology of anorexia is uncertain, although it is likely to be multifactorial involving biological, psychological and psychosocial factors.

Biological Factors

Although many have postulated the existence of a hypothalamic disorder underlying an endocrine disturbance (Russell, 1985) it is difficult to dissociate primary dysfunction from secondary effects of the disease process. More recent research has focused on genetic factors which show that sisters of anorexics have a higher incidence of the disorder than the general population (Scott, 1986) and that children of mothers with eating disorders are more at risk of developing one themselves. Twin studies have also supported a genetic contribution. In a sample of 45 twin pairs the concordance rate for AN in dizygotic twins was 5 per cent, whilst for monozygotic twins it was 56 per cent (Holland *et al.*, 1988). Higher concordance rates for BN in monozygotic as compared to dizygotic twins has also been shown (Fichter and Noegelm, 1990; Hsu *et al.*, 1990). However, there are no studies that show high concordance rates for eating disorders in twins raised apart. Clearly, interpretation of these data are not straightforward, though they suggest an interaction between genetic and environmental factors in developing an eating disorder. Future studies will attempt to identify the environmental triggers.

With the recent advent of brain imaging technology a number of studies have suggested a brain dysfunction in children that could be a primary marker of the disease. Anorexia has been shown to be associated with a functional abnormality within subcortical structures (Sieg *et al.*, 1997; Addolorato *et al.*, 1998). In the tradition of the medical model the long-term hope would be to identify the exact site of a primary organic abnormality with the view to developing specific treatments.

Psychological Factors

Most of the literature in this area has focused on the patient population where child–parent relationships are likely to be strained and parents concerned about their child's starvation may well attempt to exert considerable control. Thus anorexia has been associated with problems in upbringing, sexual abuse, family dysfunction, low self-esteem and poor self-concept, over-controlling mothers and distant fathers

(Wallin *et al.*, 1996). Anorexics fear sexual maturation, have difficulty in dealing with stress and have problems separating from the family and developing a distinct self-identity. More recent studies have examined comorbidity with depression and a tendency towards perfectionism. However, the overlap with depression and obsessive compulsive behaviour remains unclear. It is also less than clear whether these findings represent a primary dysfunction due to the illness or a secondary effect of it.

Sociocultural Factors

The development of AN and BN have been explained by biopsychosocial multifactorial models that postulate an interplay between external and internal variables (Szmukler, Dare and Treasure, 1995). These disorders are most commonly found in modern western societies and are associated with a desire to attain a shape that is both unnatural and unobtainable to the vast majority. The impact of increased exposure of the female form through the mass media has been linked to the changing trends in both appearance and image, and may have exacerbated the number of women initiating medical intervention for eating and related disorders (Vandereycken, 1986). The media provides an image of how one is 'supposed' to look, and pressure to conform to this image often results in unfavourable appraisal during self-evaluation (Hamilton and Waller, 1993). In a study of 921 adolescent schoolchildren the greatest predictor of engagement in extreme weight-loss behaviours was the desire to match up to society's current ideal body size (Wertheim *et al.*, 1992). One test of the sociocultural hypothesis is to study congenitally blind women who have never been able to 'see' their own image but hold an internal representation, albeit impoverished and systematically distorted. Visually impaired women should, according to multifactorial models, be subjected to similar risk factors of aetiology as sighted women. However, the past 15 years have only resulted in the publication of a handful of such cases (see Bemporad *et al.*, 1989, for a review), and have been interpreted in two ways. Firstly, that body-image disturbance/dissatisfaction and the sociocultural value of thinness in the etiology of eating disorders is of great significance and that it must be dependent upon external 'visual experience' (McFarlane, 1989). Secondly, as a juxtaposition, that the inability to see does not protect against or preclude the development of an eating disorder and that internal conflicts are of stronger importance (Touyz *et al.*, 1988). However, it has been shown in non-eating disordered subjects that congenitally blind women have lower body dissatisfaction scores and more positive eating attitudes compared to both women blinded later in life and sighted women who have the highest body dissatisfaction scores and most negative eating attitudes (Baker, Sivyer and Towell, 1999).

Feminist theory also contributes towards the multifactorial model and asks – Is the experience of eating disorders a result of being female? Despite the increase in awareness of male sufferers of eating disorders, it is still largely (80–95%) a female experience. During puberty the development of secondary sexual characteristics (hips, thighs and breasts) involves the depositing of fat onto these areas. In today's westernized culture little value is placed on a well-rounded figure, thinness is the desirable norm. For some, the gender role and whole experience of femaleness may be in direct conflict with biologically determined size and shape. A struggle may then ensue to live up to society's double standards and the imposition of gender specific traits. Desirable attributes include passivity, intellectual inferiority and slenderness (Lester, 1997). Cherin (1987) views the promotion of a slender adolescent male body as the female ideal, as nothing less than the total rejection by our society of 'mature womanhood'. To perpetuate female feelings of inadequacy the male-dominated fashion, diet and advertising industry continues to dictate image. This ever-changing image is unobtainable to the vast majority and requires time, money and effort in the pursuit to achieve. The pressure to conform is thus likely to adversely affect the adolescent that is seeking out and experimenting with her own identity and image.

In summary, no one theory or perspective is able to describe and explain the entire phenomenon of disordered eating behaviour. Even a multifactorial model offering an interplay between social, biological, psychological, environmental and familial factors could only hold true for a specific generation. Central themes that have emerged focus upon disordered eating not merely concerning food and weight, but as being symptomatic of far deeper issues. It is clear that in the present state of knowledge, health professionals must adopt a pragmatic approach to diagnosis and consider the condition as having roots in each of the afore-mentioned factors with different and specific weightings of each factor for each individual case.

CONSEQUENCES ASSOCIATED WITH EATING DISORDERS

Most physical consequences of eating disorders are as a direct result of self-induced starvation and compensatory behaviours. In AN, usually protein and vitamin intake are sufficient but carbohydrates and fats are severely lacking. The effects of starvation on the cardiovascular system can be fatal. In BN, medical consequences are predominantly the result of fluctuations in weight, fluid and menstrual status, and as above may prove to be fatal (Sharp and Freeman, 1993; Szmukler *et al.*, 1995). Virtually all physical complications associated with eating disorders rescind with a return to normal weight and the disuse of inappropriate weight loss behaviours – although osteoporosis may be one exception.

Cardiovascular and circulatory complications   These include: bradycardia (a slowing of the heart to less than 60 beats per minute) in order to conserve energy and slow the metabolic rate; hypotension (a blood pressure of less than 90/60 mmHg) due to a depletion of fluids through avoidance (dehydration) and purging; and cardiac arrhythmias (abnormal heart beats) primarily due to a disturbance in the balance of potassium, sodium and calcium (electrolytes), again caused by avoidance and loss of foods/fluids. Electrolyte imbalance may also manifest in the form of peripheral oedema (swelling) of the ankles, feet and hands, which may also be due to a lowering of osmotic pressure and protein levels in the blood. Anaemia may be present due to an iron deficient diet.

Gastrointestinal and dental complications   Due to persistent vomiting there is an erosion of dental enamel and an enlargement of the parotid salivary gland, which may give the individual a hamster like appearance as the glands in the side of the neck swell. Ulcers are likely to appear as a result of exposure to gastric acid. Ruptures and tears in the oesophagus can be caused following a vomiting episode and can be fatal. Due to abnormal eating patterns there is often delayed gastric (stomach) emptying which may give rise to feelings of fullness and bloating which further propels the myth or feelings of fat being deposited on or in the stomach. Constipation and/or diarrhoea may occur as a result of inadequate dietary intake and/or laxative abuse.

Muscular and skeletal complications   Osteoporosis in both AN and BN has been well-documented and represents a real and potentially severe risk of non-traumatic pathological fracture (Baker, Roberts and Towell, 2000). The precise mechanism responsible remains unclear, but factors of oestrogen deficiency, malnutrition and behaviours such as exercise have an etiological role to play. Over half of all eating-disorder patients suffer from osteopenia (thinning of the bones). The use of oral oestrogen as a prophylactic measure is unknown. Dry and discoloured skin (due to reduced collagen and dietary insufficiencies), lanugo hair and bruises or calluses on the backs of the hands (due to self-induced vomiting) are all symptomatic of behaviours linked with eating disorders.

Endocrine complications   The most obvious, and indeed important for diagnostic criteria, is the absence of menstruation. This is due to a loss of more than 15–20 per cent of ideal body weight and diminished release of hormones that are necessary for ovulation to take place. A disruption to the normal hypothalamic–pituitary–ovarian functioning occurs. The ovaries and uterus (testes in males) shrink in size. There is some evidence to suggest that polycystic ovarian syndrome is, as a result of abnormal eating behaviours, usually associated with BN. There is also evidence of increased levels of cortisol in the blood, as is commonly found during high levels of stress. Reputed hypothalamic dysfunction is responsible for inadequate temperature control. During periods of cold, core temperature fails to increase and no shiver response is evident. On exposure to heat vasodilation (opening of the blood vessels) fails to occur resulting in an abnormal rising of the core temperature. Disturbances in sleep have been recorded but may be secondary to other co-morbid psychological dysfunction including depression and substance abuse.

Central nervous system consequences   Magnetic resonance imaging (MRI) studies in both AN and BN have revealed anatomical changes to the sulcal spaces (widening), cerebroventricular enlargement, reduction in pituitary size and mid-brain area. These changes may not necessarily be consequent to reduced weight and may have pre-existed as precipitating factors. Neuropsychological functioning reveals attentional deficits, memory and visuospatial impairment as well as a general reduction in problem-solving ability and judgement skills.

Social–Psychological Consequences

Both AN and BN interfere with interpersonal relationships. This is not only due to the secrecy required to pursue one's particular behavioural practices, but is also due to co-morbidity of other psychological disorders (that is, social withdrawal and inadequacy) and as a direct result of periods of starvation. Treasure *et al.* (1992) measured quality of life in eating disordered subjects using the Nottingham Health Profile. The highest levels of impairment were found in the psychosocial domain, followed by energy and sleep. Both groups had the greatest difficulty with close relationships and reported minimal social support and small social networks. It is difficult to know if these factors precipitate or are as a consequence of the eating disorder, though either way they serve to perpetuate the condition and should be taken into account when planning treatment packages.

Treatment

Successful treatment regimes must be based upon defining and treating each area of specific concern. Each individual will vary in clinical presentation and the diagnostic label is insufficient to describe the full and complex range of disordered thoughts, beliefs and behaviours. Any refeeding programme will need to exercise caution as sudden changes in diet and electrolyte balance can cause congestive cardiac failure. Clinical assessment of the physical state will need to be closely monitored during the initial stages of weight gain. This would include blood tests, urine tests, chest x-ray and bone mineral density scanning. Psychologically the individual will require lots of reassurance as complications of refeeding (bloating and swelling) may exacerbate feelings of fatness.

Occasionally those charged with providing treatment consider it necessary to force-feed an individual. This is an issue which presents enormous ethical problems. These concern the rights of the person to refrain from feeding versus the question of the sanctity of life and the pain and distress caused to friends and family if the person's wishes not to eat are respected. An added issue is that forced feeding could be construed as abusive and a further removal of autonomy and control by the person whose refusal to eat in the first place may be linked to these matters. As such it has been argued that forced feeding may exacerbate feeding difficulties (Hoch *et al.*, 1994) as well as posing additional health risks and is therefore counterproductive. Opposing this position there are many for whom forced feeding has been an action of last resort and who have gone on to make a viable recovery.

Until the mid-1980s hospital in-patient treatment was the treatment of choice. Russell (1981) summed up the treatment philosophy by stating 'Experience teaches that the patient is unlikely to respond to psychological methods of treatment until her loss of weight has been corrected'. More recently there has been a move towards the psychologically-orientated therapies, cognitive behavioural regimes and the increasing use of day programmes. For the most severe, treatment resistive, chaotic or dangerously underweight sufferer, in-patient treatment is still the one of choice for weight gain, stabilisation or maintenance. Treatment plans can be either structured and contingent upon weight gain (see Box 8.1), or unstructured where the patient is allowed to dictate most aspects of care, and the onus is on the individual to want to change thoughts and behaviours that are consistent with eating disorders. There will still be an expectation of minimal weight gain (approximately 0.5 kg per week) and attendance at either individual or group therapeutic activity. Target weight will be set at the lowest end of the normal spectrum, that is a body mass index of 19. No punitive action occurs if weight gain is not met, but consistent failure will result in the individual being questioned on their motives for in-patient treatment and an alternative will be offered dependent upon their needs. Unstructured treatment regimes are generally not suitable for those patients that are being detained and treated against their will under a section of the 1983 Mental Health Act.

The stages of change model referred to in the previous chapter (Prochaska and DiClemente, 1984) has been applied to intervention in the eating disorders, as remission and relapse are common (Hamburg *et al.*, 1996). One application suggested to improve compliance is 'motivational interviewing' (Miller and Rollinick, 1991), which is seen as complementary to the stages of change model. These techniques could also be used as a strategy to promote readiness for change and hence compliance in treatment resistant inpatients. In fact it has recently been reported that out-patients with bulimia nervosa who began treatment in the action stage showed

BOX 8.1 In-patient treatment programme

Ms X is 24 years old and has an 11-year history of disordered eating. Her current weight is 35kg (BMI = 13). She restricts her dietary intake to 200 calories/day and only 200ml of black coffee. She participates in aerobic activity following food. She has had four previous in-patient admissions. Behaviours include secret disposal of food and hiding heavy objects (batteries) in her vagina, and drinking large volumes of water prior to being weighed to artificially increase weight. She is socially isolated and lives with her parents and older sister. A target weight of 60kg (BMI = 19) has been set. She will be weighed on Monday and Thursday each week at 7 a.m. in underwear (due to previous history). A dietitian has prescribed a 2500 calorie diet. Daily intake includes 3 meals, 3 snacks and 1 litre of fluid.

At 35kg – to remain on full bed rest. To have all meals and snacks in the room under the observation of staff, both during food/drink ingestion and for 1 hour following (to prevent food from being hidden or vomited and to prevent exercise). To use a commode. To wash at the sink in the room. No phone calls or visitors. No television but may have reading material.

At 38kg – as above with the addition of twice weekly hair wash and weekly use of the bath/shower. Parental visit for two hours per week.

At 42kg – as above with use of bath/shower three times per week. May use the phone for five minutes twice per week. Parental visits for 2 hours twice per week. Television for 30 minutes per day. Limited attendance at therapeutic activity. Allowed to use the toilet, restrictions apply (not during or one hour following meals and snacks).

At 45kg – as above. Daily use of bath/shower. Daily use of telephone for 10 minutes. Allowed off bed rest for 30 minutes prior to each meal.

At 50kg – as above. Bed rest only during and following meals/snacks. Unlimited use of phone, television and visitation rights. Allowed out of doors for 30 minutes twice per week with staff supervision.

At 55kg – as above. Full participation in therapeutic activity programme. Allowed out of doors for one hour twice per week unsupervised. May have week-end leave with parents. Meals to be eaten in the dining room.

Weight gain programme to continue until target weight achieved, then to maintain weight for two weeks prior to discharge. Attendance for eight weeks at the day hospital/programme (if available). Out-patient follow up. Failure to comply with this type of regime will result in discharge. If the individual is considered dangerously ill then treatment may be given forcibly under a section of the Mental Health Act.

greater improvement in symptoms of binge eating than did patients in the contemplation stage. There were no differences between motivational enhancement therapy or cognitive behaviour therapy in terms of developing a therapeutic alliance or increasing readiness to change over a 12-week period (Treasure *et al.*, 1999). It should also be noted that there may be a significant subgroup of severely ill people with bulimia nervosa who have a good and rapid response to intensive treatment over a short period (four weeks; Olmsted *et al.*, 1996). It remains to be established whether such a subgroup exists in treatment-resistant patients and whether it is rapid improvement rather than compliance that determines good outcome.

All forms of treatment, both in and out-patient, are based upon a multidisciplinary approach of assessment, implementation and evaluation of care or intervention. The team usually consists of a dietician, psychiatrist, nurse, occupational therapist, family therapist, psychologist and physiotherapist. There may be the additional involvement of an art or drama therapist. Cognitive behaviour therapy, psychodynamically-orientated therapy and counselling will be administered by the appropriate therapist dependant on the orientation of each treatment centre. The exact type and duration of therapy is decided by members of the multidisciplinary team following a brief period of assessment. In-patient regimes range in duration from 12 weeks to one year.

Day-patient/Out-patient Programme

This type of regime is increasingly the one of choice. This may be predominantly driven by the available national health service resources, both in terms of financial cost, numbers that can be treated at one time and staffing availability and speciality. The other benefit to this type of care is that the individual can retain links with her family and friends and take responsibility for her actions outside of clinic attendance. The individual will be subjected to similar expectations of weight gain and appropriate behaviour as the in-patient and will be expected to engage in a therapeutic and meaningful way. Each treatment centre will set its own rules regarding the number of meals eaten and how time is spent following the meal. Generally weight will be monitored by staff. Day-patient programmes can consist of many types of individual and group activity and therapy. These may include cooking and meal planning, self/personal development, body image, exercise, assertion, stress and anxiety management, family therapy and individual sessions with a key worker. Places on a day programme treatment regime are usually for a defined period of time ranging from eight weeks to one year. Once an individual has been discharged from the day programme, out-patient follow-up care will continue, this usually takes the form of two–four yearly visits to the treatment centre to see any member of the team dependant upon needs.

Primary Prevention

Attempts at primary prevention (intervention prior to development of an eating disorder) are complicated by the need to advise the consumption of healthy foods against the non-consumption of unhealthy foods. Clearly in the latter case there is a danger of recruiting vulnerable individuals into a cycle of bad eating habits. Intervention at the level of the media is now a possibility with haute couture designers openly debating the 'thin-body cult' and using models of more realistic proportions and sizes to show their clothes . A more structured approach has been to use health education campaigns in schools (Carney, 1986). Here the emphasis is on group discussion and experiential learning and the programme covers such topics as dieting, male concerns with eating disorders and sociocultural perspectives. Although there have recently been a number of similar programmes (Griffiths and Farnill, 1996; Neumark-Sztainer, 1996), there are no longitudinal data on outcome and it is therefore difficult to study the long-term efficacy of these interventions.

Another approach has been to design interventions that are aimed at closing the 'knowledge gap' amongst the general public in relation to eating disorders (Slade,

1995). For instance, the general public were uncertain about whether dieting leads to anorexia, whether drugs have a role in their treatment, the length of time for recovery and the nature of bulimia. Organisations such as the Eating Disorders Association are providing information to fill this gap. The final approach to primary intervention is to target high-risk groups and intervene in the natural history of the development of the disorders. However, because of limited numbers of case reports there are no prospective studies which can reveal robust markers to predict whether or not an individual will develop disordered eating.

Summary and conclusions

Ample evidence exists of the positive effects of exercise on physical and psychological health. As such there are major health policy initiatives to target groups who would benefit maximally from exercise; such as the young, elderly and ethnic minorities and those with risk factors for disease such as CHD. There is still a paucity of research on factors predicting exercise participation and maintenance. The current focus is to target the young (age 5–16 years) in an effort to promote exercise as a daily routine. Such strategies encourage walking to school, cycling and fun team games and in the very young physical exploration of safe and structured environments. The most powerful message that has yet to infiltrate the general population is that age is not a barrier to exercise and benefits can be obtained at any stage over the lifespan. It is still unclear as to exactly which components of exercise (e.g. group versus individual participation, light versus strenuous) provide the maximal benefits to physical and psychological health and this is further compounded by the interrelationship between physical and psychological health. Evidence suggests that positive mood changes following exercise impact on immune function which in turn impacts on physical health status.

Eating disorders present a major public health problem affecting some 1–2 per cent of the adolescent female population with increasing numbers of adolescent males also being diagnosed. As well as physical ill-health, both anorexia and bulimia interfere with interpersonal relationships, due not only to the secrecy required to pursue particular behavioural practices, but also because of accompanying psychological disorders. As for etiology, there is no one single causal factor although biological, environmental, psychological and sociocultural factors all play a role. There is widespread concern regarding the effects of continuing media representations of thinness as glamourous and desirable. Clearly there is a need for large-scale multi-centre prospective studies where diagnostic protocols and outcome measures have been defined and standardised and the efficacy of interventions can be assessed. It is only then that a systematic approach can be taken towards the prevention, diagnosis and treatment of the eating disorders.

Discussion points

A Devise a study to investigate factors that predict exercise initiation and adherence in a group of elderly subjects.

B What can be done to incorporate the health education authority recommendations for exercise into our daily lives?

C Good health is all in the mind. Discuss evidence for and against this.

D Discuss the range of interventions used in dealing with eating disorders and how their efficacy might be improved.

E Discuss the advantages and disadvantages for each type of treatment regime for eating disorders. Which do you feel is more likely to result in a good prognosis?

Suggested reading ●

Kraemer, R., Dzewaltowski, D., Blair, M., Rinehardt, K. and Castracane, V. (1990) 'Mood Alteration from Treadmill Running and its Relationship to Beta-endorphin, Corticotrophin, and Growth Hormone', *Journal of Sports Medicine and Physical Fitness*, **30**(3): 241–6.

Steptoe, A. and Butler, N. (1996) 'Sports Participation and Emotional Wellbeing in Adolescents', *Lancet*, **347**(9018): 1789–92.

Szmukler, G. and Patton, G. (1995) 'Sociocultural Models of Eating Disorders', in G. Szmukler, C. Dare and J. Treasure (eds), *Handbook of Eating Disorders; Theory, Treatment and Research*. (Chichester: John Wiley & Sons).

Health Compromising Behaviours I: Alcohol Use and Abuse

'The devil hath power
To assume a pleasing shape.'

William Shakespeare
(*Hamlet*, II, ii, 628)

NATURE AND EFFECTS OF ALCOHOL

Alcohol in the form of ethyl alcohol is one of most widely used psychoactive substances in the world; the first being caffeine (Julien, 1996). On a global scale alcohol-related diseases affect between 5 and 10 per cent of the world's population and are estimated to have accounted for approximately 3 per cent of the global burden of disease in 1990 (World Development Report, 1993). Pharmacologically, alcohol acts as a sedative, depressing central nervous system functioning, though its disinhibiting effect on behaviour leads many lay people (at least in people raised in western societies) to believe it has the properties of a stimulant (Coleman, Butcher and Carson, 1980). Sex and ethnic differences exist in how the body processes alcohol. A given dose produces a 25–30 per cent higher concentration in the blood of a woman, even after allowances are made for women's smaller body weight. In addition, women have lower levels of gastric alcohol dehydrogenase – the enzyme whose action constitutes the first stage in the metabolism of alcohol. Greater alcohol dehydrogenase activity has similarly been reported in Caucasians compared to Japanese (Dohmen *et al.*, 1996). At low doses the user experiences mild relaxation and euphoria; progressively increasing doses lead to pronounced cognitive and motor impairment and ultimately to loss of consciousness and death.

EFFECTS ON HEALTH

Alcohol is known to affect all the major organ systems of the body. Cirrhosis of the liver, chronic gastritis, pancreatitis, peptic ulcers, oesophageal cancer, diabetes, hypertension, heart disease, as well as cancers of the mouth, throat, voice box and liver, for example, are all consequences of chronic alcohol consumption. Long-term heavy consumption may lead to irreversible brain dysfunction. In extreme cases poor nutrition associated with heavy drinking may lead to thiamine deficiency, in turn giving rise to Wernicke's encephalopathy and progressing to Korsakoff's psychosis, characterised by confusion and memory loss. Drinkers may not have to wait until old age for permanent cognitive deficits to occur. Lee (1979) found evidence of cortical atrophy in 49 per cent of young adult male drinkers, whilst Parker, Parker and Harford (1991) found a relationship between increased quantity of alcohol usually consumed per drinking occasion and decreased sober cognitive performance. In recent years concern has been expressed about the effects of alcohol on the developing embryo. Fetal alcohol syndrome is a collection of symptoms (prenatal and post-natal growth retardation, small head, abnormally shaped face, congenital heart defects and various neurological and behavioural abnormalities including mental retardation and hyperactivity) found in about 6 per cent of the offspring of mothers with drinking problems (Collins, 1993). In fact a number of researchers (Charnbess *et al.*, 1989) now believe alcohol is the leading cause of mental retardation in the United States. In addition, alcohol use may lead to greater involvement in risky sexual behaviours placing people at increased risk of HIV infection.

SOCIAL PROBLEMS

Because of the behavioural disinhibition stemming from its use, alcohol has been linked with a number of social problems, including violent crime, family disruption, drunken driving and football hooliganism (Royal College of Psychiatrists, 1986). Summary data from a number of UK studies implicate alcohol use in 78 per cent of assaults, 71 per cent of drivers killed on Saturday nights, 60 per cent of parasuicides, 54 per cent of fire fatalities, 50 per cent of homicides, 43 per cent of hospital admissions with serious head injuries, 40 per cent of road traffic accidents to pedestrians, 33 per cent of domestic accidents, 33 per cent of child abuse cases and 30 per cent of drownings (British Psychological Society, 1988). When compared to other European countries some of the above figures can be considered conservative. A study in Finland for example found almost 80 per cent of both murderers and victims were intoxicated (Hagnell, Nyman and Tunvirg, 1973).

Examining the social problems arising from alcohol use creates a different impression of the problem drinker than the one which arises from the medical model of alcohol dependence (see Box 9.1). Until fairly recently, consideration of alcohol use has concentrated on the minority of people with a recognised drinking problem, estimated in the United Kingdom to be around 1 million people or 2 per cent of the population (Royal College of Physicians, 1987). In the United States the prevalence rate for dependent drinkers has been put at 3.9 per cent (Caetano and Tam, 1995), with lifetime prevalence estimated at between 8 and 14 per cent (American Psychiatric Association, 1994). These estimates, however, are not strictly comparable owing to the different criteria used to define the problem (see Box 9.2).

Population figures may, however, mask the extent of problem drinking within certain groups. For example, high proportions of mental health service users (32%: Menezes *et al.*, 1996) and men admitted to general medical wards (20%: Lockhart *et al.*, 1986) are reported to have alcohol problems. Survey data (Blaxter, 1990a) suggests those at higher risk also include young males, the separated or divorced, middle-aged single males and unskilled workers. In the United States around 2–4 per cent of elderly people meet DSM III criteria for alcohol dependence (Adams and Cox, 1995), and with an ageing population this translates to large numbers of people requiring help with their drinking behaviour.

It has been recognised for a number of years that certain occupations carry increased risks for the development of alcohol-related problems. These include workers in the brewing and catering industries, the armed forces, the medical profession,

> ### BOX 9.1   The medical model of alcohol abuse
>
> Though the medical concept of alcoholism originated in the second half of the 19th century, current usage of the term owes a considerable amount to Jellinek (1960). His original conception was wide-ranging and not restricted to biological correlates of excessive drinking. In it alcoholism was conceived as drinking which caused any damage to the individual, the society or both. Five different 'species' of disordered drinking behaviour, labelled alpha, beta, gamma, delta and epsilon alcoholism, respectively, were discerned. Only two of these, so called gamma and delta alcoholism were considered indicative of a disease state with accompanying altered biological responsiveness. In the gamma state these altered biological responses could lead to drinking which was either impulsive or lacked control, whilst in the delta state these culminated in an inability to abstain from drinking. These two types have often been distinguished from other types of problematic drinking which occur in the absence of a sustained biological adaptation to alcohol – which may include psychological dependence on alcohol or incorporate occasional drinking with disturbed social consequences (Orford 1985).
>
> Jellinek's work continues to influence the current generation of researchers and has recently been incorporated into Dean's (1996) model of addictive behaviour drawing on chaos and complexity theories. Despite this continued influence, the notion has also engendered considerable confusion, not least in the practical identification of problem drinking types. As a result, the notion of alcoholism has been replaced by the concept of the alcohol dependence syndrome (Edwards and Gross, 1976) which emphasises the interplay between altered biological responsiveness (e.g. tolerance and withdrawal), subjective sensations (e.g. craving), behaviour (e.g. relief drinking, compulsive consumption) and performance of social roles (e.g. interpersonal problems resulting from pattern of use, failure to fulfill role obligations). Despite differences between the two concepts both imply that addictive drinking stems from a pre-existing physical vulnerability. This is probably rooted at the genetic level, but may also arise from exposure to certain social environments.

travelling sales people, fishermen and restaurateurs to name but a few (Plant, 1987). Whilst there is probably an element of self-selection in some of these occupations, it is now apparent that high-risk occupations share a number of the following characteristics: the ready availability of alcohol at the workplace, social pressure to drink, work that involves separation from normal social and sexual relationships, freedom from supervision, very high or low incomes, job stresses and strains such as danger and high demands coupled with low control (Plant, 1987; Cyster, 1987; Crum *et al.*, 1995). Consequences of alcohol problems at work include absenteeism, industrial accidents and poor decision-making (Lucas, 1987; Hore, 1987). Because it has been estimated that 75 per cent of problem drinkers at any one time are in full-time employment (Kenyon, 1979) a number of organisations have developed employee alcohol policies designed to help problem drinkers at work and reduce the risks which the workplace presents for inappropriate drinking (Cyster and McEwen, 1988). In the long term the success of such interventions will depend on producing a radical shift in normal attitudes towards alcohol consumption (Roberts, Cyster and McEwen, 1988).

Consideration of the overall impact of alcohol-related harm on individuals, families, communities, industry and society as a whole has led some to question the wisdom of preventive strategies targeting individual problem drinkers (Gorman and Speer,

BOX 9.2 Assessing alcohol consumption and detecting problem drinking

Two main methods exist for estimating numbers of problem drinkers. Survey methods ask respondents to recall their consumption on a day-by-day basis over the previous week. This is then usually recorded in units of alcohol, where one unit represents the amount of alcohol contained in a half pint of ordinary strength beer, a single glass of wine or single measure of spirits. Total consumption is then compared to a predetermined critical level. Using a criterion of 56 units a week (Royal College of Psychiatrists, 1978), Wilson (1980) suggested 6% of men and 3% of women in England, Wales and Scotland were drinking at levels likely to damage their health in the long term, figures supported by other workers (Dunbar and Morgan, 1987; Blaxter, 1990a). During the 1980s the UK medical Royal Colleges' recommended levels of sensible drinking were revised downwards. Using the newer guidelines, 27% of males and 11% of females were adjudged to be drinking above the safe limits (21 units a week for males, 14 units for females) (OPCS, 1994). Although the Department of Health issued a statement in 1995 suggesting individuals consuming at levels 50% higher than these limits were unlikely to accrue any significant risk, the advice is at odds with the views of the British Medical Association and the Royal Colleges and was criticised for being influenced by commercial interests (Edwards, 1996). Though survey methods underestimate total per capita consumption, and are prone to biases in recall, attempts to use biological markers as more accurate measures of intake have not proved successful (Poikolainen, Karkkainen and Pikkarainen, 1985). To date those used appear to reflect alcohol-induced changes in the body rather than levels of intake *per se*.

Alternatively, a number of screening instruments exist to identify people with probable alcohol dependence. Perhaps the briefest and most well-known of these, the CAGE, consists of only four questions – one point is scored for each affirmative answer;

A Have you ever felt you should **C**ut down on your drinking.
B Have people **A**nnoyed you by criticising your drinking
C Have you ever felt **G**uilty about your drinking
D Have you ever had a drink first thing in the morning (an **E**ye opener).

Mayfield, McLeod and Hall (1974) found a cut-off of 2–3 points provided the maximum number of true positive (81%) and true negative identifications (89%). Other widely used instruments include the MAST (Michegan Alcohol Screening Test, and VAST (Veterans Alcoholism Screening Test). Magruder-Habib, Stevens and Alling (1993) concluded all three of these perform well relative to DSM III criteria for alcohol dependence. Caetano and Tam (1995), however, found a correlation of only 0.67 between the DSM (used to determine the US prevalence rates given in the text) and ICD-10 criteria. Because of the different methods sometimes used, caution is urged when making comparisons between countries. It is important to remember that because of the fuzzy nature of the concept of alcoholism and alcohol dependence, uncertainty surrounding estimates of prevalence is likely to continue (American Psychiatric Association, 1994).

1996). Because of their relative numbers the major part of the harm that ensues from alcohol use arises from the actions of moderate drinkers (Royal College of Psychiatrists, 1986). In addition it has been demonstrated that the proportion of people deviant with respect to various types of ill-health is frequently predicted by the population mean level of the relevant parameter (Rose and Day, 1990; Rose, 1992). The proportion of people who suffer hypertension, for example, is predicted by average blood pressure. Similarly, deaths from liver cirrhosis and the proportion of heavy drinkers are closely predicted by the average alcohol consumption in the population. In a random sample of over 32 000 adults in the 1993 and 1994 health surveys for England, Colhoun *et al.* (1997) found correlations of around 0.75 in men and 0.62 in women between mean consumption in light to moderate drinkers and the prevalence of heavy drinking across 14 geographical regions.

Should strategies for reducing the level of alcohol-related ill-health in a population therefore target, not individuals with known drinking problems, but the whole population itself? There is evidence that such a strategy might pay dividends. Data indicate that the price of alcohol in relation to other goods is an effective regulator of consumption (Ornstein, 1980; Royal College of Psychiatrists, 1986), with even the heaviest drinkers reducing their consumption in response to price increases (Kendell, de Roumanie and Ritson, 1983). Although this suggests a cost–benefit analysis has some place in the cognitions of heavy drinkers, it would be of interest to see whether this insight carries any practical significance as far as the applicability of social cognition models (see Chapter 7) in planning such preventative efforts is concerned. Such knowledge of costs is however likely to be tacit and as such not easily obtainable by researchers. Further work is, however, required to identify those sections of the population who show most price responsiveness (Marmot, 1997). In addition, as European drinking patterns move to greater homogenisation in conjunction with the harmonisation of alcohol and tobacco taxes across the European Community, the role of fiscal policies in regulating consumption in individual member states needs careful monitoring (Powell, 1988; Gual and Colom, 1997).

DETERMINANTS OF DRINKING

The material presented thus far indicates that the issues involved in understanding problem drinking are not easily separated from those which concern normal drinking. In fact we might better understand how a minority of individuals come to have a recognised 'problem with alcohol' by attending to how people in general learn and make decisions about the use of alcohol. Surveys show that approximately 90 per cent of people drink regularly, and that their consumption of alcohol is strongly tied to particular social situations. Data point to substantial numbers in the population being accustomed and indeed attached to drinking alcohol; a survey of workplace attitudes found 28 per cent of respondents were of the view that it would be difficult for them to abstain from alcohol if required to do so for their health (Roberts *et al.*, 1988). These perspectives thus move us away from a medical model of abnormal drinking and towards one with a strong emphasis on social learning (Heather and Robinson, 1985; Ogden, 1996) whereby different behaviours and cognitions are reinforced by their consequences.

Social learning theories of excessive drinking propose the origins of this behaviour in situations where an individual repeatedly experiences a lack of coping resources, the presence of cues to drink (including the ready availability of alcohol) and the belief that alcohol will have a positive outcome. From this confluence of circumstances a conditioned response is believed to ensue, with the subjective effects arising from consumption acting as a negative reinforcer for aversive states. Initially these aversive states are social – only later after tolerance has set in do they come to be based on internally-generated physiological cues. Subsequently the variety of cues to drink multiply through stimulus generalisation and secondary reinforcement. Given the widespread use and popularity of alcohol, this model may also assist us in ascertaining the reasons why people drink normally. The most commonly cited reasons for using alcohol; the relief of tension or anxiety, improving social competence, producing drunkenness and the desire to appear mature (Knight and Godfrey, 1993) are certainly amenable to a learning theory analysis – and it is not hard to see how the actual or believed consequences of drinking may come to confer reinforcing properties upon it (Lieberman, 1991). Seeman, Seeman and Budros (1988) have also found that quantity of drinking and the number of social problems arising from drinking were correlated with degree of powerlessness and the number of negative life experiences reported by subjects. In fact the relationship between aversive life experiences and subsequent alcohol use is well-established. Moncrieff *et al.* (1996), for example, found an increased risk of alcohol and drug problems in people with a past history of sexual abuse.

Weil (1988) notes a strong social learning element in drinking behaviour across cultures; observing that alcohol abuse is uncommon in cultures where drunkenness is not condoned, and where traditions, often religious, exist pertaining to its use. Mäkelä (1997) has argued that the false consensus effect in social perception whereby people exaggerate the similarity between their own behaviour and that of significant others may also play a role in developing and maintaining normative attitudes to drinking and drug-taking behaviour. This could operate to maintain either high levels of abstinence in particular communities or more liberal attitudes and behaviour in others. In addition, children learn drinking behaviour from available role models; be they parents (Orford and Velleman, 1991 and Casswell, *et al.*, 1993), friends (Keefe, 1994) or television (Austin and Meili, 1994). The contexts provided by these will be influential in shaping future drinking practices. Miller *et al.* (1990) argue that the expectancies which young children develop about alcohol use can determine their later propensity for developing alcohol problems. In fact the pattern of use amongst young drinkers before long-term problems are manifest has been a source of concern. Recent evidence from the UK shows the quantity of alcohol consumed by young drinkers on a typical occasion (Newcombe, Measham and Parker, 1995) is increasing. This has occurred in conjunction with increasing demands on National Health Service resources from the non-dependent abuse of alcohol (Hughes *et al.*, 1997). Though reasons for these are as yet unclear, some of the commonly cited reasons given above for alcohol consumption must be considered in any evaluation. The question of how to operationalise some of these constructs, however, does present difficulties for researchers – notably the desire to appear mature. In fact when conducting research into appetitive behaviours in general, the problem of how to circumvent set responding based on the demands of the question as perceived by respondents and on the understandable wish to maintain self-esteem are not to be dismissed lightly.

To interpret trends in young people's behaviour towards alcohol in terms of social stresses and pressures is too simple. In finding the consumption of designer drinks – so called 'alcopops' – linked to greater drunkenness and drinking in less-controlled environments, Hughes *et al.* (1997) expressed concern that the marketing and perception of such drinks may reinforce the tendency to drink more on single occasions. The rapid consumption of alcohol in brief periods, so called binge drinking, may also be linked to similar patterns of appetitive behaviour with respect to food or sex (see later) which together may reflect changes in learned patterns of impulse control. It is premature to conclude whether such changes are in part a response to the brand of consumerism, now prominent in the western world, which promotes the three-minute attention span and instant consumer gratification (Hutton, 1995).

What is undeniable is that normal drinking is surrounded by ambivalent attitudes. The consequences of drinking are at the same time both feared and anticipated with delight; an approach–avoidance conflict deeply rooted in our societies. This is evident in reviews of health education literature and has also affected the interpretations of data offered by scientists (*The Lancet*, 1987; Roberts, 1988). Plant, Peck and Samuel (1985), for example, in discussing the results of a longitudinal survey of the drinking habits of a group of Scottish teenagers remarked that the level of consequences amongst the study group was not unduly high, although these included 25 per cent of the study group having been involved in fighting whilst drinking in the previous two years. That such casual acceptance of high levels of antisocial behaviour associated with drinking attracted little comment from the scientific community itself reflects how ingrained are the normative attitudes to drinking behaviour.

If a social learning theory can inform us of the costs and benefits encountered on the path to problem drinking, can it be of use in assisting problem drinkers to regain control of their life? Early work by Davies (1962) suggested the answer to this question lies in the affirmative. The idea of controlled drinking would be difficult to envisage within the remit of the old 'alcoholism as disease' concept. Subsequent work utilising behaviour therapy has now established the viability of this approach with a sizeable minority of problem drinkers – usually those with less severe problems (Sobell and Sobell, 1973; Heather and Robinson, 1985). However, it remains true that whilst controlled drinking is an option, it is more favoured in some quarters than others. Professionally, psychologists are more likely to consider it than addiction counsellors (Hshieh and Srebalus, 1997), whilst geographically it is more popular in some countries (Norway and the UK) than others (in the USA abstinence remains the preferred treatment option) (Donovan and Heather, 1997). Drinkers themselves are less likely to consider it an option if they have been abstinent during the preceding year (Mackenzie, Funderburk and Allen, 1994). Whether this reflects current heavy drinkers' lack of committal to abstention or the effects of continued heavy drinking on cognitive appraisal has not been reliably determined.

Doubts about the long-term efficacy of controlled drinking remain (Miller, 1995). For example, observations made by Vaillant (1996) after a five-year follow-up suggested abstinence may be less likely to lead to relapse than controlled drinking. A number of factors have been put forward to explain variations in success rates using the controlled drinking strategy, including older age, higher self-efficacy and lower consumption (Kavanagh, Sitharthan and Sayer, 1996) as well as marital and employment status (Heather and Robinson, 1985), although conflicting findings have been reported. It is apparent that controlled drinking is far from suitable for all problem drinkers – however, the debate about its use no longer generates the heat it once did nor has the same importance attached to it. The reasons for this are complex, though the fact that the philosophy of harm minimisation now predominates in many areas of substance abuse probably has some part to play, coupled with a move away from a strict medical model of drinking as the role of cultural factors in shaping drug and alcohol use have become increasingly recognised.

We have thus described drinking behaviour as being shaped by economic, cultural, social and occupational factors, within whose influence people construct what is deemed acceptable and appropriate to given situations – situations which include the use of alcohol to modulate experiences of physical and emotional distress. Within this broad context what can be said about the role of genetic factors? Studies have to date only explored the role of genetic factors in alcohol abuse, and have not really addressed the question of individual differences in alcohol consumption. Evidence from familial studies is suggestive of a genetic vulnerability to abusing alcohol (Rosenhan and Seligman, 1989), though considerable methodological difficulties are present in such studies. Despite these a number of routes have been proposed by which a vulnerability may be realised; these include attentional deficits (Tarter *et al.*, 1984), impaired neurological homeostasis (Nasrallah, Shroeder and Petty, 1982) and differences in neurotransmitter pathways – particularly dopamine D1 and D2 receptors (Blum *et al.*, 1990; Comings *et al.*, 1997). What is clear is that because the proportion of problem or dependent drinkers is relatively small, and social and economic factors play such a large role in shaping overall consumption, current evidence would imply that genetic factors make only a small contribution to the overall burden on society arising from alcohol use.

ALCOHOL AND CARDIOVASCULAR DISEASE

Numerous studies (for example Kreitman, 1982; Marmot and Brunner, 1991; Jackson, Scragg and Beaglehole, 1991; Rimm, Klasky, Grobbee and Stampfer, 1996; McElduff and Dobson, 1977) have indicated a U-shaped relationship between the level of alcohol consumption and all-cause mortality, this being largely a consequence of lower death rates from coronary heart disease amongst moderate drinkers (see Figure 9.1). This has generated considerable debate as to whether moderate levels of alcohol confer a protective effect (Kreitman, 1982; *Lancet*, 1988; Holman and English, 1996; Rimm *et al.*, 1996) and whether some types of beverage, particularly red wine offer more of this protection (Kannel and Ellison, 1996; Constant, 1997). Previous attempts to unravel the significance of this observation have centred on controlling for possible confounders, such as smoking, educational level and social class (Marmot *et al.*, 1981) and the existence of previous ill-health in the group of abstainers. Shaper, Wannamethee and Walker (1988) for example, as part of the British Regional Heart study, found ex-drinkers comprised 70 per cent of non-drinkers (1989) and had high prevalence rates for angina, myocardial infarction, elevated blood pressure, diabetes, gall bladder disease and bronchitis. Consequently they argued that in assessing the relative risks of cardiovascular disease against varying levels of consumption it was inappropriate to compare moderate drinkers to abstainers. Whilst part of the increased risk for abstainers relative to moderate drinkers is likely to be due to the presence of sick quitters (that is, those people abstaining from drinking alcohol who now carry the burden of ill-health arising from their previous excessive consumption), this is not sufficient to explain the higher mortality of lifetime non-drinkers observed by Kono *et al.* (1986) and Klasky (1996), nor Jackson *et al.*'s (1991) finding that former drinkers had a lower risk of myocardial infarction than lifetime non-drinkers.

LDL lipoprotein is a protein involved in transporting cholesterol to the walls of blood vessels.

HDL lipoprotein is a protein involved in transporting cholesterol away from the walls of blood vessels.

Several plausible biological mechanisms have been proposed to account for the protective effect of alcohol, which the above studies seem to show. These include the action of alcohol in reducing **low density lipoprotein** cholesterol (responsible for depositing cholesterol on the artery walls) and in elevating **high density lipoprotein** cholesterol (responsible for conveying cholesterol to the liver for metabolism and associated with a reduced risk of ischaemic heart disease). Furthermore, alcohol is

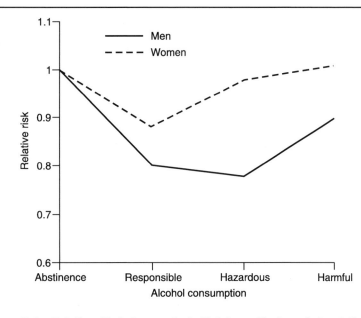

Figure 9.1   Relationship between alcohol intake and ischaemic heart disease (pooled results from 22 studies)

Source: Adapted from C.D.J. Holman and D.R. English (1996), *Journal of the Royal Society of Medicine*, **89**: 123–9, reproduced with permission of the Royal Society of Medicine.

known to inhibit blood coagulation (Holman and English, 1996). Results have been inconsistent on whether red wine offers more protection (Holman and English, 1996), most likely because of the differences in patterns of alcohol consumption associated with different types of drink and varying associations with other risk factors (Rimm *et al.*, 1996).

Whilst the evidence appears strong for a causal role for alcohol it must be remembered that the relationship is correlational and some studies have failed to produce supporting evidence (Hart, Davy Smith, Hole and Hawthorne, 1999). Little experimental evidence yet exists to show that bringing about changes in people's level of alcohol consumption reduces their risk of heart disease. Accordingly, it is feasible that as yet unknown bias or confounding effects may explain the relationship. Roberts, Brunner and Marmot (1995) explored the possibility that psychological factors (psychological well-being, social supports, hostility, affect balance, life events, satisfaction with life) could play a role in confounding relationships between levels of consumption and several established risk factors (factor 7, fibrinogen, systolic blood pressure, cholesterol, apolipoprotein B and apolipoprotein AI) for coronary heart disease. It is certainly conceivable that how someone negotiates stressful life events (for example by recourse to varying levels of social support) may be related both to their current level of alcohol consumption and to future disease outcomes. Though finding some evidence of weak confounding, the authors concluded there was not compelling evidence that the U-shaped relationship between alcohol and coronary heart disease mortality could be easily explained by psychosocial factors. Lowe (1996), however, has proposed that humour and mood enhancement may be at least partly responsible. In a study of 323 social drinkers, moderate drinkers were

U-shaped curve describes the observed relationship between the level of alcohol consumption and coronary heart disease. So called because moderate drinkers have less risk than abstainers.

found to laugh more in both laboratory and natural settings. And in a recent study by Fillmore *et al.* (1998) mortality risk was found to be similar for abstainers and light drinkers after the analysis controlled for a number of psychosocial variables. The **U-shaped curve** is still far from understood, and though evidence presently favours a biological interpretation, more research is required on the lifestyles characteristic of drinkers at different levels of consumption.

Summary and conclusions

After caffeine, alcohol in the form of ethyl alcohol is one of the most widely used psychoactive substances in the world and alcohol-related diseases affect almost 1 in 10 of the world's population. Every organ system in the body is affected by alcohol, and if consumed heavily on a long-term basis it can seriously harm health in a variety of ways (e.g. cirrhosis of the liver, diabetes, heart disease, a variety of cancers, irreversible brain dysfunction). Social learning theories suggest poor coping resources, the presence of cues to drink and the belief that alcohol will have a positive outcome contribute to excessive drinking. In contrast, the most commonly stated reasons for using alcohol amongst 'normal' drinkers include the relief of tension or anxiety, improving social competence and producing drunkenness. Building links between these two accounts is necessary in order to produce a viable developmental theory of problem drinking. A range of severe social problems (e.g. murder and violent crime, road accidents, accidental injury, football hooliganism) are also associated with alcohol consumption, and because of their more numerous representation in the population the problems are more likely to stem from the actions of moderate drinkers. When the overall impact of alcohol-related harm is considered, the wisdom of preventive strategies targeting individual problem drinkers has been questioned.

A relationship between moderate drinking and reduced cardiovascular risk is well-established. It might therefore be thought that encouraging people to consume alcohol for their health would have a beneficial impact on the public health. Commentators, however, have been unanimous in concluding that exhorting people to drink for their health is ill-advised and could lead to increasing the level of harmful effects arising from alcohol use (Kreitman, 1982; Marmot and Brunner, 1991; Edwards, 1996; Holman, 1996). This is principally because in the absence of experimental evidence that altered consumption leads to altered risk, there is the danger that making such a recommendation could lead to an increase in overall consumption levels – with the consequence that, as Rose (1992) argues, rising mean levels would predict a greater number of problem drinkers in the population.

Discussion points

A How could social cognition models be used for understanding and developing preventative strategies for controlling problem drinking?

B Should the use of alcohol be considered a form of drug use? What are the advantages and disadvantages of adopting such a perspective?

C Why has controlled drinking as a treatment option been more readily accepted in the United Kingdom in comparison to the United States?

Suggested reading

Dean, A. (1996) *Chaos and Intoxication: Complexity and Adaptation in the Structure of Human Nature.* (London: Routledge).

Gorman, D.M. and Speer, P.W. (1996) 'Preventing Alcohol Abuse and Alcohol Related Problems Through Community Interventions: A Review of Evaluation Studies', *Psychology and Health*, **11**: 95–131.

Roberts, R., Brunner, E. and Marmot, M. (1995) 'Psychological Factors in the Relationship between Alcohol and Cardiovascular Morbidity', *Social Science and Medicine*, **41**(11): 1513–16.

chapter 10

Health Compromising Behaviours II: Smoking

'There's nothing like tobacco.'

Molière (*Don Juan* I, i)

BACKGROUND

Tobacco smoking competes with alcohol as the second most commonly used psycho-active substance after caffeine (see Figure 10.1). Moreover, in terms of adverse health effects, smoking is arguably more important than alcohol since it is considered to be the single greatest cause of preventable death, at least in the developed world (US Department Health and Human Services, 1989). For example, it has been estimated that in the USA alone, approximately 400 000 people a year die from smoking-related illnesses, a source of deaths greater than the combined effects of alcohol, AIDS, car accidents, murders, suicides, drugs and fires (Grunberg *et al.*, 1997).

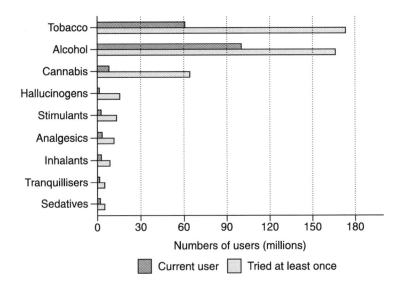

Figure 10.1   Relative usage of non-medical psychoactive drugs in the USA (caffeine excluded)

Source: Adapted from J.F. Golding (1992).

110

SMOKING PREVALENCE

From being a majority (in males at least), smokers have become a minority group (about 30%) in many countries (US Department Health and Human Services, 1989). The decline in prevalence of smoking has been dramatic, for example. in the UK 70 per cent of men were smokers in the 1950s, but by the 1990s this had dropped towards 30 per cent (General Household Survey, 1999). An example of recent trends in smoking prevalence is given in Figure 10.2a. The drop in female smoking has been less dramatic because the prevalence of female smoking was increasing until relatively recently. In many countries female smokers are approaching the prevalence rates seen in males. There has been some tendency for the remaining smokers to be heavier cigarette consumers. The reasons are obscure, but may reflect socioeconomic trends, reductions in nicotine/tar deliveries, and it may also be due to the fact that the lighter smokers are more likely to quit, thus exposing a 'hard-core' of heavy smokers who continue with the habit. Women in particular have become heavier smokers. For example, over a 20-year period in the USA, the percentage of women smokers of more than 25 cigarettes per day almost doubled from 13 per cent in 1965 to 23 per cent in 1985. Moreover, women are starting to smoke earlier. In some countries the frequency of smoking in girls is now exceeding that of boys.

On a more positive note, men in particular are giving up smoking in increasing numbers, and more men and women are not starting to smoke. Since most smokers start in their teens (Figure 10.2c), it may be expected that the growing number of those that have never smoked will remain 'never-smokers' in the years to come. Socioeconomic gradients in smoking have also become apparent; the prevalence of smoking has reduced in the professional/white-collar groups but less so for the manual and unskilled (Figure 10.2b). In less-developed countries the picture is different; the prevalence of cigarette smoking is increasing as are the numbers of cigarettes consumed per smoker.

HEALTH HAZARDS

Tobacco smoking is the largest preventable cause of death in the developed world. Epidemiological studies in many countries have consistently pointed to a strong association between smoking and serious disease. For example, for all male smokers the overall mortality ratio is around 1.7 compared to non-smokers. Heavy smokers of two packs a day show a higher mortality ratio of 2.0. Mortality ratios are generally higher for male as opposed to female smokers even when equated for daily consumption which may partly reflect greater tobacco smoke exposure in male smokers through different smoking behaviour and differences in smoke deposition patterns. The excess mortality for smokers reaches a peak in middle age with some decline towards old age. This does not imply a decreasing effect of smoking on health with old age but rather a process of selection in which the more susceptible smokers have already died (US Department Health and Human Services, 1979, 1989).

However, demonstrations of correlations or associations between smoking and excess morbidity and mortality may be consistent with but not proof of causation. Thus it is worthwhile noting that a variety of lines of evidence indicate that the smoking–mortality link is causal. First, the toxic nature of constituents of tobacco smoke has been demonstrated in laboratory animals. Secondly, the likelihood of serious disease is related to the degree of exposure, for example as expressed in

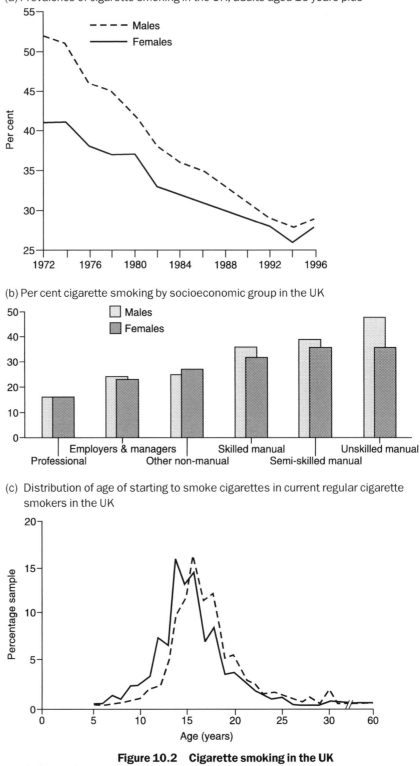

Figure 10.2   Cigarette smoking in the UK

Source: Adapted from J.F. Golding (1995), General Household Survey 1997.

BOX 10.1   Measuring smoking behaviour and smoke exposure

Methods of assessing smoke exposure include manner of tobacco use (cigarette, pipes, cigars), years smoked, numbers smoked daily, machine smoked yields (of tar, nicotine, carbon monoxide), residual butt length, butt filter nicotine, smoking behaviour (number of puffs, puff pressure profile, puff volume, depth and duration of inhalation), blood carboxyhaemoglobin, exhaled carbon monoxide, blood and urinary levels of nicotine and its metabolites such as cotinine, and thiocyanates in saliva, urine or blood. The measures employed vary tremendously in the accuracy, complexity, invasiveness and cost, and consequently in their areas of research application. For large-scale epidemiological work, self-report of type and amount of tobacco consumption has formed the basis of the well-known dose-response (e.g. 'pack-years') and mode of usage (e.g. cigarette/cigar/ pipe) relationships with mortality and morbidity. However, cigarette yields vary considerably and may change the degree of hazard to some extent. For example, low tar cigarettes may produce limited reductions in lung cancer. 'Standardised' yields are produced by machine smoking. Unfortunately, the standard cigarette yields do not take into account actual individual variation in the manner of smoking a cigarette. To take the example of low-tar ventilated filter cigarettes, the blocking of the filter perforations by fingers or lips, which is observed in 32–69% of low tar smokers, increases the yield of toxic products by 59–293%. Standard machine smoked yields do not take this into account.

Carbon monoxide and carboxyhaemoglobin measurements

Blood carboxyhaemoglobin level is a good index of the extent of recent inhalation-style smoking (it has a half-life of less than 4 hours). Exhaled carbon monoxide concentration relates linearly to blood carboxyhaemoglobin. Exhaled carbon monoxide levels greater than 8 p.p.m. are strongly suggestive of smoking and typical levels in an average smoker are around 20–30 p.p.m., depending on the number and time since smoking. An extremely heavy cigarette smoker may attain up to 80 p.p.m. carbon monoxide at the end of a day's indulgence in the habit (approx. equivalent to blood carboxyhaemoglobin of 14%). Measurement of exhaled carbon monoxide has the advantage of being quick and non-invasive, and inexpensive portable carbon monoxide gas analysers are now available (Jarvis *et al.*, 1986). When carbon monoxide is used as an index of smoking the possibility of absorption of carbon monoxide from extraneous sources (e.g. stoves, automobiles) should be borne in mind.

  Measurement of nicotine and cotinine levels of nicotine and its metabolites in biological fluids have the advantage of being the most tobacco specific of all measurements. Moreover, for cigarette smoking it is an index of the extent of particulate phase intake to the lungs since nicotine from cigarette smoke is not well-absorbed in the mouth whereas nicotine from pipe/cigar smoke can be absorbed by this route. Nicotine itself has a fairly short half-life (approx. 2 hours from venous trough levels) and so is best used as an index of recent smoking. Its main metabolite, cotinine, with a longer half-life of 19 hours, is a better index of chronic smoking and urinary or salivary cotinine sampling has the advantage of being relatively non-invasive by comparison with blood sampling. Thiocyanates from hydrogen cyanide in tobacco smoke may be measured in blood, urine or saliva. They have an even longer half-life (14 days approx.) than cotinine but the disadvantage of being less tobacco specific. Other sources include diet (e.g. cassava root, cabbage, broccoli, etc.) and less frequent industrial sources (e.g. electroplating works). The differences for regular smoking are large, e.g. typical blood levels of thiocyanate are 18 umol l^{-1} in non-smokers, 25 umol l^{-1} in vegetarian non-smokers and 80–100 umol l^{-1} in regular smokers (Golding, 1995).

'pack-years' or cigarettes per day, and it is higher in inhalers than non-inhalers. Similarly, cigar and pipe smokers show less excess mortality than cigarette smokers which is related to the lesser inhalation of cigar/pipe smoke, a pattern of exposure to the toxic constituents of tobacco smoke which is consistent with their lesser incidence of cancer of the lung as opposed to cancer of the oral cavity. Thirdly, risk of serious tobacco-related disease declines as a function of number of years elapsed since giving up smoking, reaching near-equivalence with never-smokers after 15 years off tobacco (the decline in risk is more rapid for cardiovascular disease). Fourthly, the increase in smoking prevalence amongst women smokers during the twentieth century has been followed, with a predictable time lag, by an increase in smoking-related disease such as lung cancer and coronary heart disease in women. A similar predictable rise is beginning to occur in the less-developed countries (US Department Health and Human Services, 1979, 1989). Finally, the classic epidemiological studies of smoking and non-smoking monozygotic and dizygotic twins has enabled control of genetic and psychosocial factors, leaving little doubt that the link is causal (Cederlof et al., 1977).

The catalogue of tobacco-related disease is extensive, and an example study of smoking-related mortality is given in Table 10.1. The more important diseases are cardiovascular (including coronary artery disease, cerebrovascular disease, peripheral vascular disease), neoplastic (including cancer of the lung, larynx, oral cavity, oesophagus, bladder, pancreas) and chronic obstructive pulmonary disease (COPD) (chronic bronchitis, emphysema). In addition, maternal smoking would appear to produce deleterious effects on the fetus (perhaps by fetal hypoxia) since birth weights are lower and gestation and birth complications greater, even when such relevant factors as social class and maternal weight are taken into account. Although smoking-related mortality ratios are highest for lung cancer and COPD, in terms of actual number of deaths the major contributor to cause-specific mortality amongst smokers is cardiovascular disease (Table 10.1).

Table 10.1   Smoking related mortality: example epidemiological study

Cause of death (selected causes)	Pure cigarette smokers			Pure cigar smokers		
	Observed deaths	Expected deaths	O/E	Observed deaths	Expected deaths	O/E
All causes	15091	8112	1.86	2653	2302	1.15
Cardiovascular diseases	8920	5257	1.70	1681	1522	1.10
Cancers, all sites	3138	1401	2.24	510	386	1.32
Coronary heart disease	5740	3414	1.68	1077	965	1.12
Stroke	1172	796	1.47	267	249	1.07
Respiratory disease	879	185	4.75	51	61	0.84
Bronchitis & emphysema	568	43	13.13	10	14	0.71
Lung cancer	1095	91	12.06	41	25	1.66

Source: Adapted from J.F. Golding (1995).

For cardiovascular disease the smoke components of major interest are carbon monoxide (and related hypoxaemia) and the effects of nicotine on cardiac rhythm, free fatty acids in plasma, lipoproteins, coronary vasoconstriction and the coagulability of blood. Smoking-related neoplastic diseases (for example, lung cancer) are doubtless due to one or more of the known carcinogens and co-carcinogens in tobacco smoke rather than to nicotine or carbon monoxide. COPD is probably caused by effects of substances in both the gas and particulate phases of smoke on proteolytic, interference with immune mechanisms and inhibition of mucociliary clearance mechanisms. The latter ciliotoxic effects of tobacco smoke may contribute to carcinogenicity of tobacco smoke, potentiate the effects of other environmental carcinogens such as asbestos, and increase the risk of respiratory infections. Reliable differences in indices of expiratory air-flow exist between smokers and non-smokers after age 25 years (US Department Health and Human Services, 1979, 1989). Finally, the negative association between smoking and Alzheimer's and Parkinson's disease (perhaps due to nicotine) may be noted, although these possible protective effects are trivial by comparison with the health risks of smoking (Van Duijn and Hofman, 1991).

PASSIVE SMOKING

Passive smoking is inhalation of the products of other people's smoking.

Passive smoking refers to the exposure to tobacco combustion products from the smoking of others. Tobacco smoke in the environment derives from main-stream and side-stream smoke. Main-stream smoke is first filtered by the cigarette and, in the case of the inhaling smoker, by the lungs before emerging into the environment. Side-stream smoke emerges directly into the environment. Many potentially toxic constituents are present in higher concentrations in side-stream than in main-stream smoke. Moreover, side-stream smoke contributes nearly 85 per cent of the total smoke in a room. Quantification of the exposure of a passive smoker is difficult because it is dependent on a number of factors including type and number of cigarettes burned, size of room and ventilation rate. However, elevated levels of indoor byproducts of tobacco smoke (acrolein, aromatic hydrocarbons, carbon monoxide, nicotine, oxides of nitrogen, nitrosamines and particulate matter) under realistic conditions, for example in the atmospheres of cafes, bars, restaurants, trains, cars, hospitals, and so on have been measured in a number of studies. In turn, elevated levels of markers of environmental tobacco smoke exposure such as nicotine and its metabolites, and carbon monoxide have been demonstrated in passive smokers (Cook *et al.*, 1993).

The most frequent symptom of the non-smoker's reaction to passive smoke exposure is eye irritation (estimate 69%). Headache, nasal irritation and cough are also commonly reported. Small but statistically significant acute decreases in pulmonary function have been demonstrated in non-smokers under experimental chamber conditions of moderate-to-high smoke exposure levels. However, general irritant responses occur below the levels of smoke exposure which produce these acute pulmonary effects.

In children, many studies have shown a positive relationship between parental smoking and respiratory symptoms such as chronic cough, chronic phlegm, persistent wheeze and respiratory infections. Some increased symptoms may be confounded by increased reporting of children's symptoms by parents who smoke and have similar symptoms, by the child's own smoking habits or by other related factors which may have a bearing on the child's health such as socioeconomic group and family size. However, these confounding factors have been controlled in some studies and a relationship remains. It is possible that young children represent a more susceptible population for the adverse effects of passive smoking than older children or adults. Especially important are the increases in severe respiratory illnesses in children under two years of age. Since the degree of passive smoke exposure is variable between smoking households and since exposure can occur outside the home to children of non-smoking parents, the use of objective markers for exposure to environmental tobacco smoke may reveal small effects that would otherwise be obscured. Studies of passive smoking and symptoms in patients with known pulmonary disease (for example asthmatics) have produced conflicting results of objective pulmonary measurements, although subjective symptoms such as tightness in the chest are related to passive smoke exposure (Jorres *et al.*, 1992).

The evidence that passive smoking is associated with serious health hazards, principally lung cancer, comes from epidemiological studies. Most of these studies have compared the incidence of lung cancer in various groups of non-smokers living with smoking as opposed to non-smoking spouses. A number of artefacts may distort studies of this nature. Thus smokers tend to congregate and socialize together and this extends to living together. The extent to which smokers preferentially live with other smokers rather than with non-smokers may be termed an 'aggregation factor'. Since ex-smokers can in practice be misclassified as 'never-smokers', and since they will be over-represented among non-smokers living with current smokers, the still significant elevated risk from lung cancer in ex-smokers distorts (increases) 'passive smoking' effects. Estimated allowances can be made for ex-smokers among the non-smokers 'boosting' mortality ratios. Wald *et al.* (1986) reviewed 13 case-control and prospective studies. The mean relative risk across all studies for elevated risk for lung cancer in non-smokers living with smoking spouses was 1.35 (1.0 = no difference; <1.0 = opposite effect) with a range of 0.5–3.25. Other more recent reviews of the relative risk from spousal smoking have produced somewhat lower values for excess risk of lung cancer, in the range 1.05–1.10 (Tweedie *et al.*, 1992). It has been claimed that such results are consistent with risk estimates based upon bio-chemical markers of passive smoke exposure such as cotinine.

The objective measurement of degree of passive smoke exposure, and relating this to elevated morbidity and mortality, are both qualitatively and quantitatively more difficult than the analogous measurements of smoke exposure and ill-health in active smokers. The trend of the evidence indicates that apart from the well-known irritant effects, passive smoke exposure is associated with increases in respiratory symptoms and infections in very young children of smokers and with small but statistically significant reductions in pulmonary function. For adult non-smokers living with smoking spouses some elevation of lung cancer risk has been observed which varies between studies and considerable difficulties of interpretation remain. However, if there is no level below which carcinogens cease to have an effect, it is likely that some elevation of risk for lung cancer from passive smoke exposure occurs. The USA Environmental Protection Agency has designated environmental tobacco smoke a human lung carcinogen, estimating that in the USA it is responsible for about 3000 deaths from lung cancer in non-smokers each year and an annual 150 000–300 000 cases of lower respiratory tract infections in children of smokers (*British Medical Journal*, 1992). Finally, there now appears to be some evidence for a relation between passive smoking and heart disease (*British Medical Journal*, 1997).

WHY PEOPLE SMOKE: SMOKING MOTIVATION AND MODELS

Smoking is a complex pattern of behaviour with nicotine acquisition overlaid by social and psychological factors. Theories range from the *psycho-analytical* (including 'oral fixation'), *social learning, smoking typologies*, to those placing more emphasis on particular actions of nicotine such as *arousal modulation* (and similar variants such as 'psychological tool', 'stimulus filter'), and *nicotine addiction* (including more advanced variants such as 'opponent process') as well as *genetic predisposition* theories (Mangan and Golding, 1984) None of these theories or models is sufficient individually, but abstraction of important elements from them enables some understanding to be achieved. For convenience smoking is seen in three stages: initiation, maintenance and cessation (the latter is discussed mainly under 'Prevention and Cessation').

The initiation stage usually occurs in the early teens and begins with experimentation with cigarettes. Social approval or disapproval would appear to be of overriding importance. This is the explanation for the dramatic rise in prevalence of smoking among women over this century which has parallelled emancipation in other spheres. The highly significant association between adolescent smoking and smoking by parents, siblings or adolescent peer group indicates that social forces are exerted at an immediate level through these agencies. However, this is not to deny that other individuals such as schoolteachers, high-status individuals in the media and, more mundanely, the degree of enforcement of any legal sanctions against sale of cigarettes to minors, also have a role. Within these external limiting factors there is evidence that adolescents of a more rebellious, risk-taking, outgoing nature are more likely to take up smoking, as are individuals who have more neurotic personalities.

BOX 10.2 Importance of nicotine in smoking behaviour

Evidence for nicotine being the primary motivator for smoking includes:

1. Nicotine is absorbed from tobacco smoke in sufficient quantities to produce clear-cut pharmacological effects in the brain.
2. The most popular form of nicotine self-administration, inhalation of cigarette smoke, is the most rate- and concentration-efficient method for delivering nicotine to the brain. It reaches the brain within 10 seconds after inhalation.
3. Nicotine is the only pharmacologically active constituent obtained in common from the various forms of tobacco use: inhalation of cigarette smoke, non-inhalation of pipe/cigar smoke, tobacco snuffing and tobacco chewing.
4. Nicotine replacement therapy (nicotine gum, nicotine transdermal patch) is an effective aid to smoking cessation.
5. Animals will voluntarily self-administer nicotine.
6. Self-administration of nicotine can be altered both in animals and humans by central (but not peripheral) nicotinic cholinergic receptor antagonists.
7. Smokers down-regulate and up-regulate nicotine intake (albeit imperfectly) in the face of variations in tobacco nicotine delivery.
8. Smoking or snuffing behaviour in humans is not practised in the absence of the known pharmacological rewards obtained from drugs such as opiates, cannabis, cocaine, organic solvents, or nicotine.

To highlight the importance of nicotine is not to deny the contributions of other factors in determining smoking behaviour. Other, mostly learned or associated cues add to smoking satisfaction. Tar components provide taste and smell and are responsible for the 'scratch' of inhaled smoke at the back of the throat; these may become pleasurable by a process of classic conditioned association as predictors of the arrival of nicotine in the brain. Practised smokers may use them as cues for estimating the nicotine strength of the cigarette. Manipulations of the cigarette, pipe or rolling tobacco, lighting-up routines, situational and social pressures all play a part, but these lose their motivational power without the reinforcing effect of nicotine. Thus a knowledge of the properties of nicotine is necessary to understand the motivations in smoking and cessation.

Maintenance of smoking continues through a variety of direct and indirect routes. Direct pharmacological reward from nicotine occurs, perhaps through central release of dopamine, noradrenaline and opioid peptides. Smoking may also serve as a coping strategy in the face of stress. The mechanism for the tranquillizing action of nicotine is still incompletely understood. It is possible that cigarette smokers may obtain stimulant or depressant/tranquillizing actions by varying their nicotine intake, by virtue of the biphasic dose-and rate-related stimulant vs depressant nature of nicotine action. Such effects may also explain why smoking can increase mental performance on a variety of tasks. However, a price, quite apart from physical health hazards, has to be paid by the smoker for these benefits. 'Dependence' on smoking develops in both an obvious and a less obvious fashion. The most obvious is that of physical addiction to nicotine. A definite withdrawal syndrome is experienced by most smokers for days to week(s) following cessation. To some extent, continued smoking in long-term heavy users is reinforced by the avoidance of nicotine withdrawal symptoms. Weight increase following cessation of smoking may also act as a disincentive for some individuals. However, a more subtle dependence is that many smokers will have come to learn to use smoking as a coping strategy for dealing with stress, fatigue and boredom. Indeed the personality characteristics of smokers indicate that a disproportionate number are inherently more susceptible to such mood and arousal perturbations. By default, it seems that alternative non-pharmacological coping mechanisms fail to develop or are allowed to 'atrophy' over the years in which the long-term smoker has come to use smoking as a 'psychological tool'. Given the short latency between puffing, inhalation and nicotine reward in the CNS, and given the large number (thousands) of such pairings, the various sensory aspects of smoking (motor movements, lip contact, taste, 'scratch', inhalation) acquire secondary reinforcing properties by a process of conditioning. Similarly, smoking becomes inextricably linked with a wide variety of situations, both work and social.

PREVENTION AND CESSATION

General

The majority of smokers say that they would like to give up and they also report one or more serious attempts to do so. Although it has been difficult to distinguish and demonstrate a direct effect of any particular anti-smoking public health education or media campaign, there is no reason to doubt the source and nature of the self-reported motivation of ex-smokers. This is the wish to avoid future ill health and in some cases actual ill health at the time of giving up. For many pregnant women smokers (and some smoking spouses) concern for the health of the unborn child is the motivator and opportunity to give up smoking. Social pressures to quit smoking can be exerted by the immediate family and peer group. The concern over passive smoking now also works as an additional pressure. Bans or restrictions on smoking in the workplace, in public transportation, and various other public places, have made smoking more difficult and tend to marginalise the smoker. Price of cigarettes, which may be varied by tax, is certainly a factor limiting cigarette consumption (and perhaps smoking prevalence). Socio-econometric models suggest that for every 1 per cent increase in price, consumption drops by approximately 0.5 per cent. The effects of price increases appear greatest for those with small incomes such as adolescents. Other factors affecting smoking are more difficult to quantify. Probably important are the presence or absence of cigarette advertising and the perceived status of smoking in terms of images and associations in films, television, sport sponsorship, etc. (Laugesen and Meads, 1991).

The proportion of individuals continuing successful abstinence follows a roughly exponential decline after giving up smoking. It approaches an asymptote at six months to one year, with around 10–30 per cent successful abstinence (varying between studies and type of smoker at entry, see below). This type of decline may also be observed with other drug dependencies, with relapse to alcoholism, opiate or other drug use. Individual factors indicating greater long-term successful smoking cessation include former low daily cigarette consumption in younger smokers but heavier smoking in older smokers (Coambs *et al.*, 1992), lower consumption rates of alcohol and coffee, higher socioeconomic group and less neurotic or depressive personality (US Department Health and Human Services, 1988). There is some slight evidence that women find it harder to give up smoking. Of importance seems to be the degree of self-confidence from the outset that the goal will be achieved, the absence of stressful episodes which precipitate the desire for a cigarette and the degree of social support from friends and family (Breteler *et al.*, 1996).

Aids to smoking cessation

The majority of smokers give up on their own efforts. For those who cannot manage this, a variety of specific methods has been proposed. Although initial successes have been claimed, little or no extra benefit in long-term successful smoking cessation has been shown. Methods include desensitization, progressive reduction of consumption, aversion therapy (electric shocks, rapid smoking to nicotine nausea, etc.), hypnosis, acupuncture, various counselling and psychotherapies. The major failing in these specific methods lies not so much in the initial stage of cessation but in their failure reliably to improve long-term abstinence by comparison with unaided quitting. Indeed it may be important for the majority of successful ex-smokers to feel the self-confidence that they have succeeded through their own efforts. For many novice ex-smokers major difficulties emerge after the initial 'euphoria' of successfully having overcome the first week(s) of withdrawal symptoms. The more complex task then begins of finding alternative sources of enjoyment, different coping strategies in the face of stress, and other ways of maintaining concentration during sustained tasks. If, as has been suggested earlier (see 'Smoking Motivation and Models'), many smokers have inherently poor central control systems for arousal, reward and punishment, then possible alternative strategies may involve physical sports, mental relaxation or assertiveness techniques, and different scheduling of work activities if appropriate or possible.

To date, the only drug preparations with demonstrated practical usefulness are the various nicotine replacement therapies: nicotine chewing gum and the transdermal nicotine patch and more recently the nicotine inhalators. Although some studies have failed to demonstrate the utility of nicotine gum by comparison with placebo gum, there is now sufficient evidence that, at the 4 mg nicotine strength, it increases long-term success rates (1–2 years follow-up) in heavy smokers who usually have more difficulty in giving up. The transdermal patch works about as well as the gum, and either formulation doubles success rates in trials of smoking cessation. Combining nicotine gum with the patch may be superior to either treatment alone, perhaps because the combination allows 'nicotine boosts' from the gum to be superimposed upon the steadier levels provided by the patch, avoiding to some extent a build up of central nervous system tolerance due to steady levels of nicotine. A recent study using combination treatments, demonstrated that nicotine nasal spray compared with spray placebo, increased the effectiveness of the nicotine transdermal patch in successful smoking cessation rates at one year to 27.1 per cent success (nicotine patch + nicotine spray) from 10.9 per cent success (nicotine patch + placebo spray) (Blondal *et al.*, 1999).

The powerful effect of hospital physicians' advice to a smoker who has suffered some serious smoking-related illness has been noted. For example, survivors of ***myocardial infarction*** have success rates for giving up smoking of 50 per cent. However, success rates of physician advice for unselected patients in general practice are much lower, around 5 per cent (as judged by long-term validation smoking cessation, for example carbon monoxide validation at 1-year follow-up). Nevertheless, given the large number of patients in the latter case and the minimal cost of such interventions, this approach is of potential large-scale use (Chapman, 1993). Other settings for channelling advice are dental, family planning and prenatal clinics (pregnancy is cited frequently as a reason for having given up smoking). The incorporation of face-to-face advice on stopping smoking from physicians and other health professionals has formed one element of community-based programmes for prevention of chronic disease, which involve other agencies such as schools and workplaces. Although there are methodological limitations to nearly all community studies, positive results have been obtained and it appears that person-to-person communication is a necessary part of such broadbased programmes.

Myocardial infarction is a heart attack and occurs following severe blockage of arteries supplying the heart, resulting in loss of oxygen supply and death of heart muscle.

Prevention

It is a truism that prevention is better than cessation and offers the slower but more certain long-term hope of elimination of cigarette smoking. Progress is being made. Fewer young people are taking up the habit (see 'Smoking Prevalence'), but much remains to be done. Laws restricting sale of cigarettes to adolescents require enforcement, and of great importance is the role of the image of smoking through associations in the media and advertising. The reduction of smoking's image as 'something exciting and sophisticated' is required, since this would lower motivation to experiment with cigarettes. Various specific school programmes involving 'peer teaching' and demonstration of immediate effects of smoking to offset what to the adolescent seem distant and personally irrelevant health risks have been tried, in addition to more direct health education messages. As in the case of adult-directed media campaigns it is often difficult to demonstrate specific results. However, the message does appear to be taking effect gradually, since fewer adolescents are starting to smoke. Moreover, as adult smokers become a minority, the 'role model' of smoking as an adult activity to emulate will be diminished.

Summary and conclusions

Smoking is considered to be the single greatest cause of preventable death in the developed world. The more important diseases are cardiovascular, neoplastic and chronic obstructive pulmonary disease. In many developed countries smokers have now become a minority group, though in less-developed countries the picture is different; with the prevalence of cigarette smoking increasing. Many studies show a positive relationship between parental smoking and respiratory symptoms in children. Especially important are the increases in severe respiratory illnesses in children under two years of age.

Smoking is a complex pattern of behaviour with nicotine acquisition overlaid by social and psychological factors. Psycho-analytical, social learning and personality theories have been proposed to account for it, as well as those emphasing the actions of nicotine in arousal modulation and addiction. None of these individually is sufficient. Social approval or disapproval appear to be of great importance and there is evidence that adolescents of a more rebellious and risk-taking nature are more likely to take it up. Maintenance of smoking continues for a variety of reasons; there are direct pharmacological rewards from nicotine and smoking may also serve as a coping strategy.

It is difficult to demonstrate a direct effect of any particular anti-smoking public health education or media campaign, though social pressures to quit can be exerted by the immediate family and peer group. The powerful effect of hospital physicians' advice to smokers who have suffered serious smoking-related illness has been noted, although success rates of physician advice for unselected patients in general practice are much lower. The price of cigarettes is also a factor limiting cigarette consumption and perhaps smoking prevalence. However, the majority of smokers give up through their own efforts and indeed it may be important for the majority of successful ex-smokers to feel the self-confidence that they have succeeded through their own efforts. For those who can't manage this, a variety of specific methods has been proposed. Many are based on classical learning theory, though others include hypnosis, acupuncture as well as various forms of counselling and psychotherapy. The major failing in these methods lies not in the initial stage of cessation but in their failure to improve long-term abstinence in comparison with unaided quitting. To date, the only drug preparations with demonstrated utility are various nicotine replacement therapies.

Discussion points

A   How might the data presented in Figure 10.2 of this chapter be used to target resources for an anti-smoking campaign? You may assume that these data are fairly typical of an industrialised country, but for developing countries will be different.

B   What makes smoking such an attractive option to young women?

Suggested reading

Breteler, M.H.M., Schotberg, E.J. and Schippers, G.M. (1996) 'The Effectiveness of Smoking Cessation Programs: Determinants and Outcomes', *Psychology and Health*, **11**: 133–53.

Conner, M. and Norman, P. (eds) (1995) *Predicting Health Behaviour*. (Buckingham: Open University Press).

Golding, J.F. (1995) 'Smoking', in R.A.L. Brewis, B. Corrin, D.M. Geddes and G.J. Gibson (eds), *Respiratory Medicine*, 2nd edn. (London: W.B. Saunders & Co.).

Health Compromising
Behaviours III: HIV Infection
and Sexual Behaviour

'Death has a thousand doors to let out life.'

Philip Massinger (*A Very Woman*, 1655)

AIDS or Acquired Immune
Deficiency Syndrome.
Occurs when the immune
system is weakened beyond
a certain point and follows
infection by the HIV virus
that progressively disables
the immune system.

Within health psychology the question of sexual health has largely focused upon HIV infection and *AIDS*. In considering these, however, it is important to remember that a large number of other sexually transmitted diseases exist, which though less lethal are more prevalent than HIV (Rathus and Boughn, 1994). Fortunately, from a psychological perspective many of the issues concerning prevention, risk reduction, and behavioural intervention are similar. Although this is not the first time that sexually transmitted diseases have had such a deadly impact (syphilis was responsible for the deaths of millions of people before effective anti-bacterial agents were discovered) a number of factors make the AIDS phenomenon unique in public consciousness. These include the initial absence of effective treatment options, the ability of the virus to rapidly mutate and acquire resistance to antiviral drugs (Connor, 1995), and the speed with which it has emerged on the global stage (modern air travel is one factor in this). However, the rise to prominence of AIDS as a issue of global psychological concern owes something to the way in which it has become enmeshed with a variety of additional discourses – both public and private (Adam, 1989). These cover morality, religion, the law, the nuclear family, sexual lifestyles and choices, contraceptive use, drug use, bereavement, fear of death not to mention public health policy. Fuelled by such an emotionally charged concoction and in the hands of a mass communications media, AIDS has produced widespread apprehension on a scale that is without parallel in the modern era of scientific medicine.

Between diagnosis of the first case in 1981 and late 1996, an estimated 8.4 million people worldwide have gone on to develop AIDS, approximately 20 per cent of these being children. A more indicative figure of the future burden of the disease on global health and demand for health care is provided by the figure of 33.6 million adults and children estimated to be living with HIV and AIDS in 1999 (WHO, 1999a), a figure revised substantially upwards from earlier estimates. The distribution of these cases has been skewed to poorer countries, notably in Africa (where three-quarters of the total AIDS cases to date have occurred), Latin America and Asia where the disease is now rapidly spreading (Beaglehole and Bonita, 1997). Approximately 90 per cent of all perinatal HIV transmission cases worldwide occur in Africa. In both the United States and in most of the industrialised countries of Europe the development of new cases is showing signs of levelling off (see Figure 11.1 for UK data between 1985 and 1999), although HIV epidemics have recently emerged in several

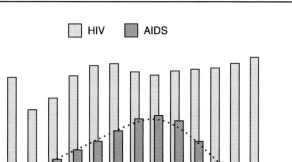
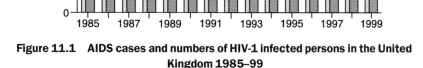

Figure 11.1   AIDS cases and numbers of HIV-1 infected persons in the United Kingdom 1985–99

Source: Communicable Disease Surveillance Centre and Scottish Centre for Infection and Environmental Health 2000.

countries of the former Soviet Union amongst injecting drug users (ECEM, 1997; WHO, 1999a).

It has been suggested that this levelling off may be due to changes in behaviour and secure blood supplies (Bonita and Beaglehole, 1997). Brody (1996), however, contends that as epidemics normally follow a bell curve of incidence with time, such a levelling off may be a consequence not so much of intervention programmes to change behaviour but of changes in the infecting pathogen and the host. Work by Sinicco *et al.* (1997) which indicates the emergence of a more virulent strain of the HIV-1 virus characterised by more rapid depletion of CD4 cells and faster disease progression may mean that Brody's optimistic interpretation of the trends is premature (see Box 11.2).

At the time of writing an effective vaccine does not exist. Combination therapies using three anti-viral agents (zidovudine, protease inhibitor and nucleoside reverse transcriptase inhibitors) have enjoyed success in reducing plasma viral load to below detectable levels in some individuals (Carpenter *et al.*, 1997) and offer promising hope for the future. However, there is no evidence to show disease progression can be completely arrested, nor that people can return to a non-infectious state with restored immunocompetence or that the health benefits offered by the multi-drug regimens can be maintained in the face of viral mutation (Graham, 1998). In lieu of the rapid viral evolution of HIV, optimism for a permanent cure must be tempered.

In the light of the difficulties facing biomedical scientists and medical practitioners, for a number of years the consensus amongst social scientists and the international medical community has been that the most effective means for limiting the spread of the virus lie in the province of behaviour change and harm minimisation. Recently the wisdom of this voluntarist approach to HIV prevention has been questioned. Danziger (1996) argued that as the possibility of viable treatments appears closer, the grounds for rejecting traditional public health measures to infectious diseases, such as compulsory testing and isolation, are no longer straightforward. Were a non-elective approach to HIV monitoring ever to be adopted within the western industrialised nations, then the leading role in prevention occupied by behavioural scientists would require reassessment. Even without such a change, the challenges to health psychology posed by the HIV epidemic are plentiful. Chesney (1996) identifies five major demands on the discipline; these include the early identification of at-risk individuals (antiviral therapy is more beneficial the earlier it is started, Van Praag and Perriens, 1996), the rising expectations of health professionals for successful behaviour change programmes, a growing population coping with chronic disease, an increasing shift from individual towards community health perspectives, and the need to address health problems on a global scale. We will now examine some of these issues.

BOX 11.1   How does HIV lead to AIDS?

Following infection, the human immunodeficiency virus begins its attack on the immune system by invading and destroying the CD4 T lymphocytes (T-cells). Before the host T-cell dies the virus turns over its replicating mechanism to the production of new viral particles, which in turn go on to infect new cells. Normally the T-cells provide signals to other branches of the immune system – the B-cells and T-killer cells – the B-cells being responsible for the production of antibodies to bind with the invading pathogen and the T-killer cells for the destruction of the infected cells. By attacking the T-cells, the virus thus strikes at the heart of the body's defence system. Recent research shows that the immune system fights a long and protracted war against the HIV virus. Ho *et al.* (1995) found that between 10^8 and 10^9 virus particles – about 30% of the total – were being cleared each day, with 2×10^9 cells being produced each day to replace those being destroyed. During the first few years following infection, the number of CD4 cells may remain relatively high. As HIV gradually disarms the immune system, however, the person becomes vulnerable to a variety of opportunistic diseases such as Pneumocystis carinii pneumonia, Kaposi's sarcoma, pulmonary tuberculosis, toxoplasmosis (a parasitic infection of the brain), invasive cancer of the cervix and AIDS wasting syndrome. Initially HIV may give rise to a complex of flu-like symptoms including fevers, fatigue and sore throats (Phillips, 1991). Eighty per cent of people infected with HIV go on to develop AIDS within 15 years, and once AIDS has been diagnosed the overwhelming majority (95%) will die within 5 years. Nearly 80% of those who die from AIDS are found on autopsy to have neuropathological abnormalities. Whilst alive about one-third of AIDS patients will develop AIDS dementia complex which is marked by severe memory loss, confusion and a variety of other cognitive effects which occasionally include hallucinations (Frude, 1998).

BEHAVIOURAL RISK FACTORS, STRESS AND HIV TRANSMISSION

To date, a number of groups have been considered to be at higher risk of HIV infection. Within Europe in 1996, the largest proportion of newly diagnosed cases of AIDS occurred in injecting drug users (43%), followed by homosexual/bisexual men (26%). However, heterosexual infections (21%) now comprise the third largest transmission group (ECEM, 1997) and mothers to infants the fourth (Hoover, 1996). From the earliest days of the epidemic when it was first identified in gay males, a tendency has existed to direct attention and responsibility for transmission of the virus onto those peoples worst affected by it. The stigmatising of HIV-infected individuals extended to individuals with haemophilia who had been infected from blood transfusions. Mistreatment, social isolation and overt violence have meant that many people infected with the virus or suffering from AIDS have been forced to leave their homes, jobs and communities and have been implicated in an increased risk of suicide (Bor, 1997). The effect of such additional stress on quality of physical and psychological well-being is far from being fully understood.

Several researchers have suggested relationships between psychological variables such as mood, and markers of immune functioning such as natural killer cell (NKC) activity (for example Valdimarsdottir and Bovbjerg, 1997). It has been hypothesised that psychological stress and low levels of social support could hasten progression from HIV to AIDS (Sodroski, Rosen and Haseltine, 1984; Solomon and Temoshok, 1987; Solomon, Temoshok O'Leary and Zich, 1987; Burack *et al.*, 1993; Evans *et al.*, 1997). Such a relationship could be mediated by the inhibitory effects of both cortisol and ACTH (the so called stress hormones) on natural killer cell activity (Nair, Saravolatz and Schwartz, 1995). However, a number of well-controlled studies have to date failed to provide supporting evidence that AIDS onset can be accelerated by stress (Kessler *et al.*, 1991; Rabkin *et al.*, 1991; Kertzner *et al.*, 1993). Psychosocial variables have been consistently associated with self-reported HIV symptoms, but not as yet with objective clinical markers (Vassend, Eskild and Halvorsen, 1997). Although it remains debatable whether stress hastens the disease onset there is currently no strong evidence that stress management can reverse it. Coates, McKusick, Kuno and Stites (1989) employed a regime of stress reduction, which included stress management, relaxation training and health habit changes in a sample of 64 men who had tested positive for HIV. No discernible changes in immune functioning were observed.

The idea that AIDS is confined to particular groups of people detracts attention from the behaviours that expose people to the virus and the contexts within which these behaviours confer risk. The principal routes by which the virus may be transmitted involve the exchange of semen or vaginal fluids through sexual intercourse (Ingham, 1994), or the exchange of blood through the sharing of needles or other paraphernalia associated with injecting drugs (Koester, 1996). Transmission of the virus from mother to infant is also believed to occur during breast feeding. The risks of transmission associated with these behaviours multiply with the frequency of the behaviour. Thus a risk of infection of 1 in 500 from one act of unprotected sex with an infected partner equates to a risk of 2 in 3 for 500 acts of intercourse (Rathus and Boughn, 1994). Similarly, the more sexual partners one has, the more likely it is that one of them will be an infected person. Moreover, it has been found that as the number of partners increases, the characteristics of these later partners are more likely to be associated with increased HIV risk (Lindblade, Foxman and Koopman, 1994).

SOCIAL COGNITION MODELS OF HIV-RELATED BEHAVIOUR

One of the major tasks confronting health psychologists is to devise interventions which will reduce or minimise the likelihood of HIV infection, based upon an understanding of the processes which underlie risk-taking behaviour. As Chesney (1996) has remarked this is an enormous challenge – not least because a number of factors external to the individual play a major role in determining risk-taking behaviour. For example, housing and unemployment problems, depression, alcohol and drug abuse, relationship status (that is, whether or not a close regular partner is involved), relationship difficulties, life dissatisfaction and low social status all raise the probability of people engaging in risky sexual behaviours and contracting sexually-transmitted diseases (Wright and Rodway, 1988; Kalichman, Rompa and Muhammad, 1997).

Several models which explore the cognitive determinants of sexual behaviour in the context of HIV and AIDS have been used. As well as the Health Belief Model and Theory of Planned Behaviour (see Chapter 7), the AIDS Risk Reduction Model (Catania, Kegeles and Coates, 1990) has recently entered the fray. To date applications of the health belief model to HIV/AIDS have yielded disappointing results. Siegel *et al.* (1989), for example, found drug use and previous sexual behaviour were more important predictors of future safe or risky sexual practices in gay males than either attitudes or knowledge. The importance of past sexual behaviour received further support from Aspinall *et al.* (1991). Over a six-month period they found over half the variance in the reported number of partners was explained by the previous number of partners. Similar negative findings have also been reported with hetero-sexual adolescents – health belief variables failing to predict condom use (Abraham and Sheeran, 1994; Sheeran and Abraham, 1996). The theory of planned behaviour has been more successful: attitudes and subjectively perceived social norms have been found to predict HIV-related intentions and behaviours (Jemmott and Jemmott, 1991), intentions to predict future condom use (Van der Velde, Hookyaas and Van der Plight, 1992), and a further independent relationship found between perceived self-efficacy and safer sexual behaviour (O'Leary *et al.*, 1992; Terry, Galligan and Conway, 1993). The strength of these relationships, however, still falls far short of what these models originally promised to deliver. As a result, Abraham *et al.* (1994) have called for further clarification of the components of safer sexual behaviour and to other aspects of personal competence which may impact on them.

The deficiencies in the social cognition models we highlighted in Chapter 7 are readily apparent when their predictive utility with respect to safe sexual behaviour is examined. So, for example, if one considers the perceived severity of the threat of HIV infection it is found that although most people acknowledge the severe consequences of HIV infection, they simply don't perceive themselves to be at risk. The media has undoubtedly contributed to this perception with its depiction of AIDS as a disease which strikes gay males and drug users. However, it cannot be ignored that the risk to the population at large is not spread evenly, and too little attention has been paid to the accuracy or otherwise of people's subjective estimates of their probability of infection and the grounds on which these estimates are based. Sexual behaviour may also be quite different from other health-related behaviours such as deciding whether or not to visit a dentist. So while models have enjoyed a degree of success in predicting some less emotionally charged behaviours, quite different constructs are required to deal with the emotional and social nature of sexual encounters. The difficulties which clinicians and researchers face in confronting the deep rooted and often inflexible patterns of responses which surround human sexual expression may be partly determined by a biologically set vulnerability to classical and operant conditioning in this domain.

Unlike the above models the AIDS risk reduction model was developed to specifically address issues of sexual health. In so doing it intends to provide a more complete picture of the process of behaviour change while explicitly acknowledging the importance of contextual variables. Within it, three stages to behavioural change are proposed; labelling, commitment to change and enactment (Flowers, Sheeran, Beail and Smith, 1997). The first two of these stages incorporate elements from both the health belief model and the theory of planned behaviour. Labelling comprises the acknowledgement of personal susceptibility to HIV infection, the belief that HIV/AIDS is undesirable, and knowledge of the activities associated with HIV transmission. Similarly the commitment stage – the decision-making phase between problem perception and action – incorporates cost–benefit analysis, which in turn is dependent upon both social norms and the perceived efficacy of adopting particular actions. Only in the final stage of enactment does the AIDS risk reduction model clearly move beyond earlier formulations. It does so by postulating a process beyond intention formation – the implementation of intentions in sexual contexts, which may be affected by social influences – such as relationship status or degree of social support. Movement between the three stages as well as maintenance of behaviour change is construed as under the influence of context – social factors, emotional states, drug use and mass media representations. This model, while certainly a conceptual advance upon the health belief model or theory of planned behaviour, does suffer from some of the same difficulties – principally how to operationalise and measure the constructs, and this is most apparent where issues of context are being considered.

Knowledge and understanding of context is vital because viable opportunities for safe behavioural alternatives cannot be engineered without it. The efforts to change behaviours associated with HIV risk have by and large enjoyed only limited success. Evidence continues to show that despite the wealth of information in the public domain, large numbers of people are putting themselves at risk of contracting HIV (Rosenthal and Fernbach and Moore, 1997), and that even amongst those sections of the population where behaviour change has been readily undertaken, maintaining those changes is proving to be difficult (Davies and Hickson, 1993; Hart, 1996). An explanation for the relative failures of HIV preventive efforts to date must stem in part from the narrow individualistic focus adopted in the initial years following the discovery of HIV-related disease. The limiting horizons imposed by politics, economics, society, and indeed biology on the form and content of human sexual and social relationships have too frequently been ignored by psychologists. Psychological theories of behaviour change if they are to be of use must seek integration with models of other social processes. At present, the AIDS risk reduction model offers one of the best hopes of this. As Ingham remarks:

> The integration of individual and societal levels of analysis is essential if real progress is to be achieved, especially in an area as replete with moral, ideological and emotional issues as the field of sexuality and sexual activity. (1994, p. 80)

HIV PREVENTION

From a practical point of view if no other, we are now in a position to ask what characteristics effective HIV prevention must present. From the foregoing it would seem a prerequisite that health interventions for HIV function at a variety of levels. Changes must be encouraged at the level of the individual, the community and the wider social and political environment (Rhodes, 1996). At the individual level, information can be given, awareness of risky behaviours and alternatives can be provided, people can be counselled to raise their esteem and self-efficacy and encouraged to act in cohort with others. Community action may encompass needle-exchange schemes for injecting drug users, action in schools and centres where young people associate, or targeting of perceived at-risk groups in the local community such as commercial sex workers (Barnard and McKeganey, 1996) or sexually abused young people

(Futterman *et al.*, 1993). Community interventions have as their aim changes in the norms and practices of members of those communities. They rely inherently on the social networks between people and encourage peer support and participation. Qualitative research in the form of participant observation and in-depth interviews has a vital role to play. This can uncover the contexts within which behaviour relevant to HIV transmission occurs, establish what behavioural norms exist within a community and which behaviours can be effectively targeted and changed, as well as what obstacles stand in the way of making persistent changes. Such research and community action may go hand in hand.

Friedman, Des Jarlais and Ward (1994) outlined two broad types of social process whereby behaviour can be changed in cultures of risk. These include social diffusion whereby preexisting leaders and/or influential people are recruited to promulgate changed norms within a culture and collective self-organisation instigated wholly from within a particular group. At present such initiatives have enjoyed greater success within the gay community, in part because of the strong shared cultural and political identity of many gay people, which perhaps provides a firmer basis for the practice of reciprocal altruism. The stigma and the very hidden nature of associations within the IV-drug using community on the other hand probably make the task of social diffusion that much harder to achieve (Jose *et al.*, 1996).

The importance of change at broader social, cultural and political levels for HIV transmission can be seen in the consequences of increased urbanisation in Africa in recent decades. War and famine have been two of the principal forces driving people to cities for food and work. Women excluded from traditional lineage at the village level and driven to towns and cities may be forced into prostitution in order to obtain work and money. The marked cultural changes experienced by people moving from rural communities to cities may also include a breakdown of traditional restraints on sexual behaviour which have operated at a local level. Together such changes provide fertile ground for the proliferation of HIV. Coupled with these the strong pressure to have children in many African societies may lead to a reduced inclination to use condoms (Potts, 1990). Yet another example is provided by examining the acceptability and availability of condoms and needle-exchange schemes in different parts of the world (Bonita and Beaglehole, 1997). Syringe-exchange schemes remain legally prohibited in a number of countries, including parts of the United States and Sweden. Religious influences have meant family planning measures such as condom use are unavailable or culturally proscribed in many regions – often the very same places where HIV is running out of control. In the United Kingdom, failure to provide condoms and syringe-exchange schemes has contributed to the spread of HIV in the prison population. The UK Government has also so far refused to make sex education a compulsory part of the National School Curriculum (Ingham, 1994).

The nature of these influences poses serious challenges to Health Psychology as a discipline. Many of the models which have been put forward as possible solutions to the problem of understanding the pathways to HIV risk behaviours have been too narrowly focused for the level of complexity on offer. Their failure raises serious questions not only as to whether health psychology has become preoccupied with the health threats facing the populations of the western industrialised nations, but also whether in the rush to confront the problems of HIV infection, the global dangers posed by the return of previously controlled infectious diseases are going unchallenged (Wilson, 1995). We will return to this theme when considering the future of health psychology in the final chapters of the book. Only by a thorough examination of all the mechanisms – social, economic, political, cultural and behavioural – through which the HIV virus has been propagated globally can psychologists appreciate the quite proper role they have in contributing to thoughtful and necessary behavioural change.

Summary and conclusions

The phenomenon of AIDS has acquired a strong place in public consciousness. Major reasons for this include the initial absence of effective treatment options, the mutability of the virus and its resistance to antiviral drugs, the speed with which it has spread globally, as well as the manner in which it has become enmeshed with a variety of additional discourses such as morality, the law, the family, sexual lifestyles, contraceptive use, drug use, fear of death and public health policy. Estimates from the World Health Organisation in 1998 suggested over 30 million adults and children were living with HIV and AIDS. With no effective vaccine against the virus the consensus amongst workers in all fields has been that the most effective means for limiting its spread lies in the province of behaviour change and harm minimisation.

The idea that AIDS is confined to particular groups has detracted attention from the behaviours that expose people to the virus and the contexts in which these confer risk. A major task for health psychologists is to devise interventions for reducing or minimising the likelihood of HIV infection, based on an understanding of the processes underlying risk-taking behaviour. Several models exploring the cognitive determinants of sexual behaviour in the context of HIV and AIDS have been used. None of these has yet to meet the high hopes which have been invested in them, though a recent development, the AIDS risk reduction model offers better prospects of predicting behaviour. A major difficulty is that past behaviour remains a strong predictor of current behaviour. Researchers have called for further clarification of the components of safer sexual behaviour. The integration of individual and societal levels of analysis is also essential if real progress is to be achieved. Some headway has been made in understanding the social processes whereby behaviour can be changed in cultures of risk. These include social diffusion whereby preexisting leaders and/or influential people are recruited to promulgate changed norms within a culture and collective self-organisation instigated wholly from within a particular group.

On a somewhat different front, psychosocial variables have been associated with self-reported HIV symptoms, but not with objective clinical markers, and a number of well-controlled studies have to date failed to provide supporting evidence that psychological variables such as stress can hasten the onset of AIDS, or that stress reduction can delay it. Further research is likely to clarify this picture.

Discussion points

A What are the options if behavioural control of HIV infection is not successful?

B At what age should young people be educated about HIV and AIDS?

Suggested reading

Davies. P.M. and Hickson, F.C.I. (1993) *Sex, Gay Men and AIDS.* (London: Falmer.

Rhodes, T. and Hartnoll, R. (1996) *AIDS, Drugs and Prevention: Perspectives on Individual and Community Action.* (London: Routledge).

12

Health Promotion and Behaviour Change

'The role of an intellectual is to be critical of their own ideology.'

Umberto Eco

INTRODUCTION

It should be apparent from the preceding chapters that the antecedents of health-related behaviours are complex, and that interventions intending to modify them must be cognisant of this complexity. Early attempts at health education relied upon the assumption that supplying the relevant information would bring about attitude change and with it behavioural change (Bagnall, 1987). Thus in both practical and policy terms the intention was to use communicational activities which would provide people with knowledge which would enable them to make informed choices about their health and lifestyle. This framework received serious criticism for failing to intervene or monitor changes in social, cultural or economic domains (Green, 1979), for dis-empowering people by shifting control over health from the individual to experts who possessed the all-important information (Aggleton and Homans, 1987) and for not being very effective (McEwan and Bhopal, 1991).

A broader notion of Health Promotion therefore developed from the recognition that health education alone did not provide a sufficient basis for behaviour change. As a term this now covers a range of activities which are intended to both enhance health and well-being and prevent ill-health (Simnett, 1996). Downie, Fyfe and Tannahill (1991) have suggested that the promotion of good health comprises three overlapping spheres of activity; health education, health prevention and health protection. Prevention may occur through screening and immunisation for example, and is intended to reduce the risk of occurrence of particular kinds of ill-health or injury. Health Protection on the other hand comprises legal controls, public health measures and voluntary codes of practise. Whereas education and prevention largely target individuals, protection is directed at populations.

As the stars of health psychology and health promotion as distinct specialities have risen together during the recent historical period, it is not surprising to find that there has been considerable overlap in the areas of health which they address, nor indeed to find that health psychology now occupies a crucial role in health promotion. In the United Kingdom, for example, *The Health of the Nation* document (Department of Health, 1992) setting out the government's agenda and targets for achieving health improvement by the end of the century, gave impetus to work in five specified areas – coronary heart disease and stroke, cancers, mental illness, HIV/

AIDS and sexual health and accidents. The main fields of advice to emerge from these endeavours comprise diet, drug intake, personal body maintenance and leisure activities (Davison, Frankel and Davey Smith, 1992). Health education and prevention continue to occupy a preeminent position despite criticisms (Rush, 1997). This status quo rests on a number of suppositions, which ironically may actually threaten the viability of health promotion in the future (Kelly, 1996). The first of these has been to maintain a somewhat defensive posture about the suitability of scientific methods for evaluating health promotion activities (see Boxes 12.1 and 12.2).

BOX 12.1 Is scientific evaluation of health promotion possible? The politics of health promotion research

The relationship between the functions of health promotion as a branch of public health policy and within more overtly political agendas, places obstacles in the way of effective scientific appraisal. It can be argued that many evaluations have sacrificed rational assessment at the expense of producing a positive conclusion of any kind (Smith, 1987). For example, of 65 available outcome evaluations of sexual health interventions for young people (between 1982–94) only 18% were judged methodologically sound (Oakley *et al.*, 1995). Many lacked random control groups, failed to present suitable baseline or post-intervention data and did not address high attrition rates (50% in many cases). Of these 18% ($n = 12$) only two reported changes in sexual behaviour as a result of the intervention. Despite this the original authors were considerably more upbeat about their findings than the reviewers. Similarly, a review of 7 community action studies examining cancer risk factors found none fulfilled all the criteria for rigorous scientific evaluation (Hancock *et al.*, 1997). It would be an easy matter to criticise the authors of these studies, however the context in which much health promotion has occurred has been one in which the notion of individual responsibility for health has been championed by local health authorities and governments of the day (Roberts, Mayer and McEwen, 1989), and uncritically accepted by many lay people (Blaxter, 1997). While public policy frequently demands that health action be visible, the question of whether it is effective or not has been relegated in importance. It cannot be surprising, therefore, that few evaluations have been independent – that is, conducted by researchers with no vested interests in the outcome. In such a climate it cannot be considered surprising if some practitioners seek to justify their work by displaying undue optimism about what their data actually reveal. In turn this optimism may deter others from disseminating their findings when the negative tone of these is seen as being at odds with the emphasis on success.

All too easily the question of 'Does it work?' has been replaced with 'How can we show it works?' Commitment to scientific objectivity in evaluating health promotion doesn't mean that investigators must adopt a narrow perspective nor a neutral stance with respect to the aims of a programme. What is required is that scientists be disengaged from the vested interests possessing a stake in the outcome (Savan, 1988). Suitable questions can be posed which address the effects an intervention has at several levels and which seek to ascertain whether people's control over their health and the processes which influence it has been augmented or not. It is possible for scientific investigation itself to be embedded in a framework of social action and social investigation without compromising its own standards.

BOX 12.2   Is scientific evaluation of health promotion possible?: Methodological constraints

Political constraints aside, the issue of whether evaluation in the form of experimental method is appropriate has been raised by several commentators (e.g. Dignan, 1986; Whitehead, 1995; Fraser, 1996; Britton *et al.*, 1998). It is certainly true that numerous methodological constraints and difficulties are present. Level of exposure may be difficult to quantify – particularly amongst those not directly targeted. The relevant exposure variable may not be a simple reflection of the degree of air time, newspaper space etc., but to what extent a message is taken up in popular discourse and is present in the immediate interpersonal vicinity of a person. Both Type 1 and Type II errors can result from these difficulties (i.e. effects may be considered to be present when they are not and, alternatively, real effects may be masked because of simultaneous effects on the target and comparison group). Despite these limitations comparison of measures taken before and after an intervention is possible, but caution is urged as any differences could be due to regression to the mean (baseline measures may have been either artificially low or high to begin with, and subsequently will tend to regress to their more typical level).

Two further issues are important. Firstly, at what level should an outcome be evaluated; individual, social, political, community, cultural or economic? Secondly, what should the outcome measures of interest be at each of these levels? Clearly for some social interventions experimental control of variables is neither possible nor desirable. However, observational methodologies where statistical rather than experimental control is possible are available and are equally scientific (see Chapter 2). Where the nature of an important social network is itself poorly understood qualitative methods may be useful at a prior stage in teasing out what the variables of interest are. One area of tension in this debate has been the view that the form and objectives of an evaluation must accord with the participants. Whilst it is important and ethical that participants be fully informed about the nature of a study, and that the aims themselves are benign, it is not necessary that participants themselves set the evaluation agenda – this would be to confuse respect for common-sense perceptions with the best available means for evaluating their basis in reality.

In addition it is assumed that provision of information and guidance on healthy lifestyles gives the general public an adequate platform from which to decide and embark upon rational courses of action. It is further assumed that following such guidance will in the long run have the desired impact on health and life expectancy. The general ineffectiveness of information provision in changing behaviour has already been noted. One response to the lack of compliance with health advice has been the development of interest in lay theories of disease causation.

LAY THEORIES OF HEALTH AND ILLNESS

If people fail to comply with sound health advice, so the argument runs, perhaps the reason can be found in the nature of the beliefs which people hold about health and illness. If people believe that the causes of ill-health lie outside their influence then they may also deny the relevance of personal behavioural change. Workers following this line of reasoning have therefore utilised psychological models of change such as the health belief model and the theory of reasoned action (see Chapter 7). Concepts such as fatalism and internal locus of health control have also been proposed to explain the continued maintenance of unhealthy behaviours (Pill and Stott, 1981; Blaxter and Paterson, 1982). Davison *et al.* (1992), however, have argued that by labelling as 'fatalism' a less than total belief in individual behaviour as the determinant of health status, supporters of health promotion implicitly suggest that non-behavioural explanations of the cause and distribution of disease are somehow not rational or scientific. Studies of different social groups though have demonstrated that lay ideas of health and illness far from being simplistic, in fact incorporate a number of sophisticated tenets found in modern epidemiological theory; including knowledge of the causes of specific diseases (for example bronchitis and coronary heart disease), awareness of the multifactorial nature of disease, and that predictors of ill-health in groups provide a weak basis for individual prediction – what is usually called '*the ecological fallacy*' in scientific research (Unschuld, 1986). That prediction on an individual basis is so clearly difficult in part underlies the apparent recalcitrance of people to change their behaviour (see Box 12.3).

BOX 12.3   The prevention paradox

The notion of the prevention paradox is recognised by many researchers. Rose (1992) illustrates this in discussing men at 'high risk' for CHD (though the arguments are equally applicable to many other conditions). Of these only 7% actually develop trouble in the following five years – the remaining 93% keeping well. Additionally, only about one-third of future cases will display the risk factors. As a consequence of these proportions, most people will be exposed to numerous examples of individuals which are contrary to the pattern of disease expected from health promotional messages. On this basis the construction of luck as a 'cause' of ill-health may well be a reasoned response to the perceived evidence – and of course scepticism may well ensue. This does not mean that the statistical models which depict associations between risk factors and disease outcomes are erroneous – rather that the greater predictive ability of the models compared to chance isn't sufficiently strong to be apparent in everyday experience. The paradox lies in the fact that a preventive strategy aimed at only a small section of the population is likely to be ignored by the majority and will, even if taken up by the minority, have almost no discernible effect on the population incidence of disease; whilst one which addresses a substantially larger proportion of the population will produce readily observable effects in only a small number. A kind of cyclic relationship may thus ensue; with large numbers of people targeted, few take notice and more people become susceptible to disease – as these numbers increase, people are more likely to take notice of the intervention, which in turn will produces fewer cases. With few cases, people take less notice, etc. An oscillating relationship of this kind between two populations (in this case numbers responding to preventive messages and numbers effected by the target disease) is observed in many natural systems (the prey–predator system is one example) and is described mathematically as a 'limit cycle' (Stewart, 1997). The specific dynamics of the 'prevention paradox' are likely to vary considerably between different disease outcomes. For example the greater perceived threat of a disease (e.g. AIDS) may mean there is more elasticity in the system before a decline in incidence induces people to change their behaviour.

What is generally agreed from readings of lay accounts of the origins of ill-health is that the role of the social structure in disease is not adequately represented (Calnan, 1987; Blaxter, 1997). It has been suggested that this may even be because health promotional messages have afforded them no prominence. Recent work, however, challenges this view that lay understanding does not include knowledge of the effects of the social structure on health and illness. Roberts *et al.* (1998) surveyed a group of 480 people from a variety of occupational backgrounds, all of whom were asked to estimate their own life expectancy. Workers in manual jobs estimated their life expectancy to be almost four years lower than their counterparts in non-manual jobs (73.4 vs 77.2 years). This difference remained after adjustment was made for respondents' current mental and physical health or current health behaviours (exercise, smoking, alcohol and drug use). This data is intriguing first of all because of the accuracy of respondents' judgements, which compare favourably with real mortality data from UK social classes (Hattersley, 1997). Secondly it suggests that the estimates have not been based on subjects' own health behaviours. If not from their own behaviour, then it is possible that the differences derive from subjects' own tacit recognition of an association between social status and health. Further work is required here, though one implication is that social cognitive models of health behaviours might be enhanced by incorporating such tacit knowledge. A clear challenge is to devise means whereby it could be operationalised.

From the foregoing the reader could be forgiven for concluding that we view the prospects for behaviour change as slim. Doubtless it is no easy matter, but we would maintain that under favourable circumstances change is certainly possible – and one of the major tasks for psychologists and others concerned with promoting better health is to discover how this is achievable. At this point we wish to ask on a more general level – what kinds of approaches work in what kinds of situations?

ENVIRONMENTAL INTERVENTIONS

Economic

There is clear evidence that economic policies can induce behaviour change at the population level. Elasticities of price and income provide a useful yardstick for assessing the prospect of controlling consumption of health-damaging products such as tobacco and alcohol by fiscal means. Price elasticity, for example, refers to the percentage change in demand which accompanies a 1 per cent increase in price. For tobacco, both price and income elasticities are thought to be low (between –0.2 to –0.5 for price, and in the region of 0.2 for income; Maynard, 1986; US Department of Health and Human Services, 1989; Peterson *et al.*, 1992). With low elasticities the impact of fiscal policies is quite small, though there is more uncertainty where large percentage price changes are recorded. Further information is also needed on the operation of elasticities within specific demographic groups – there is some evidence to suggest that price rises amongst the young have a greater deterrent effect (Lewit, Coates and Grossman, 1981). It is noteworthy that in western industrialised countries, as demands grow for greater controls on smoking in public places and tighter regulations governing the sale and advertising of tobacco (Chapman, 1996), cigarette manufacturers have been dumping their products into developing countries at low prices. Mackay and Crofton (1996) draw attention to the need to develop national control policies in the poorer regions of the world by pointing out that if current smoking patterns continue, 70 per cent of the expected 10 million annual deaths from tobacco will occur in developing countries.

Where alcohol is concerned, data also suggest consumption is responsive to relative shifts in prices and incomes. The magnitude of price and income elasticities are highest for spirits (–1.39, 2.5) and wine (–1.1, 1.8) and lowest for beer (–0.2, 0.7) (Ornstein and Levy, 1983; Maynard, 1986). Similar relationships probably underlie the consumption of illicit drugs – the cheap price of the heroin flooding into European and American cities in the 1980's being one factor behind its increased take up. Besides the effects stemming from elasticities of price, demand for goods may also be influenced by absolute income levels; low income makes it substantially more difficult to buy healthy food. James *et al.* (1996) point out that for the 20 per cent of income-support claimants with compulsory deductions for rent and fuel, their diet is far below the reference nutrient intake for iron, calcium, dietary fibre, folate and vitamin C. For those who smoke within this group it is lower still. For those lacking access to a car, this may be compounded by the movement of major retailers away from city centres and by the necessity to shop locally where food prices are on average 30 per cent higher than in supermarkets (Piachaud and Webb, 1996). Wilkinson (1996b) has argued forcibly that health benefits would result from redistributive economic policies which cut the magnitude of income differentials between different sections of the population (see Chapter 13). In a similar vein, both Haines and Smith (1997) and Logie (1997) have called for the cancelling of debt in the poorer countries of the world where social spending has been diverted to service debt repayment.

Mass-media

Despite the controversy surrounding their influence on human behaviour, mass-media campaigns have frequently been at the forefront of health education efforts. This is simply because of their ability to reach so many people in a short period of time. Research undertaken with a random sample of over 14 000 subjects from 15 member states of the European Community found that televison and radio (29%) closely followed by newspapers and magazines (27%) are the most frequently selected sources of information on healthy eating (de-Almeida *et al.*, 1997). This apparent advantage aside, several workers have called for caution in using the media. Kinder, Pape and Walfish (1980) reviewed a large number of drug-education campaigns and noted several instances in which the campaigns appeared to exacerbate drug use. Many have been scathing of the value of anti-drug and AIDS campaigns launched through the television networks (Davies, 1986; Marsh, 1986). Unlike other approaches the indiscriminate nature of television means that targeting specific groups is difficult – with the additional danger of conveying unintended messages to non-target groups or conveying no useful information at all. In the early TV campaigns against AIDS produced by the UK government and the Health Education Authority, the initial failure to include subtitles meant that many deaf people were left bemused about the succession of images of graveyards which the promotional film contained. In discussing mass-media campaigns on HIV and AIDS, Banyard (1996) concluded that the nature of the campaigns were more likely to please politicians and administrators than lead to effective health promotion.

At present too little data exists concerning the appropriate evaluation of mass-media campaigns. Double-blind randomised controlled trials are clearly inappropriate, not to say impossible for assessing putative effects. However, a minimum prerequisite for any proper analysis must include baseline and follow-up data on the thing to be combatted, be it unsafe sexual behaviour, drug use or smoking. Secondly, data on the success rate (numbers of people reducing giving up the behaviour concerned) needs to be balanced against the false positive rate (possible inducements to others to experiment or try out the undesired behaviour). Thirdly, any apparent trends that emerge from the data must be treated in a circumspect manner.

While positive health gains arising from media influences are difficult to demonstrate, there is evidence that curtailing influences such as advertising may lead to beneficial health outcomes – certainly where smoking is concerned (Pekurinen, 1989). The role of cigarette advertising in influencing young people's behaviour has been of paramount importance in health promotion. Several studies show a relationship between frequency of cigarette advertising and smoking in school-age children. Because of the cross-sectional nature of some of these earlier investigations (for example Chapman and Fitzgerald, 1982), a causal relationship could not be clearly established. However, a recent longitudinal study of 1450 11 to 12-year-old children in England (While *et al.*, 1996), found that girls who previously were able to name more heavily advertised brands were, at follow-up one year later, more than twice as likely to have started smoking when compared to those naming less-advertised brands. Vaidya, Naik and Vaidya (1996) have also established a link between tobacco sponsorship of sporting events and subsequent smoking in schoolchildren. In response to the growing evidence of adverse health effects a number of countries have set about enforcing bans on the advertising of tobacco products through sponsorship. Sporting events, however, are not the sole means by which positive images of smoking are conveyed to young people; media portrayals may also be influential. Substantial amounts may be paid for product placement in motion pictures; the US company Philip Morris, for example, paid US$350 000 to have its Marlboro cigarettes appear in the film Superman II (Cancer Society of New Zealand, 1995), whilst a content analysis of music videos by DuRant *et al.* (1997) found glamorous images of tobacco and alcohol use were frequent (26% of MTV videos) and often associated with sexuality. In addition to this, in instances where tobacco companies have acquired control of news media the presentation of smoking in them has changed to appear more as a forbidden fruit (Dejong, 1996).

Legal/Civic Controls

Proposals to counter negative influences emanating from the mass-media and commercial sector include the curtailment of advertising, restricting media portrayals and reducing access to tobacco and alcohol in young people through legal and other controls (Bennett and Murphy, 1997). In contrast to these active measures to change the social environment the provision of health messages or information on products appears to carry little weight. Few smokers even know the tar levels of the cigarettes they smoke (Cohen, 1996) and nutritional information is frequently not understood, particularly by those with low incomes and low education (Glanz *et al.*, 1995). Simply asking for age and identification, however, has been found to be an effective means for decreasing minor's access to tobacco (Landrine, Klonoff and Alcaraz, 1996), while more rigorous checks for under-age drinkers by police has been shown to be effective in reducing alcohol-related crime (Jeffs and Saunders, 1983). There is also some evidence that well-publicised road checks especially those incorporating educational programmes can significantly reduce both crash and fatality rates

(Bennett and Murphy, 1997). Legislation for compulsory wearing of seat-belts has been argued to be a major factor behind the decline in fatal accidents to both drivers and passengers, although this interpretation has been questioned by McCarthy (1989) whose analysis despite showing a downward trend in accident mortality points to little influence from the law. Instead it is argued there is a complex interaction between the driver and the physical environment of the car, in which driver behaviour alters in response to the changing safety features in automobile design. As well as changes to the interior environment of the motor vehicle, changes to the external physical environment have also been called for. Roberts *et al.* (1994), for example, claim that traffic-calming measures are a more effective means of reducing pedestrian accidents than educating pedestrians.

Community Interventions

We saw in the previous chapter that community initiatives have offered the best prospect of containing the spread of HIV infection and maintaining low-risk behaviour. Both social diffusion and collective self-organisation were advanced as models of change within a community (Friedman, Des Jarlais and Ward, 1994). When successful, diffusion is believed to follow an S-shaped trajectory, slow initial uptake followed by rapid acceptance and finally a slow move towards the maximum level of uptake. This pattern may reflect not only distinct sub-groups of the population taking up the new behaviour (innovators, conformers, resistors), but also the differing motivations which lead people to change their behaviour (Bennett and Murphy, 1997). These concepts may also be applicable in contexts as diverse as schools and workplace sites. Appropriate evaluation of these ideas would require longitudinal studies, probably combined with in-depth qualitative work to establish the nature of the social processes at work. Unfortunately these have been few and far between. Peer-led interventions have long been recognised as one of the most effective channels for drug-abuse prevention work in schools (Bachman *et al.*, 1988; Sussman *et al.*, 1995) in part because relationships with drug-using peers are one of the strongest predictors of hard drug use (Jenkins, 1996). The introduction of employee-assistance programmes and health promotional policies in the workplace have also been an effective means of intervention (Cyster and McEwen, 1987). Those with restrictive smoking policies combined with smoking education and cessation programmes have proven effective (Fielding, 1982), though programmes have generally worked best when a number of areas for health improvement have been targeted together. Workforce interventions targeting weight loss and diet have generally fared less well (Klesges *et al.*, 1989; Hebert *et al.*, 1993) although this may be because the motivational structures underlying these behaviours differ substantially from those dealing with tobacco and alcohol consumption, as well as the behaviours themselves being embedded within a quite different social discourse - in which concerns of appearance, self-esteem and attraction outweigh matters of health.

Individual interventions: Lifestyle

Historically, psychologists have devoted most attention to those interventions which have sought to instigate change in the habits and lifestyles which pose risks to the health of individual people. As such, individuals rather than communities, population sub-groups or nations have usually been the preferred target for change.

As previously discussed some of the reasons for this are political in nature, though it should not be forgotten that theories and technologies of behavioural change have been well-developed within psychology for the best part of the twentieth century (Lieberman, 1991) and provide an important framework for the design and implementation of programmes for changing behaviour. The biggest setback for this approach emerged from the disappointing results from the Multiple Risk Factor Intervention Trial (MRFIT) conducted across 18 American cities during the late 1970s. Six years of intensive intervention devoted to 12 866 highly-motivated men in the top 10 per cent risk category for coronary heart disease, for example, produced only minimal changes in their diet, exercise and smoking behaviour (Multiple Risk Factor Intervention Trial Group, 1982; Syme, 1996). In addition the study found no relationship between the much vaunted Type A behaviour pattern (TABP) – no matter how it was measured – and coronary heart disease. Even where behaviour change was successful the ensuing changes in mortality were much smaller than anticipated.

Although positive results have been reported on occasion where studies have been well-designed and potential confounding factors controlled for, the findings have more typically been disappointing. Baxter *et al.* (1997), for example, claimed reductions in smoking and increased use of low-fat milk in areas where a health promotion campaign (*Action Heart*) to reduce coronary risk factors had been active, in comparison to a control region with similar social deprivation and standardised mortality ratios. Davey Smith and Ebrahim (1998), however, argued that the areas were not well-matched and that the differences in smoking rates which were observed were more likely to be an effect of the different characteristics of the areas. Ebrahim and Davey Smith (1997) also reviewed nine multiple risk factor interventions (comprising counselling, education and drug treatments) for reducing coronary heart disease where both disease events and changes in risk factors were measured as outcomes. Pooled effects of multiple risk factor intervention were found to be insignificant. Beneficial effects were observed in high-risk groups (for example people with hypertension), though for low-risk members of the general population the small treatment benefits may be outweighed by treatment risks (Davey Smith and Egger, 1994). Along with data gathered from studies of secondary prevention (modifying risk factors after myocardial infarction and angina) these results support the contention that interventions are only likely to be beneficial where there is a noticeable health threat and the ensuing motivation to change behaviour is high.

Despite the dubious value of lifestyle interventions in the area of coronary heart disease, encouraging results have been obtained in other quarters. Brunner *et al.* (1997) reported the results from a ***meta analysis*** of 17 randomised controlled trials of dietary interventions involving 6893 subjects in all (3817 in the intervention groups). Intervention groups were encouraged to consume a diet intended to change patterns of fat, sodium or fibre consumption. In all the trials, which lasted at least 3 months, subjects were either randomly or systematically allocated to the intervention or control group. The nature of the interventions themselves varied considerably, including weekly teaching sessions, individual advice from physicians and dieticians, group discussion, self-help (plus telephone support), and face-to-face counselling. A variety of outcome measures were also used. These included serum cholesterol, diastolic blood pressure, urinary sodium, and calories from fat as a percentage of total non-alcohol calories. Overall the results suggested that dietary advice can lead to diet change and modest risk reduction amongst healthy adults. In accordance with the health belief model, more substantial changes were observed in those

Meta analysis is a system in which the results from different studies investigating a particular hypothesis are pooled to examine the consistency of effect sizes reported and whether the pooled results (treated as if from a single study) are statistically significant. Studies to be pooled must be critically selected.

subjects participating in breast cancer prevention trials. The authors remark that as there is little evidence on maintenance of change following dietary intervention beyond 18 months, it is too early to state whether these risk-factor reductions will translate to fewer disease outcomes. However, even if they do, a question mark must remain on how feasible such intensive interventions are in routine practice (Ebrahim and Davey Smith, 1997).

Individual interventions: screening

In addition to changing lifestyle risk factors, the other strand of preventative action concerns health screening and immunisation. Both of these are more likely to be utilised by white-collar educated people (Greenland *et al.*, 1992; Benzeval *et al.*, 1995). In addition a substantial body of work does point to a significant role for psychological factors. Health beliefs have been implicated in the take-up of a wide range of prevention services, including influenza vaccination, screening for cervical cancer, hypertension and sexually-transmitted diseases, as well as counselling for a number of genetic diseases (Conner and Norman, 1995). One such study is described in Box 12.4.

BOX 12.4   Psychosocial correlates of health screening: an example study

In a recent study, Shiloh, Vinter and Barak (1997) used both the health belief model and the theory of self-regulated motivations (Leventhal, 1970; Leventhal, Diefenbach and Leventhal, 1992) to explain attendance at four types of health screenings; dental check-ups, blood pressure and cholesterol checks, pap smears and mammography. The health beliefs of perceived severity, susceptibility, benefits and barriers (costs) in conjunction with motivations for controlling danger and fear were most effective in accounting for variation in dental check-ups (75%), and least successful in addressing blood pressure and cholesterol checks (31%), though even here the observed effect sizes were substantially greater than those which are usually obtained in investigations of preventive behaviour (Harrison, Mullen and Green, 1992). The data also suggested the presence of an interaction between type of screening and motivation to attend. Both danger and fear-control motivations were generally higher amongst attenders than non-attenders, though fear motivations in the dental group or danger control in the blood pressure and cholesterol checks did not distinguish between attenders and non-attenders. Health beliefs also differed between groups, with the dental group higher in susceptibility beliefs and the mammography group lowest and the blood pressure and cholesterol groups lowest in benefits and costs.

A consistent difficulty with much of the work conducted on screening lies with the nature of the study design. In the example cited in Box 12.4, as in many investigations, the data were collected after the fact of attending or not attending for screening. As such it is possible that the expressed beliefs reflect rationalisations for attendance or non-attendance. Because of these and other difficulties confirmation of the results must await more carefully designed longitudinal studies. It must also be noted that the extensive use of regression analyses in cross-sectional health research without demonstration of any subsequent predictive validity to address the same behavioural outcomes is a significant problem in health psychology (Roberts and Brunner, 1998). In the absence of replication, the mere presence of an interesting or indeed a complicated model to explain an important behaviour cannot be taken as sufficient evidence of the validity of the explanation. If psychological attributes are really associated with some outcome, then this fact needs to be demonstrated with data collected on another (future) occasion.

In future, genetic testing may be used to identify those whose behaviour confers elevated health risks. Recent work by Krauss (quoted in Wise, 1998) indicates genetic differences in how people respond to low-fat diets, with people possessing the low-density lipoprotein (LDL) subclass B pattern having a three-fold higher risk of coronary heart disease compared to those with larger forms of LDL cholesterol. From this he argued that diet plans and drug regimens may be tailored to people with particular genetic predispositions. Such developments may not only benefit those at high risk but avoid unnecessary deployment of health promotional resources on those unlikely to benefit. The introduction of genetic screening on a wide scale would, however, have enormous psychological consequences. In order to take maximal advantage of these developments people will need a good understanding of the concept of risk, as well as informed knowledge of what are appropriate steps to take given a specific test result be it positive or negative (Macdonald *et al.*, 1996; Humphries, Galton and Nicholls, 1997).

ETHICS AND HEALTH PROMOTION

Psychologists have naturally shown interest in identifying and highlighting the most successful means for producing persuasive messages, rather than in identifying the most effective ways to resist them! The so-called 'Yale model of communication', for instance, identified five important elements (Zimbardo, Ebbesen and Maslach, 1977). These concern the source of the message (e.g. the source should be credible); its nature (e.g. short clear and direct; it should be one sided where the audience is sympathetic and two-sided where it is not); the medium in which it is delivered (e.g. is it personal, or on radio television etc.); the intended target (e.g. conclusions explicitly stated are more effective unless the audience is well-informed); and the situation in which it is received (home, cinema etc.). Using the knowledge of what makes a communication maximally effective lays the communicator(s) open to the charge of manipulation.

It is customary to assume that health promotion is in everyone's best interests; that failure to direct behaviour towards healthier ends is the only rational course of action. This perspective, however, ignores the fact that maximising health status is but one of many potential goals, and even when other goals are acknowledged it is rarely questioned whether there can be a rational conflict of interest between them and the pursuit of better health. That health should occupy the prime position amongst the numerous competing motivations in life is certainly open to question. Unhealthy behaviours such as smoking or drinking may clearly seem unhealthy from one vantage point – but if construed as methods for coping with stress in the absence of other less harmful means, their elimination may no longer be so straightforwardly desirable, certainly as far as the person smoking or drinking is concerned. Exhorting people to eat healthily, drink sensibly, refrain from smoking and practice safer sex whilst ignoring the functions which particular behaviours have in people's lives or the situational factors (usually social, economic or emotional) which govern them, is at once both a poor method of promoting health and an arrogant one. In this field, as in psychology as a whole, there is a real danger that empirical issues of how people *do behave* can get turned into moral issues of how they *should behave* (Leahey, 1991). Morality, of course, points in both directions – and just as there is a legitimate concern for the welfare of individuals faced with the demands of larger social organisations, there is the issue of how individual's behaviours impact on others. Whether it be public drunkenness or the presence of infectious disease, the state and behaviour of an individual may have serious consequences for the well-being of numerous other people. Just how the needs of the larger social good are to be balanced against the needs and freedoms afforded to individuals is a difficult matter – but one that is worthy of the attention and thought of psychologists as well as moral philosophers.

Summary and conclusions

A broader notion of Health Promotion developed from the recognition that health education alone did not provide a sufficient basis for behaviour change. However, substantial difficulties stand in the way of good scientific evaluation, as most campaigns are not amenable to the use of randomised controlled trials – the gold standard of medical intervention evaluation. This often means that finding suitable control groups with which to compare the effects of campaigns and interventions is almost impossible. Where an intervention in different geographical areas is under scrutiny, then it is important that accurate matching is performed and, where this is imperfect, appropriate statistical procedures are used to gauge its effect. Qualitative evaluation – for example how media information was appraised, and how this varies with personal or social characteristics – can be a useful adjunct but should not be the sole aim of an evaluation, as it is asking too much for people themselves to be aware of what might be quite subtle changes in their behaviour as well as the problem of demand characteristics inherent in a situation where people know that the intention was to change their behaviour.

The review in this chapter has suggested a number of possible routes whereby people's health may be enhanced. These include economic, mass-media, legal/civic, community and individual routes. Psychological factors have indirect roles in the chains of causation leading from economic, mass-media and legal measures, and more direct roles in community and individual measures. Although lifestyle factors are strongly implicated in ill-health, the evidence suggests that the targeting of general and specific populations through community, economic and legally enforced measures are more effective in changing behaviour than the direct targeting of individuals through lifestyle changes and health screening. Ebrahim and Davey Smith (1997) argue that health protection through national fiscal and legislative changes should have a higher priority than health promotion interventions applied to general and workforce populations and counsel against exporting the current paradigm to poorer countries as a means of preventing chronic disease.

Discussion points

A   Consider the role health psychologists might have in understanding people's responses to genetic testing.

B   In what other areas of health psychology are an understanding of people's lay theories of health and illness of practical benefit?

Suggested reading ··

Davison, C., Frankel, S. and Davey Smith, G. (1992) 'The Limits of Lifestyle: Reassessing "Fatalism" in the Popular Culture of Illness Prevention', *Social Science and Medicine*, **34**(6): 675–85.

Part 4
Society and Health

Attempts to justify the growth of Health Psychology in the late twentieth century usually extol the relationships existing between behavioural factors and health outcomes (Taylor, 1995). More often than not students are presented with a research digest of the principal means by which the health of individuals will be compromised, less often discussion may turn to the various means by which health and well-being may be actively enhanced. Another strand which underlies the expansion of health psychology addresses the changing nature of the delivery and evaluation of health care. Useful as these frameworks have been for equipping students with a knowledge of the role psychological factors may play in health and illness, or indeed for championing the cause of health psychologists in the health-care system, they really only provide half the story.

To look behind the social distribution of health is not simply to seek alternative levels of explanation for causes of ill-health (though that is one possibility), but to discover how people's psychological responses to life are shaped by the wider social, historical and economic milieu. One interpretation of the role of science is to explain variation in the occurrence of natural (or social) phenomenon (Liebert and Liebert, 1995). If we restrict our endeavours to understanding variations in health outcomes or determinants of health outcomes which occur at the level of the individual, then we may never come to understand how variations in these attributes may themselves be following patterns which exist at more broader levels of abstraction, such as community, culture or society. Such a strategy is in fact implicit whenever researchers seek explanations for psychological (or indeed social) phenomena at the biological level. Our principal aims in this section are therefore to examine the relationships between health and various forms of social, cultural and economic organisation.

chapter

13

Social Class and Health

'Grinding poverty takes the edge off most things including life.'

Tom Baker (*Who on Earth is Tom Baker?*, 1977)

INTRODUCTION

Preeminent amongst the organising principles which exist in all human societies is the idea of social status. Following Weber (Gerth and Wright Mills, 1970) sociologists identify three defining characteristics of social hierarchies – class, status and power – reflecting in turn, ownership and control of resources, social importance and power to shape events in society. Several schemes have been proposed to operationally define social position (Marshall *et al.*, 1989), and though each presents its own difficulties, health researchers are agreed that the construct is an important and useful one, whether defined through educational level, housing tenure, car ownership, income or socioeconomic status (see Box 13.1). The most frequently utilised model of social class in the United Kingdom has been the Registrar General's, a hierarchy of occupations graded by level of occupational skill. Assigning occupations to socioeconomic groups in this way is an imperfect process, with reliability in the

---

BOX 13.1 Indicators of socioeconomic status

Herrnstein and Murray (1994) constructed an index of socioeconomic status based on those variables most frequently used to assess it; education, family income and occupation. In a sample of 7447 subjects, the composite index derived was found to be highly reliable (Cronbach's $\alpha = 0.76$). The correlations are shown below:

	Mother's Education	Father's Education	Parental Occupation
Father's education	0.63		
Parental occupation	0.47	0.55	
Family income	0.36	0.40	0.47

region of 80–90 per cent (Leete and Fox, 1977; Goldthorpe and Payne, 1986a). Recently the Office of National Statistics has introduced a new system for classifying socioeconomic position in response to the changing nature of industry and occupations (Sacker *et al.*, 2000) (see Table 13.1).

Table 13.1   Measurement of social class in the UK

(a) Registrar General

Class	Description	
1	Professional occupations	**Non-manual**
2	Intermediate occupations	**Non-manual**
3N	Skilled occupations	**Non-manual**
3M	Skilled occupations	**Manual**
4	Partly skilled	**Manual**
5	Unskilled	**Manual**
6	Armed forces	–

(b) Office for National Statistics

Class	Description
1	Higher managerial and professional
2	Lower managerial and professionals
3	Intermediate occupations
4	Small employees and own account occupations
5	Lower supervisors, craft and related occupations
6	Semiroutine occupations
7	Routine occupations

INEQUALITIES IN MENTAL HEALTH

It has been known for a long time that various types of mental ill-health show relationships with indicators of social class. Hollingshead and Redlich (1958) found class gradients in the diagnosis of schizophrenia. Hare (1956) discovered that prevalence rates (existing cases) for the disorder were approximately eight times higher in areas of low socioeconomic status, whilst incidence rates (new cases) were three times higher. In their classic study, Brown and Harris (1978) found depression to be almost three times more common in working-class women.

Data taken from the Health and Lifestyles Survey (Blaxter, 1990b) of 9003 respondents in England, Scotland and Wales are presented in Figure 13.1. These show a strong linear relationship between socioeconomic position and psychological disturbance, identified using the 30-item version of the General Health Questionnaire. The lower the socioeconomic position the higher the probability of severe psychological disorder. Data from the same survey also find manual occupational groups consume significantly more alcohol per week. The most striking feature of the data depicted in the figure is not simply that those in the lowest socioeconomic category exhibit poorer mental health than those in the highest, but that there is a gradient from the lower to the higher classes. Whilst it would be legitimate to invoke absolute levels of poverty or material deprivation as possible explanations of differences between the highest and lowest groups, these types of explanation cannot be offered as

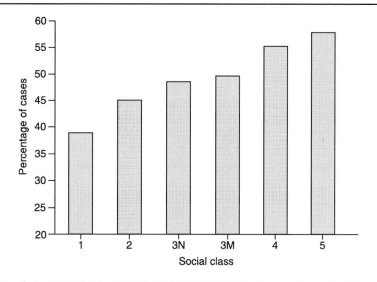

Figure 13.1   Psychiatric cases identified by GHQ30 scores by Registrar General's social class

plausible accounts for a gradient. A similar problem will be encountered when we come to consider physical health.

Gradients in psychological health have been found in other studies. In the White-hall II study of 10 308 civil servants, socioeconomic status was denoted by six employment grades ordered in terms of decreasing salary (Marmot *et al.*, 1991). Stansfeld and Marmot (1992) found the prevalence of minor psychiatric disorder (as measured by the GHQ and Affect Balance Scale) to be greater in lower grades, though only for men, echoing findings from a number of other European countries of an association between psychiatric disturbance and social position (Hodiamont Peer and Syben, 1987; Vázquez-Barquero *et al.*, 1987). Significant age-adjusted trends for declining well-being with occupational position have also been reported for social functioning (Hemingway *et al.*, 1997), satisfaction with life, positive affect, hostility, job satisfaction and various forms of social support (Marmot *et al.*, 1991). Relationships with low social class have also been reported for suicide and para-suicide (Gomm, 1996; Drever, Whitehead and Roden, 1996).

These data paint a picture of increasing risk of mental ill-health the further down the socioeconomic ladder one moves. To make matters worse, not only are work-ing-class people more likely to be diagnosed psychotic as a consequence of this, but once they come into contact with the mental health services, they may then be deemed more suitable for physical treatments (Goldberg and Huxley, 1980).

On the face of the above evidence, it might be thought that a straightforward relationship would exist between happiness and social class. A number of studies, however, have found at best a weak to moderate relationship between the two (Argyle, 1994; Harding, 1985) although it is the very rich who are usually found to be the happiest (Diener *et al.*, 1993). In poorer countries the relationship is stronger, which perhaps suggests that as the level of material scarcity in a society diminishes and physical survival into adulthood is relatively assured, the potential sources of happiness multiply and intercede to weaken the basic relationship. When examin-ing the relationship between social class and happiness one must be alert to the possibility that the meaning of the term happiness itself varies with class.

The existence of socioeconomic differentials in so many areas of mental health raises the hope that common causal pathways underlaying them could be identified. An explanatory framework of this type must of necessity be formal – identifying only the gross general features in diverse forms of disturbance. The goal of producing such a framework would certainly be in accord with the dominant paradigms in psychology and medicine for understanding mental health, a paradigm in which the study of the content of mental experience has, according to some commentators, frequently been relegated to the fringes of scientific activity (Boyle, 1996). Examples of such general formal constructs which could be invoked to account for class differences include stress (Tarlov, 1996), control (Syme, 1990) or, more broadly still, negative life events.

Hopes of elucidating common pathways, however, must be tempered by the realisation that although most forms of psychological distress show the pattern of poorer psychological functioning with declining social standing, there are very notable exceptions. Preeminent amongst these are disorders associated with eating. Both bulimia and anorexia nervosa are more usually to be found amongst middle-class educated women (Cohen and Hart, 1988). Manic depression, too, appears to be more prominent in the middle classes (Gomm, 1996). And yet another aspect of psychological well-being, self-esteem, shows only a weak relationship with social class (Gecas and Seff, 1990) – the strength of the relationship being in part dependent upon the method of assessing class (education is a more powerful predictor of self-esteem than either income or occupation). Finally, the Type A behaviour pattern (TABP) identified as a risk factor for coronary heart disease (see Chapter 21) actually shows a social class gradient in which it is more commonly found in people of higher social status (Marmot *et al.*, 1991), although the risk for cardiovascular disease (as we shall see later in this chapter) decreases markedly with increasing socioeconomic status. The space commonly allocated to TABP in health psychology texts (for example Sarafino; 1995, Taylor, 1995; Sheridan and Radmacher, 1992), being substantially greater than that given over to social class, both overstates its importance and illustrates the difficulties which psychologists have had in appreciating the impact of wider social forces on human health. As a further illustration of this, a leading textbook of abnormal psychology (Rosenhan and Seligman, 1989) and a recent health psychology text (Banyard, 1996) contain no mention whatsoever of social class in the books' indexes.

Difficulties for formal models do not end with the problems presented by the nature of the variation in different psychological indicators. They are further compounded by potential uncertainties surrounding the meaning of social class, notably in relation to gender. In a meta analysis conducted by Kessler (1982), earned income emerged as the strongest predictor of mental health in men, whilst for women it was level of education. These differences may arise in part because women's employment chances are structured differently to men's (Goldthorpe and Payne, 1986b), but also because under certain circumstances women may actually be less inclined to affirm themselves as members of a particular class (Marshall *et al.*, 1989). Moreover, social class may be better understood, not as an enduring fixed identity, but as a developmental pathway through a landscape whose social, occupational, economic and psychological characteristics are inextricably interwoven. Social class then is less a thing – more the outcome of a complex social dynamic. The relevance of the various pathways whereby people arrive at a particular social location are accentuated when we consider gender precisely because the journey to the different social classes is so different for them (Roberts *et al.*, 1993).

The diverse relationships between forms of psychological well-being and class – the fluid nature of class itself, the attendant inevitability that class identity and class position must be actively constructed by social actors – all these mean that in order to understand class inequalities in mental health we must turn to the study of content, the actual substance of people's lived experience. Much of the data gathered by anthropologists and social psychologists, dealing with variations in communicative style (Coupland, 1984), non-verbal behaviour, linguistic codes (Bernstein, 1971) and social interaction within and between social classes (Argyle, 1984), have not adequately informed us of how people actually go about making sense of their lives in a society organised on class lines. Useful published accounts of working-class experience in different occupations are rare (for example Ryan and Sackray, 1984). Perhaps the most well-known and enduring of these is Sennett and Cobb's (1972) classic study of blue-collar workers in Boston, revealing the 'hidden' psychological damage which the class system inflicts on its subjects.

That these works draw their strength from qualitative analyses is perhaps no accident, but before we can consider further the importance of qualitative studies in unravelling the links between class and health we must first review the relationships between social class and physical health.

INEQUALITIES IN PHYSICAL HEALTH

Work documenting socioeconomic differences in physical health have a long history (Fox and Benzeval, 1995). More recently, interest in the topic of health inequalities within the United Kingdom received renewed vigour from publication of the Black Report (Townsend and Davidson, 1982) which summarised available knowledge and examined a number of possible explanations. Whitehead (1987) provided a further update and suggested that inequalities had widened in the intervening years. This situation is not unique to Great Britain. A substantial body of evidence gathered over different periods of time and across a diverse range of countries shows raised mortality for those of low socioeconomic status (Wilkinson, 1986; Fox, 1989; Illsley and Svensson, 1990; Mackenbach, 1992; Macintyre, 1997; Whitehead and Diderichsen, 1997). Mortality gradients can be found for nearly all causes of death. Death rates from approximately 80 per cent of the most important 80 causes of death are more common in blue compared to white-collar workers (Wilkinson, 1996b). Some of the steepest gradients are found for behavioural causes: drug dependence, non-dependent drug abuse, mental disorders, accidents (caused by fire and flames) and homicide. Figure 13.2 shows a comparison of Standardised Mortality Ratios in the UK for men in social classes I and V between 1991 to 1993 (Office for National Statistics, 1997). Considered in toto, the likelihood of a premature death for people in unskilled occupations and their children is considerably greater than for professionals (Figure 13.3). In the first Whitehall study (Marmot *et al.*, 1984), where a more sensitive measure of socioeconomic status was employed, even steeper gradients were observed. Alternative measures of socioeconomic position such as the Cambridge Scale which assess social position based on social and material advantages, as well as lifestyle as reflected in friendship choice, provides a better predictor of mortality in women where steeper gradients are found than when the ONS system based on occupation is used (Sacker *et al.*, 2000).

Mortality is of course a very crude indicator of health. The general pattern observed in mortality statistics, however, is repeated when morbidity is considered. Examples

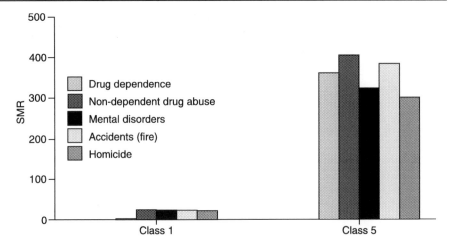

Figure 13.2   Comparison of standardised mortality ratios for men in social class I and V (United Kingdom, 1991–93): selected causes

Source: Adapted from *Health Inequalities*, Office for National Statistics, Crown Copyright 2000.

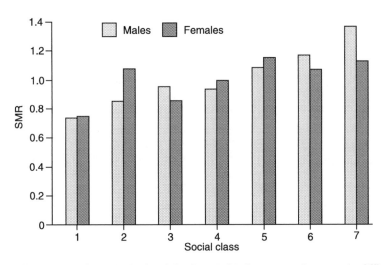

Figure 13.3   Age-adjusted relative risk of mortality for men and women by Office for National Statistics social class (United Kingdom)

Source: Adapted from A. Sacker *et al.* (2000), *British Medical Journal*, **320**; 1303–7, with permission from the BMJ Publishing Group.

of these include angina, diabetes, ischaemic heart disease, physical symptoms reported in the preceding two weeks (Marmot *et al.*, 1991), chronic bronchitis (Davey Smith *et al.*, 1991), dental caries (Marcenes and Sheiham, 1992), hypertension, lung function (Cox *et al.*, 1987), obesity (Blaxter, 1990b), long-standing illness (Lahelma *et al.*, 1994), general physical health (Aiach and Curtis, 1990), perceived health (Hunt, McEwen and McKenna, 1985b; Marmot *et al.*, 1991), self-reported pain and physical functioning (Jenkinson *et al.*, 1993; Hemingway *et al.*, 1997), risk of low birthweight (Botting, 1997) and sickness and absence from work (Stansfeld *et al.*, 1995). There is even evidence to suggest that available instruments for measuring general health such as the SF-36 actually underestimate social class differences, because of ceiling effects in the responses of members of higher socioeconomic groups to some of the scales (Hemingway *et al.*, 1997). As with mental health, where such a general pattern is found, the question for researchers is whether explanations should be sought in terms which stress a general susceptibility to ill-health, or whether a diverse set of specific explanations is required (Haan, Kaplan and Syme, 1989; Marmot, 1996).

ORIGINS OF SOCIAL CLASS DIFFERENCES IN HEALTH

Four categories of explanation are usually advanced in explanation of the relationship between socioeconomic inequality and health (Townsend and Davidson, 1982; Carroll, Bennet and Davey Smith, 1993). These are described as *artefact, selection, material/structural* and *cultural/behavioural* explanations. These categories largely deal with characteristics of lifestyle and environment acting in adulthood (Bunker *et al.*, 1989) or on the long term effects of circumstances in early life (Barker *et al.*, 1990).

1. Artefactual explanations

These explanations argue that methods of measuring class are responsible for inflating the magnitude of health inequalities. One example of this is *numerator denominator bias*. Standardised mortality ratios which are calculated on the basis of deaths per social class divided by the numbers from each class as determined by census returns may introduce error due to inaccurate reporting on the census of the deceased person's occupation by surviving relatives, who may elevate the dead person's social status. Specific investigations to examine this possibility have, however, produced little supportive evidence that these could account for mortality differences between the classes (OPCS, 1978).

Accounts based on the changing size of social class groups have been similarly unsuccessful. Although social class V has declined in size, this cannot explain the widening of inequalities over time; when classes IV and V are considered together evidence of widening inequalities is still present. Similarly, between 1971 and 1981 class I grew as a proportion of the total population and yet the mortality rate declined (Davey Smith *et al.*, 1991).

2. Selection theories

Selection theories try to explain the disproportionate presence of mental and physical ill-health in people of lower social standing as a consequence of health-related social mobility. Social mobility may be related to health in at least two ways: firstly, ill-health may function as a barrier to upward social mobility, and, secondly, it may lead to downward social drift.

The 'social drift' hypothesis contends that the relationship between socioeconomic status and ill-health is brought about by people with severe health difficulties drifting down the social scale through being unable to meet the role demands and expectations of their class position (Pilgrim and Rogers, 1993). With regard to mental health, research has produced equivocal findings (Goldberg and Morrison, 1963; Fox *et al.*, 1986; Fox, 1990; Jones *et al.*, 1993) with recent arguments focusing on the methodologies employed for estimating the mobility of the mentally ill compared to the general population (Rodgers and Mann, 1993; Fox, 1993). With regard to physical health there is evidence that people with chronic illness (Meadows, 1961; Roberts and Brunner, 1996) move down the social hierarchy. However, the interpretation that this is somehow a consequence of their inability to perform adequately in their social or occupational roles is not supported by the evidence. Moreover, Bartley and Owen (1996) found that the chronically ill were more likely to be excluded from the workforce during periods of high unemployment and to remain excluded during periods of economic recovery. This strongly suggests the presence of institutional barriers to the employment of people with chronic illness and disability, rather than it being a matter of abilities or qualities which reside in individual people.

The weight of the evidence thus suggests that even where social drift occurs, explanations couched at the level of the individual will not suffice. In addition, compelling reasons exist for believing selection could at best make only a small contribution to observed inequalities. Fox, Goldblatt and Jones (1985) found social class differences exist after retirement, when there is no opportunity for social mobility and as Blane *et al.* (1993) point out, the years during which ill-health is most prevalent do not match the years in which mobility is most common.

3.   Behavioural/Lifestyle theories

Theories of this kind have in recent years received a great deal of attention. There are many reasons for this, quite apart from the failure of selection and artefact hypotheses to account satisfactorily for social class variation in health. Bartley (1985) describes the emergence of lifestyle explanations in the United Kingdom as a consequence of the apparent failure of the welfare state to eliminate health inequalities. Psychologists came into this scientific and political arena with a tradition of examining behaviour divorced from the wider social context in which it occurs, firm in the belief that the appropriate domain of psychological investigation is the individual or relations between individuals. Such a stance has not been without its critics (Bannister and Fransella, 1971), though even social psychologists, where this tradition is weaker, have been reluctant to venture beyond the study of group dynamics or interpersonal behaviour.

Lifestyle theories have enjoyed strong political support, notably during the 1980s (Blane *et al.*, 1996). This support has been bestowed because of the political convenience which comes from envisaging the poor health of many as a consequence, not of inequitable social organisation with its attendant economic, psychological and material disadvantage, but the consequence of people's own propensity to damage themselves. There is also of course a wealth of scientific data to link social class with unhealthy behaviours. The further down the social hierarchy one looks, the more likely are people to smoke, take less exercise, follow poorer diets, be obese (Pekkanen *et al.*, 1995; Argyle, 1994; Marmot *et al.*, 1991) and to avoid taking preventive health care measures (Benzeval *et al.*, 1995). Marmot, Shipley and Rose (1984) found that differences in smoking, obesity, physical activity, blood pressure and plasma cholesterol, however, could explain only a small part of the social class gradient for heart attacks (see Box 13.2). Similarly, in the Alameda County study in the United States, Haan *et al.* (1989) found death rates were still one and a half times greater in the poorest groups compared to the richest after controlling for smoking, drinking and exercise. The evidence clearly suggests that though lifestyle factors play an important role, they fall a long way short of providing a complete explanation for class differentials, not withstanding the fact that there are numerous instances in which the elevated risks of death in lower socioeconomic groups have not been related to lifestyle (Marmot *et al.*, 1984; Davey Smith *et al.*, (1991).

BOX 13.2   Explaining social variations in health

When researchers attempt to understand differences in ill-health between groups they use methodologies whereby the health outcome is modelled in terms of a small number of predictor variables which are used to try and explain either variation in the health outcome (when it is measured on an interval scale), or to describe the relative risk of undergoing it (when it is measured on a nominal scale). In these techniques, based on a form of statistical analysis called multiple regression (see Lewis-Beck, 1980), 'explanation' does not necessarily provide a causal explanation of the health outcome, but provides a 'statistical' explanation of the degree of variation (the variance) associated with it. Essentially it is a more complex form of correlational analysis. Once social class differences have been observed, for example, a model is produced in which the health outcome of interest is expressed in relation to social class. Other variables are then added to this model in an attempt to reduce or eliminate the observed socioeconomic gradient. In the study referred to in the text, Marmot *et al.* (1984) found they could only account for 40% of the variation in heart attacks between the different occupational groups by using lifestyle variables. In a similar manner, Brunner *et al.* (1993) were able to account for between 43% and 70% of the variance in one of the risk factors for cardiovascular disease (apolipoprotein AI) by using a statistical model based on health-related behaviours.

The existence of class differentials in behaviours, however, ignores a more fundamental question – which is why those differences exist in the first place. An instructive example is provided by social class gradients in cigarette smoking, which in the earlier part of this century were the reverse of how they appear now (Davey Smith *et al.*, 1991). Smoking was then regarded as an esteemed activity which conferred social status on its consumers, and vestiges of these notions remain in our current attitudes towards the smoking of cigars. The increased take up of smoking which occurred in lower socioeconomic groups can thus be seen as an attempt to mitigate low esteem bound up with people's view of their own social standing.

Concerns have also been expressed about attempts to exhort people on low incomes to take up healthier lifestyles without examining whether the financial possibilities exist for them to do so (Davison *et al.*, 1992), or whether a belief system emphasising the importance of lifestyle above psychological comfort is viable within the confines of certain social, economic and cultural circumstances. Some workers (for example Calman, 1987; Blaxter, 1993, 1997) have drawn attention to how economically disadvantaged people have internalised the lifestyle message so as to believe themselves responsible for their own health, whilst at the same time many seem unable to accept that unskilled workers do have poorer health than professionals. Regrettably, however, the health belief model (Fishbein and Ajzen, 1975) has often been criticised for ignoring people's social environment and the conditions under which people's health beliefs are acquired (Furnham, 1988). Lifestyle theories have therefore not only had limited success in explaining class differences in health, but have also made it harder for the victims of inequality themselves to see the material origins of their plight.

4. Material structural explanations

Explanations of this type posit the relationship between class and health to be an expression of the material inequalities built into society by the partitioning of social groups into hierarchies. Opinions vary as to whether childhood circumstances and early life experiences are the antecedents of later inequality, or whether the procession of class-based circumstances occurring throughout life hold greater importance. In this context there is great difficulty in disentangling effects arising from social class position in childhood and social class position in adulthood, when these two are known to be correlated (Power *et al.*, 1996). Results obtained by Van de Mheen and colleagues (1997) in the Netherlands are consistent with adult health differences between educational and occupational groups stemming principally from the childhood environment, the principal determinants being financial circumstances, father's occupation and mother's education. Van de Mheen *et al.* were unable, however, to distinguish direct (social causation) from indirect (selection) effects. Direct effects may operate, for example, when health problems in childhood arising from unfavourable socioeconomic conditions relate to social position in adulthood through a lowering of educational opportunities (Wadsworth, 1986). Indirect effects on the other hand may exist when circumstances in childhood, such as material deprivation, separately influence both later occupational success and health in adult life.

A wealth of information now exists on the relationship between social and material deprivation and health. Within this framework, different operational indicators of deprivation have been constructed. These include Jarman underprivileged area scores (Jarman, 1983), the Carstairs index (Carstairs, 1981) and the Townsend index (Townsend *et al.*, 1988). All these indices are used to describe variations in conditions within geographical areas. The Townsend index, for example, is constructed from four variables: the percentage of private households not owner occupiers, the percentage of private households possessing a car, the percentage of private households containing economically active members who are unemployed, and the percentage of private households with more than one person per room. These constitute measures for wealth, income, unemployment and overcrowding, respectively. With the Carstairs index strong associations have been found between levels of deprivation and mortality (Carstairs and Morris, 1989), whilst use of the Townsend index has suggested that local levels of deprivation may account for around two-thirds of the variation in health between electoral wards. Sloggett and Joshi (1994), meanwhile, have argued that all excess mortality in deprived areas can be accounted for by the concentration of individuals with poor personal or socioeconomic circumstances.

There is no doubt that ecological factors such as homelessness, unemployment, poor housing, poor nutrition, pollution and dangerous working conditions place heavy burdens on the health of people exposed to them. Such indicators can explain the concentration of ill-health in lower socioeconomic groups, but accounting for the gradients in health which run from higher to lower groups is not so easy. Attempts to understand these social patterns call for the data to be looked at differently. In recognition of this, workers have turned to the psychosocial environment. Sapolsky and Mott (1987) have even provided evidence of the importance of this in wild living baboons. Differences in high-density lipoproteins usually protective against cardio-vascular disease were found to vary with dominant or subordinate social status; the dominant animals having the higher levels. Low-status animals also evidenced pro-longed elevation of blood pressure and glucocorticoid levels after a stressful encoun-ter. Differences in lipoprotein levels have also been reported in human populations (Brunner *et al.*, 1993). Sapolsky and Mott attributed the source of the differences they observed to the chronic stress of competing for social and material resources, and analogies with the dynamics of human social organisation can easily be made in this respect. However, Lynch *et al.* (2000) are careful to remind us that the effects on health of living in a social hierarchy are contingent on the relations between social position and material living conditions, which themselves comprise a whole matrix of unequally shared social and material resources such as health services, transporta-tion, environmental controls, housing quality, food and so forth.

Some workers have attempted to delineate the main features of the psychosocial environment, invoking variables which describe important aspects of the working environment (e.g. control over work, job satisfaction), social circumstances outside work (e.g. difficulty paying bills, negative aspects of social support) in addition to health behaviours (Marmot *et al.*, 1991; Marmot *et al.*, 1997a). This strategy has en-joyed mixed success. In the Whitehall II study, the addition of the above variables explained about half of the variation in self-rated health (itself a good predictor of mortality), all of the variation in depression and eliminated differences between occupational grades in whether they found little meaning in life (Marmot *et al.*, 1997a). They did not, however, have much impact upon the distribution of smoking by occupational grade – an indication that they would be unable to account for re-lationships existing between social position and smoking-related diseases. However, recently Marmot *et al.* (1997b) using logistic regression found that they could pro-vide a complete account of the excess coronary heart disease in men and women in lower occupational grades by using a model incorporating psychosocial factors in the workplace, height and coronary risk factors.

An interpretation consistent with the data which has been gathered to date, is that different factors operate to produce ill-health at different levels of the socio-economic hierarchy. At the lower end direct material deprivation may have a stronger role – with the distribution of broader environmental and social resources (psychosocial factors among them) playing an increasing role as material needs are met. This is, of course, a somewhat simplified picture. The success in accounting for variation in aspects of well-being may be a step forward, though it does not provide us with an explanation of exactly how psychosocial factors bring about poor psycho-logical well-being. Rather it may tell us something of the general nature of the causal pathways which we must seek to construct. There are further reasons for caution too. Associations between predictor and outcome variables can arise spuriously when the predictor variables themselves are capable of serving as proxy measures for what is being predicted. Thus, where psychological well-being is concerned, feeling satisfied with work or feeling in control could both be construed as dimensions of happiness. In this respect the relationships between these variables and happiness could simply be tautological and as such be of little help in understanding the pathways which link social class to well-being.

This concurs with the conclusion reached earlier that research must engage further with the detailed contents of people's lives. Given that social class appears to be a major stressor, it would be instructive to examine the myriad ways in which social hierarchies function on a day to day basis to determine the context of living; shaping people's attitudes, self efficacy, hope, confidence and access to personal and social resources. Additional support for this contention comes from Wilkinson (1992, 1996a, 1996b), Kawachi *et al.* (1997) and Wolfson *et al.* (1999) who have shown a strong relationship between income distribution and life expectancy; countries and regions with wider income distributions exhibiting poorer overall levels of health. Recent work by Kennedy *et al.* (1998) showing a correlation between income distribution and self-rated health across the 50 states of the United States strongly suggests that this relationship is not a result of confounding by individual variables such as ethnicity, education or income, but stems rather from the direct effects of income inequalities on structuring the social environment – possibly through a disinvestment in various forms of social capital; such as civic participation, trust and norms of reciprocity between community members (Kawachi *et al.*, 1997). Such a relationship appears to be predicated upon a shift in developed countries from absolute to relative standards of living. The rise to prominence of relative standards carries with it the implication that above the satisfaction of the essential material prerequisites for living, active evaluation of one's position in society relative to others can have detrimental effects when the result is a lower evaluation of oneself relative to some arbitrary but valued social criterion. These processes of evaluation and their initial effects must by definition be psychological – and their end results may well be physical ill-health (Tarlov, 1996).

The importance of psychological constructs, though, is not that they are necessarily the primary causes of health inequalities, far from it, but that they are but one pathway mediating the effects of the social structure on the health of individuals (Lynch *et al.* 2000) – that is, one avenue through which the consequences of the social structure (understood as the myriad of ways in which social and material resources are unequally distributed) are conveyed to people in psychological and psychosocial ways. A prime example is the unequal distribution of stressors and the means to cope with these (Stronks, Van de Mheen, Looman and Mackenbach, 1998). Without the introduction of qualitative methodologies it is difficult to imagine how the dimensions of society, social change or social power as they appear on the ground can be fully appreciated and subsequently used to bridge the gap between social, psychological and medical models (Roberts, 1996). But it is important to underline the fact that the role for health psychologists here is in producing understanding, not directing interventions to tackling inequalities. Carroll, Bennett and Davey Smith (1993) explicitly caution against inferring from the data anything but a minor role for psychological interventions, and warn of the dangers of victim blaming which might ensue should such strategies be followed. It is therefore regrettable that in some quarters (for example Phillips and Pitts, 1998) health psychologists have already set about turning this message on its head.

Summary and conclusions •

Gradients in physical and psychological health exist for a wide range of conditions. These show trends of declining well-being with decreasing social status however social status is measured. Some of the steepest of these gradients exist for behavioural causes of death. A variety of types of explanation have been advanced to explain this association, which include measurement artefact, health selection, behavioural and material factors. The evidence to date suggests that only a small role exists for social (health) selection, though behavioural factors are believed to play a big role. Psychologists' interest in health inequalities has deepened as research suggests that in addition to material factors the psychological disadvantages associated with relative material inequality play a major role in transmitting physical ill-effects from the social hierarchy to the population. Understanding of the causal routes by which the effects of the social structure are conveyed to individuals is incomplete. Qualitative investigations concerned with the details of people's lives may be needed to reveal important aspects of these processes.

Whilst research on the social patterning of health has been predominantly concerned with class, there are other important social dimensions which also embody differences in social power and social status – gender, physical disability and ethnicity. It is to these that we will now turn.

Discussion points ·

A   Are social gradients inevitable in human societies?

B   Is ill-health an inevitable consequence of any hierarchy?

C   On the basis of the material presented in this section, suggest several intervention strategies which might be employed to reduce the extent of health inequalities

(D) Why should psychologists be interested in social class differences in health?

Suggested reading ·

Argyle, M. (1994) *Social Class*. (London: Routledge).

Blane, D., Brunner, E. and Wilkinson, R. (eds) (1996) *Health and Social Organisation: Towards a Health Policy for the 21st Century*. (London: Routledge).

Carroll, D., Bennett, P. and Davey Smith, G. (1993) 'Socio-Economic Health Inequalities: Their Origins and Implications', *Psychology and Health*, **8**: 295–316.

Marmot, M. and Wilkinson, R.G. (eds) (1999) *Social Determinants of Health*. (Oxford: Oxford University Press).

Wilkinson, R. (1996) *Unhealthy Societies*. (London: Routledge).

14

Gender and Health

'Where did we go wrong? The women on tablets, pills and tranquillisers, the men who don't feel human 'til they've had a drink.'

Trevor Blackwell and Jeremy Seabrook (*A World Still to Win*, 1985)

INTRODUCTION

We have seen in the previous chapter that the primary causes of the unequal social distribution of health arise not from fundamental differences in biological constitution, but in forms of social organisation. If we consider differences in health between males and females we face a situation where the undoubted biological differences between the sexes are confounded with the different social environments in which males and females are reared, come to maturity and live as adults. However, the study of gender and health cannot be restricted to a simple review of health differences – for this presupposes a commonality of health outcomes. A number of authors have sought to redress what they see as the political domination of medical theory and practise by men in favour of a psychology of women's health and health care (Nicolson and Ussher, 1992). The development of interest in health care issues for women whilst obviously welcome leads one to ask whether it is possible for an understanding of men's and women's health issues to proceed within a common explanatory (and indeed methodological) framework, or whether we are to see distinct psychologies of men and women's health emerging. This is no idle question. The future development of psychology must contend not only with the gendered nature of human existence, or the desire to distinguish nurture from nature in accounting for gender differences in health, but also resolve the increasingly acrimonious debate as to what are the most appropriate methods for a scientific investigation of personal and social life. The issue of qualitative versus quantitative methodology is particularly pertinent in the present context precisely because how people make sense of their lives appears to be of central importance to their physical and emotional well-being. Before touching on some of these broader issues in investigations of gender and health we will begin by reviewing some of the main findings concerning differ-ences in health between males and females where common reference points are available.

HEALTH DIFFERENCES

Mortality

It has commonly been observed that mortality for men occurs earlier than for women, although the extent of this difference varies across countries (Whitehead and Diderichsen, 1997). In the United Kingdom between 1987–91, mean life expectancy at birth for males, at 72.3 years, was 5.6 years less than for women (78.9 years). In the United States in 1996 the disparity was 6.2 years (Kranczer, 1997). This gap of approximately six years occurs across a number of countries including the Netherlands (Whitehead and Diderichsen, 1997) and Japan (Marmot, 1996) irrespective of the absolute levels of life expectancy, although in some poor countries, particularly in South Asia, men outlive women (Doyal, 1995). Here systematic economic and cultural discrimination against females – including in extreme cases female infanticide – have resulted in the erosion of whatever biological advantage they possess. Within the United Kingdom the difference has remained fairly constant, although between the early 1970s and 1990s 12 industrialised countries witnessed a narrowing of sex differences in life expectancy at birth (Trovato and Lalu, 1996). In contrast to this, in Russia, where life expectancy has declined rapidly in recent years, gender differences have widened (Leon *et al.*, 1997; Walberg, McKee, Shkolnikov, Chenet and Leon, 1998).

To seek explanations for the pattern of gender differences a number of questions can be posed. Where life expectancy is changing, is the change uniform across all sections of society or are some groups (whether by age or socioeconomic position) more exposed to the possibilities of change than others? In brief, where in the life-cycle is death most likely to occur and to whom? We can also inquire into the degree of overlap which exists in the causes of death for each gender and what the determinants of life expectancy are for males and females. If we consider Russia as an example, increases in mortality have been greatest between 40 and 50 years of age with the largest increases occurring for alcohol-related deaths, accidents and violence (Leon *et al.*, 1997). In addition, the fall in men's life expectancy shows a strong relationship with increasing unemployment and recorded crime and occurs most notably in areas with unequal distributions of household income. This illustrates the need to link structural, economic, cultural and psychological explanations of health outcomes. The question for psychologists is not simply why do men drink heavily under stress – but why in this particular culture at this point in time is this seen as a viable option for men to cope with the stresses engendered by economic change? In this context it is necessary to know the nature of the different stresses which impact on men and women, and to understand the behavioural pathways which are open to them within their cultural system. If behaviour is not considered within its social context, it loses meaning both within any wider explanation of events and within the nexus of meanings in which it is situated for each individual – a lesson we have already abstracted from our discussions of health promotion.

Comparisons of cause-specific mortality for males and females shows males are considerably more likely to die from cardiovascular disease, injury and poisoning, suicide, violence and AIDS (see Table 14.1). As Edwards (1996) discusses, risk-taking and aggressive behaviour commonly exacerbated by alcohol are more prevalent among men and are thus likely to explain the higher fatalities from accidents and violence. Furthermore, men are more likely to have unhealthy lifestyles – drinking too much alcohol, smoking and eating a less-healthy diet (Wright, Harwood and Coulter, 1992)

Table 14.1   Major causes of death 1991–93, in UK men and women aged 20–64

	Males (%)	Females (%)
Diseases of circulatory system	39.5	14.8
Malignant neoplasms	31.4	29.8
External causes of injury and poisoning	12.0	3.7
Violence	6.1	<1.0
Diseases of respiratory system	5.5	3.6
Suicide and undetermined injury	4.2	1.6
HIV infection	0.7	0.0

Source: Adapted from *Health Inequalities*, Office for National Statistics, Crown Copyright 2000.

with there being evidence to suggest that at least some of the gender differences in alcohol consumption arise from gender differences in sensation-seeking and coping styles (Watten, 1997). Gender differences are also found in childhood; males having an elevated perinatal/early childhood death rate, a greater proportion of congenital birth defects, greater vulnerability to sex-linked disorders, a higher accident rate from childhood onwards, and a higher incidence of behavioural and learning disorders (Verbrugge, 1988). This evidence implicates both biology and lifestyle acting in concert to produce the observed differences in death rates.

It would be erroneous, however, to believe that biology and lifestyle alone explain all of the differences in death rates. Reviewing available evidence on biological (e.g elevated plasma lipids, lipoproteins, blood pressure, oestrogen levels) and behavioural risk profiles (e.g. smoking, diet, exercise, alcohol consumption), Weidner (1998) noted that they were able to explain only 40 per cent of the variation in the gender ratios of coronary heart disease across communities, and proposed psychosocial variables such as coping styles, social support, psychosocial stress and gender roles as plausible candidates to explain the additional variance. One of the limitations in such attempts is that studies which have sought to identify risk factors for cardiovascular disease have generally focused on men – probably at the cost of more accurate models being developed. The focus on men has doubtlessly arisen as a result of their higher death rate, although because of women's longer lifespan their lifetime risk is in fact almost equal (Tunstall-Pedoe *et al.*, 1997) and in post-menopausal women is the single most important cause of death (Doyal, 1995). The emphasis in recent research on the psychosocial environment is to be welcomed, although an analytic strategy which continues to rely on factors which are localised in individuals is unlikely to be successful in accounting for variations between communities. The correlation between regional variations in risk factors with levels of coronary heart disease mortality (Crombie, Smith, Tavendale and Tunstall-Pedoe, 1990), for example, strongly suggests that ecological variables should figure in any explanatory model.

Data from the Scottish Heart Health study provides a further instance where contextual factors are likely to play a differential role in cardiovascular disease outcomes for men and women. Although coronary risk factors for men and women in this study were similar, **Type A behaviour** in women was associated with lower coronary risk (Tunstall-Pedoe *et al.*, 1997). The reasons for this may lie in reported gender differences in the psychosocial components of Type A behaviour (Knox and Follman, 1996). Davidson, Hall and MacGregor (1996) also found differences in these: hostility scores derived from a structured interview were related to higher systolic

Type A behaviour pattern is behaviour characterised by hostility, impatience, competitive drive and vigorous speech. In contrast, the so-called Type B pattern comprises a relative absence of these charateristics. Has been investigated for its possible connection with coronary heart disease.

blood pressure in men, but lower systolic blood pressure in women. This suggests that it is not simply the cognizance of hostile feelings and intentions which is important, but how these are expressed. Sherman, Higgs and Williams (1997) have also summarised important differences between men and women in their locus of control. For men this is more likely to be internal and shows a stronger relationship to achievement motivation. Men are also more likely to believe themselves capable of controlling uncontrollable events and to score higher on unrealistic perception of personal control. Locus of control thus shows differential gender relationships to two of the three components of Type A behaviour, which supports the contention that Type A behaviour has a different meaning in women's lives than it does in men's. Significantly, Toves, Schill and Ramanaiah (1991) found that internality appears to mediate the relationship between stress and symptoms only in males. If Type A behaviour is seen as a manifestation of individuals' attempts to control stressful experiences (Sarafino, 1998), then a fuller understanding of gender differences in coronary heart disease will need to address gender differences in risk appraisal and coping responses together with the different sources of psychosocial stress and the situations in which they are faced. Many situational influences on risk factors (Bages, Warwick-Evans and Falger, 1997) as well as the actual overt behavioural differences in men and women's lifestyles are rooted in the interpretations, expectations and correlates of gender-typed behaviour, which as Weidner postulated adversely affects male mortality. Waldron (1976) has even suggested that three-quarters of the difference in life expectancy can be accounted for by sex-role related behaviours, with up to one-third of this stemming from differences in smoking.

While a thorough review of the social psychology of sex-role differences is beyond the scope of this chapter, some relevant themes from this literature can be identified. Brannon (1976) highlights four themes to the male role – the need to be different from women, to be superior to others, to be independent, self-reliant and to be more powerful than others – through violence if necessary. It takes little imagination to construct links between these dispositions and health-related behaviours and outcomes. Women's greater propensity to consult their general practitioners for most illnesses (Bradlow, Coulter and Brookes, 1992), for example, can be construed as a consequence of males avoiding behaviours which may connote vulnerability or weakness, though this is unlikely to be a simple matter of conscious decision-making. Females are not only more emotionally expressive than males but more able to decode emotions (Manstead, 1992), which means that in the present psychosocial environment men appear less able than women to recognise physical and emotional distress. Added to this, women receive more emotional and practical support (Pikó, 1998) and possess more awareness of relationship issues replete with greater skills in consoling those in distress (Brehm, 1992).

Morbidity

While mortality data can be interpreted unambiguously to denote real gender differences in underlying health, the evidence with respect to morbidity is not so clear. Until recently, prevailing wisdom held that women's rates of morbidity were greater, covering amongst other things the reporting of symptoms, rates of acute illness, numbers of chronic conditions, self-evaluation of health, use of outpatient services and consumption of both prescription and non-prescription drugs (McIntyre, 1993; Sweeting, 1994). So ubiquitous have these different patterns become, that as

McIntyre, Hunt and Sweeting (1996) point out it has become almost standard practice to analyse data for males and females separately (see for example Roberts *et al.*, 1995) and in so doing to overlook the nature and extent of any differences between them.

However, on re-analysing data from the *Health and Lifestyle Survey* (Cox *et al.*, 1987) and the West of Scotland Twenty-07 studies (West, Ford, Hunt, McIntyre and Ecob, 1994) McIntyre *et al.* found that the customary picture was far from accurate. With the exception of migraine (for which there was a female excess at all ages), no sex differences at any age were found for a variety of chronic conditions currently experienced – respiratory disorders, diabetes, hernia, epilepsy, cancer or high blood pressure. Variable differences according to age were obtained for asthma and stomach troubles, arthritis/rheumatism, and ulcers or gastric problems (McIntyre *et al.*, 1996). A similarly unexpected pattern was observed when examining symptom reporting in the previous month. Although overall symptom reporting conformed to the expectation of greater reporting by females at all ages, when the data were categorised as either physical (constipation, colds/flu, bladder/kidney problems, stiff/painful joints, sinus/catarrh/blocked nose, trouble with eyes, trouble with ears) or 'malaise' (sleep problems, concentration difficulties, nerves, worrying over every little thing, always tired) a female excess in physical symptoms only appeared at 39 years in the West of Scotland study, and at 56–60 years in the Health and Lifestyle study (see Table 14.2), though a female excess for 'malaise' appeared at all ages. Hence this re-analysis shows an excess for females at all ages only in the more psychological dimensions of health. This pattern has been interpreted by other workers (for example Verbrugge, 1989) as showing that men tend to suffer from an excess of serious disability and disease – the kinds of conditions which might shorten life – whereas women's excess tends to be in symptoms and less serious conditions.

McIntyre *et al.*'s and Verbrugge's reading of the data carry important implications for understanding sex differences in mental health – where women are more likely to be diagnosed with neurotic disorders, affective psychoses and vague mental disorders in contrast to men, for whom schizophrenia, alcoholism, personality and psychosomatic disorders feature more prominently. What exactly do these differences

Table 14.2   Mean number of symptoms reported: Health and Lifestyle and West of Scotland Twenty-07 survey

Symptoms	West of Scotland			Health and Lifestyle		
	Age	Males	Females	Age	Males	Females
All	18	2.80	***3.56	18–22	1.98	***2.64
	39	2.07	***2.62	36–40	2.04	***2.81
	58	2.77	***3.40	56–60	2.61	***3.86
'Malaise'	18	0.72	***1.02	18–22	1.06	***1.30
	39	0.65	***0.92	36–40	0.56	***1.02
	58	0.80	***1.16	56–60	0.73	***1.30
Physical	18	1.33	1.43	18–22	1.02	1.09
	39	0.69	*0.83	36–40	0.88	0.95
	58	1.09	1.17	56–60	1.07	***1.42

*** $p < 0.001$ * $p < 0.05$

Source: Adapted from *Social Science and Medicine*, **42**(4): 617–24, S. McIntyre, K. Hunt and H. Sweeting, 'Gender Differences in Health. Are Things Really as Simple as they Seem?' Copyright (1996), with permission from Elsevier Science.

represent? One suggestion is that such gender differences represent the outcome of different, socially learned coping styles and strategies (Coleman, 1995). Similarly it can be argued that women are more able to articulate and express symptoms of distress and discomfort. From this it might be posited that the expression of milder degrees of emotional distress might protect women from developing more serious forms of psychological disorder. Such a hypothesis would concur with classical Freudian theories on the functional benefits of catharsis as well as with more modern variants such as are contained in co-counselling (see for example Jackins, 1985). Whilst this is open to debate, one interpretation which can be rejected is that the excess of symptom reporting or of mental distress amongst women merely denotes a greater readiness to complain given equal levels of distress. This assertion can be readily contradicted as research shows no gender differences in the likelihood to recognise and respond to cancer symptoms in those with cancers of the colon or rectum – in fact women were more likely to delay seeking care (Marshall and Funch, 1986) and among people with x-ray evidence of osteoarthritis it was men who were more likely to report pain than women, independent of disease severity (Davis, 1981). Finally, in a double-blind comparison, men were more likely to over-rate the severity of cold symptoms when compared with ratings made by a trained clinical observer – and this bias was not associated with age, class or marital status (McIntyre and Pritchard, 1989).

Overall, it is hard to avoid the conclusion that the data contained in the research base strongly supports a role for the socialisation patterns cast over males and females in explaining at least some of the differences in health (Gove, 1984). This is most apparent in the preponderance of females suffering disturbances of body image and in eating disorders (McCauley, Mintz and Glenn, 1988). As women increasingly challenge their allotted place within this scheme one will expect the balance of these differences to shift. Arber's (1997) model of structural influences upon women's health (Figure 14.1) provides a useful guide to where such shifts in health are likely

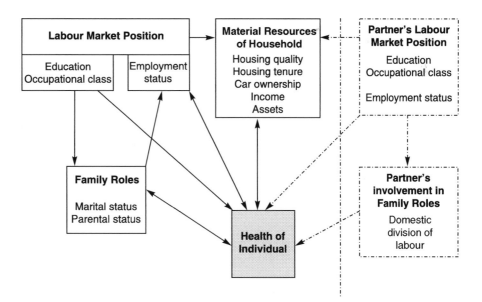

Figure 14.1   Factors Influencing women's health

Source: After Arber (1997).

to originate; summarising as it does the relationship between women's social and economic relationships (family roles, labour market position, available material resources, partners involvement in family roles and partner's labour market position) and health. Numerous studies attest to the relationship between inequalities in women's health and the roles they occupy in family and occupational life. Married women usually have better health than previously married women (both divorcees and widows), mothers are usually healthier than childless children, and women employed outside the home are generally healthier than women not so employed (El stada, 1996). A common finding is that marriage benefits men more than it does women (Gove, 1984; Haavia-Mannila, 1986). Berkman and Syme (1979), for example, found that marriage was associated with significantly decreased mortality in men but not women. A somewhat different view has been offered by Wood, Rhodes and Whelan (1989) who concluded that whilst women appear to suffer more in marriage than men (that is, they experienced more negative consequences) they also experienced more positive feelings – a result endorsed by Mookherjee's (1997) findings that married women report more satisfaction than married men. Women's elevated experience of distress in marriage compared to men also appears to be associated with decrements in immune function (Mayne *et al.*, 1997).

As psychologists have preoccupied themselves with the health problems of men and women in industrialised societies – indeed they have sought justification for their existence in understanding and addressing these – it can be easily forgotten that the impact of structural factors upon health are felt more keenly in poor countries. As noted earlier, in many poor countries women's health is constrained by the operation of cultural and economic barriers to the material and social resources necessary for good health. The effects of this are particularly acute in the area of reproductive health and family life. In India, for example, early marriage and childbirth are a major determinant of women's health and play a substantial part in maintaining socioeconomic underdevelopment. Maternal deaths frequently stem from socioeconomic factors – lack of antenatal care being just one aspect of this – with further unequal consequences for male and female offspring. When the mother dies, statistically this doubles the chances of death for her surviving sons and quadruples it for her daughters. It is argued that women's empowerment at all levels of society is now urgently required to improve health and nutrition (Buckshee, 1997), although the scope for self-empowerment by women may be highly place-specific and dependent upon such factors as the personal characteristics of community leaders, cultural norms regarding the acceptability of women's political action, local histories of such action and the social, economic and cultural composition of the local community (Asthana, 1996). The importance of these factors has also been borne out by the responses of the gay community to the HIV/AIDS epidemic.

Education is a potent weapon in the struggle for improved resources and health, as the literacy levels of women are known to affect reproductive behaviour, contraceptive use, child-rearing practises, hygiene practises and access to jobs. An analysis by Hobcraft (1993) of 25 developing countries found that mothers' education exhibited a linear relationship to the survival chances of her offspring. Against this the ravages of poverty may leave young children, especially girls vulnerable to prostitution, drug use and drug trafficking with all the attendant risks of HIV infection, and severe emotional disturbances. Chikwem *et al.* (1988) in a study of 767 prostitutes in Nigeria found that less than 18 per cent of them had any secondary school education. The health risks associated with prostitution are not of course confined to sex workers in poor countries. Although in the UK at present HIV/AIDS does not appear to be a significant issue for prostitutes, amongst those who inject drugs it most certainly poses a threat, alongside hepatitis B and other infections (Barnard and McKeganey, 1996). Neither should the risks to sex workers be seen as one confined to infectious diseases; violence, robbery and rape are ever-present dangers. In view of the risks and human misery which this type of work entails, the prospect in the UK at least that education may become a risk factor for engaging in prostitution as one of the consequences of increasing debt for students must be viewed with considerable unease (Roberts, Towell, Golding and Weinreb, 1999).

GENDER ISSUES IN HEALTH RESEARCH

Amongst those interested in exploring relationships between health and gender, a core theme is how people make sense of their experiences of health and illness – how our perceptions and interpretations of our mental and physical states are allied or become allied to our sense of who we are as males and females, and how dominant or important schemas of masculinity and femininity are in shaping and directing our responses in matters of health. The social implications of the increasing bodily differences between boys and girls which accompany development have been the subject of extensive research (Crawford and Unger, 1995) with cross-cultural data illuminating the role of social pressures on women to maintain thinness. Non-white women, for example, appear to be at less risk, as white standards of beauty are deemed less applicable (Root, 1990). Indeed, the patterning of psychological disturbance across gender which we have referred to above owes something to the internalisation of widespread negative evaluations of the normal female body shape. Low self-esteem, body dissatisfaction and depression are just some of the sequellae.

A failure over many years within the mainstream academic community to address issues of power in relationships between men and women and how these have shaped the psychological discourse on men and women has led in recent years to the development of feminist psychologies. Critics have argued that work has tended not only to equate patterns of male behaviour with normative standards (and in so doing ignores women), but has also prescribed a male research agenda in choosing the questions for scrutiny and determining how they should be investigated (Kahn and Jean, 1983) (see Box 14.1). Thus despite heart disease being a major cause of mortality in women it has been construed as essentially a male disease with the ensuing result being that many clinical trials have failed to include women. Women are also less likely to receive kidney transplants and to be referred for diagnostic tests for lung cancer – even after adjustment is made for smoking status (Pitts and Phillips, 1998). Mental health issues have been similarly denuded of the gendered context in which they arise; recognising that the relative frequency of depression in women owes something to learned patterns of behaviour does not go far enough. What is generally missing from such accounts is that depression and learned helplessness are responses to situations where there is an imbalance of power. Miller (1986) stresses that what are seen as feminine characteristics – lack of initiative, passivity, the desire to please others and dependency – are all psychological consequences of subordination. The determining influence of power relationships – in their nature and their strength – for individual functioning is an insight from social psychology which might equally be applied in other areas of health where questions of social power arise (for example social class, disability and ethnicity). Given the neglect in health psychology of the question of power and dominance it comes as no surprise to find that in one of the few areas where this should have been an obvious issue – health communication between experts and lay people – gender is also frequently omitted (Gabbard-Alley, 1995).

BOX 14.1 How should sex differences be studied?

A major theme in contemporary psychology concerns the appropriateness of methods for studying humans (Cooper and Stevenson, 1998; Morgan, 1998). There are a number of reasons why the debate over the use of quantitative and qualitative methods has relevance for studying health in males and females. Firstly, qualitative methods may be extremely useful for getting a handle on how men and women, boys and girls experience their gendered condition and their relationships to the wider culture which in proscribing their roles determines so much behaviour. As such, data derived from qualitative methods may constitute an important source for understanding behaviour in its everyday context and how people make sense of their experience (Green and Britten, 1998) and which thereby is also useful for generating hypotheses. Secondly, the debate has frequently crystallised into a dispute between the methods favoured in the natural sciences which are seen as quantitative, reductionist and 'masculine', and those on the other hand which are seen as qualitative, discursive and 'feminine' – the latter not surprisingly at the forefront of feminist research into women's health, while comparative work on men's lives is lacking.

Writers critical of traditional scientific methods have argued that they are impersonal, positivistic, ideologically biased, cement a power imbalance between researcher and researched, rely on an assumption that the world of subject and object can be neatly partitioned, that personal meaning or the creation of meaning between actors cannot be adequately understood by using them, and furthermore that prediction and control are undesirable goals for a human science (Gillett, 1996). One cannot doubt the dangers present in objectifying human beings – 20th century history stands as a sad exemplar of this. However a crucial aspect of this debate centres on the degree to which it is useful to assume the existence of an objective world, regardless of individual human perspectives. Many who have taken up residence in the qualitative camp reject outright the notions of validity and reliability implicit in scientific measurement and argue for the elevation of subjectivity to preeminence in psychological discourse (Sherrard, 1998). It is true that many non-scientific disciplines – e.g. history, literature and drama express truths about the human condition that are difficult to imagine being rendered with equal clarity or poetry by scientific endeavour, but this is no argument for rejecting scientific method – unless the scientific project truly favours omniscience as its only goal and denies the validity of other forms of knowledge in their own domain.

Gödel's theorem, known within the scientific community for the best part of this century, formally acknowledged the impossibility of capturing all truths within any one axiomatic system, yet it is widely recognised that this provides no rationale for abandoning science. Regrettably this debate repeats many fundamental mis-readings of what doing science is all about. Chamberlain, Stephens and Lyons (1997), for example, contend that qualitative methods emphasise meaning over measurement. But how can you have meaning without measurement? Those who have utilised Personal Construct Theory (Kelly, 1955; Bannister and Fransella, 1981) recognise that understanding meaning is central to any psychological undertaking and moreover, because meaning is construed as an act of differentiation between aspects of the recognisable world, it sits comfortably with scientific measurement. Furthermore, courses in research methods begin by

BOX 14.1 **Continued**

imparting an understanding of nominal levels of measurement for which numbers are arbitrarily assigned; too much of the disdain for scientific method which some proponents of qualitative methods advance appears to devolve from a dislike of using numbers to understand relationships between events or perceived elements.

Science, though, is not just about using numbers – far more fundamentally it is a method of thinking which seeks to produce knowledge about relationships existing between events in the world, knowledge which is in principle broadly replicable and which points towards a reality which exists irrespective of opinions. If this position is rejected then there are no clear grounds for favouring one point of view over another – even within the qualitative domain – and it becomes all a matter of who has the most political clout to impart their preferred 'knowledge' (Morgan, 1998). Hopefully, rather than treading too far down the post-modernist pathway, the way ahead will involve some fusion between the richness of qualitative methods and the rigours of scientific method with which they must be tested in order to cement useful knowledge into the scientific culture.

In an attempt to redress the bias in the research agenda, feminist researchers have concentrated on events unique to women such as pregnancy, childbirth and menstruation which have been appropriated as medical events within the biomedical framework (Smith, 1992). It should be noted in passing, however, that there is still relatively little research into non-reproductive conditions that affect women such as incontinence and osteoporosis (Doyal, 1995). What is characteristic of these new approaches is that they question the validity of pathologising natural events and ignoring the meanings which individuals construct from them. The concept of post-natal depression (PND), for example, has been challenged by a number of writers (Nicolson, 1986; Ussher, 1992). Like many other psychiatric diagnostic entities (see Chapter 5) its validity is not clear cut. No distinct reasons have been given as to why PND should be considered different from any other depression, in fact the major predictors of PND – relationship difficulties, low social support, life stress and previous depression – are all strong predictors of depression in general (Whiffen, 1992). Nor for that matter have the demarcation lines been clearly drawn for how close the depressive episode needs to be to childbirth in order to be classed as PND. Such uncertainties in diagnosis lead to wide variations in estimates of prevalence which currently range between 3 and 25 per cent (Nicolson, 1989). But at the heart of this critique is the collision between two fundamentally opposed viewpoints; whether the misery and melancholia in women which can accompany childbirth is best characterised as flowing from internal mechanisms or the meanings which these events have. The very concept of PND itself seems to preclude any resolution of this question outside the biological realm – for although men can undoubtedly become depressed following the birth of a son or daughter they can never receive a diagnosis of PND. An examination of the social context of care-giving finds men who raise children or care for elderly and sick relatives can suffer depression (Richman, Raskin and Gaines, 1991; Ussher, 1992). After reviewing available evidence, Lee (1997) concluded that the high rates of depression in mothers of newborns and indeed young children is largely a consequence of the social expectations surrounding parenthood which leads to the act of raising children being envisaged as the almost exclusive concern of women who must also sacrifice their own needs in the interests of their children. And these expectations are created and in turn reinforced by the planned sexual division of labour in our society involving as it does the scarce allocation of social resources to 'women's work'. This conclusion sits uncomfortably within modern medicine whose prevailing orthodoxy places women at the mercy of their biological destiny – usually conceptualised as hapless victims of 'raging hormones'. It can be argued that the self-empowerment for women, involving their recognition of the constraints imposed by ideology and organisation – in rich and poor countries of the world – depends upon a psychological liberation from dependence on medical technology and medical theory which the orthodoxy promotes.

Does this then mean that biological considerations have no relevance at all where mood disturbances in mothers are concerned? Some (for example Lee, 1997) have argued that post-partum psychosis, rare as it is, is very likely a consequence of the biological processes of childbirth – although this conclusion seems to have been reached more on the basis of an absence of evidence showing a role for social factors rather than convincing biological evidence in its own right. There has also been considerable controversy around the concept of premenstrual syndrome (PMS); like its cousin PND there is also no agreement as to what constitutes the syndrome. Ussher (1992) notes the dilemma facing those who advocate its existence as a neatly definable set of symptoms:

> The guru of PMS, Katrina Dalton, has described it as 'the reoccurrence of any symptoms at the same time in each menstrual cycle' ... yet as there are over 150 different symptoms which have been associated with PMS with little agreement as to core symptoms, this definition could describe a myriad of different 'syndromes', each quite distinct. (Ussher, 1992, p. 41)

Again problems abound in defining the relevant time period in which the problems can be diagnosed – whether it be three days, five days, seven days prior to menses, or the entire second half of the menstrual cycle. No clear cut biological aetiological factors have been found – with a plethora of inconsistent findings. Bloch et al. (1998), for example, examined basal levels of several hormones (for example beta-endorphin, ACTH) previously reported to differ in women with PMS compared with controls. Mood and behavioural symptoms were assessed by daily self-ratings and objective ratings. The study failed to find abnormalities in plasma levels of either ACTH or beta-endorphins in women with PMS and also failed to replicate a previous observation of high free testosterone levels in women with PMS. The authors concluded that the results do not support the hypothesis of a primary endocrine abnormality in PMS. A severe methodological difficulty in double-blind placebo-controlled studies in this area is the possibility that subjects in their randomly allocated groups may be able to hypothesise on the basis of the subjective sensations they experience (or do not experience) due to treatment, which group they are in, thus rendering interpretations of results unclear. Results also show no evidence of poorer cognitive performance (attention, memory, cognitive flexibility, overall mental agility) compared to controls, even though PMS sufferers may have more subjective feelings of inadequacy compared to a matched group of controls (Morgan et al., 1996).

Breast cancer is another area which has attracted the interest of workers involved with women's health issues. In the United Kingdom breast cancer deaths comprise 28 per cent of all cancer deaths in women (Office for National Statistics, 1997). Breast cancer can of course have a significant impact on body image. Ganz et al. (1998), however, found that breast cancer survivors, though reporting more frequent physical and menopausal symptoms compared to age-matched women, reported comparable levels of general health and sexual functioning. One factor which may be influential in women's psychological adjustment to cancer is whether they are able to actively participate in deciding their treatment. Fallowfield *et al.* (1994) found that the risks of anxiety and depression were significantly reduced in those women who had been treated by surgeons favouring breast conservation or who offered choice of either chemotherapy or mastectomy in comparison with those treated by surgeons who favoured mastectomy. What women will make of recent advances in the mathematical modelling of the natural history of breast cancer – work which suggests surgery may actually provoke relapse (Bonn, 1998), particularly in women with large tumours – should prove interesting.

With rapid advances in reproductive technology and changing social relationships around childbirth and parenthood, increasing attention is being devoted to the psychological consequences of infertility. There is evidence that this may impact worse on females: Link and Darling (1986), for example, found 40 per cent of wives and 16 per cent of husbands had scores indicative of clinical depression, whilst Harrison *et al.* (1984) found women, but not men, in infertile partnerships reported higher state anxiety scores than controls. Part of women's sense of failure may derive from the plethora of testing and the exposure to technological procedures which may be sources of considerable stress (Johnson, 1996; Eimers *et al.*, 1997). Regrettably the literature which has explored the psychological consequences of infertility has been characterised by a number of flaws, including over-sampling of women, small sample sizes, non-representative samples, an overreliance on self-reports, a failure to study those who have not sought treatment and poor statistical analyses. It is argued that future investigations need to consider both the duration of infertility and the duration of treatment (Greil, 1997). Boivin (1997) contends that the widespread idea of the stressful nature of infertility may have been overstated based on the unrepresentative experiences of a few highly distressed people who feel overwhelmed by their plight, in contrast to a majority who manage to cope well despite some degree of distress. Certainly very few patients actually take up offers of psychosocial counselling. It is difficult to resist the notion that the subject of infertility has become burdened with an over-importance that owes much to stereotypical notions of womanhood and maternity that are endemic in our society, and which receive regular reinforcement from media coverage of the latest medical 'breakthroughs' in infertility treatment.

In contrast to women's health, the health concerns of men have not been explicitly linked to a political context. In part this is due to the reluctance of male researchers to adopt qualitative methods in their work, though it must be acknowledged that the lack of impetus derives in part from the hegemony which men's health has enjoyed as the default option in health science for so many years. Paradoxically, this dominance has not prioritised the study of behavioural risk factors in men which are heavily linked to their sex-role – as if questioning the structure of the male sex role has been somehow off-limits. Recent interest in men's health as with women has been directed towards reproductive and sexual health – examples being HIV and AIDS, and cancers of the testes and prostate glands. It is apparent that with prostate cancer a lack of data has hampered the initiation of a decisive public health response. Uncertainty surrounds the best treatment options for early detected cancers (Lu-Yao and Yao, 1997) and whether a widely available screening service would be effective in reducing mortality (Dearnaley and Melia, 1998; Charatan, 1998). Difficulties have stemmed from whether screening based on prostate-specific antigen (PSA) can predict whether a man has a cancer that will progress to cause ill-health or death (Morris, 1998). There is a pressing need for this matter to be resolved as prostate cancer looks set to increase – it is predicted to be the most common cause of cancer death in males by the year 2010 (*The Lancet*, 1998) and it cannot be doubted that the psychosocial consequences for men are serious. Work in this area has been sparse, though Clark *et al.* (1997) using focus groups suggested three major areas of concern for men – self-perceptions, anxiety about the effects of treatment, and concern with the process of decision-making and treatment. They supplemented this with formal psychometric analyses which indicated several specific dimensions of prostate cancer-related quality of life – masculinity, body image, sexual problems, partner affection, partner anxiety, cancer-related self-image, cancer distress and cancer acceptance. Professionally-led support groups have been shown to be effective in reducing anxiety, providing a feeling of being involved with treatment, enhancing coping and providing a more positive outlook for people with the disease (Grégoire, Kalogeropoulos and Corcos, 1997). More research is awaited in this area. Given the resource implications which such groups would have, it would undoubtedly be of interest to compare the effectiveness of professionally-led groups with ongoing peer support networks. Comparison between groups of male patients with colorectal and prostate cancers and women with colorectal and breast cancers has highlighted gender-specific concerns with quality of life. For men, vitality and personal resources have been found to be particularly salient, and for women psychosocial well-being and physical competence (Dibble *et al.*, 1998). These clearly reflect concerns about the challenges which these cancers present for the ability to fulfill key aspects of the gender role – for males the need to be independent and for women to maintain physical appearance and social interaction with others.

Where gender issues in health have come in for scrutiny, the lion's share of the attention has been devoted to adult health. Interest in children's health has had to contend with a shortage of suitable instruments for assessing subjective health. Of late a number of projects have made significant progress in correcting this oversight, including the Child Quality of Life (CQOL) questionnaire (Graham, Stevenson and Flynn, 1997), although unfortunately no analyses by gender are reported with this, and the Child Health Questionnaire, a new instrument developed at the birthplace of the SF-36. Use of this latter instrument has found few differences (boys scored significantly poorer on bodily pain) in general health between boys and girls. Interestingly, ratings made by parents indicated that they thought more health differences existed between the sexes than did the children (Landgraf and Abetrz, 1987). By their very broad nature, however, such generic assessments may well fail to detect important differences in the social environment that may impact on well-being. In trying to explain sex differences in referral rates for gender-identity disorder (almost seven times as many boys as girls are likely to be referred), Zucker, Bradley and Sanikhani (1997) were unable to find differences on several indices of general behaviour problems on the Child Behaviour Checklist. They also found that the percentages of boys and girls meeting DSM-III-R criteria for gender-identity disorder were comparable. However, they noted cross-gender behaviour was tolerated less in boys than girls by both peers and adults. Disadvantages for boys were also found in the disabled community, where Sobsey, Randall and Parrila (1997) reported boys were more likely than girls to be represented amongst the neglected and abused (physically and sexually) compared to non-disabled children. Among the non-disabled it is girls who are some two to three times more likely to be sexually abused (Finkelhor, 1994). The introduction of disability into the equation opens up a whole new set of issues which have considerable bearing on how people respond to the psychosocial environment in which they live and how responsive that environment is in meeting people's differing physical and psychological needs. Thus in the following chapter we will be examining the social context of disability and how psychologists have viewed the lives and problems of disabled people.

Summary and conclusions

Substantial differences in life expectancy exist between males and females, and in advanced industrial societies females enjoy an advantage of some six years. Males are considerably more likely to die from cardiovascular disease, injury, suicide, violence and AIDS. Risk-taking and aggressive behaviour are more prevalent among men and may explain the higher fatalities from accidents and violence, whilst unhealthy lifestyles may contribute to earlier death from CHD. Gender differences in childhood suggest a role for biological factors in explaining the differences, though biology and lifestyle alone are unlikely to explain all the differences. Further psychosocial variables (coping styles, social support, psychosocial stress and gender roles) have been postulated as additional explanatory variables. The evidence for gender differences in morbidity is less clear cut. Some researchers have interpreted the data to argue that males suffer from an excess of serious disability and disease – the kinds of conditions which might shorten life – whereas women's excess tends to be in symptoms and less serious conditions. Data does not support a view that this excess amongst women denotes a greater readiness to complain given equal levels of distress.

Research on ill-health has been criticised for failing to adequately address issues of power in relationships between men and women and how these have shaped scientific discourse. This has led in recent years to the development of feminist psychologies in which critics have argued that a male research agenda exists influencing the questions asked and how these should be investigated.

Discussion points

A To what extent are the questions posed by health psychologists and the methods they use affected by the cultural influences acting on them as males and females?

B How far can differences in life expectancy between males and females be explained by psychosocial factors?

C Why has interest in cardiovascular disease in males received so much attention compared to women, while at the same time prostate cancer has been relatively ignored?

Suggested reading

Arber, S. (1997) 'Comparing Inequalities in Women's and Men's Health: Britain in the 1990s', *Social Science and Medicine*, **44**(6): 773–87.

Buckshee, K. (1997) Impact of Roles of Women on Health in India', *International Journal of Gynaecology and Obstetrics*, **58**(1): 35–42.

Doyal, L. (1995) What Makes Women Sick: Gender and the Political Economy of Health. (London: Macmillan).

Nicolson, P. and Ussher, J. (eds) (1992) *The Psychology of Women's Health and Health Care*. (London: Macmillan).

Disability, Health and Illness

'Non-disabled people feel that our differentness gives them the right to invade our privacy and make judgements about our lives. Our physical characteristics evoke such strong feelings that people have to express them in some way. At the same time they feel able to impose their feelings on us because we are not considered to be autonomous human beings.'

Jenny Morris (*Pride against Prejudice*, 1991)

INTRODUCTION

Including a chapter on disability in a book on health psychology might easily be interpreted as lending support to the medical model of disability – where the focus is on individuals and the nature of their impairments. The psychological questions posed within that framework inquire into people's adjustment (or lack of it) to being disabled, the wider context of which extends only to whether their impairment can be reduced or cured by medical intervention (Oliver, 1998). An increasing number of workers, not to say disabled people themselves, have become dissatisfied with the limitations which this imposes. We therefore wish to review the literature on disability from another vantage point, one which examines the lives of disabled people primarily from within a social model of disability. This sources the major restrictions on people's functioning in the social and economic realm and not the physical. Thus this asserts that disabled people are an oppressed minority group in society and that much of their psychological well-being or lack of it results from the oppression.

ADJUSTMENT AND DISABILITY

Criticism of the status quo in disability research is not itself new. Stubbins, (1977) noted that psychologists frequently view the problems facing disabled people as ones which can be overcome by the right attitude and motivation, and over twenty years later this is still the most frequently used model in psychological studies of disability (Johnston, 1995) where theoretical treatments of disability still focus intensely on 'adjustment' – particularly emotional adjustment. The case against this was eloquently expressed some time ago,

> Adjustment is seen to be the major prerequisite for a happy life for people who are disabled. It refers overtly to the capacity of the individual to accept the fact that s/he has a

disability, and get on and make the most of it. People who complain or are depressed or angry are seen as not being well adjusted. People who try to do something that the professional is convinced is too difficult are seen as not being well adjusted. As one explores the concept further, however, one finds that it actually means accepting the social environment that exists for people who are disabled, rather than accepting the disability itself. Thus someone who has recently become disabled is regarded as not yet having good adjustment if s/he is still complaining about the fact that s/he can no longer find work; if s/he admits defeat and adopts a new hobby that can be done in the home and stops grumbling about the sudden loss of income, then that person is deemed to be well adjusted. (Cross, 1981, p. 457)

This kind of cognitive set can lead to situations where disabled people are caught between a rock and a hard place – subject to criticism for being passive and apathetic or for being troublesome and independent. As Stubbins (1977) realised, this can mean that disabled people frequently have to contend with situations where what they are experiencing (impossible demands) and what they are led to believe they are experiencing (good care) do not coincide.

The adjustment framework, with its pernicious idealisation of normality, embodies two key features of medical models of mental health. Firstly, in assuming that people's behaviour can be adequately understood without a detailed knowledge of their circumstances (current or historical) and, secondly, in that the standards of 'expected' behaviour are value laden – determined by prevailing normative attitudes rather than empirical data – a recurring motif in the psychology of the oppressed. But is the slavish adherence to medical values sufficient to explain the compliance and lack of imagination exhibited by psychologists in this field or do more disturbing motives stalk the intellectual landscape? As health psychologists seek increasing professional recognition and a place at the table with the medical elite this is an important if uncomfortable question. How much does acceptance of psychological values in medicine depend on an investment by the profession in the existing structures of power? Herein lies a question which all those who work with users of social and health services must face, that of deciding to whom is their primary allegiance – the clients? themselves as workers? or the institution to whom their services are contracted? Regrettably it appears to be the institutions which often come out ahead. A national survey of cancer counsellors in the UK, found that the stated goals of the counsellors related to the setting in which they worked (Roberts and Fallowfield, 1990). Those working in a voluntary capacity were more likely to have goals oriented to empowering clients, in contrast to those working in hospice, hospital or community settings where goals were more likely to pertain to service provision, development, maintenance or expansion. A significant proportion (12%) had explicit goals directed towards getting patients to respond as they (the staff) wished. This was often stated in terms of getting people to accept their limitations and to try and live normally. This was the case whether working directly with the clients or in the case of children through their parents.

It is claimed that the philosophical underpinning of the medical model of disability stems from the World Health Organisation's (1980) distinction between impairment (the objective difficulty), disability (the effects of the impairment on everyday activities) and handicap (the effect of the impairment on social roles). Whilst psychologists have with few exceptions been content to work within this system – we have seen for example attempts to integrate the WHO model with models of coping and with social cognition models (see Figure 15.1) (Johnston, 1995) – disabled people themselves have forcefully rejected it. They have done this because in all the models

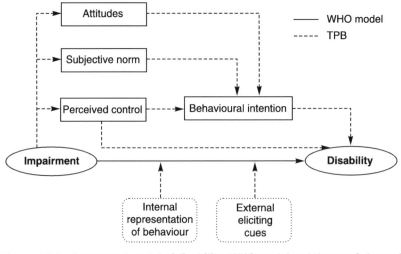

Figure.15.1   Integrated model of disability: WHO model and theory of planned behaviour

Source: Adapted from M. Johnston (1995) *The Psychologist*, **9**(5): 205–10. Reproduced with permission.

the direction of influence moves from the impairment towards disablement. In some respects the newer psychological models are actually a regression from the WHO model, which at least includes the social environment as a relevant dimension of concern. In the model illustrated, perceived control, attitudes and subjective norms are depicted as arising from the objective impairment. This significantly misrepresents how people come to construe the behavioural possibilities open to them as disabled people. Whether an impairment is congenital or acquired later in life it is incontestable that the behavioural repertoire for that person is in part determined by the social environment and the degree of investment which has been allocated to meeting people's needs. As Oliver (1998) observes, a lack of publicly available transport is disabling for the physically unimpaired. If it is the design of the physical environment in which humans live which precludes activity for people with specific impairments which would otherwise be attainable with adequate resourcing, then it is absurd to talk about the internal attitudes and perceived levels of control as central (psychological) variables determining the level of disability construed as an article of behaviour. That different health-related quality-of-life measures may produce significantly different profiles of social impact when administered to the same group of disabled respondents (Ziebland, Fitzpatrick and Jenkinson, 1993) merely confirms the inadequacy of determining the degree of social limitation without recourse to an assessment of the impact which the social environment itself makes. The model also oversimplifies how attitudes themselves may be formed within a nexus of interpersonal relationships, influenced by the process of others reflecting back to us their views of our own potentialities.

THE SOCIAL MODEL OF DISABILITY

The new perspective which the disabled peoples' movement demands sees disability as the result of physical, social and psychological barriers which prevent or reduce the opportunities to participate in community life for people with impairments (Oliver, 1996). Disabled people are certainly disadvantaged in the labour market (Blane, Davey Smith and Bartley, 1993) and have to contend with unemployment rates which are extremely high – a likely consequence of employer discrimination at the recruitment stage (Barnes, 1991). Those who are in work are also frequently in low-paid, low-skilled jobs which are unrewarding and undemanding. Work conducted in the UK has also found that people with chronic or long standing illnesses were excluded from the workforce as unemployment increased, but did not re-enter it as it fell (Bartley and Owen, 1996). Much work remains to be done on how occupational opportunities for people with specific impairments or chronic illnesses operate, although there is evidence that people with diabetes are disproportionately more likely to suffer downward occupational mobility and to be passed up for promotion (Roberts and Brunner, 1996). Further analysis demonstrated that this relationship held after controlling for social class, level of educational attainment, mental health, self-reported health status, and sickness absence in the preceding year. The results of this and other studies (see also Songer *et al.*, 1989) suggest that health-related social mobility is not a simple consequence of the intrinsic characteristics of those with chronic medical conditions or impairments, and that assumptions about their abilities to work productively or meet the role demands of employment should be questioned. As well as discrimination in the employment field the construction of the physical environment plays an important role in determining levels of functional disability (Porter, Alder and Abraham, 1999). Few public buildings or houses have been constructed with an active consideration of people's needs to gain access to them and to move about and use the facilities within them with ease. Other such shortcomings include inadequate public transport provision, inaccessible lifts, entrances to buildings which are too narrow and lack ramped access, steep kerbs and absences or shortages of taped literature in libraries.

Many people with sensory impairments such as blindness and deafness or those which restrict mobility only gain access to basic education through the Special Educational Needs system (Department of Education, 1994). The very language used here seems to imply that people with impairments are gaining something special in comparison with children in mainstream schools. In fact reports suggest that special schools in fact offer poorer educational resources than those in the mainstream sector (Barnes, 1991). However, no bed of roses awaits disabled people who enter the mainstream system where they may be marginalised by their peers and differentiated from other students by their teachers (Maras, 1995).

A well as occupational, educational and physical restrictions, the social and interpersonal environment can also create disabilities. Morris (1991) provides a lengthy list of assumptions which the non-disabled may bring to their interactions with disabled people. We mention just a few of these: that disabled people feel ugly, inadequate and ashamed of their experience; that their lives are a burden to them; that they crave to be normal; that they constantly suffer and lead naive, tragic and sheltered lives; that daily necessities are pursued as a challenge through which to prove their capability; that hopes for a cure are without end; that it is amazing if they laugh or are cheerful; that disability leads to the psychological consequences of being bitter and twisted; that the needs for privacy are somehow less acutely felt by disabled people; and that disability equals asexuality.

The philosophical and cultural origins of these discriminatory ideas and attitudes, as well as the practices enacted towards those with impairments can be traced back to the societies established in ancient Greece and Rome – their maintenance in the modern era owes a considerable amount to the activities of the media, including television, film, literature and the advertising industries (Morgan, 1987; Oliver and Barnes, 1998). Commonly occurring stereotypes abound (Shakespeare, 1994; Davidson, Woodill and Bredberg, 1994) and include images intended for specific consumption by children. Disabled characters make regular appearances in fiction as criminals, monsters, powerless and pathetic victims or else as superhuman individuals overcoming immense personal tragedy or else possessing uncanny psychic abilities. The corresponding emotions evoked by these images are fear, horror, pity and pathos. In the news media, stories predominate of medical interventions for specific impairments, or else present tales in which heroic individuals (usually but not always children) triumph over what are alleged to be insuperable odds and come out smiling. Furthermore, disabled people are largely absent from mainstream advertising. Finally, many major charities promote the view of disabled people's lives as public property, fit for public consumption, which require only the financial beneficence of the general public to rise inestimably towards greater happiness. That many of these charitable organisations are in the charge of non-disabled people cannot even be considered with irony. Little wonder then that the public at large has in all probability lost contact with the reality underpinning disabled people's lives – and continues to equate disability with the existence of medical problems.

In the face of this psychological onslaught we might pause to consider what identities disabled people are constructing for themselves. Central to these endeavours are the attempts to legitimise physical and functional differences (see Campling, 1985; Saxton and Howe, 1988), and in so doing to challenge the presumption that one's physicality is but a signal of limited abilities when compared with the aesthetic preferences of the dominant body culture. In its current ascendency the latter continues to pervade the lives not only of those with impairments but legions of non-disabled women and increasingly younger men who have internalised the desire for an ideal physique. The obsession with the human body and sex which so pervades our society is central to this and lies behind the equation of asexuality with disability. Lacking the desired body beautiful, disabled people are seen not to be interested in sex and therefore are prone to being treated as children. Seen as lacking a sexual life they may also be construed as being happy to receive sexual advances from anyone in order to be 'fulfilled'. Recent research into disabled women's sexuality suggests that these perspectives need to be considered seriously as factors behind the higher incidence of sexual abuse of disabled women (Gillespie-Sells, Hill and Robbins, 1998).

Sutherland (1981) makes the point that any clear-cut distinction between 'the disabled' and 'non-disabled' is not possible – at least not in terms of how people's bodies actually work. In our society, being normal, for example, can encompass having hay fever or short sight but not mild epilepsy. Likewise, no consistent distinction can be made between chronic illness and impairment. It might be argued that people with chronic illnesses are treated differently than 'the disabled', though there are numerous examples where social and institutional barriers to participation in society have been placed in the way of people with chronic illnesses (for example HIV infection). Though it is probably true to say that people with impairments are treated differently and perceive themselves to be different than those who are seen as chronically 'ill', this will depend on the nature of the impairment, the social network lived in, the physical restrictions relevant to a given condition or state of health and the socially enacted responses which exist around specific impairments or chronic illnesses.

The distinctions the non-disabled world have imposed on the notion of disability really tell us more about how being physically normal is construed by the self-defined normal majority than anything intrinsically useful about the reality of physical differences. A further difficulty for any clear-cut distinction is that every person must inevitably contend with the ageing process, where physical limitation, chronic illness and disability blend imperceptibly together. Although the issue of how people come to make sense of disability (their own and that of others) is a subject ripe for investigation, and would doubtlessly yield useful insights into how people prepare and cope with the likelihood of impending ill-health and impairment, sadly it is one where health psychologists have contributed little. Instead we have examples of uncritical research accepting the framework of disability bequeathed by the medical model. It has, for instance, seemed more interesting to some to examine parental attributions of blame for the birth of children with Down's syndrome, following health professionals' failure to detect the syndrome on screening (Hall, Bobrow and Marteau, 1997) than to inquire why a child with Down's syndrome should be viewed so negatively in the first place. In the face of this, the workable solution adopted by disabled people has been to define themselves on the basis of the discrimination and mistreatment they receive. In this endeavour extensive parallels have been drawn between the political nature of both women's and disabled people's personal lives – suggesting a feminist perspective may be useful to both understanding and empowering people who are disabled. For this analogy to yield fruit, however, Morris (1996) calls for a greater inclusion of disability issues in the women's movement and a recognition that a great number of disabled people are in fact female.

The issue of prenatal screening is one area where the ideals of the apparent right to choose to have a healthy baby advocated by many feminists does not sit comfortably with the experiences of disabled people who have frequently received the message that they should never have been born or been allowed to live (Bailey, 1996). It is an uncomfortable truth that the 'euthanasia' programme in Nazi Germany to kill disabled children was the operational forerunner for the mass extermination programmes directed predominantly against the Jews in Europe and constituted an important element in the training of those who were to carry out major duties in the death camps (Sereny, 1974). Mindful of this, many disabled people have been vociferous in pointing out that attitudes towards disability carry implicit attitudes towards human life in general and thereby contain implications for how all of us may (or may not) be allowed to lead our lives.

ABUSE, DISABILITY AND INSTITUTIONAL LIFE

Thus far we have provided an indication of the disabling context of ordinary community life. In addition to the varieties of social exclusion documented, evidence shows that children with a wide variety of disabilities are more likely to be abused than those without disabilities – estimates put the rate of maltreatment at up to 10 times that for non-disabled children (Sobsey et al., 1997). In reviewing data linking disability with abuse one possible source of confusion is whether the disability existed before injury or arose as a consequence of it (Cross, Gordon, Kennedy and Marchant, 1993). There is evidence which indicates physical violence to children is a major cause of disability. A ten-year follow-up of abused infants by Elmer (1977) found 24 per cent had neurological problems and 47 per cent significant learning difficulties. Diamond and Jaudes (1983) in their study of children with cerebral palsy estimated that 9 per cent of the disabilities probably resulted from abuse. Newlands and Emery (1991) meanwhile suggested that around 10 per cent of fatalities from Sudden Infant Death Syndrome – so-called cot deaths – are the consequence of infanticide through smothering, with private estimates from paediatric pathologists put at between 20–40 per cent (Green, 1999). Thus for those who survive, brain damage may be the result.

It remains true, however, that for large numbers of disabled people their existence unfolds not within the community but in a variety of institutional contexts (hospitals, residential homes, schools and hospices) (Morris, 1995) and that in many ways the model of mistreatment enshrined in the larger social system cannot be separated from the extreme forms which have developed in institutions. In these settings abuse may take many forms. Residents may not be allowed to wear their own clothes, for example; they may be frequently left unwashed and unchanged; their relationships with others prescribed by staff; their personal possessions subject to theft by staff and other residents; and their personal space disregarded by physical beatings, sexual abuse and inappropriate intimate care. Instances have been recorded of children being forced to swallow their own vomit and being subsequently denied treats such as horse-riding and swimming when their parents complained (Sobsey, 1994; Westcott and Cross, 1996).

Far from being based on isolated incidents or on events remote in time and place from our own, evidence from the United States suggests that the prevalence for maltreatment of disabled children in institutions is high. Verdugo, Bermejo and Fuertes (1995) estimate this at 11.5 per cent, whilst a US study of 40 211 schoolchildren by Sullivan and Knutson (1999) put the rate of abuse amongst disabled children at 31 per cent, 3.44 times the rate for non-disabled children. Little information currently exists on the institutional abuse of disabled people in the UK, though a survey conducted under the auspices of the NSPCC into child abuse in residential care and educational settings in England and Wales between March 1991 and February 1992 leaves no room for complacency. Over one-third of the cases involved children who were learning and/or physically disabled – and practically all of these had experienced some kind of sexual abuse in care.

A variety of approaches have been taken to understand why such events occur. Some have argued that institutions are inherently abusive, and support for this view comes from the long and disturbing history of institutional abuse in many countries (see for example Howard, 1929; Goffman, 1961; Peterson, 1982). Goffman (1963) took the view that by virtue of the uniformity of rules and procedures adopted in the face of the different needs of individuals housed inside its confines, institutions were unavoidably dehumanising and were thereby likely to disinhibit coercion and violence towards residents. Several additional factors which exacerbate the potential of institutions to abuse their clients have also been posited. One of these is the general level of trust that the public bestows on institutions entrusted with caring for others. It is a deeply and widely held conviction that institutions provide safe havens for the people within them; yet collective inaction and resistance of politicians, bureaucrats, administrators and staff towards investigating allegations of abuse and mistreatment means that evidence to the contrary rarely surfaces into public consciousness. Sobsey (1994), in fact, notes that administrative structures in many places *de facto* facilitate and encourage abuse – at times by sanctioning the punishment of those who report it. Against this backdrop, human contact in institutions is also characterised by detached social relationships which can hardly help staff to find common human cause with those whose care they are charged with. Young children reared in institutional settings typically encounter between 50 and 80 caregivers before they have reached school age (Rutter, 1989), caregivers moreover who will provide less eye contact, touching, rocking and vocalisation compared with natural caregivers (Roe, Feldman and Drivas, 1988). The institutions themselves may also be situated in relatively remote areas – so enhancing the sense of isolation from normal human affairs and with perhaps a corresponding isolation from the normal moral standards governing conduct. The prevailing patterns of behaviour within institutions may also go unchallenged for a sufficiently long period that an abusive subculture persists even after identifiable problem staff have left (McGrath, 1991). Wardhaugh and Wilding (1993) contend that what they call the corruption of care in institutional settings is a direct failure of management – and that abusive care is facilitated by inward-looking undemocratic organisations lacking clear demarcation lines and mechanisms of accountability. Crossmaker (1991) remarks that the power and control dynamics of institutionalisation are in fact practically identical to those that characterise sexual assault and abuse. An explanation that has been advanced on more than one occasion (for example Rusch, Hall and Griffin, 1986), that abuse arises from individual carers' frustrations in dealing with difficult people, is however difficult to reconcile with the evidence of widespread sexual and physical abuse of children and adults in institutional settings.

Pilgrim and Rogers (1993) note that what distinguishes institutional clients and patients such as the mentally ill, drug users, abused children and disabled people from physically-ill patients, and which thereby renders them more vulnerable to abuse, is principally the prior stigma attached to the group in question, combined with the curtailment of opportunities for educational and social (particularly intimate) contact as well as the sheer degree of contact with services. Westcott (1993) similarly locates the abuse of disabled children within a wider context of prejudice, stereotyping and discrimination, maintained by inequalities of power between the disabled and non-disabled. Middleton (1992) completes this picture in proposing that the abuse of disabled children is made easier by virtue of their physical, geographical and social isolation, and is compounded by the psychological 'training' in institutions which instill compliance and obedience as good behaviours, gives people little control over their own lives and furnishes them with little useful general or sexual education.

EMPOWERMENT

Without doubt the preceding picture is an uncomfortable one – and because the reality of the attitudes underlying it is seldom spoken of publicly it will be one which many will find difficult to acknowledge. The lack of transparency of this cultural knowledge (at least to the able-bodied population – the disabled are all too aware of it) poses particular problems to social scientists trying to understand it, though these problems have been evident in other fields too – they have, for example, been a major preoccupation for cognitive cultural anthropologists (for example Goldhagen, 1997). Our view here is that the wealth of behavioural data and reported personal experiences of disabled people confer sufficient validity on our presumption that the attitudes discussed reflect cognitive structures of disability widely held in western societies. From recognising the current situation, the resultant challenge must be to identify steps which can bring about change as rapidly as possible. In this regard Westcott and Jones (1999) note a welcome change in emphasis in recent studies towards disabled children's rights to protection and an understanding of the social context in which mistreatment occurs. For example, rather than highlighting the disabled child as an additional 'stress' factor in fraught families, attention is now turning to how health, education and welfare systems create situations and dynamics which accentuate the possibilities for abuse.

Some of the necessary steps undoubtedly concern issues of civil rights and must involve the pursuit of anti-discrimination legislation in the political arena (for example as regards physical barriers to participation in work and community life), though saying as much should not be interpreted to mean that health psychologists can continue to sit on the fence pretending to be disinterested impartial observers of the political process. An explicitly active role can also be taken in creating environments that are open to criticism and scrutiny (Westcott and Cross, 1996), that have clear definitions of good practice and which seek to empower individuals to resist abuse – the latter can include training in assertiveness, self-esteem, social, communication and personal safety skills, sex education, individual rights and self-defence (Bregman, 1984; Blackburn, 1993; Cross, 1998), areas where psychologists have considerable expertise. Fryer, Kraizer and Miyoshi (1987), for example, found high self-esteem to be a good predictor of less-vulnerable responses to a simulation procedure of leaving a building with a stranger and Foxx and McMorrow (1985) in a follow-up study of social skills training for adults with 'mental retardation' (*sic*) found levels of skill acquisition had been maintained or even surpassed over six months later. Active consultation with disabled people – both children and adults – is a fundamental prerequisite for translating all of these aims into effective practise and will require a shift towards action research.

Summary and conclusions ●

In closing this chapter we would like to reiterate what we believe are its central messages. First of all, methods of studying 'the disabled' which have excluded disabled people themselves from framing what are seen by them as more relevant questions have been harmful and led to an emphasis on the adjustment of individuals to disabling and oppressive social and civic circumstances (e.g. Cross, 1981; Westcott, 1993). Models which have focused on adjustment without addressing these features of social organisation have been harmful. As a result, disabled people's relationships with professionals working within this framework have been marred by a disjunction in perspectives, with psychologists tied to a belief in their professional scientific expertise while disabled people contend with situations where what they are experiencing and what they are lead to believe they are experiencing simply do not coincide. A further downside has been a lack of a concern with what actually happens to disabled people. A wealth of data shows that disabled people are at high risk from physical and psychological abuse – this is widespread in many societies, though it seems particularly exacerbated in institutional settings. Several factors which exacerbate this have been posited – detached social relationships between care-givers and those cared for, undemocratic, rigid, administrative and managerial structures in institutions, their geographical remoteness from centres of population, political resistance to change, as well as the persistence of abusive sub-cultures unchallenged by outside agencies.

Finally, in a call to our fellow professionals in this field, psychologists could play a more useful role by addressing the behaviour and attitudes of non-disabled people and listening to disabled people who are working to change organisations and empower individuals. Adopting the social model of disability which directs attention to the disabling aspects of the social structure through education, employment and physical access and interpersonal relationships will be a more helpful theoretical tool to assist this endeavour.

Discussion points

A   What ethical objections may be raised to the planning of designer babies?

B   In studying disability, has the language adopted by psychologists been helpful or harmful?

C   To what extent is the treatment of disabled people and the conseqences of this treatment similar to sexism?

Suggested reading

Oliver, M. (1998) 'Theories of Disability in Health Practice and Research', *British Medical Journal*, **317**: 1446–1449.

Sobsey, D. (1994) *Violence and Abuse in the Lives of People with Disabilities.* (Baltimore: Paul H. Brookes).

Wardhaugh, J. and Wilding, P. (1993) 'Towards an Explanation of the Corruption of Care', *Critical Social Policy*, **13**: 4–31.

16

Ethnicity, Culture and Health

'The dominant racism of our society is reflected not just in the theories and practices of psychiatry but in its very structure: white consultants, Asian junior doctors, black nurses and domestics.'

Roland Littlewood and Maurice Lipsedge (*Aliens and Alienists*, 1989)

INTRODUCTION

This chapter will examine data which addresses how racism and the position which ethnic minorities occupy in our society contributes both to their physical and psychological malaise and to our difficulties in adequately assessing it. In addition we will question the role of the health care system in addressing and responding to people's needs as these relate to their specific cultural identities. Because health professions are governed by ethical codes that emphasise their humanitarian duties, many find the charge that health care is discriminatory hard to bear. However, there is ample evidence that the charge is warranted (Bhopal, 1998) and some of this will be reviewed shortly. Before proceeding, however, we wish to make clear that though we utilise the concept of ethnicity in this chapter we recognise that it is problematic and lacks demonstrable validity (see Box 16.1). Survey questions on self-identified ethnic group membership have usually yielded useful information only to the extent that people have been willing to answer them (Bhopal, 1997). Distinct to the biological conception of race, ethnicity is intended to convey an identity based on an ill-defined confluence of geographical, social, cultural and class characteristics. Its use as a proxy for lower social status despite variation in social strata amongst ethnic minority groups has been of little help in discerning whether health differences between groups result from biological or social influences. Confusion has abounded in existing systems of measurement which have confused skin colour with nationality (for example the Census in Great Britain has used both White and Chinese as ethnic categories) or else preserved some culture or ethnic free domain for groups of white people with specific European ancestry – notably the English. In US classifications, for example, the absence of a designated ethnic category for Americans with British heritage has passed without comment – so that whilst Irish Americans, Greek Americans, Italian Americans and African Americans amongst others see their heritage and identity proclaimed in official statistics and record-keeping, would-be English Americans remain hidden. Because of the fuzziness intrinsic to the idea of ethnicity and the confusion surrounding it, data currently in the public domain must be interpreted cautiously. The story they tell informs us as much about current forms of social organisation and their consequences as any objective picture of variations in health between different human groups. With this in mind we will now review some of the principle features of this tale.

> ## BOX 16.1 Why is ethnicity so difficult to measure?
>
> In this book we have gone to some lengths to stress the importance of using suitable measures when carrying out research. The two desirable properties for any measurement system to possess is that the measures are both reliable, i.e. they yield consistent results when applied to the same phenomenon, and that they are valid, that is they measure what they purport to measure. The difficulty with ethnicity lies squarely within the domain of validity. Academics in line with many others have realised that the concept of race has no valid biological basis – it is a social construct which was used to justify the differential discriminatory treatment of people from varying cultural and geographical backgrounds to the dominant one. Although the concept of race has been reinforced in scientific discourse, the repercussions of the concept are still in force in society and are actively felt by those on the receiving end of it – in the arena of health and health care amongst others. If this is to be recognised and steps taken to improve matters, then data must be collected on some basis. Ethnicity is one such attempt – however, it must be recognised that the concept has no external validity, it is a concept with face validity at best, required only as long as the divisions which currently exist continue to persist. The system of measurement, however, can be improved. A culturally unbiased yardstick should give no special place to specific categories of white people – nor confuse colour with nationality. Such a system must therefore allow for the emergence of new ethnic groups as people come to realise for whatever reason that they have a distinct cultural, geographical and historical identity which requires recognition. To incorporate such a system of measurement into mainstream research poses challenges for social scientists of many persuasions.

ETHNIC DIFFERENCES IN HEALTH

Evidence of poor mental and physical health in members of black and ethnic minority communities has been gathering momentum for several years. Life expectancy in African Americans is estimated to be seven years less than it is for whites and rather than decreasing appears to have increased over time (Drever and Whitehead, 1997). This has occurred despite the US Government in 1989 setting an explicit target to reduce the gap to four years. Though improvements in mortality have occurred in several areas, these have been overwhelmed by the adverse impact on the black community of HIV infection, homicide, diabetes and pneumonia (Whitehead and Diderichsen, 1997). The homicide rate for black people, for example, in 1992 stood at 39.4 per 100 000 population – over 6 times that for the white population. Reported incidence of AIDS (104.2 cf 17.9 per 100 000) manifests a similar ratio. So why have these differences persisted?

Historically, researchers sought to account for health differences between ethnic groups in terms of the presumed biological inferiority of black people. More recent approaches (though by no means the majority) have instead asked whether the generally lower social status of ethnic minorities is sufficient to explain their increased mortality and morbidity (Lillie-Blanton and Laveist, 1996). Socioeconomic inequalities between ethnic groups are widespread – almost half the black population (46.1%) under 18 years of age in the US currently live in poverty (Whitehead and Diderichsen, 1997), and unemployment rates are also considerably higher both in the United States and Europe. In the US National Health and Nutrition Examination Survey, Otten, Teutsch, Williamson and Marks (1990), however, were able to account for 31 per cent of the excess mortality in blacks by several established risk factors (smoking, systolic blood pressure, cholesterol level, body-mass index, alcohol intake, and diabetes) and a further 38 per cent by family income. In a study exploring ethnic disparities in low birth weight (itself a major predictor of infant mortality), Lieberman, Ryan, Monson and Schoenbaum (1987) found that 40 per cent of the variance was due to four socioeconomic factors (age less than 20 years, single parenthood, welfare support and educational attainment). When these risk factors pertaining to an individual woman were taken into account, ethnicity was no longer a significant predictor of premature birth. Other studies (for example Rawlings and Weir, 1992) have found no differences in black and white infant mortality rates when the parents are living in similar social conditions.

Data from the United Kingdom pertaining to the period between 1991 and 1993 also show considerable variations in health by ethnic group membership. In a comparison of migrants to the UK by country of birth, overall mortality for men from the Caribbean was found to be low (**SMR** = 89) though it was high for all other groups (see Table 16.1). Although mortality for the migrant groups was in all cases substantially higher in manual classes, adjustment for social class explained very little of the excess mortality in the migrant groups – which for Irish men was highest at 35 per cent. For Scottish, West African and East African men the excess mortality was between 20 and 30 per cent (Harding and Maxwell, 1997). Earlier data from the UK shows a similar picture (Marmot, Adelstein and Bulusu, 1984) and more recent data from the United States also indicates that ethnic differences in mortality are only partly attributable to social stratification (Pappas, 1994). What characterises much of this research is that where health differences in ethnicity have been adjusted for social class, it has been rare for researchers to attempt further explanation in terms of health or other behaviours or indeed other environmental effects. Specifically there has been little attempt to directly measure exposure to racism, although this is likely to account for at least some of the unexplained variance present in some of the studies.

Standardised mortality ratio (SMR) is a measure of how likely a person is to die in a particular population compared to other people of the same age and sex. The SMR is the ratio of the actual number of deaths in a group to the expected number of deaths in the group. It is multiplied by 100 for ease of interpretation.

Table 16.1 Standardised mortality ratios for men by country of birth (England and Wales 1991–93)

	Non-Manual	Manual
Caribbean	83*	102
West/South Africa	128*	137*
East Africa	113*	136*
India	96	135*
Pakistan	106	128*
Bangladesh	144*	201*
Ireland	102	169*
All countries	77*	124*

* denotes SMR's significantly different from 100.
Source: Office for National Statistics, 1997.

A recurrent finding where specific causes of ill-health have been investigated is the higher incidence of cardiovascular disease amongst black people (Sarafino, 1998). In the United Kingdom higher than average mortality rates from strokes have been reported in men from the Caribbean, West/South Africa, and the Indian sub-continent (Drever and Whitehead, 1997). In a comparison of deaths from cardio-vascular disease in New York during 1991 for which satisfactory data was available for ethnicity, hypertensive vascular disease was determined as the cause of death in 42 per cent of blacks compared with 23 per cent of whites – a highly significant difference (Onwuanyi *et al.*, 1998). Although black and white men did not differ in mean age at death, black women were on average 6.8 years younger (54.7 cf 61.5 years). Several strands of evidence point to racism as a major factor behind these differences. A study by Harburg *et al.* (1973) found no differences in blood pressure between blacks and whites living in low-stress neighbourhoods, whilst the highest readings were those obtained for black people living in areas with high crime rates and low incomes. Further work has found high blood pressure in black men is associated with perceptions of low job security, lack of job success and discrimination (James, Lacroix, Kleinbaum and Strogatz, 1984) with skin colour and blood pressure correlated for black men and women of low social class (Klag *et al.*, 1991). Work in which black and white subjects have been initially matched for age, initial blood pressure and body mass index has failed to find any differences in hypertension over a seven-year period (He, Klag, Appel, Charleston and Whelton, 1998). In itself this supports the suggestion that health differences between ethnic groups only appear when the groups are unequally matched in the first place.

As well as being implicated in the development of disease, racism is also prominent in the systems which deliver health care. Although black women have a lower incidence of breast cancer than white women, they are more likely to die from it (Doyal, 1995). Evidence from widely disparate areas of treatment show that black people receive poorer health care – this includes sickle cell disease (see Box 16.2), renal failure, pneumonia, bladder cancer and heart disease (Bhopal, 1998). With regard to the latter, US black patients have been found to have lower rates than whites for coronary angiography, coronary artery bypass grafting (Wenneker and Epstein, 1989), coronary revascularization (Ayanian *et al.*, 1993) and general invasive cardiac surgery even after controlling for disease severity (Hannan *et al.*, 1991). Ensuing debate has concerned whether these disparities reflect a tendency to over-treat white people or to under-treat black people. Either possibility probably owes something to the relative social positions of blacks and whites and the nature of a health insurance system whereby whites pay more into the system (and receive more in return) because of their greater wealth.

BOX 16.2   Sickle cell disease

An indication of how attitudes about race permeate research and treatment of ill-health in ethnic minorities can be gleaned from a consideration of sickle cell disease. This refers to a family of haemoglobin disorders, primarily affecting individuals of African and Afro-Caribbean descent. These disorders, the most prominent of which is sickle cell anaemia, arise from inheritance of the sickle β globin gene (β^s), which is spread throughout Africa, the Middle East, Mediterranean countries and India, with population movements responsible for carrying the gene to the Caribbean, North America and Europe (Davies and Oni, 1997). The gene has

BOX 16.2   continued

reached high frequencies in West Africans (25%) and Afro-Caribbeans (10%) because in its carrier state the gene confers a degree of protection against malaria. Sickle cell disease occurs where this gene has been inherited either in the homozygous state or in compound heterozygous states with the gene for haemoglobin C or ß thalassaemia (Weatherall, 1997). People with sickle cell disease encounter a variety of problems stemming from vaso-occlusion leading to a sickle cell crisis; severe pain usually in the arms, legs, back and joints which may last 5–10 minutes or in worst cases generalised attacks lasting weeks and requiring hospitalisation. Early death is not unusual for those aged over 20 who are homozygous for sickle cell anaemia with life expectancy severely reduced for both men (42 years) and women (48 years). In the heterozygous state life expectancy is also compromised. Currently no preventative treatments exist and a variety of methods are used to manage pain. Both biofeedback and self-hypnosis have been reported to reduce emergency visits and length of hospital stays (Midence, Fuggle and Davies, 1993) though such studies have employed small samples and lacked controls for disease severity.

Problems in treating people with sickle cell disease have occurred on several fronts. Poor communication characterised by mutual mistrust and conflict between patients with sickle cell disease and health carers has been noted with issues of race and culture compounded by the disparities in socioeconomic status between staff and patients. A survey of patients in the London area revealed that a majority felt their General Practitioner had little knowledge of the disease and was either unable or unwilling to provide the level of pain relief and support needed. (Maxwell and Streetly, 1998). Patients have also complained of being given poor or delayed treatment for pain in accident and emergency departments by staff who appear to mistake them for drug addicts on the basis of the urgency and vehemence with which they request pain killers such as pethidine (Waters and Thomas, 1995). It has also been suggested that morphine and pethidine are too frequently prescribed and at doses carrying risks of addiction for patients (Clare, 1998; Agble, 1998). These doubts have, moreover, been more frequently voiced by staff familiar with the cultures of sickle cell patients. Without question the psychosocial and cultural aspects of living with this group of diseases have not received sufficient attention (Harris, Parker and Barker, 1998). In fact it has been argued that sickle cell disease itself receives a disproportionately smaller share of resources than conditions of similar prevalence existing in the white population – for example it has often been compared with cystic fibrosis (Anionwu, 1995). With knowledge in short supply, many medical personnel remain unaware of the social and interpersonal context within which the condition occurs. In a wider climate of discrimination faced by ethnic minorities the lack of such knowledge can but exacerbate tensions between staff and patients and add to feelings of injustice. In contrast to this emphasis on neglect, Bhopal (1997) contends that where interest in the health of ethnic minorities has been expressed it has in fact concentrated too much on so called 'ethnic problems' such as sickle cell disease, and overlooked the impact of more extensive health threats to ethnic minorities such as are posed by heart disease, alcohol and smoking, thus reinforcing the tendency to stereotype blacks as exotic.

MENTAL HEALTH IN ETHNIC MINORITIES

During the 1980s, concern was raised about what was seen as the excessive incidence of mental illness in certain ethnic minorities (Littlewood and Lipsedge, 1988). This data indicated that West Indians were more likely to be admitted to psychiatric hospital (Harrison *et al.*, 1988) and once admitted were between three and five times more likely to be given a diagnosis of schizophrenia. Depression and psychosomatic illnesses were also more common, although suicide among Afro-Caribbeans was less frequent than among whites (Merrill and Owens, 1988). Once in the psychiatric system, Afro-Caribbeans are also more likely to be given physical treatments (electro-convulsive therapy and higher doses of medication) and less likely to be offered psychotherapy. Many of these findings have been extensively replicated. A logistic regression analysis conducted by Singh, Croudace, Beck and Harrison (1998) found Black Caribbeans were more than twice as likely to be compulsorily detained compared to other ethnic groups even after adjustments were made for age, sex, social class, type of diagnosis and risk of committing violence; and a recent study by Harrison *et al.* (1998) indicated that subjects born in the Caribbean, or who had one or both parents born in the Caribbean, had a greatly elevated risk (incidence ratios above 7) for all psychotic disorders and for schizophrenia.

More recent research on depression has yielded less clear cut results. Jones-Webb and Snowden (1993) report a greater risk for middle-age blacks belonging to non-western religions in comparison to whites, though social cultural variables were less potent explanatory variables than demographic variables and life events.

Substance use problems in ethnic minorities have also been the subject of extensive investigation, possibly because of the preconception (arising either from racist attitudes or because of the presumed effects of social deprivation) that they constitute a more vulnerable group. The United States National Household Survey on Drug Abuse found that although crack cocaine use was more common in African and Hispanic Americans compared to whites, no differences where found when comparing ethnic groups exposed to similar social conditions (Lillie-Blanton and Laveist, 1996). This of course does not imply that there are no culturally specific factors relevant to substance misuse. Work in the UK does show definite variations in alcohol use by ethnicity among first-generation migrants to England and Wales, which are not explicable in terms of social class (Harrison, Sutton and Gardiner, 1997). Rates of alcohol-related mortality are slightly higher for those born in the Caribbean compared to native British and are substantially raised for those born in Ireland and the Indian subcontinent. Whilst it is legitimate to attribute part of this excess to the stresses of racism, the absence of consistent behavioural disorders across all groups which are exposed to racism mean that there must be more complex cultural and historical reasons why particular groups come to express their problems by way of specific behaviours (Littlewood and Lipsedge, 1989).

Several explanations have in fact been put forward to explain the over-representation of ethnic minorities in the mental health system. One contention holds that migrants form an atypical group compared to other people either in their country of origin (for example people with severe mental health problems are more likely to migrate) or in the new country. Scant evidence exists though that those who seek to migrate are a more vulnerable group (Littlewood and Lipsedge, 1989). A more plausible view is that the stresses involved in the process of migration and adaptation to the new country produce particular mental health problems. To examine this proposition a clear understanding of the component stresses of migration is necessary. Bagley (1971) identified five such aspects: community integration, status isolation, discrimination, under-reporting of illness and prior mental illness. Determining the weighting to be attached to each of these factors is a problem that has not received the attention it deserves. One obvious problem is that various groups may differ in the weightings which they attach to these events. Nevertheless, using a simple summated rating, Bagley did find a relationship between the sum of these problems and the relative frequency of mental ill-health in different immigrant groups.

A further proposal is that mental health problems in ethnic minorities are more likely to be misdiagnosed. In the USA, black people in in-patient settings are more likely to be diagnosed schizophrenic, though general population studies provide no basis for the attribution (Fernando *et al.*, 1998). Mukherjee *et al.* (1983) found that despite there being no significant differences among ethnic groups in terms of anger, violent and destructive behaviour, persecutory or bizarre delusions and ideas of reference, black and Hispanic patients were at higher risk than whites for a mis-diagnosis of schizophrenia. Black patients were also significantly more often to be misdiagnosed as paranoid schizophrenic. There is also a strong indication that depression in black people is under-diagnosed (Fernando, Ndegwa and Wilson, 1998). To what extent such under diagnosis arises as a consequence of the propensity to attribute psychotic rather than neurotic disorders to black people cannot be answered with any certainty at the present time. The tendency for preconceptions of black people to influence diagnostic procedures is most clearly revealed by the propensity with which some British psychiatrists have diagnosed cannabis psychosis in young people of West Indian descent (McGovern and Cope, 1987a,b). Over a quarter of males received this diagnosis, though it was virtually absent in white and Asian patients. No corroborating evidence existed to support these diagnoses. The belief that cannabis smoking was more prevalent in the Afro-Caribbean groups was not substantiated. Littlewood (Littlewood and Lipsedge, 1989: 266) reports that examination of the case notes of some of these patients suggested that the diagnosis had been made without even determining whether cannabis was present in the urine – a curious omission in a discipline which by and large has proclaimed its loyalty to a biological model of mental ill-health. However, cannabis psychosis is but the latest in a long line of abuses of psychiatry in particular (and science in general) to serve racist ideologies. In the nineteenth century this included the diagnosis of drapeto-mania in runaway slaves – characterised as the irresistible urge to run away. It would be rather too simple for us to think of our societies as incapable of this kind of crass judgement. But decreed wisdom is something which accrues more easily from studies of the past than the present.

ISSUES IN METHODOLOGY

At the time of writing the logical and methodological prerequisites for a dispassionate study of ethnic differences in health do not appear to be present; a number of formidable obstacles currently stand in the way of this. The broad range of data which exist – particularly where morbidity is concerned – are contaminated by differences in the health-seeking behaviour of different people. We have already encountered this problem in an earlier chapter when discussing gender issues. It would be surprising if such behaviour was not affected by people's perceptions of the care delivered by the health service. As we have seen, treatment appears skewed in many areas in favour of white people. The entry of more ethnic minorities into the health services may have some affect on this in the long term, though it cannot be assumed that in the race for places at medical schools, ethnic minority candidates will not have to face additional hurdles to other candidates (McManus, 1997).

As indicated earlier, the categories for studying ethnic differences are themselves dependent upon the societal division of people into groups on the basis of their presumed racial or cultural identity. As Bhopal (1997) has stressed, this has only yielded worthwhile data to the extent that people continue to experience oppressed lives on the basis of these groupings and are consequently willing to treat the categories as meaningful. This presents a considerable ethical challenge for researchers, who must be clear about the purposes for which their data is being collected – and even this may not be sufficient. Governments and indeed the scientific communities which function under their jurisdiction have a long history of using such data to support inhuman and oppressive policies. Further difficulties arise because owing to the 'racist' nature of the categories, researchers are apt to seek corroborating evidence for associations between these and other characteristics such as mental ill-health or dangerous which themselves fall short of possessing established validity. Indeed such searches can become self-fulfilling prophesies as our society's proclivity to alienate and estrange people from the productive processes and social intercourse of everyday life gives rise to people who feel alienated, unwanted and angry. Their behaviour in turn is then taken as prima facie evidence for the different nature of the alienated 'other'. Such considerations apply equally to issues of class, gender and disability as they do to ethnicity.

Summary and conclusions ●

Previous chapters in this part of the book have reviewed how people's health experiences vary according to gender, physical disability and the position they occupy in the social strata or their ethnic origin. Implicit in these discussions has been the assumption that an appreciation of this state of affairs requires an understanding of how different groups in our societies occupy different positions of power and privilege. How people are oriented with respect to these does more than describe their relative access to and control over material resources or their relative exposure to stimuli which either enhance or compromise health. Just as important are the psychological concomitants which flow from these. This includes the awareness which people have of their own situation in life – their social destiny as it were. How we make sense of who we are structures the psychological means through which we as individuals will explore life and pursue our goals. At one extreme we may make ourselves slaves of our interpretations – and at the other open doorways to realms beyond our wildest dreams. Alongside our individual choices run the pathways which society maps out for people of varying cultures – the constellations of family and social life, beliefs, attitudes, language and behaviour which, though taking relatively stable forms through time, are dynamic and changeable (Fernando, 1998). The choices made from within different cultural domains may thus accord with those prescribed by the dominant society or stand in opposition to them. The different psychologies of class, gender, disability or 'race' which have appeared in recent years and infused psychology with fresh vigour have been products of rebel minds – constructed from a discourse of opposition to the prevailing system of values. The concept of culture is central to uniting these disparate psychologies within the bounds of a common framework. Before we can proceed on this course, though, we must clarify the concept of culture in the area where it has found its most frequent application – race and ethnicity.

Although the notion of race as a biological reality has been superceded (Gould, 1996), – its existence as a social reality still informs much medical research. Confusion is widespread. Though the modern variant of race – 'ethnicity' – in fact reflects geographical, social, cultural and class distinctions rather than biological ones (Bhopal, 1997), within medical discourse its principal use has been to seek differences in health between different ethnic groups, on the presumption that these will lead to insights about the biological rather than social vectors of health or illness. A corresponding confusion has seen the notion of culture restricted to groups of differing ethnic and national status. Such a brand of multiculturalism in which varying cultures are in fact synonymous with racial groups threatens to reinforce the strand of racism it was intended to challenge (Fernando, 1998). An exemplar of this latter error occurs in what has come to be called transcultural psychiatry – though the same muddled thinking can also be witnessed in the products of forensic psychiatry. Littlewood and Lipsedge (1989) in an otherwise commendable exposition of the limitations and racist assumptions of orthodox psychiatry, fail to follow the implications of their own reasoning. Having delineated how appropriate cultural-historical frames of reference can clarify the presentation of psychological distress in various ethnic minorities – ways which have often been misread as unintelligible symptoms of psychotic disorder – they do not stop to consider whether other categories of identity (gender, social class or geographical location for example) could offer equally potent cultural frames of reference to be set against the culture of orthodox psychiatry. In so doing they cling to the notion that the western psychiatric enterprise really does mirror reality in some fundamental way. Thus the psychology (and psychiatry) of ethnic minorities remains an exotic outpost from the safe haven of knowledge embodied in the medical model. In short, by restricting the notion of culture to ethnic minorities, Littlewood and others commit the very act which they profess they wish to avoid – that of treating ethnic minorities as somehow different from the rest of us whilst protecting the medical fraternity from questioning whether their professional values are indeed biased by white male middle-class mores. So dominant have these been that, like water for fish, they seem to constitute the very bedrock of reality even for those who advance the cause of cultural relativism. Such errors aside, the notion of cultural relativism is we believe central to understanding how health and well-being is unfairly shared in our societies, and how the health care system responds to this. If this notion of culture is to be advanced on a broad front then its synonymous relationship with race and ethnicity must be broken.

Discussion points

A   An unemployed working-class man resident on a housing estate in the north of England is adamant that the Queen has been visiting him over a period of several months to take tea and biscuits and discuss the state of the nation. How might an understanding of the culture and symbols of social class life shed light on the nature of the distress being presented?

B   How could exposure to racism be measured?

Suggested reading

Bhopal, R. (1998) 'Spectre of Racism in Health and Health Care: Lessons from History and the United States', *British Medical Journal*, **316**: 1970–3.

Fernando, S., Ndegwa, D. and Wilson, M. (1998) *Forensic Psychiatry, Race and Culture*. (London: Routledge).

Littlewood, R. and Lipsedge, M. (1989) *Aliens and Alienists: Ethnic Minorities and Psychiatry*, 2nd edn. (London: Unwin).

Social Relationships

(with Antje Mueller)

'A faithful friend is the medicine of life.'

(Ecclesiasticus, 6:16)

INTRODUCTION

Each of us owes our existence to the attraction that once existed between a man and a woman, and because we are dependent upon others from our entry into life to its end, the duration and quality of each of our lives is continuously affected by the answers to the question of who likes and loves us, who is indifferent, dislikes or even hates us (Berscheid, 1985). Throughout the intellectual history of psychology, from Aristotle through to the present day, the subject of social relationships has consistently received attention.

To the discipline of psychology, an understanding of relationships and friendships has been vital because human life is conceived, lived and terminated within social relationships, and thus most human behaviour takes place within a social context. Considering the importance of social relationships it is understandable that the social, behavioural and health sciences have become increasingly interested in studying the association between satisfying relationships and mental and physical health. Argyle (1987) concluded from his own review that 'social relationships are a major source of happiness, relief from distress, and health' (p. 31). In a National survey, involving more than 2000 Americans, Campbell, Converse and Rodgers (1976) found that marriage and family life were the best predictors of overall life satisfaction. The association of friendship with happiness is so compelling that Myers (1992) speaks of this as a 'deep truth' (p. 154) when referring to it.

The concern of the present chapter is to reflect on adult social relationships and well-being, rather than a consideration of, for example, developmental aspects of this relationship. Within this, we aim to reflect on the nature of the social phenomena itself and review broader issues of theory and method. A word of warning may be placed here. The focus in the present essay lies on social relationships rather than on the equation 'satisfying relationships equals psychological and physical well-being'. Elsewhere in this volume we have referred to the diverse contexts in which epidemiological evidence links social support to health; for example coping with diabetes, coronary heart disease, cancer, degenerative disease, bereavement and trauma and how other broader factors such as social class, gender and ethnicity shape the pattern of social support that is available. Although these epidemiological studies are extremely valuable in identifying an important phenomenon, they have limited ability

191

to enhance our understanding of the relevant processes and to guide the design of interventions. It is for that reason that health is discussed here in a broader framework. Before going further, it may be useful to anticipate both the flavour of the conclusion which shall be reached and a little more of the theoretical perspective upon which this review converges. Understanding how social relationships impinge on adults' well-being is surely a vital challenge for psychology, and yet the literature reviewed here creates a sense of only modest progress. Part of the problem may lie in the fact that there is no agreed definition of what constitutes a friendship or relationship, let alone the question when is a friendship of good quality and thus satisfying for both people.

Our argument is that if we are to gain more knowledge about the association between social relationships and health, attention must be directed towards a number of areas, which have rarely been discussed together. The three which appear most prominent to us are, firstly, the negative components of relationships and their consequences; secondly the historical, cultural and social context in which friendships and relationships are investigated; and, thirdly, the precise nature and role of social support within social relationships. All these must be better understood before the implications for health of social ties can be fully comprehended. Below we will briefly discuss some of what we do know about social support and health. This will focus on the role of close personal relationships and the meaning of these relationships to an individual. Such a focus should not only contribute substantially to our understanding of the support process, but also enable enhanced prediction of the effects of social support.

A necessary prerequisite for evaluating the effects of social relationships is a clear understanding of what we mean when we refer to friendships, relationships and support. Though the definitions we provide will facilitate communication (see Box 17.1) it must be noted that these are not universal. It will become clear in the remainder of this chapter why this is the case.

BOX 17.1 Definitions of relationship, friendship and support

The term relationship, as used in this chapter, contains superficial friendliness and casual friendships in the sense of 'associative friendship' as used by Reisman (1981). These relations are characterised by an absence of loyalty or a sense of commitment to seeing that the friendship endures much beyond the circumstances that bring the parties together (work, neighbourhood, being part of the same organisation). Yet should one of the friends move or depart, there is little effort to keep in touch. Friendship may be defined in the sense of 'reciprocal friendship' (Reisman, 1979), characterised by loyalty and commitment between friends who regard one another as equals. One would hope that reciprocal friendships are not truly rare but as yet no definitive answer can be given to this. Cobb (1976) described support as what leads a person to believe that they are 'cared for and loved . . . esteemed and valued and belong to a social network of communication and mutual obligation'.

A limitation in reviewing the social support literature is that so much of it has been conducted in western industrialised societies with people who stand on the middle rungs of the socioeconomic ladder. Thus caution is urged in generalising these findings beyond the populations from which they were gathered.

THE MEANING OF SOCIAL RELATIONSHIPS IN ADULT YEARS

The health protective effects of social ties have been noted in a number of industrialised countries (Veiel and Baumann, 1992). However, for much of the world, where the geographic dispersion of primary kin and friendship groups has not occurred, social ties have not been conceptualised as being so important to health as they have in western cultures. In addition, Neugarten and Datan (1974) have drawn attention to the fact that how the adult years and the needs for social relationships are viewed depends on the socioeconomic status the person holds. People with high and medium socioeconomic status see young adulthood as a period of exploration and groping for identity, intimacy and a career. Individuals with lower socioeconomic status may focus more on finding the right partner to marry and settle down. People of medium socioeconomic status see maturity (between the ages of 30–40) as a time of accomplishment and for establishing oneself, whereas people from lower social classes see it as a decade for becoming older, quieter and wiser. Likewise middle age (between 40 to 60 or 65) is for middle and higher social classes the prime of life, whereas people with lower socioeconomic status see it as a period of decline both emotionally and physically. Finally old age (over 60 years of age) is perceived as a richly earned vacation by the former group and a wretched time for making-do and battling illness by the latter.

In young adulthood (20–30 years) the major developmental task is to complete one's education and, together with beginning one's career, the growth of an intimate relationship, the process of courtship and marriage, and beginning a family. In this period of life, education, marriage and career may require moving to communities far from home and being separated from the family and one's usual friends and neighbours; with consequent disruptions and subsequent losses of relationships (Reisman, 1981). Perhaps in many cases people have to move from rural to urban areas where social life is differently organised and more anonymous. Moving was the reason most frequently given by the respondents to the *Psychology Today* questionnaire for terminations of their friendships (Parlee, 1979). Although this survey was conducted some years ago it is unlikely that things are different today, in fact if anything geographical mobility has probably increased. Packard (1972) speculated that the process of friendship formation may be accelerated among individuals who find themselves in transition, since they share similar uncertainties, disruptions and pressures to make friends quickly.

ADVERSE EFFECTS OF SOCIAL RELATIONSHIPS AND FRIENDSHIPS

Investigators in the 1970s and early 1980s often described only the positive features of friendship, but there is compelling evidence that interpersonal relationships can have a darker side. Berndt (1996) supposes that this bias probably resulted from the emphasis on positive features in both Piaget's and Sullivan's theories, and in the classical writings on friendship. When researchers asked more balanced questions they discovered that many supportive relationships are sources of significant problems for people (Rook, 1984). As Berndt put it, these researchers portray friendship inaccurately when they 'accentuate the positive and eliminate the negative' (p. 354). Clearly, to study the process accurately, researchers must be prepared to give equal significance to both positive and the negative features of relationships. But despite the wealth of evidence that relationships are peoples' most frequent source of both happiness and distress, there is inadequate evidence of the causal mechanisms responsible and of the types of relationships that are most beneficial or harmful, even though these issues form the core of much theorising and research.

Troubled relationships are indeed the most common presenting problem of psychotherapy seekers (Rook and Pietromonaco, 1987; Cupach and Spitzberg, 1994). More specifically, Veroff, Kulka and Douvan (1981) found that 40 per cent of the people seeking professional help were individuals who had problems with their spouse or marriage, whilst Cramer (1998) estimated about 11 per cent of the people who were or had been married had sought professional help for marital difficulties. Geiss and O'Leary (1981) asked a random sample of 116 members of the American Association of Marriage and Family Therapists to estimate the percentage of couples, seen during the past year, who had expressed complaints in 29 spouse or marriage-related areas. The seven most common problems were: communication (84%), unrealistic expectations of marriage or spouse (56%), demonstration of affection (55%), lack of loving feelings (55%), sex (52%), power struggles (52%) and decision-making and problem-solving (49%). This study, however, can only be seen as indicative. One must be cautious about the reliability and generalisation of the study because the sample size is simply to small to allow for any overarching conclusions.

The plethora of research that has examined the association between well-being and relationships has focused on marriage, partly because marital status can be ascertained easily and accurately in surveys and because of the importance of the marital relationships to individuals and society. Hence, there is a substantial lack of research concerning cohabiting relationships and other important relationships in our social network that may impact on one's psychological and physical health. However, studies relating marital status to general well-being have identified two gender differences. First, marriage seems to be associated with somewhat greater benefits in global happiness for women than for men (Wood, Rhodes and Whelan, 1989); married women report higher life satisfaction than married men do, although they also report higher negative affect (Bernard, 1972; Glenn and Weaver, 1988), a finding that Wood and colleagues attribute to women's greater sensitivity to emotional factors in relationships. Second, whereas simply being married accounts for most of the increase in well-being among men, marital quality appears to be a more salient predictor among women (Gove, Hughes and Style, 1983) (see also Chapter 13). This suggests that important differences exist in the concept of marriage between women and men, but little empirical evidence is available to support this position. Further, the majority of the studies in this field are correlational and therefore do not allow any inferences to be made about the causal mechanisms. Thus we are left without a clear understanding as to why and how these social relationships have the negative or beneficial effects which they do.

SOCIAL AND CULTURAL CONTEXT IN INVESTIGATIONS OF FRIENDSHIP

The issue of cultural context in the investigation of relationships and friendships has received relatively little attention in the literature; there is little knowledge about how the features and effects of relationships and friendships vary with culture. However, a term for friendship seems to be available in nearly every language of the world, and an examination of the philological root of the word 'friend' in different cultures may reveal interesting and important aspects of notions of friendship and how these have evolved in different cultures (see Box 17.2 opposite).

BOX 17.2 The word 'friend' and its connotations in different cultures

The word 'friendship' or 'friend' exists in nearly every language of the world. When translating the word into our mother tongue, we often overlook the fact that the original words bear cultural particularities and differences, and these may be revealed by examining the philological roots of the words (Krappman, 1996). Below is a brief overview of the philological roots of the word friend in four European cultures (German and English, and Latin and Greek).

German and English

The modern English word 'friend' as well as the German word 'Freund', are derived from the Germanic word 'Frijond' meaning 'friend'. The word Frijond, however, also means 'kinsman', namely, a relative from a widespread kinship network and, therefore not just one of the very few persons whom we recognise today as our relatives. The German word 'fri', which still means 'free' or 'frei' in modern German, was also developed from this root. Thus, the aspect of voluntariness connected with friendship relations is embedded within the word 'friend'.

Latin and Greek

The Latin word 'amicus' is derived from the verb 'amo' (I love), which is based on 'ama'. Ama is the same word as 'mama' or 'mamie', phonemes from the child's first attempts to express affection for the mother. The Greek word 'philos' means friend, but also means 'belonging to' and 'one's own'. Therefore, the 'philli' are an individual's own family, relatives and friends. Unlike in German, however, the word for voluntariness in Greek and Latin is unrelated to the word for friendship.

The history of a particular word and its relation to other words of the same language, that are derived from the same source, suggest underlying meanings of the word that are often unknown even to native speakers. One might propose that these networks of meanings, linked with the respective words for friends, may also affect the behaviours of the members of each distinct culture. Moreover, it becomes subject to convention between those who share and use it.

Cohen (1966) examined 65 non-western societies and demonstrated that the conceptions and functions that friends perform for each other differ across these societies. The different society-specific priorities ranged from material exchange, support in love affairs or marriage arrangements through to child adoption. Suttles (1970) speaks of the 'contrastive structures' generated by friends, which on the one hand are private cultures opposing usual conventions, but on the other hand are intrinsically shaped by the overarching meanings, ideals, expressive symbols and the language that together constitute culture. In other words, friendships may be unique but they are nevertheless embedded within a larger cultural context. Cultures also circumscribe the leeway that friends have as they balance social demands and concerns with individual desires (Krappman, 1996).

The social process of friendship is manifested in a myriad of ways and reflects the weaknesses and strengths of the surrounding context. This means that cultural differences may be seen both between societies, such as those one might find in different parts of the world, as well as within societies (Krappman, 1996). The behaviours of the members of a society are not simply derived from the proclaimed common values and norms of that society, but are influenced by the outcome of these norms and values, for example the importance of socioeconomic status, ethnic traditions, religious affiliations, occupational and leisure subcultures, and age or gender specific standards. Thus, it is vital to investigate the patterns of friendship that are found in different sections of western societies. The great variety of forms of friendship to be found there is largely due to the variability in cultural values that derive from a multicultural climate. An ethnographic study conducted by Liebow (1967) illustrates this. The focus of the work was upon the friendships within a group of young black men who gathered on the sidewalk in front of a take-out restaurant ('Tally's Corner'). The men all lived under marginal, disadvantaged social conditions. These circumstances lead to the desire for reliable support from 'true' friends while at the same time severely restricting the objective and subjective capabilities of those concerned to overcome crises in relationships. He observed that these close relationships, perhaps because of the fragility of friendships, are often not declared to be friendships but are transformed into kin relationships. Good friends may consider themselves brothers and others treat them as if they were brothers. At the same time, friendships are idealised; friends claim that they will share every misfortune, give everything to the other, and will protect the friend against every danger. In reality these relationships are easily broken when unfavourable circumstances occur or selfish interests arise. Then, it becomes apparent that these people do not know anything really personal about each other. What they know about each other, whether or not they are friends, is what is known to everybody strolling around Tally's Corner (Krappman, 1996). There is no substance in the relationships to which friends can appeal when they are in conflict; thus the social situation among these men is very unstable, contrary to the claimed myth. These men try to stabilise their relationships by applying kin terms, idealising them, and ascribing long histories to them, but their friendships are in fact of another quality than is claimed by the individuals. Krappman remarked that although Liebow attempted to describe nothing more than life at Tally's Corner, his analysis demonstrated that miserable living conditions as experienced by these men can produce a situation which elicits hopes about close relationships but cannot be realised under just these conditions. This may be a relevant aspect in the actual social life of many individuals because contradictions between one's personal desire and socially offered opportunities are ubiquitous (Krappman, 1996).

This clearly shows the cultural and/or social diversity of friendships. Therefore it is necessary to examine friendships with respect to the social location of groups within one society and its culture. The content and performance of friendships are much more determined by sociocultural factors than is typically recognised within the usual narrow focus of psychological research. Psychological research must draw on etymological studies to grasp the differences of meaning connected with the phenomena of friendships. Interviews and questionnaires that take for granted that every person asked about friendships will respond on the basis of a shared meaning of the word will not be useful as long as these people come from different cultural worlds (Krappman, 1996). Should relationships between social bonds and health then be found to vary between cultures, it is difficult to be certain as whether this is due to different intervening variables modifying the relationship or simply that the essential meaningful aspects of friendship have not been measured with the same precision. To uncover some of the social collective nature of the processes which underlie our understanding and representations of the social world, it would be helpful to study friendships historically and to conduct studies in various sections of social life such as in different professions or institutions, and at times of great social change.

SOCIAL SUPPORT, SOCIAL RELATIONSHIPS AND HEALTH

To date, a substantial body of empirical evidence indicates that there exists an association between social support and health status (Burman and Margolin, 1992; Uchino, Cacioppo and Kiecolt-Glaser, 1996; Stansfeld, 1999). The absence of meaningful social connections, however this term may be defined, is thought to predispose the individual to emotional problems, psychiatric disturbance and poor physical health. Despite this now widespread empirical confirmation of the importance of social relationships for psychological and physical health, surprisingly little agreement exists about how to conceptualise or assess the potent elements of these relationships. 'Social support' is the most popular term, but its definition eludes consensus.

Heller and Swindle (1983) reflected upon the diverse meanings of the term and suggested that 'facets' of support, such as social connections, skills in accessing and maintaining social networks, support appraisals and support-seeking behaviours should be distinguished conceptually and empirically. This has rarely happened and the multiple meanings of the term have made it difficult to integrate diverse findings. Perhaps most striking is the lack of theoretical substance to the various definitions that have been proposed. The literature is largely descriptive in nature, demonstrating repeatedly that various aspects of social relationships influence health outcomes, without providing much insight into why these effects occur (Heller and Rook, 1997). This implication has some serious consequences. First, it represents a gap in our basic knowledge about the processes inherent in human well-being (Reis, 1984). Second, as Heller (1979) has cogently pointed out, the outcome of therapeutic interventions is likely to be uncertain when the explanation for the underlying phenomenon is unknown.

Sarason, Sarason and Gurung (1997) argue that social support is not simply membership in a social network, assistance that is exchanged among network numbers, or an appraisal of that assistance; neither is it only one's perception of what network members may potentially provide. Instead, social support should be seen as a reflection of a complex set of interacting events and processes that include behavioural, cognitive and bodily components. Despite this complexity, one finding emerges consistently; the qualities of personal relationships, their meaning to the individuals involved, and how that meaning is communicated are active, crucial ingredients in the social support equation. An adequate understanding of social support processes must specify the role of these qualities of social relationships in the provision, receipt, and appraisal of social support. As Heller and Swindle (1983) pointed out a number of years ago, social support is a process that involves an interaction among social structures, social relationships and personal attributes.

Newcomb (1990) views social support from an interactional perspective, arguing that it is a resource that evolves throughout life and is shaped in a reciprocal, bidirectional process between the individual and significant others. Perceived levels of social support are joint products of personal characteristics and interactions with the social environment. Personality variables may play an important role, not only in the stressors individuals encounter but also in the quantity and quality of individuals' social support networks – the frequency with which they receive support when needed, and the nature of that support – be it practical or emotional for example. Further, close personal relationships are likely to be the source of most support received (Cutrona, 1986) as well as what is perceived to be available.

Following from this, an understanding of social relationships is particularly important to an understanding of perceived support. The level and type of perceived support and the associated models of the world which people hold are likely to be based on a significant degree of earlier life experiences, especially those within the family. The work of Bowlby (1969, 1980) and later researchers (Kobak and Sceery, 1988; Hazan and Shaver, 1987) suggests that the working models that people hold in regard to themselves and towards the behaviour of others are a potent force in determining relationship behaviour in adulthood. Baldwin *et al.* (1993) have viewed these working models in terms of the internalisation of significant relationships, self-constructs and the scripts which people form of their interactions.

Elaborating on this, Sarason, Sarason and Gurung (1997) believe social support should be viewed as a set of working models of one's self as someone with certain competencies and characteristics that imply worthiness of the support and caring of others, expectations of the social forthcomingness of others, and the qualities of the relationships expected with particular people. These working models lead a person to conclusions about the degree to which she or he is valued. These conclusions then influence (1) the development of current relationships with others, (2) the acquisition of feelings of self-efficacy – feelings that are both generalised and related to specific tasks, (3) the perceived availability of social support across a range of tasks, and (4) effectiveness in coping with stress and maintaining a task focus. If this is the case, as Sarason *et al.* suggest, then it would be helpful to assess aspects of social relationships and friendships and for this information to be used in predicting health outcomes, thereby increasing our understanding of the way in which support functions with respect to health.

Summary and conclusions

The scientific study of personal relationships and friendships is in its infancy and consists largely of descriptive data derived from questionnaires and interviews with samples of unrepresentative adults. Research has not given equal attention to the positive and the negative features of these relationships. Given the diverse forms that social relationships can take and the variety of ways that people can either help or hinder one another, perhaps it should not be surprising that definitions of supportive relationships vary so greatly. However, it makes little sense to develop programmes to 'increase support' (grafted support through interventions) without some sense of what aspects of social relationships tend to be health protective, neutral, or perhaps even noxious. Until the structure and detailed content of social support is fully understood, research will remain impaired, and the fullest protective *and* healing functions of social support will not be realised. Additionally, the content and performance of friendships are much more determined by sociocultural factors than is typically recognised within the usual narrow focus of psychological research. Research from other disciplines provides evidence that friendships differ with respect to societies and their cultures as well as to the social location of groups within one society. Individuals almost universally are searching for others with whom they can establish a particular relationship, that is, a close friendship. For that purpose they use a culturally-based shared meaning system because it enables them to negotiate their relationships in a way that offers the best balance of personal desires and others' demands in a given context. Thus, researchers must look at the social collective nature of the processes which underlie our understanding and representations of personal relationships.

Discussion points ●

A   Is a friendship of inferior quality better than none at all?

B   Have non-kin relationships become more important in western society over the last century?

C   What limitations do current conceptions of social relationships place on understanding the relationship between social ties and well-being?

Suggested reading ●

Cupach, W.P. and Spitzberg, B.H. (1994) The Dark Side of Interpersonal Communication. (Hillsdale, N.J.: Erlbaum).

Duck, S. (1997). *Handbook of Personal Relationships: Theory, Research and Interventions.* (New York: John Wiley & Sons).

Stansfeld, S. (1999) 'Social Support and Social Cohesion', in. M. Marmot and R.G. Wilkinson (eds), *Social Determinants of Health.* (Oxford: Oxford University Press).

Doctors and Patients

'What is happening to the human relationships between GP and patient is part of the same process which is making the quality of life so much worse for the urban have-nots.'

David Widgery (*Some Lives*, 1991)

INTRODUCTION

The delivery of medical care has always been dependent on interpersonal relationships and, though this has been acknowledged in the importance accorded to 'the bedside manner' of physicians, it has seldom been recognised in medical theory. Two historical developments now dominate the human interaction between physician and patient. Firstly, the increasing technological transformation of society has created a deep rift between the art and science of medical practice. Not only has the human element in medicine been subordinated to the technical, but the very nature of human relationships themselves are being re-engineered along with the new medical technology. Secondly, as the human touch takes an increasingly back seat to the hi-tech face of scientific medicine, paradoxically the power accorded the role of medical practitioner in the minds of the public remains very strong and continues to mask the reality of the human beings enacting it. The training of doctors as technicians has important implications for the way their patients respond to them and to how successful their interventions will be in improving health and well-being. In this chapter we will examine how features of the doctor–patient relationship influence the progress of the consultation and relate to the subsequent management of health.

MEDICAL COMPLIANCE

Over 200 different factors have been associated with compliance to medical treatment (Homedes, 1991). These include demographic variables, the psychological characteristics of the patient, their social context, the interactions between care providers and patients and situational demands from particular diseases or ailments (Sheridan and Radmacher, 1992). Non-compliance, however, is usually conceived as originating with patients. This is probably because the term compliance already implies that the measure of successful outcome in a medical consultation is the patient subscribing to the view provided by the physician and doing what they say. This is certainly questionable. We have already seen evidence (Chapter 2) that physicians' judgements of the quality of life of a variety of patient groups frequently does not concur with their patients. Treatments designed to alter patients' quality of life may not therefore be necessarily what is best for them. Though the term *adherence* is now favoured over *compliance*, it is doubtful whether the change in terminology has been accompanied by any underlying change in meaning regarding the power or the expert status of doctors. Indeed in some quarters the term adherence is already being replaced by concordance in a further attempt to downplay inherent imbalances in power between the parties. Whilst there can be no doubting that failing to follow prescribed treatments may carry serious health risks, there are also occasions when following the advice of physicians does likewise. Illich (1977) draws attention to the huge impact of medically-induced ill-health in the population. One example results from the unnecessary over-prescribing of antibiotics which has led to greater microbial resistance and increased health risks. A study by Butler *et al.* (1999) found that doctors justified the prescribing of what they knew were ineffective treatments on the grounds that they did not wish to jeopardise the doctor–patient relationship. Many commented that they felt the risk of over-prescribing antibiotics was a community health problem and not one for individual patients – a strange piece of logic if ever there was one. The same study, in fact, found that amongst patients attending for sore throats or upper-respiratory-tract infections satisfaction was not related to whether or not they received antibiotics, but whether they received reassurance, information and pain relief. Dissatisfaction pertained to feeling rushed and the lack of provision of clear explanations for their treatment.

The issue of adherence, then, cannot be considered apart from the question of whether it is always rational to follow medical advice. It is therefore important to distinguish between intentional (for example a desire to avoid or reduce unpleasant side-effects associated with a given medication, such as occurs for example with anti-hypertensive medication or anti-psychotic drugs; a wish by patients to reduce their expenditure on medicine by extending the length of time it is used for; or discontinuing medication when it is believed it is no longer needed or no longer effective) and non-intentional compliance (for example as results from a range of emotional and cognitive factors such as the ability to correctly recall the instructions for use, how much information has been given and so on) (Pitts, 1998b). Identifying factors behind compliance or non-compliance depend on reliable and valid ways to measure it in the first place. Interview methods will inevitably be biased by social pressure to overstate the extent of compliance. In general, patients' self-reports suggest a level of non-compliance of around 22 per cent, whilst more objective methods such as pill counts, blood and urine tests produce estimates of over 50 per cent (Ley, 1988).

The failure to carry through an intended medical intervention must also be considered from the perspective of health-care providers as well as patients. The effects of long waiting lists for treatments and frequently cancelled or late appointments on patient morale and confidence have received scant attention in recent years, though there is no reason to believe that compliance levels and satisfaction levels will not be affected by these. An early study by Geersten, Gray and Ward (1973) found compliance levels with medical advice fell sharply as waiting times in the surgery increased. No doubt the lack of attention to delays or failures to administer treatment says much about the power dynamics inherent in medical research – it is much easier to blame patients when things go wrong, and to see this view in widespread circulation. Indeed there appears to be an assumption of inherent rationality behind all health-care provision. However, this assumption is erroneous – and the debate over evidence-based medicine in recent years has drawn attention to the fact that there are complex reasons for initiating and maintaining treatments other than any scientific evidence of efficacy. Dinant (1997) notes that physicians are frequently confronted by patients taking multiple long-term medications for which there is no proper evidence on when drug cessation may be appropriate. In addition, no gold standards exist for many treatments, and young and elderly people are frequently underrepresented in clinical trials with the ensuing result that no proper evidence exists regarding the suitability of certain treatments for them.

DOCTOR–PATIENT COMMUNICATION

It is disconcerting to see that the manner of communication between doctor and patient is still a major cause of dissatisfaction – having been identified as an important reason for non-compliance many years ago (see for example Davis, 1968) and replicated many times since (for example Ley, 1982; Cecil and Killeen, 1997). In a study by Phillips (1996) of 320 patients on obstetrics and gynaecology wards, almost half reported dissatisfaction with the care received. Complaints concerned insensitivity to subjects' conditions, evasion of direct questions, deliberate use of medical jargon and unwillingness to give information. This style of interaction may be more typical of male than female physicians. Female physicians have been shown to spend more time with patients, be more likely to facilitate patient participation, in addition to including feelings and the wider psychological and social context of patients' lives in discussions (Roter and Hall, 1998). One of the problems is that physicians still see good communication as inefficient and as something that gets in the way of what they perceive to be their main role – which is to practise clinical medicine. Good communication, however, has been shown in numerous studies to have positive effects on a number of health outcome measures; including pain, anxiety, functional status, blood pressure and blood glucose level (Stewart *et al.*, 1999).

PATIENT SATISFACTION

Research shows that one of the undoubted problems facing doctors is the matter of identifying what the patient actually requires when they come for a consultation. In one sense this is hardly surprising when so little research has actually been done asking patients what they want. All too often in both clinical and research settings it is simply assumed. Given the widespread levels of dissatisfaction reported – a review by Ley (1988) put this at 41 per cent for hospital patients and 28 per cent for general practice patients – it is surprising that more concern has not been evident. Some commentators believe current surveys in fact already overestimate levels of satisfaction owing to factors such as social desirability bias, patients' reluctance to express opinions and because of the wording of the questions (Avis, Bond and Arthur, 1997). Williams and Calnan (1991), for example, found that asking patients about their overall satisfaction is more likely to elicit positive replies, whereas asking them about specific details of care can lead to critical comments. Concern has been expressed that the concept of patient satisfaction itself may lack validity and doesn't allow patients to express in their own terms how they perceive and evaluate the care they receive. A further difficulty is that satisfaction levels may change over time as patients come to reconstrue their earlier experiences as their own knowledge about their condition develops. Perhaps what is called for is a more patient-centred mode of evaluation, where patients actively set the agenda for what is to be evaluated and play an active role in the research process. Despite these limitations, 'satisfaction' research has yielded some valuable information about the nature of physician–patient interactions. A factor analysis by Ware and Snyder (1975) reported finding 18 dimensions to patient satisfaction. Subsequent work has led to the identification of eight attributes of health care – accessibility and availability, financial arrangements, time spent with providers, choice and continuity, communication, interpersonal aspects of care, technical quality of care and outcomes of care (Davies and Ware, 1991). These can be grouped in terms of provision, interpersonal aspects of provision and outcome which resemble two of the three main components to patient satisfaction proposed by Ley (1988) – competence, emotional support and understanding, and explanation and information – which have provided a useful framework for teasing out what appears to be going wrong in medical consultations.

Emotional Support

The provision of adequate emotional support is no doubt hampered by the fact that psychological problems presented to general practitioners frequently go unrecognised. In part this is likely to be due to the fact that many doctors do not see themselves as appropriate providers of psychosocial care (Bower, West, Tylee and Hann, 1999). Why is this? It is not easy to say to what extent this is a consequence of inadequate training for doctors or to what degree it stems from the selection of people for medical training who come with unsuitable interpersonal styles in the first place. Certainly training appears to be inadequate. Only 16 per cent of a sample of house officers (those in their first hospital appointment after medical school) reported being taught assessment of psychosocial factors during their first clinical year (Williams *et al.*, 1997). Some have argued that doctors' poor use of communication and social skills stems from the stressful effects of their excessive workload and that the solution to the problem of poor communication will not come from skills training for doctors but from more doctors and investment in health care. Parsons (1999) puts the case succinctly:

> If we want doctors to be empathic, approachable and effective communicators they have to be treated properly. (p. 717)

Calnan (1988) identified two contrasting orientations amongst physicians. Those with a social orientation were more likely to see their role in much broader terms – encouraging health education and screening as well as taking an interest in the social aspects of their patients' lives. In contrast, those with a medical orientation concerned themselves more with organic disease, the financial rewards of medical practise and were less interested in the personal or social concerns of the patients. Clearly Calnan's findings lead to questions about whether the right kind of people are being recruited for medical careers. In the UK, increasing attention has been devoted to researching the selection process of medical students and the evidence currently suggests candidates from lower socioeconomic groups and ethnic minorities are disadvantaged (McManus, 1997) at the entrance stage, with women disadvantaged later on for more senior positions (Kværner, Aasland and Botten, 1999). It is not hard to see from this that in terms of their demographic characteristics, medical practitioners are not representative of the general population and the underrepresentation of people from lower socioeconomic backgrounds – itself ignored in all subsequent commentaries on this paper – is likely to be a contributing factor in the degree of empathy established between patient and doctor.

Information

Accessible written information regarding their medication is desired by a majority of patients (Weinman, 1990) and a majority of studies show it to have an affect in increasing compliance. It is preferable to verbal communication alone which a number of studies show quickly results in over half the information being forgotten (DiMatteo and DiNicola, 1982). Written information may also be effective in reducing post-surgical pain (Boore, 1979). However, only a small proportion of time is

BOX 18.1   What information should patients be given about medication?

Berry *et al.* (1997) presented 16 categories of information that people wanted to know about prescribed medication. Eighteen doctors (including general practitioners, hospital registrars, senior registrars, and consultants) were asked to rate these from 1 (not at all important) to 5 (vital). From these, the categories were rank-ordered in terms of their importance. These were then compared to those from a group of patients. The data are presented below.

Categories	Patients ranking	Doctors ranking
Possible side effects	1	10.5
What the medication does	2	10.5
Lifestyle changes	3	3
Detailed questions about taking medication	4	2
What is it (e.g. drug type, active ingredient)?	5	15
Interaction with medication for long-term use	6	1
What to do if symptoms change/don't change	7	10.5
Probability medication will be effective	8	14
Any alternatives to medication	9	16
Is it known to be effective?	10	13
Does medication treat symptoms or cause	11	6.5
What if I forget to take or take too much?	12	6.5
Interaction with non-prescription items	13	4
Risks of not taking medication	14	8
Interaction with currently prescribed medication	15	5
How will I know if medication is working?	16	10.5

A rank-order correlation between patients' and doctors' rankings shows almost no relationship between the two (*Rho* = 0.02, *n* = 16). There are few areas where there is any noticeable degree of agreement. These are: principally lifestyle changes consequent on taking the medication, the details of how to take the medication and whether the treatment is known to be effective (though the latter begs the question of by what criteria efficacy is judged) and how important are these to the patient. The most frequently requested information item by patients – the possible side effects of the medication – received a very low ranking from the doctors.

actually spent imparting information to patients, though doctors think the amount of time is greater than it actually is (DiMatteo, 1985). This still leaves the matter of deciding what kind of information to provide. Research by Berry, Michas, Gillie and Forster (1997) (see Box 18.1) suggests that patients' needs for particular types of information about their medication is not being met, whilst Falvo and Tippy (1988), found in a high proportion of medical interviews (38%) the physicians failed to specify the amount of medication prescribed, with half of these not even providing information about the length of treatment. This work raises a number of important questions, chief among which must be the means through which doctors form their views about patients' needs – in this instance for information. An obvious answer would be through their experience with their patients. Given that the evidence suggests low agreement in this area in addition to the widespread general dissatisfaction with communication between physician and patient, an inescapable conclusion is that a good deal of doctors' opinions about patients' needs are not derived from listening to their patients. An alternative candidate lies in the system of medical education. There is currently little or no data concerning the nature of and the manner in which psychosocial skills are acquired or lost during medical training. Of concern must be the suggestion that more recent entrants to medical schools appear to have less clinical experience than in the past (McManus, Richards and Winder, 1998).

Of course it must be remembered that optimal medical consultations do not simply comprise in giving patients what they want – but it is reasonable to expect that patients' emotional and informational needs are at least recognised and attempts made to address them. Overall, the medical consultation can be considered to have three different purposes: making treatment-related decisions, exchanging information, and creating or maintaining a good interpersonal relationship (Ong, de Haes, Hoos and Lammes, 1995). Even after a considered reciprocal exchange of information (from the patient regarding their symptoms and needs), and from the doctor (information about treatment choices and outcomes) there is no reason why one should necessarily expect complete agreement. Patients in Berry et al.'s (1997) study, for example, indicated that they would be less likely to take prescribed medication were the explanations to contain negative information.

Competence

The presumed competence of those charged with our medical care is extremely important to patients, it cannot always be taken for granted. A few studies have shown that some doctors may have inaccurate knowledge about the anatomical location of certain organs (Boyle, 1970) or that their knowledge of specific diseases (for example asthma) may be inaccurate (Anderson et al., 1983). Health professionals, then, do not behave in a uniform clinical manner; they may frame a given problem differently, may be more or less likely to arrive at a particular diagnosis, and when a diagnosis has been made may differ in the treatments they prescribe (Ogden, 1996). This variability is due not only to differing levels of expertise and knowledge; different information about reported symptoms may be used to form hypotheses, and different criteria used to confirm or refute the hypotheses made. This may then lead to different decisions about what clinical actions to take. Several studies also suggest the clinicians' own health beliefs influence the course of treatment arrived at. This was evident in the earlier discussion regarding the overuse of antibiotics.

The question of how to assess clinical competence is a vexed one. Simple audits which involve making comparisons between different surgeons in terms of their respective success rates or mortality rates for specific operations may be misleading unless adjustments are made for the duration and severity of the condition being treated, the presence of other illness, patient characteristics such as age, gender and social class and the socioeconomic characteristics of the region where the patients are being treated. It may even be necessary to take account of the level of experience of the surgeon. Should one really expect comparable performance between consultant surgeons of say 5 and 15 years experience? Some exploratory work has been undertaken to measure physician competence. In one employing written assessment by patients, peer physicians, referring physicians and co-workers, Vilato *et al.* (1997) reported promising psychometric properties for the measures. Notzer, Eldad and Donchin (1995) used four instruments (peer assessment, self-assessment, written examination and interview) to assess competence of those providing emergency care under field conditions and found significant but moderate correlations between results of a written examination and peer evaluation and between peer and self-assessment. Though still in its infancy, this type of work warrants further consideration, though clearly the pencil and paper methods should also be linked to appropriate measures of clinical outcome.

Summary and conclusions ●

Providing medical care is highly dependent on interpersonal relationships. To date over 200 factors have been associated with compliance to medical treatment, covering a range of demographic variables, patient characteristics, interpersonal aspects and situational and contextual demands. Despite this, failure to follow medical advice is usually considered the responsibility of the patient with the complexities of the power dynamics of the relationship between medical practitioner and patient given less attention. In considering this matter it is helpful to distinguish non-intentional from intentional compliance. The latter cannot be considered separately from the question of whether it is always rational to follow medical advice. Identifying factors behind compliance or non-compliance depend on reliable and valid means of assessment. Interview methods are biased by social pressure. Patients' self-reports suggest lower levels of non-compliance in comparison to objective methods such as pill counts, blood and urine tests.

Although it may seem a simple matter to ask patients how satisfied they are with the treatment they have had, a number of considerations must be borne in mind. How and when one asks the question can in large measure determine the kind of response received. General closed questions are more likely to produce positive responses, which may mask how patients feel about the details of their consultation/treatment. More open questions which allow patients to voice any concerns may be more likely to detect them. Inquiring immediately after treatment is also more likely to produce higher levels of satisfaction. Work to date indicates emotional support, information and competence are important components of satisfaction. However, as in many areas of health psychology it is important to obtain people's own assessments of the components of quality and how important each of them are, before asking how satisfied they are with each of them. Many studies suggest communication between doctor and patient is still a major cause of dissatisfaction Complaints concerned insensitivity to subjects' conditions, evasion of direct questions, deliberate use of medical jargon and unwillingness to give information. There is evidence that good communication may have positive effects on a number of health outcome measures.

Discussion points

A What factors do you think influence doctors' levels of satisfaction with their work?

B What difficulties arise in trying to assess levels of patient compliance?

C Suggest ways for assessing clinical competence.

Suggested reading

Calnan, M. (1988) 'Images of General Practice': The Perceptions of the Doctor', *Social Science and Medicine*, **27**: 579–86.

Ley, P. (1988) *Communicating with Patients* (London: Croon Helm).

Ong, L.M., de Haes, J.C., Hoos, A.M. and Lammes, F.B. (1995) 'Doctor–Patient Communication: A Review of the Literature', *Social Science and Medicine*, **40**(7): 903–18.

Roter, D.L. and Hall, J.A. (1998) 'Why Physician Gender Matters in Shaping the Physician–Patient Relationship', *Journal of Women's Health*, **7**(9): 1093–7.

Part 5
Managing Chronic Illness

As Health Psychology achieves greater prominence, a number of distinct challenges are emerging. Several of these have been outlined in previous chapters – particularly the relationship between psychology and other health sciences which have more explicitly recognised the role of social processes in engendering health or illness. A related matter concerns what research methods are appropriate to the study of psychological processes affecting health and health care. These problems are predominantly theoretical in nature. Given that one of the driving forces behind the rise of the discipline has been the urgent need to solve practical problems – it should not be considered altogether surprising that these theoretical issues are only just gaining ground. However, the practical problems which it was hoped health psychology would address should not be underestimated. Chief amongst these are the demands placed upon health services by the growing populations coping with chronic diseases. The following chapters will survey the role of psychological processes in a number of areas, examining those areas of ill-health which in many ways have become the staple diet of research work in health psychology – cancer, diabetes and heart disease. Subsequently we will review work which addresses the psychological demands and management of two major chronic neurological diseases – Alzheimer's disease and multiple sclerosis.

In addition to providing the clinical background to these conditions we set out to consider three principle issues. First of all we wish to enquire into the role, if any, which psychological factors play in increasing susceptibility to these types of ill-health. Secondly, we ask what psychological demands do these illnesses place on those who experience them? Related to this is the question of how people can be supported psychologically and socially, so that their lives as people with these conditions may proceed as optimally as possible.

Cancer

'That experience changed me. I realized how fragile everything in life is.'

Federico Fellini (*I, Fellini*, by Charlotte Chandler, 1994)

The term cancer refers to a group of nearly two hundred different diseases, all of which are characterised by unrestricted cell proliferation which usually leads to the formation of a malignant neoplasm (cancerous tumour). It is useful to classify these into four main types: *sarcomas* which are malignant neoplasms of muscle, bone or connective tissue; *carcinomas* which develop from skin cells or the cells lining organs; *lymphomas* which arise in the lymphatic system; and *leukaemias* which are cancers of the blood-forming organs (Sarafino, 1998). Metastases refer to secondary cancers which are formed in parts of the body as a result of the migration of cancerous cells from other sites through the blood or lymphatic system. The most prevalent cancers are those of the lung, colon, rectum, bladder, prostate, breast and skin.

CANCER: BELIEFS, ATTITUDES AND PERSONALITY

Cancer as a generic disease is considered the most psychologically threatening in western societies. In a study of medical staff's views, Crary and Crary (1974) found cancer was rated as worse, less happy and more worthless than death. It is without doubt a widespread disease – around 30 per cent of people will probably develop some form of cancer in their lives. While Pitts (1998) suggested this psychological dread has occurred because of the declining threat of infectious diseases and the increase in life expectancy during the last century, Calnan (1987) contends that fear of cancer has grown from the mystery surrounding the cause, the insidious way it develops and the inability to cure it. These are obviously important factors although they are unlikely to tell the whole story. Sontag (1979) states quite starkly that cancer as a disease is regarded with shame – a testament perhaps to the failure of our quest to conquer nature and to transcend the body. Cancer now serves as a metaphor for physical, psychological and social decay in many areas of life. Like their real biological counterparts, such metaphorical cancers can be slow or quick-acting. Either way they have come to symbolise the threat of impermanence and decline in aspects of our socially constructed reality – an impending demise often precipitated by some invasive agent. In a society that appears to elevate the impossibility of eternal youth, economic stability and continual competition and struggle above so many other things it cannot be surprising that the symbol of cancer has become so potent.

People's beliefs about cancer have received increasing attention in recent years. Given the socioeconomic trends in mortality and morbidity for many cancers at all stages of life (Davey Smith, Hart, Blane, Gillis and Hawthorn, 1997; Faggiano, Partanen, Kogevinas and Boffetta, 1997; Kunst *et al.*, 1998) it is surprising that little work has examined class or cultural differences in the nature of these beliefs. In fact little general social context of any kind has been provided when examining people's representations of cancer. In one notable exception, Blair (1995) found middle-class respondents were more likely to emphasise psychological factors like stress, anxiety, worry or not expressing feelings as factors behind the causes of cancer. Working-class respondents were conversely more likely to emphasise physical factors like pollution, too much alcohol, smoking and poisonous chemicals. In their views on treatment efficacy, middle-class respondents, rated psychological treatments like therapy or talking, support from family and friends considerably more effective than did the working-class respondents, who were more likely to consider luck a factor in recovery and gave less value to personal control. That clear class differences appear to exist in lay representations indicate the importance of considering these in efforts to promote better health – whether through exhortations for people to change or adopt healthier behaviours, or to take up screening options which afford the possibilities of early disease detection and better survival rates. Beyond their value in informing health promotional practice, lay representations of cancer are of additional interest because they may tell us something about how people may respond to having cancer. Faller, Lang and Schilling (1996), for instance, found that cancer patients who were more likely to make psychosocial causal attributions were also more likely to suffer depression and emotional distress. These latter factors have themselves been implicated as agents influencing cancer progression.

The idea that psychological states can influence the development of cancers has a long history – it was for example considered by the Greek physician Galen in the second century (Walker and Eremin, 1995). Nowadays it is most readily expressed in terms of the cancer-prone personality, which has generated considerable work, not to say controversy (Box 19.1). Fernandez-Ballesteros, Ruiz and Garde (1998) noted that over 300 journal articles and 68 books and book chapters had been published on this subject between 1974 and 1995. The putative personality type in question – sometimes labelled as the **Type C personality** involves the suppression of negative emotions, notably anger and anxiety and hopelessness or helplessness in the face of stress and passivity (Eysenck, 1994). Eysenck argued that this link between personality, stress and cancer is likely to be mediated by the immune system – with chronic stress acting to suppress immune function. Differences between cancer patients and controls consistent with this hypothesis have been found in a number of studies. Fernandez-Ballesteros *et al.* (1998) found women with breast cancer exhibited greater emotional defensiveness and need for harmony compared to healthy controls. Compared to a group of healthy controls, Phipps and Srivastava (1997) also found paediatric oncology patients scored lower on depression and anxiety and higher on defensiveness, characterising a repressive coping style. Cross-sectional studies such as these, however, must be considered inconclusive as links between cancer and personality variables could have arisen as a consequence of psychological reactions to the disease, rather than the latter occupying an antecedent role. Phipps and Srivastava, (1997) however, did report that repressive adaptation did not appear to be related to the time which had elapsed since diagnosis.

Several studies have employed prospective designs – comparing premorbid personality data with subsequent disease status, and a number of these have provided

Type C personality The putative cancer-prone personality, otherwise known as the Type C personality, involves the suppression of negative emotions – notably anger and anxiety, as well as hopelessness or helplessness in the face of stress, and passivity.

Suggestions of a causative role in cancer formation from a repressive coping style has aroused controversy for several reasons. Above all there is concern that this will lead to people being blamed for having cancer – a possibility which can only make matters worse for those suffering from the disease. Whilst victim blaming is to be deplored, if evidence of a causal relationship does withstand critical scrutiny then it is the action of victim blaming which should come under attack, not the research itself. At the present moment interpretation of the research is open to question on several fronts. Besides the ambiguous nature of the cross-sectional data, many of the studies have inadequately controlled for either age or disease severity and consensus has been lacking as to whether the association between psychosocial factors and cancer relates primarily to disease onset or disease progression. A role for personality variables in disease progression in no way logically implicates these in prior disease causation. What the variables characteristic of the Type C personality actually denote is still unclear. If they represent a tendency for behavioural inhibition of felt emotion this would imply conscious decision-making. By contrast, repression of the relevant emotions would not (Fernandez-Ballesteros, Ruiz and Garde, 1998). A further problem in interpreting the relationship is whether to treat personality as an efficient cause of the cancer – or whether personality itself should be regarded as an intermediate step in a causal chain leading from earlier formative experiences. There have been suggestions that other psychosocial characteristics such as social inhibition (Denollet, 1998), negative life events (Cooper, Cooper and Faragher, 1986), depression (McGhee, Williams and Elwood, 1994) and self-efficacy (De Boer *et al.*, 1998) are related to cancer development. Whilst the links between depression, social inhibition and cancer appear more well-founded, they have not been found in all studies (e.g. Barraclough, Pinder, Crudddas, Osmond, Taylor and Perry, 1992). Evidence with respect to self-efficacy is promising but requires further study. A meta analysis of 29 studies by Pettigrew, Fraser and Regan (1999), however, found little evidence of any reliable association between adverse life events and breast cancer, suggesting instead that the seemingly pathogenic effects reported in many studies are an artefact of poor methodology. More work is obviously called for in this area. Whilst there does seem sufficient evidence to accept that psychological factors play some role in the development of cancers, it has not been established that this is true for all cancers, or that the physical effects can be reversed by psychological intervention.

stronger evidence. Dattore, Shontz, Franklin and Coyne (1980) compared premorbid MMPI records from 735 cancer and 125 non-cancer patients. Those who went on to develop a cancer, irrespective of its site, were distinguished from those without cancer on the basis of lower scores on the repression-sensitisation scale. In a similar design, Kavan, Engdahl and Kay (1995) found veterans who subsequently developed colon cancer were distinguished from those who did not in terms of aggressive hostility and phobia scores, while Greer and Morris (1975) found women with short survival times following a diagnosis of breast cancer tended to be hopeless and helpless in contrast to survivors who displayed a more fighting spirit. One rather interesting possibility which this work throws up is that the lower survival rates for breast cancer which are found in the UK (Sant *et al.*, 1998) might owe something to aspects of the British national character noted for the tendency to withhold emotional expression. Other factors must certainly be considered (Richards, Sainsbury and Kerr, 1997), though the hypothesis has testable implications. A meta analysis by McKenna *et al.* (1999), however, examining data from 46 studies investigating the relationship between psychosocial factors and the development of breast cancer, found only a modest association between them and concluded that they did not support the conventional wisdom that personality and stress influence the development of breast cancer.

COPING WITH CANCER

The process of coping with cancer begins with receiving the diagnosis from a health professional. The manner in which this is conveyed is very important, not only for reducing the stress of the situation for the patient, but for longer-term adjustment, selecting from appropriate therapeutic options and complying with treatment (Ford, Fallowfield and Lewis, 1994). It was commonly believed for many years that patients should not be told bad news – and that neither would they want to be told. However, research does not support this. In a study of 101 patients newly referred to a medical oncology out-patient department, the overwhelming majority (94%) expressed a desire to be given as much information as possible – be it good or bad (Fallowfield, Ford and Lewis, 1995). Unfortunately, many physicians receive little training in the communication skills necessary for delivering bad news, and evidence suggests they are not good at detecting distress in their patients or estimating the amount of information that they require (Ford *et al.*, 1994). Greater training in counselling skills would be helpful in this regard – at all levels of the medical hierarchy – but it is also evident that despite the enthusiasm of some physicians, adherence to the medical model has meant and is likely to continue to mean that the psychological aspects of clinical consultations remain relatively neglected in medical training. This has too often been justified on the basis of good communication being time consuming and interfering with real clinical care (Fallowfield and Clark, 1994).

Above and beyond receiving a diagnosis of cancer, the psychological and psychosocial demands on patients are severe. These come from both the impact of the disease and the treatments for it. The disease poses questions about our own mortality, about the image we hold of ourselves constructed from how our bodies look, feel and function, and of the nature of our relationships with others (Fallowfield, 1991). All these have to be rapidly re-evaluated. The adaptation demanded will depend on many factors – the stage of the cancer, the age one has attained, the level of available social support, the interpersonal skills one has mastered in life as well as the meanings and attitudes one has constructed towards health, illness and important life goals. Not surprisingly cancer patients show high morbidity for psychological distress, with an indication that the level of distress is greater for those who have encountered the disease in other family members (Gilbar, 1997). It has been estimated that almost one-fifth of patients will be so affected, with mood disorders such as anxiety and depression the most common (Ogden, 1996). As a result there have been calls for greater psychological interventions as part of routine cancer treatment (Fallowfield, 1995d) – although some voices have cautioned against an uncritical acceptance of the benefits of different approaches (Moynihan, Horwich and Bliss, 1999). The intention is for these to be directed towards improvements in patients' quality of life (Greer *et al.*, 1992), although some have even suggested there may be added benefits in longevity (Fawzy, Fawzy, Arndt and Pasnau, 1995). Greater evaluation of a whole range of general and specific interventions is required, although these have been slow in forthcoming, and many nurses who are best placed to deliver psychological care have been poorly trained or lack training altogether (Fallowfield and Roberts, 1992).

Amongst the reasons for this have been a constellation of views held by many medical practitioners that subjective data are unsuitable for scientific measurement, that anxiety and depression should be regarded as normal reactions to cancer and that dwelling on emotional issues upsets patients. However, as quality-of-life evaluation gathers momentum and assumes increased importance in clinical trials this picture is likely to change. Ogden (1996) lists a number of areas where psychological intervention is appropriate, including pain management, social support, the treatment of classically conditioned nausea and vomiting, body-image counselling, cognitive adaptation strategies, relaxation training and use of mental imagery. To this list could be added psychological support for health service workers where the risks of burn out and distress are also high (Fallowfield, 1995e). It should be noted, however, that evidence for the efficacy of interventions in all the listed areas does not as yet exist and considerable methodological problems exist in conducting such evaluations. People receiving psychological interventions may proceed to alter their behaviour in other crucial ways that may be difficult for researchers to track (for example improved diet and exercise), and it is these that may be responsible for any change in outcome.

CANCER PREVENTION

As we have seen, the question of personality correlates of cancer has provoked debate regarding cancer patients being blamed for their condition. Surprisingly this debate has not been so apparent in those areas where people's behaviour has unquestionably increased their risk. Cigarette smoking is an obvious example. International comparisons show lung cancer death rates closely follow the prevalence and duration of smoking in previous decades (Kubik and Plesko, 1998). Smoking trends in females in many European countries (particularly central, southern and eastern Europe) are giving cause for concern as these predict increasing lung cancer mortality in the next few decades (La Vecchia and Boyle, 1993; Jubik, Plesko and Reissigova, 1998). In addition to smoking, diet (Senior, 1997), alcohol consumption and sexual behaviour are also related to cancer risk.

Diets low in fresh fruit and vegetables have been associated with cancers of the respiratory and digestive tracts. La Vecchia, Tavani, Franceschi, Levi, Corrao and Negri (1997), for example, estimate that a poor diet of this kind may account for 10–15 per cent of oral cancer cases in Europe. High fat diets have been linked with both skin and breast cancer (Black, 1998; Pitts, 1996). Slattery, Boucher, Caan, Potter and Ma (1998), meanwhile, provide epidemiological evidence that western dietary patterns typified by a greater intake of total energy and dietary cholesterol, together with a higher body mass index, are associated with an elevated risk for colon cancer in men and women. Encouraging dietary change in adults presents considerable difficulties for psychologists (see Chapter 12), not least because the psychosocial correlates of healthier eating may differ depending upon the type of food consumed (Trudeau, Kristal, Li and Patterson, 1998).

Heavy alcohol consumption has been linked to cancers of the mouth, throat, voice box, oesophagus, liver and breast (Royal College of Psychiatrists, 1986; Bowlin, Leske, Varma Nasca, Weinstein and Caplan, 1997; Seitz, Pöschl, and Simanowski, 1998),

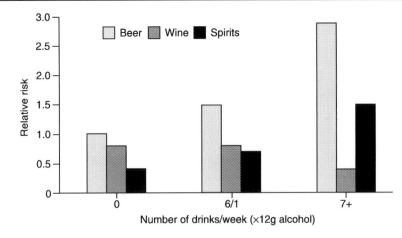

Figure 19.1   Relative risk of upper digestive tract cancer according to intake of beer wine and spirits, adjusted for age, sex, smoking habits and education

Source: Adapted from M. Grønbæk *et al.* (1998), *British Medical Journal*, **317**: 844–8, with permission from the BMJ Publishing Group.

with equivocal findings regarding prostate cancer (Lumey Pittman and Wynder, 1998). The presence of dose–response relationships between the level of consumption and the relative risk for many of these cancers, after adjustment has been made for other known risk factors, is strongly suggestive of a causal relationship. The apparent beneficial effects of alcohol on coronary heart disease, means that consumers are faced with complex decisions about the relative benefits and costs at different levels of intake regarding their health as a whole. Little research has as yet been conducted on how people balance their assessments of risk in these matters. This picture may be even more complicated by the observation that different types of alcoholic drinks present different risks (wine appears to be less malignant) for tumour development (Grønbæk, Becker, Johansen, Tønnesen, Jensen, Thorkild and Sørensen, 1998)(see Figure 19.1).

Sexual behaviour too has been linked to cancer – notably of the cervix – with the risks increasing with number of births, number of partners and early age at first intercourse (de Sanjosé, Bosch, Muñoz, and Shah, 1997; Parazzini *et al.*, 1998). From these data many have been quick to identify female promiscuity as a 'cause' – however, in reality the risks women face also relate to the sexual habits of their male partners. Some work has suggested that the relative risks of contracting the disease are elevated by a factor of eight if the male partner has had at least 15 partners outside marriage (Doyal, 1995). Evidence linking human papillomavirus (HPV) in the male partners of women to cervical cancer is strong – suggesting over 90 per cent of cervical cancers can be attributed to certain HPV types (Chichareon *et al.*, 1998). Preventative efforts here face many of the same hurdles as attempts to minimise the spread of HIV and AIDS, and not just the time lag between behaviour and health outcome. But as with many of the aforementioned cancer risks the underlying behaviours appear highly resistant to change, perhaps because of the highly emotionally charged nature of learned appetitive behaviour (Orford, 1985). It is not surprising, therefore, that much greater success has occurred with preventative efforts which have been directed at detecting cancers at an early enough stage.

CANCER SCREENING

Cancer screening has largely been directed towards detecting cancers of the cervix and breast, and these have been supported by programmes which have encouraged women to undertake breast self-examination. To a lesser degree steps have also been taken to urge men to undertake testicular self-examination, as cancer of the testes is now the most common malignancy in young males and has doubled in the last 20 years (O'Callaghan and Mead, 1997; Peate, 1997). Uptake of screening services appears to be related to a complex array of factors. Social class is one such influence, with most studies showing a higher pattern of uptake amongst more advantaged groups for both breast cancer and cervical cancer screening (Benzeval, Judge and White-head, 1996). These inequities are, however, not inevitable. As part of a general health study of almost 60 000 UK Post Office employees, Welch *et al.* (1999) examined the uptake of screening for cervical cancer, breast cancer and frequency of breast self-examination amongst women and testicular self-examination in men. Whilst the usual gradients for attendance for cervical screening and breast self-examination were present, trends for utilisation of breast cancer screening followed the reverse pattern – with lower occupational grades attending in greater proportions for mammograms, and amongst male workers testicular self-examination was more prevalent amongst blue-collar workers. These relatively unusual findings followed intensive health interventions organised within workplaces throughout the country and suggest that specific occupational initiatives if carried out within a favourable organisational culture can yield dividends.

In addition to social class a number of workers have explored the potential of psychosocial factors – particularly those specified in the Health Belief Model for pre-dicting screening uptake. Self-efficacy, perceived vulnerability and perceived barriers (for example fear of the negative consequences of performing a health behaviour) have been found to be the most powerful predictors for practising breast self-examination and attending for cervical screening (Fulton *et al.*, 1991; Murray and McMillan, 1993). The means by which people are exhorted to attend for screening, however, needs to be undertaken carefully. Bunker, Houghton and Baum (1998) drew attention to public information campaigns which have presented grossly inflated risks of developing breast cancer, and which have failed to present appropriate data on the relative risks at different ages. This could conceivably result in women ignoring more serious health threats. Other work suggests that people's appraisals of the risks and benefits to be accrued from screening are strongly affected by the manner in which the information is presented to them. Focusing on cognitive factors, of course, assumes that screening itself is an effective means for reducing breast cancer, and while this has been readily apparent in clinical trials, national screening pro-grammes have usually taken some time to reach the same level of detection – and in a recent analysis of a 10-year-old screening programme in Sweden, no significant re-duction in breast cancer mortality was apparent even after this time (Mayor, 1999). This is likely to be a result of the length of time necessary to train sufficient numbers of workers to the necessary skill levels for adequate detection.

Summary and conclusions ●

Cancer is considered the most psychologically threatening disease in western societies. In recent years people's beliefs about what causes it have received growing attention although little work to date has examined class or cultural differences. The idea that psychological states can influence the development of cancers is embodied in the idea of a cancer-prone personality type, labelled the Type C personality, characterised by the suppression of negative emotional states, repressive coping and passivity when faced with stress. There is some evidence to support this view and the immune function has been suggested as a plausible mediator of such a relationship. However, this is still controversial and further prospective studies are needed to clarify matters. What is clear is that the psychological and psychosocial demands on cancer patients are severe, both from the disease and the treatments for it. Many cancer patients will be affected by disturbances of mood with anxiety and depression the most common. Several areas where psychological intervention may be appropriate have been proposed, including pain management, social support, body-image counselling and classically conditioned nausea and vomiting following chemotherapy. Evaluating such interventions is problematic. Designing a study requires careful thought and the choice of suitable outcome measures. Randomised controlled trials are not considered appropriate for ethical reasons. Caution is also required when interpreting results as patients receiving interventions may have changed their behaviour in other important ways (e.g. diet and exercise) which may actually be responsible for any change in outcome.

A number of lifestyle factors are implicated in the development of certain cancers, ranging from smoking and alcohol consumption to sexual behaviour. Preventive efforts face large hurdles as the underlying behaviours are highly resistant to change. Cancer screening has usually been aimed at detecting cancers of the cervix, and breast. These have been supported by programmes encouraging women to undertake breast self-examination. Self-efficacy, perceived vulnerability and perceived barriers have been found to predict who attends for cervical screening and who practises breast self-examination.

Discussion points

A   If personality does predispose to cancer, does it make sense to say that people are responsible for their health?

B   If randomised controlled trials are unsuitable for ethical reasons, how can psychological interventions be suitably evaluated?

Suggested reading

Eysenck, H.J. (1994) 'Cancer, Personality and Stress: Prediction and Prevention', *Advances in Behaviour Research and Therapy*, **16** (3): 167–215.

Fallowfield, L. (1991) 'Counselling Patients with Cancer', in H. Davis and L. Fallowfield (eds), *Counselling and Communication in Health Care*. (London: John Wiley).

Fawzy, I.F., Fawzy, N.W., Arndt, L.A. and Pasnau, R.O. (1995) 'A Critical Review of Psychosocial Interventions in Cancer Care', *Archives of General Psychiatry*, **52**: 100–13.

McGhee, R., Williams, S. and Elwood, M. (1994) 'Depression and the development of Cancer – a Meta Analysis', *Social Science and Medicine*, **26**(3): 441–7.

20

Diabetes

'The experience and communication of distress requires a theoretical
model which emphasises the contextual nature of such experience.'

Alan Blair (in A. Radley (ed.) *Worlds of Illness*, 1995)

INTRODUCTION

Diabetes is a disease
characterized by chronically
elevated blood sugar levels.
Two types are recognized.
In Type 1 (insulin-dependent
diabetes) the pancreas
ceases to produce insulin,
and in Type 2 (non-insulin-
dependent diabetes) the
body can still produce insulin
though not in sufficient
quantities.

Although knowledge of **diabetes** now enables it to be more effectively controlled
than ever before, it remains a prevalent disorder with serious consequences –
chronic and potentially fatal which are not widely understood outside of the circle of
those immediately affected by it. Diabetes is in fact the fourth leading cause of death
in developed countries, with severe reductions in overall life expectancy for those in
whom the disease develops – particularly so if this occurs in childhood (Hixenbaugh
and Warren, 1998). Two types of diabetes are recognised – Insulin dependent
(IDDM) and non-insulin dependent (NIDDM). These are sometimes referred to as
Type 1 and Type 2 diabetes. In the first type the pancreas ceases to produce insulin,
thus daily injections are required to regulate blood glucose levels. Though this can
occur at any time, its age of onset is more frequently under 30 years. Non-insulin
dependent diabetes on the other hand, which comprises the overwhelming majority
(85%) of diabetes cases, is more likely to develop after 40 years of age. In this type
the body can still produce insulin though not in sufficient quantities, so that people
with this type still require medication in the form of tablets or injections, as well as
following carefully prescribed diets and exercise patterns.

Evidence points to both environmental and genetic factors playing a role in the
manifestation of the disease. Twin studies appear to show a genetic susceptibility to
underproduction of insulin in both types of diabetes (Sarafino, 1998) and low birth
weight has been suggested as a risk factor for NIDDM (Poulsen, Vaag, Kyvik, Müller,
Jensen, Beck and Nielsen, 1997). In some instances IDDM may be the expression of
an auto-immune dysfunction in which a viral agent is stimulated to attack pancreatic
cells (Conrad *et al.*, 1994). A variety of environmental agents have been identified in
NIDDM, including diets high in fat and sugar, over-production of a protein that impairs metabolism of sugars and carbohydrates and stress. These all play a part in
accounting for the relationship between diabetes and socioeconomic status (Brunner,
1996). Work in this area has also revealed social gradients in the pre-diabetic state of
impaired glucose tolerance, which appears to be mediated by work-related stress
(Nanchahal, 1994). Further evidence for the importance of environmental variables
also comes from the observation that disease prevalence has been increasing amongst

middle-aged and elderly populations, though not amongst younger groups. Diabetes in adults now constitutes a global health problem – moderate (3–10%) or high (11–20%) prevalences have been observed in many populations worldwide and populations of developing countries, minority groups and disadvantaged communities in industrialised countries appear to be at greatest risk (King and Rewers, 1993).

Although widely-recognised treatments are available, there are considerable complexities to their effective implementation, not least the considerable demands placed on sufferers. These begin with diagnosis – where work suggests almost a third of new patients have concerns which suggest cognitive or emotional problems in coming to terms with their diabetes (Benett, 1993). The demands are particularly acute where type I diabetes is concerned. For example, in order to use appropriate quantities of insulin for regulating blood glucose levels, frequent blood glucose testing is required (at least four times per day is recommended) with several injections of insulin per day (Bradley, 1994a; Hixenbaugh and Warren, 1998). Such routine monitoring at set times, however, carries the risk that episodes of hyperglycaemia (high blood glucose) or hypoglycaemia (low blood glucose) can be missed. Because of this, research has been exploring the capacity of patients to recognise when their own blood glucose levels fall outside of an acceptable range (Gillespie, 1991). It appears that most people if they are not already accurate at this can learn to do so successfully through close monitoring of physical symptoms and moods, which though they are idiosyncratic are nevertheless reliable for individual patients.

The diabetic regimen is, however, merely one source of stress that must be contended with. The medical complications of the disease itself are numerous. Prolonged hyperglycaemia may lead to *retinopathy* or neuropathy, causes of blindness and kidney failure respectively (BDA, 1988), while macrovascular complications such as strokes and coronary heart disease are also more prevalent in the diabetic population. Sexual problems have also received attention. Much of this has focused on erectile dysfunction in males where evidence appears to show a significant interaction between organic and psychological influences (Rubin and Peyrot, 1992). The investigation of sexual problems in women with diabetes is a relatively recent undertaking and results are less clear-cut. Schreiner-Engel, Schiavi, Vietorisz and Smith (1987), for example, found women with IDDM were no more likely to report sexual problems than non-diabetics, although those with NIDDM did report lower levels of sexual desire, sexual satisfaction and orgasmic capacity compared to controls.

Retinopathy is a disease of the retina and may occur in diabetes.

PSYCHOSOCIAL ASPECTS OF DIABETES

Interest in the physical sequelae of diabetes is now giving way to a concerted attempt to understand the psychosocial aspects of diabetes. Poor adherence and metabolic control have been repeatedly reported in the literature (Stenström, Wikby, Andersson, Rydén, 1998) and have prompted greater awareness of the importance of personal and social factors in the maintenance of good glucose levels. Psychological modelling of the processes involved in adhering to treatment regimens have focused on the cognitions which are presumed to underlie self-care behaviours. Although locus of control has been posited as a key variable here, research in the diabetic field has produced contradictory findings with some studies reporting positive relationships between internal locus of control and metabolic control (Konen, Summerson and Dignan, 1993) and others negative relationships (Evans and Hughes, 1987). This inconsistency may have arisen for a number of reasons, not withstanding the fact that theoretical grounds do exist for believing potentially adverse coping patterns could ensue in persons with high internal control when faced with feedback indicating poor metabolic control. First of all, as Stenström *et al.* suggest, contrary findings could result from a lack of standardisation in measuring locus of control. The difficulty of controlling for attenuating biological, social and situational variables is likely to be a further influential factor and, lastly, the non-uniformity of the different (mostly convenience) samples which have been employed serve to further highlight the complexity of the task facing researchers. With respect to this latter point, the interpersonal circumstances of patients will vary significantly with demographic and other lifestyle characteristics and the relevance and meaning of various self-monitoring activities which could both impact upon and be affected by these circumstances is likely to vary accordingly.

SOCIAL IDENTITY AND DIABETES MANAGEMENT

The psychosocial context of diabetes in a number of social groups is not well-understood. In one sense this is surprising given the wealth of information on how group processes – their dynamics and meaning – vary with socially prescribed identities. This lack of understanding could be looked on as a consequence of the hegemony with which the medical model functions – through its effective isolation from other forms of knowledge in the social and behavioural sciences it dominates all forms of discourse relating to health. The importance of individual and social differences in disease presentation and management cannot be overemphasised. The omission of such variables from many studies (ranging from evaluations of stress management programmes to testing social cognition models) is probably responsible for some of the inconsistency in the results which have been generated.

Connell, Storandt and Lichty (1990) discuss how older adults have largely been ignored in the debates on social factors in diabetes. This is less true for younger people where the demands of maintaining a prescribed diet and careful exercise regimen are likely to impose considerably different demands than for people whose working lives have had a considerably longer time to unfold. Young children are thought unlikely to understand the nature of their condition until eight to ten years of age, and interestingly do not see themselves as being different from other children (Sarafino, 1998). Research on how this self-image changes would be valuable and might also provide us with an additional rationale for believing psychological change in the non-diabetic populations might equally be the focus of interventions. There is also no indication that before adolescence metabolic control is seriously affected by adverse life events (Goldston, Kovacs and Obrosky, 1995).

For older adolescents metabolic control appears to be poorer – as diabetes brings additional problems to the challenge of developing independence from the family. Coupled with a progressive withdrawal from formal health service input which may occur and the psychological pressures of adolescence this may be a critical time, leading to feelings of lower self esteem, isolation, reduced contact with routine services and possibly increased complications because of poorer self-care (Tattersall and Lowe, 1981; Olsen and Sutton, 1998). Encouragingly, a 10-year follow-up from diagnosis of a group of young adults (aged 19–26) compared with a group initially presenting with a moderately severe acute illness, found no differences in psychiatric symptoms, although the diabetes group showed lower self-esteem and sociability with differences also found in humour and physical appearance (Jacobson, Hauser, Willett, Wolfsdorf, Dvorak, Herman and de Groot, 1997).

The picture of adaptation facing young adults with diabetes would be incomplete without further consideration of the influence of variables associated with gender. For women with diabetes, dealing with food and managing the cultural pressures of maintaining appearance, weight and body shape involve an additional layer of complexity. Because insulin treatment may lead to weight gain, omitting it may appear to be an option worth pursuing for those women with diabetes who perceive themselves as needing to lose weight. Not surprisingly, disordered eating attitudes and behaviour are common and persistent in young adult females with IDDM and pose additional health risks, including a three fold elevation in the risk of diabetic retinopathy (Striegel Moore, 1993; Daneman et al., 1998). A cross-sectional study by Jones et al. (2000) found eating disorders were over twice as common in adolescent females compared to controls, with dieting and insulin omission the most common methods used to control weight.

Fortunately evidence does exist to show the potential of weight management programmes in people with NIDDM – and these deserve greater attention (Bradley, 1994a). In younger children work suggests boys may have poorer metabolic control than girls, although reasons for this are unclear (Grey, Lipman, Cameron and Thurber, 1997). This contrasts with the situation found in adults, where few gender differences in adherence to self-care have been found (Fitzgerald, Anderson and Davis, 1995). Where they have, women have reported greater satisfaction with diabetes-related aspects of their lives (Trief, Elbert, Grant and Weinstock, 1998) and differences in the concerns which they take to their physicians. Amongst those with the disease for under 10 years men seem more likely to indicate difficulty in adjusting to the disease and women to be more concerned with diabetic control (Benett, 1993). The available data therefore might tentatively be described as showing a cyclical pattern in how the consequences of diabetes impact differentially on gender roles at different points in the life span.

Type 2 diabetes is around four to five times more common in south Asians compared to Europeans (McKeigue, Shah and Marmot, 1991), probably because of a genetic vulnerability (Simmons, Williams and Powell, 1992). Few studies, however, have looked at how cultural issues interface with management of the condition. Obvious difficulties may involve communication. Wilson, Wardle, Chandel and Walford, (1993) and Hawthorne (1994), for example, found over 48 per cent of 500 Asians with diabetes studied in a northern English town had not been offered an interpreter, and over half reported communication problems. Language barriers may be further compounded by unsympathetic attitudes amongst health professionals who do not understand the cultural location of diabetes within the Asian community, where high fat diets and fasting during religious festivities create acute problems for glycaemic control (Chandalia, Bhargav and Kataria, 1987).

The centrality of the social environment is readily apparent from the above examples, and again underscores the difficulty of using theoretical models which are not situated within a continually changing interpersonal context. Many studies have failed to find support for social-cognition models for example (as in Harris and Linn, 1985), and thus this means that in the diabetic context these will have limited clinical relevance. Neither has the addition of self-efficacy to such models resulted in any marked improvement in consistency. From the wealth of conflicting findings some have argued that the dynamic nature of the relationship between beliefs, behaviour and context means that these models are unlikely to be useful in predicting behaviour (Shillitoe and Miles, 1989) (see Box 20.1).

BOX 20.1 Explaining health behaviour – the need for a fresh approach?

In several places in this book the shortcomings of rational models of human decision-making in health contexts have been highlighted. The repeated failure of these models to explain a substantial proportion of the variability in health-related behaviour ought to raise fundamental questions about whether the scientific aims in proposing them are being achieved. With few exceptions this has not occurred, and many psychologists enter the health arena hoping to establish their credentials through using these models – welded to a psychological mode of analysis. According to Eiser (1996), researchers have become caught in a conceptual morass in which constructs pertaining to self-appraisal and self-efficacy are enmeshed with presumed mental calculations predicting the future consequences of action deriving from health-related behavioural schemas. This 'blueprint' entails that attitudes are regarded as objects located in a mental space dissociated from the external world which must be bolted on as some necessary addition before any attempt to explain what happens in this external world can be launched. This misalliance of constructs from different levels of analysis could be circumvented by avoiding the apparent necessity to employ psychological constructs as the starting point for theoretical explanation in the first place. We have repeatedly argued that human health-related behaviour is always context-dependent, situational and interactional in nature. A more appropriate stance, as Eiser contends, might be to use a framework which embodies these relational aspects at the outset. Systems theories offer one such possibility. Rather than making variability in individual human behaviour the purpose of explanation – why not shift towards examining variation in person–situation interactions? This would of course require a radical reappraisal of what the goals for health psychology should be. The different implications of diabetes across a range of social and cultural groups would be a suitable place for exploring this shift in aims.

INTERPERSONAL AND ORGANISATIONAL INFLUENCES

A more promising line of enquiry has been to take the situation as the focal point rather than the patient. Warren and Hixenbaugh (1996), for example, observed that degree and adequacy of social support varied substantially across situations. A number of studies suggest the working environment for people with diabetes is one situation which is not conducive to their well-being – they are more likely to experience difficulty getting a job, to remain in the same job, or to be promoted if they do, despite few differences in sickness absence (Robinson, Yateman, Protopapa and Bush, 1990; Roberts and Brunner, 1996).

Several studies have focused on family functioning in adults and children. In studies with children, good glycaemic control appears to be related to family cohesion, although the relationship only holds for those with short disease duration (Hanson, Henggeler, Harris, Burghen and Moore, 1989). In adults, the level of glycaemic control has been directly related to good family functioning (Edelstein and Linn, 1985; Cardenas, Vallbona, Baker and Yusim, 1987), although methodological problems, particularly in the design and methods of analysis used, make the interpretation of such studies difficult. A more carefully designed study by Trief *et al.* (1998) using the SF-36 found no direct relationship, although supportive family behaviours were positively associated with psychosocial adaptation. The importance of the support provided in close friendships has not been extensively investigated though this may change as the nature of the family in western societies moves towards smaller-size units in response to economic, social and occupational pressures (Fonagy, 1996).

The immediate social environments of paramount importance for people who have chronic illnesses include health workers, as well as the family, close friends or colleagues. Yet despite a plethora of findings relating good patient communication to positive health outcomes, many patients feel that their emotional needs are not given due consideration by health professionals. Hixenbaugh, Roberts and Castle (2000) found that the strongest effects determining attendance at a diabetes clinic were associated with health professionals' behaviour – with criticism and lack of consultation predominantly discouraging attendance. This concurs with work which suggests treatment approaches emphasising only medical care and information-transfer are less-effective, may reduce clinic attendance and lead to an increased risk of complications (Jacobson and Leibovitch, 1984; Jacobson, Adler, Derby, Anderson and Wolsdorf, 1991).

Several reasons may underlie patients' dissatisfaction. The effects of lack of training and support for health professionals to utilise psychological skills in patient care (which was also evident in the care of cancer patients) is a likely contributory factor. It is also true that basic counselling skills alone are not sufficient, and must be supplemented by knowledge of the patient and their individual psychological needs (Hixenbaugh and Warren, 1998) – thus continuity of care would seem to be an important element. This is supported by a study which compared the preferences of diabetic patients in quality of care with those of physicians specialising in diabetes. Of ten aspects of care, continuity was ranked second only to treatment effectiveness by the patients, but only sixth by the physicians (Casparie and Van der Waal, 1995). Gender age and duration with the disease did not effect these judgements, although the importance of continuity of care differed greatly with socioeconomic position – it being ranked foremost by people from lower socioeconomic groups. Guidelines for facilitating a more whole-person approach to diabetes management have been provided by a working group of the World Health Organisation and include improving communication, protecting patients' self-esteem, responding to individuals' needs, motivating self-care and monitoring psychological well-being (Bradley, 1994b; Bradley and Gamsu, 1994). At present, recognition of the importance of psychological factors in diabetes management is still in its infancy. In the immediate future, however, we can expect an increasing number of studies to further clarify the nature of these relationships in a wide variety of contexts; the evaluation of psychosocial interventions in diabetes care designed on the basis of this knowledge; and increased pressure towards the inclusion of appropriate training in psychological skills for health professionals.

Summary and conclusions

Diabetes is one of the leading causes of death in developed countries. Two types are recognised – insulin dependent (Type 1) and non-insulin dependent (Type 2). Stress, diets high in fat and sugar, carbohydrates and over-production of a protein that impairs metabolism of sugars are implicated in the Type 2 variant. Social gradients exist in both diabetes and in the pre-diabetic state of impaired glucose tolerance, which appears to be mediated by work-related stress. Treatments are available, but place great demands on sufferers. Almost a third of new patients may have cognitive or emotional problems in coming to terms with diabetes. Poor adherence and metabolic control are frequently reported and have led to greater interest in the importance of personal and social factors in maintaining good glucose levels.

Psychological pressures on young people with diabetes have been noted, beginning with the need to adopt restricted diets and eating patterns, balanced against the energy demands of exercise combined with careful monitoring of glucose levels through the day. Risks of non-compliance increase as children age. Hormonal change during adolescence may make glycaemic control difficult, though the social pressures on young people at this time are more important – the need to maintain self-esteem and a good self-image, forming social relationships and developing independence from the family. Family atmosphere and available support may also be important influences in psychological adaptation. Young people must also begin the task of constructing a sense of how having diabetes will affect their future lives. These pressures may affect males and females differently – as pressures to conform to media images of thinness are more keenly felt by females this can result in eating disorders, although males are not immune from this. In other settings, the psychosocial context of diabetes is poorly understood. Older adults, for example, have largely been ignored from the debates on social factors. And although Type 2 diabetes is more common in South Asians compared to Europeans, few studies have looked at how cultural issues interface with managing the condition. Several studies have suggested the working environment is not conducive to the well-being of people with diabetes – they are likely to experience difficulty getting a job, and are less likely to be promoted if they do, despite few differences in sickness absence. Social-cognition models have received little support in the diabetic context, whilst work does suggest that treatment approaches emphasising only medical care and information-transfer are less-effective, may reduce clinic attendance and lead to an increased risk of complications.

Discussion points

A   Consider how the quality of the doctor–patient relationship impacts on treatment adherence in patients with diabetes.

B   In what contexts and in what specific situations might glycaemic control be difficult for a 38-year-old woman?

Suggested reading

Bradley, C. (1994a) 'Contributions of Psychology to Diabetes Management', *British Journal of Clinical Psychology*, **33**: 11–21.

Bradley, C. (ed.) (1994b) *Handbook of Psychology and Diabetes: A Guide to Psychological Measurement in Diabetes Research and Practice*. (Reading: Harwood).

Jacobson, A.M., Hauser, S.T., Willett, J.B., Wolfsdorf, J.I., Dvorak, R., Herman, L. and de Groot, M. (1997) 'Psychological Adjustment to IDDM: 10-year Follow-up of an Onset Cohort of Child and Adolescent Patients', *Diabetes Care*, **20**(5): 811–18.

21

Coronary Heart Disease

'Knock there, and ask your heart what it doth know.'

William Shakespeare (*Measure for Measure*, V, i)

INTRODUCTION

In western societies, deaths from cardiovascular diseases far outweigh those from other causes. In the United States in 1996 they accounted for 47.4 per cent of all male deaths and 52.7 per cent of all female deaths (American Heart Association, 1999). These figures cover a range of conditions: coronary heart disease (CHD), high blood pressure, stroke, rheumatic heart disease, congenital cardiovascular defects and congestive heart failure. Data from for the United States are by no means the most alarming; wide international variations exist and, as can be seen from Figure 21.1, particularly high death rates are found in the Russian Federation and countries of Eastern Europe.

Coronary heart disease (CHD) itself encompasses two types of disorder: angina

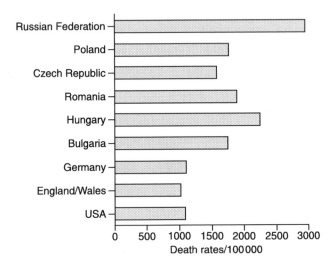

Figure 21.1   Death rates for cardiovascular diseases (per 100 000) for selected countries

Source: American Heart Association (1999).

pectoris and myocardial infarction (MI). Both of these are conditions which result from narrowing and blocking of arteries which supply the heart, usually as a result of the build up of plaques of fatty material – a process called atherosclerosis. Where the blockage is incomplete or temporary, painful cramps in the chest, arms, back or neck may ensue. These cramps are indicative of angina pectoris and may be brought on during exercise or stress. With more severe blockages a myocardial infarction (heart attack) can result where the supply of oxygen to parts of the heart causes part of the muscle there to die. Coronary heart disease has attracted considerable attention because it is seen as a preventable cause of death which kills a significant number of people in middle age. Behaviour and lifestyles have been implicated as risk factors in a considerable number of studies. The major behavioural factors include smoking, alcohol consumption, diet and exercise (Twisk, Kemper, Mechelen and Post, 1997) and together these explain between a quarter and a half of all the variation in biological CHD risk factors and CHD mortality (Brunner *et al.*, 1993).

TYPE A PERSONALITY

As we saw in Chapter 13, psychologists have devoted a good deal of attention to the Type A behaviour pattern (TABP), although this contributes relatively little to the population distribution of risk of CHD. The construct of the Type A personality came to prominence in the 1950s and 1960s and was strongly implicated as a risk factor for coronary heart disease in the Western Collaborative Group Study of the 1970s (Rosenman Brand, Sholz and Friedman, 1976). The notion of the coronary-prone personality itself, however, has its origins in the late nineteenth century (Gatchel, Baum and Krantz, 1989).

The construct was first measured by means of a structured interview (SI) which was designed to reveal the core components of the behaviour pattern. Assessment is difficult and requires supervised training, chiefly because it is the respondents' manner of saying something as much as what they actually say that is the focus of the interview. Aspects of the interview schedule can be questioned on ethical grounds as they are encouraged to provoke, annoy and challenge the subjects. Inter-rater reliability has varied between 75 and 90 per cent in classifying Type A or B behaviour (Rosenman, 1978). The components of the TABP are considered to be hostility, impatience, competitive drive and vigorous speech (Friedman and Rosenman, 1959). In contrast, the so-called Type B pattern comprises a relative absence of these characteristics. Alternative means of assessment have been devised, including the Framingham Type A scale measure (see Box 21.1) (Haynes *et al.*, 1978) and the ***Jenkins Activity Survey*** (Jenkins, Zynanski and Rosenman, 1979). Both are pencil and paper tests designed to provide a more objective system of measurement. Unfortunately the two types of measure do not correlate highly (correlations seldom exceed 0.3 and the agreement on classification varies between 50 and 75 per cent; chance agreement is 50%) and have produced quite different results. Relationships between Type A classification and health outcomes using self-report methods are not consistent and appear weak. It has been argued that the reasons for these inconsistencies stem from response bias whereby socially undesirable characteristics such as impatience and hostility are underreported. In contrast, using the interview method such bias is minimised as behaviour is being assessed 'in vivo' (Evans, 1998). However, another source of bias is being introduced as the behaviour in question is in part being provoked by the interviewer.

Jenkins Activity Survey is a means of measuring the Type A behaviour pattern

BOX 21.1   The Framingham Type A measure

For each question (1–5) will you indicate by means of the appropriate number to show whether each trait describes you **Very well** (4) **Fairly well** (3) **Somewhat** (2) or **Not at all** (1).

1. Being bossy or dominating
2. Having a strong need to excel (be best) in most things
3. Usually being pressed for time
4. Being hard driving and competitive
5. Eating too quickly

For questions 6–10 please answer **yes** (1) **or no** (0).

6. Have you often felt pressed for time?
7. Has your work often stayed with you so that you were thinking about it after working hours?
8. Has your work often stretched you to the very limits of energy and capacity?
9. Have you often felt uncertain, uncomfortable or dissatisfied with how well you were doing in your work?
10. Do you often get quite upset when you have to wait for anything?

For the next two questions (11–12) please use the following to indicate how well each statement applies to you; **Not at all** (1), **Somewhat** (2) or **Very much** (3)

11. When you are faced with slow people, do you feel agitated or irritable?
12. When you are being held up in a queue do you feel agitated or irritated?

Scoring
Simply sum the scores. When added together these yield a total Type A scale score. The higher the score denotes a stronger Type A personality.

A number of investigations of high-risk subjects who have already suffered a myocardial infarction have failed to show relationships between TABP and subsequent stroke. Cohen, Ardjoen and Sewpersad (1997) reviewed 10 such studies involving almost 6000 subjects. Four of the studies showed no relationship between post-MI morbidity and mortality and TABP; four found an association with non-Type A behaviour; one study found reduction in TABP was associated with reduced cardiac risk; and one whereby greater Type A behaviour was related to sudden cardiac death. In general, however, whilst much of the data concerns the relationship between TABP and MI, there is little on the relationship between TABP and coronary death. Those that have, find that it is Type B behaviour which is more likely to be associated (Spicer, Jackson and Scragg, 1997). Consequently, data seem to provide better evidence of a relationship between Type B behaviour and post-MI events. Cohen *et al.* (1997) hypothesise that this may arise from previous Type A individuals changing their behaviour as a consequence of having a stroke. Another suggestion is that the history of stress-induced arousal experienced by Type A individuals somehow affords them physiological protection against coronary death, whilst paradoxically increasing their risk of MI (Spicer *et al.*, 1997).

If Type A individuals are capable of modifying their behaviour to such a degree this does call into question the very notion that the TABP behaviour constitutes a personality trait of some kind. This then begs the further question as to what extent situational factors are influencing coronary-prone behaviour – Bages, Warwick-

Evans and Falger (1997), for instance, reported evidence that behavioural responses (anger and TABP) to stressful stimuli at home or at work differed and may also be perceived differently by others. Given the inconsistent nature of the database with respect to the TABP, some researchers have sought to examine its components to see if these can be more clearly related to coronary risk. Indeed, given the multidimensional nature of the behaviour pattern it could be considered surprising that this strategy took so long to emerge. Comparing a variety of methods for measuring Type A behaviour (the Jenkins Activity Survey, Framingham Type A scale, and the Survey of Work Styles (SWS), Gray, Jackson and Howard (1989) identified three independent bipolar typal dimensions and suggested that a single dimension or classification of the TABP is an oversimplification.

Of the Type A components hostility has emerged as the most favoured candidate for explaining coronary risk. Amongst low-risk populations correlations between the potential for hostility and coronary heart disease have reliably been reported between 0.08 and 0.18 (Miller *et al.*, 1996). One reason for believing this to be a more important variable than the broader Type A construct comes from studies on social class and health (see Chapter 13). In the Whitehall studies, Type A behaviour was found to be more frequent in higher occupational groups, whilst hostility and cardiovascular risk are more prominent in lower grades (Marmot *et al.*, 1991). Further evidence indicates that hostility is linked to two important cardiovascular risk factors (apolipoprotein AI and fibrinogen) via health behaviours (Brunner *et al.*, 1993; Brunner, 1996). This is important because it suggests that the negative effects on health do not necessarily arise from hostile, angry behaviour *per se*, but from other behaviours which are associated with this. It is plausible, for example, that continual hostility depletes people's personal resources to care for their health in other ways. The fact that hostility itself is a broad concept should also not be overlooked – possessing as it does connotations of anger, aggression and a chronic negative outlook. Aspects which may encompass behaviours, feelings and cognitions, and which may require additional coping resources to deal with.

As with the TABP, there are real dangers in viewing relationships between measures of hostility and risks to health as indicating a primary role for personality in creating ill-health. Accordingly, it is too easy to interpret evidence for the role of psychological factors such as hostility in ill-health as favouring interventions at the individual level. An alternative stance is to address the situations which for example engender hostility. As we know, hostility is more common in lower social classes. It seems (to us as least) that to explain the socioeconomic distribution of hostility without reference to the frustrating features of life in lower social classes would not only be doomed to failure but would be a prime example of behavioural scientists burying their heads in the sand in order to talk up a role for themselves in health care. We believe the most important role for health psychologists in these matters is primarily to ask the right questions and gather evidence. This does not then preclude psychologists in clinical settings working with patients to reduce their individual levels of risk – but it should be clear that this route alone is not adequate to tackle any problem at a population level.

At present there is no compelling evidence that behavioural interventions have a definite effect in reducing coronary risk. The Recurrent Coronary Prevention Project (Friedman *et al.*, 1986) did find direct attempts to modify Type A behaviour were associated on follow-up with decreased anger and reduced mortality from myocardial infarction in treatment groups. However, these findings cannot be considered conclusive. A number of other more global measures, such as self esteem and social support, were also found to vary between treatment and control groups and may well have occupied an antecedent position in bringing about change. This has not deterred some (for example Evans, 1998) from arguing for retention of the Type A construct because of its association with these broader patterns of behaviour rather than just those associated with coronary risk. In practice, achieving lasting change via an individual-based intervention (probably cognitive-behavioural) directed at such a broad spectrum of behaviours is likely to be difficult. There are several reasons for this. Firstly, as the complexity of a behavioural system extends more and more into the social sphere (the importance of other people for social support, self-esteem and emotional expression make this true for the TABP) the corresponding degrees of freedom for change are likely to decline with it. Even Evans accepts that consideration of TABP in isolation from its social context is fairly meaningless. Furthermore, should rigorous research conclusively demonstrate the possibility of changing TABP in at-risk populations and reducing their coronary risk, the feasibility of achieving the same in a clinical context would still remain to be shown.

WORK STRESS AND HEALTH

While interest in the TABP has generated conflicting findings and interpretations, the concept of stress, whilst being difficult to define, appears to be a more powerful concept to utilise for addressing the role of psychological and psychosocial factors in engendering cardiovascular disease. Different approaches have been adopted in the attempts to operationalise stress (Sarafino, 1998). In one the stimulus characteristics of specific stressors are employed, so that for example specific life events or major catastrophic events are deemed to be stressful. In another it is the response to stressors that forms the focus of research, so that here both physiological components of arousal (for example perspiration, elevated heart rate, dryness of mouth) are considered along with psychological ones (such as feeling tense or nervous). Transactional models of stress examine affairs in terms of a mismatch between demands and resources and are particularly evident in studies of work stress.

Within the research community, the role of psychosocial resources as an indicator of exposure to stress have grown in importance. This is particularly evident in the transactional model of job stress first proposed by Karasek (Karasek, 1979; Karasek and Theorell, 1990) (see Table 21.1). In this scheme, the work environment is described along two dimensions – demands and control. Increasing demands by themselves does not necessarily increase cardiovascular risk – in fact high demands in the presence of high control are seen as beneficial to health, possibly because these contribute to what makes work interesting and rewarding. The model has found widespread support with respect to predicting mortality and morbidity (see for

Table 21.1 Job strain model

Control and Variety of skill use	Psychological demands	
	Low	High
Low	Passive jobs	High-strain jobs
High	Low-strain jobs	Active jobs

Source: After Karasek and Theorell (1990).

example Kristensen, 1989) although inconsistent findings have been reported for several aspects of cardiac reactivity (for example Seibt, Boucsein and Sheuch, 1998). Additionally, high-strain jobs (high demands, low control) have been associated with lower vitality, poorer mental health, greater pain and increased risks of physical and emotional role limitations (Amick *et al.*, 1998). In assessing the meaning of the Karasek model an important question arises as to whether it is the objectively assessed levels of work characteristics or how these are subjectively perceived that are important. As with quality-of-life assessment, Marmot and Feeney (1996) report low correlations between self-report and external assessments. Although both have been related to sickness absence from work, it is not currently known which of these shows the stronger relationships with cardiovascular disease and whether these truly represent independent risks.

A number of improvements have been suggested to the Karasek model. To control and demands, Kristensen (1989) added lack of meaning, lack of predictability and conflict as forming the chief stressors of organised work. Lack of meaning and unpredictability, however, may simply be the principal cognitive responses to finding oneself situated in work environments objectively defined by combinations of demands and control as stressful. Accordingly, these may play a key role in mediating the illness response. The two-factor model has also been extended to take account of job support thereby arriving at the concept of iso-strain (Johnson and Hall, 1988) which has been used to predict ischaemic heart disease in many studies. Östergren (1991), however, has argued that although social support is related to mortality (see for example Berkman and Syme, 1979) it is important to distinguish social support from related variables such as social participation, contact frequency and social anchorage, which though related are distinct. With these three factors the model embodies two distinct approaches to predicting health outcomes. In one, ill-health ensues from high demand, low control and low social support. In contrast to this, high control and high social supports may buffer the effect of potentially negative influences on health (van der Doef and Maes, 1998). The latter has been less extensively studied.

Siegrist and colleagues (Siegrist *et al.*, 1990) have developed an alternative two-factor model of work stress that directly incorporates motivation and which emphasises the relationship between effort and reward. Effort is conceived as a function of both external demands and intrinsic motivation. Similarly, this model predicts high effort and low reward lead to increased risk of CHD. Both these models were compared in a prospective study (Whitehall II) of British civil servants, where an imbalance between personal effort (defined as competitiveness, work-related, over-commitment, and hostility) and rewards (poor promotion prospects and career obstacles) was associated with a more than two-fold greater risk of new coronary heart disease (Bosma, Peter, Siegrist and Marmot, 1998). Neither job strain nor high job demands were related to coronary heart disease. Low job control, however, was related to new coronary heart disease, with the risk greater for self-reported than externally assessed control.

These models of work stress clearly warrant further investigation, and require psychologists to examine the appraisal processes which are enacted by people with particular skills, resources and coping mechanisms when situated in environments which vary in the types of demands they impose – be they interpersonal, occupational, intellectual or physical. Furthermore, these models could also fruitfully examine the take-up of risky behaviours by workers as well as just concentrating on health endpoints. At present psychologists have been slow to realise the significance of these models, either for their theoretical or for their potential practical import- ance in creating more favourable working conditions which could affect the future health of employees. Indeed, van der Doef and Maes (1998) remark that it is now time for intervention studies to proceed to address these aspects. The political and organisational difficulties involved in actually implementing such experimental efforts on the ground, however, should not be underestimated.

COPING WITH HEART DISEASE

The psychological consequences for an individual who discovers they have heart disease or who has suffered a heart attack are immense. The majority experience high levels of anxiety, and initially coping reactions may include shock and denial. In a study of myocardial infarction patients, those displaying high initial denial sub- sequently exhibited less cardiac dysfunction and spent fewer days in intensive care (Taylor, 1995). Further demands, however, also come from surgical interventions or rehabilitation programmes designed to offer patients the opportunity to reduce their risks of subsequent MIs. For those undergoing surgery, social support does predict recovery. A review by Hemingway and Marmot (1999) of work over 30 years (1966–97) found most studies (9 out of 10) showed a prognostic role for social sup- ports in coronary heart disease, though the means by which it engenders beneficial effects are poorly understood (see Chapter 16). Some have argued that optimistic self-beliefs may be more important and may play a larger role than social support in predicting social coping (Schröder and Konertz, 1998). Rehabilitation programmes intend to bring about changes in lifestyle – through smoking cessation or reduction, weight loss, dietary change, reduced alcohol consumption and exercise. These are targeted because they are regarded as modifiable risk factors. As we have already seen in this book, however, maintenance of these behaviours is difficult; 50 per cent of cardiac patients, for example, discontinue exercise programmes within six months, and only 30–40 per cent MI patients reduce or quit smoking (Sarafino, 1998). Of those who do successfully maintain the new lifestyles there can be notable benefits. The demonstrable benefits of exercise maintenance in cardiac patients, for example, include lower diastolic blood pressure, lower resting heart rates, improved self- concept and perceived health.

Behavioural adaptation to cardiac illness though does not end with health be- haviours. Work, social life, social and sexual relationships, leisure activities and daily routines all face potential disruption. Where prior difficulties existed these may become worse, leading to the possibility of cycles of blame in which the prior prob- lems are blamed for the heart problems – leading to poorer adjustment later (Croog, 1983). A contrasting difficulty may see the person with heart disease accepting the illness role, restricting their activities and acting helpless and dependent. Not surprisingly the many new demands subsequent to MI can result in high levels of depression over a year later (Wicklund, Sanne, Vendin and Wilhelmsson, 1984), and even five years later up to one-third fail to achieve emotional adjustment (Havik and Maelands, 1990). Depressive symptomology appears to be influenced by social sup- port directly from family members, work colleagues and broader social networks, and indirectly through active coping strategies such as positive reappraisal and problem-solving (Holahan, Holahan, Moos and Brennan, 1997) (see Box 21.2). There is evidence, too, that those with persisting psychological problems are more likely to experience subsequent cardiac problems.

BOX 21.2 Coping assessment

Findings on the role of coping depend in part on how it has been conceptualised and operationalised (already at least 30 definitions of coping have been proposed). De Ridder (1997) has argued that resolving psychometric issues around scale construction will not solve the fundamental conceptual problems. One of the more central of these is the old dichotomy of the person versus the situation; whether to view coping as a dynamical process between the individual and their constantly changing environment of internal and external demands, or whether it is better characterised as an habitual style of responding adapted by individuals. Currently more evidence exists to support the transactional rather than the trait approach (e.g. Folkman and Lazarus, 1985). Another is the matter of coping assessments which have largely been empirically driven – these have suggested a number of coping functions including emotional regulation, behavioural confrontation, reappraisal and avoidance (Ferguson and Cox, 1997). An approach derived from clear theoretical principles would enable clearer links to be drawn across the whole range of situations, not just within the health domain, where human beings are asked to call on their resources and cope. Such theory must surely relate to people's goals and aspirations throughout life and therefore embody a developmental perspective. Though presenting a considerable challenge for psychologists this would once more demand that health psychologists step outside the self-imposed boundaries of their discipline. We will discuss the wider ramifications of this matter in greater depth in the final chapter.

Summary and conclusions ....

In western societies cardiovascular disease outweighs all other causes of death, and has attracted attention because it is seen as a preventable cause of death which shortens the lives of large numbers of people in middle age. Behaviour and lifestyles have been implicated as risk factors in many studies. Major behavioural factors include smoking, alcohol consumption, diet and exercise which explain between a quarter and a half of all the variation in biological CHD risk factors and CHD mortality. Psychologists have devoted a good deal of attention to the Type A behaviour pattern (TABP), though this contributes little to the population distribution of CHD risk. A variety of methods for measuring Type A behaviour have been advanced, which have produced inconsistent results. Work suggests that construing the TABP is an oversimplification. Of the Type A components hostility has emerged as the most likely candidate to explain CHD risk, though this does not necessarily mean that a primary role exists for personality in creating ill-health. As yet, behavioural interventions have not been conclusively shown to reduce coronary risk.

Research which highlights the role of situational factors in influencing coronary risk behaviour opens up the possibility of more powerful structurally based interventions. Such work has largely occurred in occupational settings because of the greater ease in specifying testable environmental variables. Some of the most influential work has used Karasek's job control–job demands model. This embodies a transactional notion of stress whereby the fit between a person's resources (both individual, e.g. cognitive; prior history and social, e.g. social support) and the environmental demands upon them (e.g. work load, work variety) determine the likely health outcomes. Another useful formulation is the effort–reward imbalance model of Siegrist (high effort and low reward are predicted to lead to increased risk of CHD). These models of the work environment merit further investigation – whereby psychologists could examine the health behaviours and appraisal processes enacted by people with particular skills, resources and coping mechanisms when situated in environments which differ in the interpersonal, occupational, intellectual or physical demands they impose.

The psychological consequences for an individual who discovers they have heart disease or who has suffered a heart attack are considerable. A majority experience high levels of anxiety and, initially, coping reactions may include shock and denial. Behavioural adaptation to cardiac illness involves more than changing health behaviours. Work, social life, social and sexual relationships, leisure activities and daily routines all face disruption. There is evidence that those with persisting psychological problems are more likely to experience subsequent cardiac problems. For those undergoing surgery social support predicts recovery, though the means by which it engenders beneficial effects are poorly understood.

Discussion points

A Which is more important, the person or the situation?

B Does the concept of the Type A personality have validity?

Suggested reading

Cohen, L., Ardjoen, R.C. and Sewpersad, K.S.M. (1997) 'Type A Behaviour Pattern as a Risk Factor after Myocardial Infarction: A Review', *Psychology and Health*, **12**(5): 619–32.

Karasek, R. and Theorell, T. (1990) *Healthy Work: Stress, Productivity and the Reconstruction of Working Life* (New York: Basic Books).

Miller, T.Q., Smith, T.W., Turner, C.W., Guijarro, M.L. and Hallet, A.J. (1996) 'A Meta-Analytic Review on Hostility and Physical Health', *Psychological Bulletin*, **119**: 322–48.

Psychological Factors in Degenerative Neurological Disease

(with Dawn Baker Towell)

'Make the most of yourself, for that is all there is to you.'

Ralph Waldo Emerson

INTRODUCTION

Multiple sclerosis is a degenerative neurological disease involving the progressive demyelination of nerve fibres affecting both sensory and motor systems. Cognitive impairment is often present.

Alzheimer's disease is a chronic degenerative neurological disease characterized by a profound deterioration in intellectual and linguistic functions with accompanying personality change.

Degenerative neurological diseases include Parkinson's disease, **multiple sclerosis, Alzheimer's disease**, motor neurone disease and Huntingdon's disease although there are many others. They share a number of core features in that they are gradually progressive, may affect one or more aspects of physical, sensory and cognitive function and can shorten the lifespan. In many cases the aetiology is unknown (see Tran and Miller, 1999) although these disorders can have a devastating effect on the lives of sufferers and those closest to them, in particular family, friends and carers. The aim of rehabilitating people with a degenerative neurological disease is to facilitate their adjustment to their condition by teaching them how to maximise their day to day functioning within the limits placed on them by the illness. By the very nature of the condition readjustment will not only affect the patient but also those closest to them. Current views on health consider the interaction between the individual and the social and physical environment. Current research recognises this interaction and the possible influence of both individual and external factors in shaping the onset, course and presentation of physical and psychological signs and symptoms. By implication, intervention strategies for this population are best designed for the maximum benefit of the individual and his/her caregivers.

DISEASE DESCRIPTION AND COMMON FEATURES

Alzheimer's disease

Alzheimer's disease is the most common cause of dementia affecting as many as 10 per cent of people aged 65 years and over (Knight, 1992) which is projected to rise with the increasing geriatric population. It causes a severe and irreversible deterioration in the cognition, personality and behaviour of sufferers, with motor and sensory functions being spared until the later stages (Small *et al.*, 1997). Depression is seen in around 25–65 per cent of cases and psychosis in up to 38 per cent of cases (Finkel *et al.*, 1997). Dementia may also be seen in other neurological diseases. Some make the distinction between subcortical dementia (as in Parkinson's disease, multiple sclerosis,

Aphasia is the partial (sometimes referred to as dysphasia) or complete loss of linguistic ability.

Apraxia is a disorder of movement, usually due to neurological disease or trauma.

Agnosia is a defect in recognition caused by neurological disease – can occur in any perceptual or cognitive system. Auditory agnosia, for example, refers to an inability to recognise or interpret the meanings of speech.

Huntingdon's disease and AIDS dementia) where depression, apathy, slowed mental processing speed, forgetfulness, reduced spontaneity and the absence of **aphasia**, **apraxia** or **agnosia** are the characteristic features. In contrast, Alzheimer's disease results in cortical dementia with patients experiencing much less depression, showing reduced insight into their illness and experiencing a more profound deterioration in intellectual and language functions (Rao, Huber and Bornstein, 1992). All patients are reported to have marked personality changes (Finkel *et al.*, 1997). Progression of the disease places increased burdens on carers which may be physically and emotionally overwhelming – particularly as they must not only cope with the physical and behavioural consequences of the disease on the person (sleep disturbances and incontinence are not uncommon), but also the gradual loss of signs of the active personality of the person that they love.

Multiple Sclerosis

Multiple sclerosis involves the progressive demyelination of nerve fibres affecting both sensory and motor systems and can often present with cognitive impairment. Onset is typically in the third or fourth decade of life. The presentation, course and outcome are unpredictable and may be characterised by periods of remission, progression and relapse. Symptoms include muscle weakness and spasm, bladder dysfunction, paraesthesia (pins and needles), numbness and so on, together with variable cognitive deficits, emotional and personality changes. Euphoria is also seen in about 10 per cent of patients with MS, as is pathological laughing and crying (Feinstein, Feinstein, Gray and O'Connor, 1997) defined as sudden involuntary laughing or crying. These states are more common in those where a greater decline in IQ has been evidenced and are to be distinguished from emotional lability. As such they are thought to be associated with neurological insults rather than psychological reactions to the disease (Minden and Schiffer, 1990).

Motor Neurone Disease

Motor neurone disease results in progressive damage to both lower and upper motor neurones leading to muscle weakness, spasticity, fatigue and loss of function. The main features are usually deterioration in mobility, problems in communication and pain from muscle atrophy. Bulbar onset motor neurone disease affects predominantly the respiratory muscles resulting in dysphagia (difficulty swallowing), and dysarthria (difficulty speaking) the result of which leads to an excessive production of saliva. The prognosis for this form is usually poor, with a life expectancy of between two and five years. Cognitive skills are usually spared while physical abilities rapidly deteriorate. The disease usually presents between 55 and 60 years with death ensuing within five to ten years for the non-Bulbar forms.

Parkinson's Disease

The clinical characteristics of Parkinson's disease are a disturbance of voluntary movement due to pathological changes in the basal ganglia starting in middle or old age. Abnormal cell loss may also occur in other parts of the brain and may contribute to the incidence of dementia, cognitive dysfunction and depression. In early stages the disease is well-managed with drugs that attempt to replace brain dopamine. In later stages the disease is more difficult to manage with drugs revealing tremor, shuffling gait and in some cases a mask-like expression.

Symptom Reporting

The symptoms associated with degenerative neurological diseases vary between disorders and can be difficult for patients to describe to physicians. The communication between doctor and patient is important for the accurate report of symptoms, and many studies have reported patient dissatisfaction in this area on the grounds of inadequate investigation, explanation and treatment (Fitzpatrick and Hopkins, 1981). However, when patients are informed of illness this can lead to increased symptom reporting. In situations where illness occurs on a cyclical basis, such as MS, people may experience symptoms because they expect them to occur. In a questionnaire study of 325 patients with Parkinson's disease and their relatives, Ellgring *et al.* (1993) found that social anxiety and stress-induced increase of symptoms resulted from an interaction of psychological and somatic factors. Patients who made use of structured psychological interventions were able to change dysfunctional behaviours and cognitions. Depression is often seen in this group of diseases but some of the symptoms of the neurological illness such as fatigue and sleep disturbance may interfere with diagnosis. A further complication is whether affective disorders in patients are the direct result of physical changes to the nervous system (endogenous hypothesis) or whether they result from normal emotional reactions to having a degenerative neurological disease (indirect or reactive hypothesis). In reality, depression may be a result of both (Dupont, 1997). This is further compounded in Alzheimer's disease where in its early stages the presentation is often one of depression. Differential diagnosis between depression and early onset Alzheimer's is predominantly through psychometric testing of cognitive ability combined with clinical opinion.

Coping with a Degenerative Neurological Disease

It has been proposed that before the onset of illness, control derives from physical strength and abilities and from a variety of social, economic and environmental resources (Devins and Seland, 1987). Following the onset of a chronic disease the person's ability to control can become severely compromised and the degree to which symptoms or progress of the disease are predicted can be important in determining how well a person can mobilise resources to cope. Lazarus and Folkman (1984) suggested two ways of coping. Problem-focused coping that is directed at changing the troubled relationship between the person and their environment, and emotion-focused coping which is aimed at managing the distressing emotions themselves. Emotion-focused coping can take a number of different forms such as denial, avoidance, relation therapy and seeking emotional support from other individuals. In a recent cross-cultural study of Alzheimer's disease examining coping strategies and associations with caregiving distress, four coping factors were reliably found – behavioural confronting, behavioural distancing/social support, cognitive confronting and cognitive distancing. Shanghai and San Diego caregivers endorsed similar rates of coping but Shanghai caregivers reported fewer symptoms of depression and anxiety (Shaw *et al.*, 1997). One of the significant issues in caring for those with Alzheimer's disease is whether they should be told when diagnosed (Box 22.1).

> **BOX 22.1 Should patients be told they have Alzheimer's disease?**
>
> Currently fewer than 50% of psychiatrists (Clafferty, Brown and McCabe, 1998) and only 5% of GPs (Vassilas and Donaldson, 1999) routinely tell their patients if they have Alzheimer's disease. This contrasts with terminal cancer where 27% of GPs tell the patient the diagnosis. In a survey of 100 family members accompanying patients diagnosed with Alzheimer's disease, only 17% expressed a wish for the patient to be told the diagnosis (Maquire *et al.*, 1996). The principal rationale given by the majority of those who thought not, was that the diagnosis would upset the patient. When considering themselves, however, 71% indicated that they would wish to be told. There are considerable ethical issues here; should the doctors give more weight to the wishes of their patients in this respect? Informing the patient may give them the opportunity to make important decisions about health care and financial planning before further cognitive deterioration occurs.

Caregivers of persons with MS experience a range of negative effects similar to those reported by other groups of carers of persons with degenerative neurological diseases (Knight *et al.*, 1997). The behaviours causing most distress to the carers were associated with motor problems, sudden mood changes, the partner upsetting other people, incontinence and pain. Satisfaction with coping and social support were predictors of the perceived burden consistent with the stress–appraisal–coping model of Lazurus and Folkman (1984).

PSYCHOLOGICAL INTERVENTIONS

The main categories of degenerative neurological diseases are untreatable and progressive; therapeutic intervention is therefore largely palliative. The ultimate aim is to facilitate comfort, dignity and promote the best possible quality of life for the individual and their family and or carers. Social and environmental situations can accentuate the impairment of neurological damage. This includes not making decisions for the sufferer, treating them like a child (infantilisation) and invalidation of their wishes and opinions. Person-centred approaches retain choice, respect and independence (Kitwood, 1990). A wide variety of factors need to be taken into account when carrying out an assessment that aims to facilitate any improvement (or further loss) in one's quality of life (see Figure 22.1).

One such approach to care-giving has sought to enhance the happiness and spared functions of patients through *Reality Orientation* (RO) Therapy (Folsom, 1968). Reality orientation is a process where each interaction with the person is seen as an opportunity to present current information and to involve the person in what is happening around them, by providing a commentary on what is happening and reinforcing the person's awareness of and interest in their environment. Reality orientation can either be given on an individual basis as a continuous process (24-hour or informal RO) or in small groups (classroom or informal RO). Environmental aids include

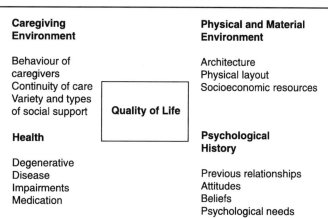

Caregiving Environment

Behaviour of caregivers
Continuity of care
Variety and types of social support

Quality of Life

Health

Degenerative Disease
Impairments
Medication

Physical and Material Environment

Architecture
Physical layout
Socioeconomic resources

Psychological History

Previous relationships
Attitudes
Beliefs
Psychological needs

Figure 22.1   Factors influencing needs assessment

clocks, calenders, pictures and signs. Language is intended to be kept to short and simple sentences that are specific and to the point with any responses from the patient encouraged. Holden and Woods (1995) carried out a systematic review of 21 studies in which reality orientation was compared with either no-treatment or alternative interventions. They found general cognitive improvement and improved verbal orientation.

More recent interventions include *Reminiscence* therapy that involves semi- or un-structured recall of past events and life experiences to encourage the use of long-term memory. Evidence supports the efficacy of reminiscence groups in producing significantly high levels of engagement when compared to other ward activities (Woodrow, 1998). This would appear to confirm that reminiscence provides an enjoyable, meaningful and stimulating activity for people even with very severe cognitive impairment.

Validation therapy was developed in the USA by Naomi Feil (social worker and actress). The core technique is to listen to the 'feelings' behind what is said rather than focusing on the content. 'Validate the feelings. Forget Facts'. The process is very demanding and involves high levels of commitment, and close attention needs to be paid to body language and all forms of non-verbal communication. Unlike reality orientation the staff should not disagree or change the subject when they are unsure of what is being said. Validation should be viewed as an approach to inform thinking rather than a set of proscribed skills.

Dementia care mapping is a cooperative venture between observers and client advocates, organisation managers and hands-on care staff, in order to improve the care process (Kitwood, 1996). It is client-centred in that data is coded to highlight needs and is useful for policy-makers as well as providing feedback to staff. Direct observation is used to assess quality of care considering the relative 'ill-being' or 'well-being' of the person being observed. Each individual is assessed in a variety of settings and situations (20 in total) and this should be carried out at different times of the day on different days. The assessments include verbal interaction, social involvement, creative activities, mobilisation and sleep patterns. Areas of need and function are then highlighted. Dementia care mapping is limited in the respect that it does not include aspects of personal care, and is not designed to be carried out in the person's home. Medication is not taken into consideration, which may be of importance if a side effect impinges into daily life. Ethically there appear to be no dilemmas as the process is intended to work towards improving the life of dementia sufferers.

Out-patient rehabilitation as an intervention has been tested on health-related quality of life in two groups of patients with chronic progressive MS. One received weekly comprehensive out-patient rehabilitation for one year and the other did not receive rehabilitation. The treatment group showed improvement in six of the SF-36 subscales (see Chapter 2). Out-patient treatment was the sole predictor of positive outcome for energy/fatigue and change in general health, and the treatment group was also associated with a positive outcome in social function and social support (Di-Fabio *et al.*, 1997).

PHARMACOTHERAPY

Pharmacological intervention for motor neurone disease focuses mainly around relief of physiological symptoms associated with the disorder; for example, to relieve muscle spasm, to inhibit excessive salivation and analgesia for prolonged spasticity and atrophy. General management is palliative and based upon prediction of needs with progression of the disease. One strategy of intervention in the UK has been the establishment of specialised centres for care and research. These have been funded by the Motor Neurone Disease Association and they provide access to a multi-disciplinary team that are able to carry out systematic assessment of both deficit and ability and to provide a care package dependent on ever-changing needs. No strong evidence exists for effective pharmacotherapy in Alzheimer's disease (Ballard and O'Brien, 1999), although **neuroleptic** and antidepressive medications have been found in some cases to reduce the behavioural difficulties such as irritability, aggression, restlessness, hallucinations and wandering which are a source of stress for care-givers. There is an urgent need for better-controlled trials focusing on specific psychological disturbances in dementia.

Neuroleptics is another term for the group of drugs more usually used to treat psychoses.

Summary and conclusions ●

Degenerative neurological diseases share a number of core features in that they are gradually progressive, may affect physical, sensory and cognitive function and can shorten life-span. These disorders can have a devastating effect on the lives of sufferers and those closest to them. The behaviours causing most distress to the carers are associated with motor problems, sudden mood changes, the partner upsetting other people, incontinence and pain. Creating an understanding of any degenerative neurological disease and the adjustment that a person has to make takes time and should be patient-driven, enabling them to develop a representation of both the disease and the available support. Care and treatment must incorporate a psychological framework in order to understand symptoms, their meaning and presentation, and the cognitive, emotional and behavioural processes that patients make use of when trying to adjust to their condition. Given the complex nature of these disorders it is important to incorporate a multitude of factors into psychological care and treatment programmes – and that these be comprehensively evaluated. Efforts to do so are in their infancy and must contend with the methodological difficulty which a continuing change in maximal achievable quality of life presents. An important ethical issue is the maintenance of quality of care whereby the person with the condition is treated as a fully human member of the community and afforded the same needs for love, care, dignity and respect.

Discussion points

A Consider the psychological consequences on someone of receiving a diagnosis of Alzheimer's disease in its early stages.

B How can quality of life be evaluated for someone with a degenerative neurological condition?

Suggested reading

Holden, U. and Woods, R. T. (1995) *Positive Approaches to Dementia Care.* (Edinburgh: Churchill Livingstone).

Maguire, C.P., Kirby, M., Coen, R., Coakley, Lawlor, B.A. and O'Neill, D. (1996) 'Family Members' Attitudes Toward Telling the Patient with Alzheimer's Disease their Diagnosis', *British Medical Journal*, **313**: 529–30.

Rao, S.M., Huber, S.J. and Bornstein, R.A. (1992) 'Emotional Changes with Multiple Sclerosis and Parkinson's Disease', *Journal of Consulting and Clinical Psychology*, **60**(3): 369–78.

chapter 23

Issues in Palliative Care

'Knowledge alone is not going to help anybody. If you do not use your head and your heart and your soul, you are not going to help a single human being.'

Elizabeth Kübler-Ross (*On Life after Death*, 1991)

'When we die, we die. The wind blows away our footprints, and that is the end of us.'

Kalahari Bushman

Palliative care is concerned with treatment that does not cure but relieves. It is most frequently used to describe the care of those with terminal or chronic disease and incorporates management of pain, both traditional and alternative; the psychosocial adjustment of the individual and their family/carers to the disease and the associated impact on their quality of life; to encourage the individual to make their own choices about how and where they die; and to assist the family during the period of bereavement. In a recent study where the meaning and definition of palliative care was explored amongst health professionals three common themes emerged: first there has been a recognition of life-threatening and life-limiting conditions within the definition; second there is an implication within the definition that there should be a responsive package of care, multidisciplinary in nature and based upon the needs of the individual and family; and third the definitions highlight an enhancement in the quality of life for the patient and their family. Amongst a wider sample of health professionals responding to a questionnaire based on these themes, it was found that as well as terminal cancer palliative care should be increasingly provided to a range of other conditions such as motor neurone disease, multiple sclerosis and AIDS, and that care should be given throughout the disease trajectory and not just in the later stages (Jones and Faulkner, 1996).

MANAGEMENT OF PAIN

Of the three aspects mentioned above, management of pain in palliative care has probably received the most attention by health professionals as it is an issue that directly impinges on quality of life. The management of pain in any situation must take account of the impact on patients' lives and this is particularly relevant with chronic pain which is sometimes defined as pain lasting more than six months (Russo and Brose, 1998) (see Box 23.1). Although issues of dependance to strong opioid analgesia may not be important in the terminally ill, the side effects of such treatments can be distressing to patients. For instance, in a randomised open, multi-centre, cross-over study comparing transdermal fentanyl with sustained-release oral morphine in 202 cancer patients, fentanyl was associated with significantly less constipation, less daytime drowsiness but greater sleep disturbance and shorter sleep duration. However, significantly more patients preferred the fentanyl patches despite the problems with sleep (Ahmedzai and Brooks, 1997). Many palliative care centres now include a range of complementary therapies that are used in

BOX 23.1   Pain and mood: implications for treatment

Chronic pain is usually associated with lowered mood, which can present as depression. Sensitivity to acute experimental pain (the pain threshold), such as induced by a laser, is greater in depressed than non-depressed subjects and when depression is reversed sensitivity is normalised (Mel'nikova, 1993). Furthermore, endurance of acute pain (pain tolerance) is much lower (by 44% on average) in depressed compared to control subjects (Pinerua-Shuhaibar et al., 1999). It should be no surprise, therefore, that numerous studies show negative mood is related to severity of chronic clinical pain (Shacham et al., 1984) and that mood disturbance scores are correlated with chronic pain ratings (Glover et al., 1995). When negative mood is reversed by use of antidepressants (Harrison et al., 1997), induction of positive mood states (Urba, 1996), or relaxation (Constant et al., 1998), pain tolerance can be increased in chronic pain patients. Overall stressful life events, in particular those that arouse feelings of helplessness, seem to contribute to greater pain intensity (Varni et al., 1996; Lampe et al., 1998). Transient mood manipulation by a variety of means including exposure to films can also modulate sensitivity to experimental pain in normal subjects (Velten, 1968). Induction of positive mood states based on elation and well-being has been associated with increased pain tolerance to cold pressor, whilst induction of negative mood has been associated with a reduction in pain tolerance (Weisenberg et al., 1998). In addition, induction of humour in normal subjects while being exposed to an aversive stimulus produced lower negative affect, lower tension and reduced psychophysiological reactivity (Newman and Stone, 1996). Humour has also been used as a cognitive technique to increase pain tolerance in normal subjects (Weisenberg et al., 1995). However, the effects may be short-lived. Mood-induction procedures using films with longer exposure times (30–45 minutes) have shown physiological effects on immune function (Mittwoch-Jaffe et al., 1995) as well as optimal changes in mood (Weisenberg et al., 1998) suggesting that short exposure to mood-induction procedures may act only as a cognitive distractor.

Nowadays pain is likely to be treated using a multidisciplinary approach in a pain clinic. The main rationale for psychological intervention is that if suffering from pain can be minimised by specific manipulation of the emotional aspect of pain (despite continued sensory activation) then the meaning of pain in terms of disruption of quality of life is reduced. Psychological treatments include operant techniques, relaxation and biofeedback, cognitive techniques, hypnosis and insight-orientated psychotherapies. Where access to pain clinics is not possible or desirable, self-management programmes for chronic pain could provide an alternative treatment strategy. In a randomised controlled trial of 110 patients with chronic pain there were significant improvements in pain, dependency, vitality, role functioning, life satisfaction, self-efficacy and resourcefulness as compared to a waiting-list control group (LeFort et al., 1998).

combination with the more traditional approaches. However, assessment of their efficacy is complicated by a lack of well-designed cross-over studies (Botting and Cook, 1998). For example, with cancer patients, their wide-ranging needs such as personal and physical demands, support, relaxation and distraction have claimed to be met by hypnosis but this has yet to be tested empirically (Pattison, 1997).

ADJUSTMENT TO DIAGNOSIS AND DISEASE

Adapting to a terminal illness with good psychological outcome for the patient and carers is a major goal of palliative care. It is often assumed that adaptation is easier in old age and harder in the young, and that in the latter case there has been a tendency to 'protect' the dying child by withholding information about their prognosis. However, there is evidence that children are aware that they are dying and are sensitive to cues from carers who may give them less time and attention compared to non-terminal children (Waechter, 1971). Good and open communication will establish a workable therapeutic alliance between the family and health professionals and increase the chances of a good psychological outcome (Wooley et al., 1989). Children are usually less upset when cared for at home although children's hospices can provide high quality care when medical and nursing needs cannot be met at home or when the needs of siblings or others do not allow it (Black, 1998). The stress surrounding the care of a dying child can increase the risk of psychological disturbance and this has to be addressed by information and support. Older children and adults with life-threatening illnesses experience a series of losses as the illness progresses, including security, physical functions, body image, power, self-esteem, independence and respect from others (Parkes, 1998). The work of Elizabeth Kübler-Ross (1970) has been instrumental in providing a stage theory of adjustment to dying (which she argues is also applicable to issues of loss in general) that includes denial, anger, bargaining, depression and acceptance. These stages do not conform to all patterns of dying and some patients will stay in denial and expect to get better whilst others will be accepting of death. In practice, most patients will oscillate between stages. However, a positive health promotion approach to palliative care has been proposed to help the patient and family approach the last stages of life with hope and possibly fulfilment based on advocacy, enabling and mediacy. The nurse as patient advocate can ensure that their wishes are met, enabling can ensure that key decisions are inclusive, whilst mediacy between caregivers ensures death occurs in the right setting for the individual (Russell and Sander, 1998).

QUALITY OF LIFE

Quality of life is the appraisal of those components of life (e.g. physical, financial, psychological, social, occupational) which constitute well-being. A variety of disease-specific and generic measures are used to measure it.

The cornerstone of palliative care is the issue of **quality of life**. Problems with definition and measurement are dealt with in Chapter 2. However, although current definitions of palliative care include quality of life as a central theme, the research into this area often fails to take into account the individual perspective of the patient on their own quality of life. This has been addressed by developing instrumentation that evolves from the perspective of the patient at any given moment in time (O'Boyle and Waldron, 1997). A number of studies have assessed patients using a variety of quality-of-life measurements during the final days or weeks of life and found that good pain management can be achieved and that patients are generally less anxious than spouses. A desire to attribute 'meaningfulness' to the situation has been demonstrated for both patients and spouses (Axelsson and Sjoden, 1998). Other approaches have looked at symptom prevalence in the last week of life with the view that it is important to redefine the goals of care as previously present symptoms may increase and new ones appear. In a sample of 176 terminal patients the most frequent end-of-life symptoms (present in more than 50% of cases) were anorexia, asthenia, dry mouth, confusion and constipation with the majority of patients dying at home (Conill *et al.*, 1997). In a well-studied cohort of 170 dementia patients investigated during the last year of their life the symptoms most commonly reported were mental confusion (83%), urinary incontinence (72%), pain (64%), low mood (61%), constipation (59%) and loss of appetite (57%) (McCarthy *et al.*, 1997). Interestingly, in randomised trials with quality-of-life endpoints where doctors ratings of symptom severity were compared against those given by patients, the doctors consistently underestimated symptom severity by around 15 per cent (Stephens *et al.*, 1997). This adds to the increasing body of evidence that challenges the ability of health professionals to accurately assess other people's quality of life (see Chapter 2). A number of studies have now looked at caregivers' quality of life in relation to the burden of caring for terminally-ill patients. One such study investigated the effects of a transmural home-care intervention on caregivers' quality of life. The transmural care intervention optimised the cooperation and coordination of intramural and extramural health care organisations to provide a more integrated information and support system. Transmural care was compared with standard care and was found to contribute significantly to caregivers' quality of life after initial discharge from hospital and three months after the patient's death (Smeenk *et al.*, 1998).

INDIVIDUAL CHOICE

There is now an increasing acceptance of the right of patients to refuse life-sustaining treatment. This is widely achieved through the 'living-will' that instructs practitioners not to use extraordinary life-support measures. Most individuals also chose an agent or 'proxy' who would make decisions on their behalf if they were unable to. There is also a movement as a corollary right to the living-will that patients have a right to physician-assisted suicide (Bernat, 1997), a matter of much recent debate. However, there seems to be some disagreement between what the public wants and what clinicians are prepared to provide. In a cross-sectional survey by postal questionnare of 387 clinicians and 910 community members from the Queensland electoral roll, clinicians were consistently more conservative about active voluntary euthanasia, physician-assisted suicide, and changes in legislation surrounding these issues (Steinberg, 1997). In light of the ethical and legal controversies surrounding physician assisted-suicide and voluntary euthanasia some have proposed voluntary stopping eating and drinking and terminal sedation as ethically superior responses of last resort that do not require changes in professional standards or the law (Quill *et al.*, 1997). It is clear that this debate will continue, though the reasons for the gradual shift in the opinions of the general public towards acceptance of euthanasia are not yet fully understood. Further research in this area is called for.

BEREAVEMENT

Given the one certainty that we will all die and suffer the loss of friends and relatives during the course of our lives it seems amazing that such little attention has been given to the issue of bereavement. After such a major loss around a 25–30 per cent of us will suffer detrimental effects on physical and mental health (Jacobs, 1993). The cost to society is enormous with increased risk of heart disease and psychiatric morbidity (Clegg, 1988). What then is the normal reaction to such loss and grief and should this take its course and be viewed as a normal adaptive response without need of intervention? Conversely, what are the complications of bereavement and what can one do to intervene?

Grief is an expression of social and cultural norms as well as a unique personal experience to us all. Central to the grieving process is the need to look back and reprocess past experience, opposed by the need to look forward into unchartered waters and discover what can be carried forward from the past. The normal course of grief has been conceptualised by classic phase theorists such as Bowlby (1980) into four phases: numbness, pining, disorganisation and despair, and reorganisation. Whilst it may be useful to think in these terms, the phases should not be regarded as a rigid sequence but rather a repeated process that may not necessarily be in phase order nor occur in series. The behavioural consequences of grieving after major loss can be seen as initial weight loss with disrupted sleep cycles that normalise after a few months. Recovery is perceived by most individuals as happening during the second year. There are a number of factors that have been identified as increasing risk after bereavement. These can generally be thought of in terms of traumatic experiences such as unexpected deaths, be they multiple (disasters), suicide, murder or manslaughter or in terms of the vulnerability of the individual such as low self-esteem, previous psychiatric morbidity and lack of social support. The complications of bereavement can be seen as physical and/or psychiatric. Physical complications such as the impairment of immunocompetence has been linked to the development of upper respiratory tract infections, as well as increased vulnerability to stress. Psychiatric complications caused by bereavement are clinical depression, anxiety disorders and PTSD, which may ocurr either in isolation but may often co-exist. Some have classified two categories of griever; 'avoiders' who avoid issues surrounding the grief and 'sensitisers' who are characterised by a tendency toward obsessive preoccupation (Horowitz, 1986).

There has been some attempt to isolate factors that may prevent complicated grief. This has been focused on 'anticipatory guidance' where members of health care teams can prepare individuals for losses that are to come. When imparting such information the goal is to strike a balance between avoidance and confrontation of painful realities through considering factors such as available social support and location of the meeting, imparting of information in a manner that is comprehended and giving time to assimilate the information and react accordingly. Of course support is required immediately after the death, and reassurance should be given that intense sobbing and expressions of hurt and anguish are entirely appropriate reactions in one person as is denial in another. The first anniversary of death is a particularly sensitive time but in most people it is a landmark to move forward without feelings of guilt or betrayal.

Summary and conclusions

Palliative care is most frequently used to describe the care of those with terminal or chronic disease. As well as terminal cancer, it is increasingly provided for people with a range of conditions including AIDS. It incorporates pain management as well as the psychosocial adjustment of the individual, their family and their carers. Many palliative care centres now include a range of complementary therapies that are used in combination with the more traditional approaches, though assessment of efficacy is complicated by a lack of well-designed studies. Adapting to terminal illness with good psychological outcome for patient and carers is a major goal of palliative care. Though it is assumed this is easier in old age and harder in the young, there is evidence that children are aware that they are dying and are sensitive to cues from carers who may give less time and attention compared to non-terminal children. Open communication between the family and health professionals increases the chances for a good psychological outcome.

Older children and adults with life-threatening illnesses experience a series of losses as the illness progresses. Kübler-Ross has been instrumental in providing a stage theory of adjustment to dying which includes denial, anger, bargaining, depression and acceptance, whilst Bowlby has described the course of grief in four phases: numbness, pining, disorganisation and despair, and reorganisation. Psychological complications consequent to bereavement include depression, anxiety and PTSD. These may occur either together or in isolation. Central to grieving is the need to look back and reprocess past experience, in conjunction with the need to look forward and discover what can be carried forward from the past. Some have classified two categories of griever; 'avoiders' who avoid issues surrounding the grief and 'sensitisers', characterised by a tendency towards preoccupation. Work has attempted to isolate factors that may prevent complicated grief. This has focused on 'anticipatory guidance' where members of health care teams prepare individuals for impending losses. The goal is to strike a balance between avoidance and confrontation of painful realities.

There are several major ethical issues in palliative care. With more open debate of physician-assisted suicide and voluntary euthanasia there is an increasing pressure on palliative care to confront these issues. However, the pursuit of terminal treatment practices and standards can only be achieved through democratic and legal means. This does not, however, offer much hope to the family or patients on the receiving end of care who feel that they have a right to make decisions about their own death. The question of whether people have a right to die when this seems to fly in the face of the Hippocratic oath taken by medical practitioners is a difficult one. There seems to be disagreement between what the public wants and what clinicians are prepared to provide. Evidence suggests clinicians may be more conservative about active voluntary euthanasia, physician-assisted suicide and changes in legislation surrounding these issues. More research into the reasons for the shift in public opinion towards acceptance of euthanasia is needed. This will likely involve questions of the (public) resources devoted to maintaining people's quality of life as well as which aspects of quality of life are more influential when making decisions about one's own and other people's manner of living and dying.

Discussion points

A Should physician-assisted suicide and voluntary euthanasia be offered as part of the palliative care package?

B What role can health psychologists play in the delivery and development of palliative care?

C How influential do you think high-quality social support and companionship are when considering voluntary euthanasia?

Suggested reading

Black, D. (1998) 'Coping with Loss; the Dying Child', *British Medical Journal*, **316**: 1376–8.

Kübler-Ross E. R. (1970) *On Death and Dying.* (London: Tavistock).

Part 6
Deconstructing Health Psychology

In this final part of the book, we wish to present an alternate view of the rapid development of health psychology as a discipline. Here we will be concerned less with the body of knowledge which has been accumulated about the importance of psychological or psychosocial factors in the genesis, maintenance or experience of health, and more with the context within which this body of knowledge has developed, with attendant claims to be a distinct discipline. Thus far we have accepted the legitimacy of these claims, albeit with arguments to further extend the scope of activities with which health psychologists have concerned themselves. In any discipline it is vital that claims – those which pertain both to matters of fact and to the wider social, political and moral discourses within which these facts are embedded – are subject to intense scrutiny before they can be accepted as adding constructively to our store of knowledge. To date it can be strongly argued that health psychology has yet to subject itself to such a searching examination. What follows, therefore, will be an attempt to locate the discipline within wider terms than the scientific rationale that is usually presented (see Chapter 1). We leave readers to decide for themselves where the 'field' of past influences is taking us; whether possible courses which these map out lead to a viable future and who stands to benefit from health psychology.

The Future of Health Psychology

(with Antje Mueller)

> 'Who controls the past controls the future
> Who controls the present controls the past.'
>
> George Orwell (Party Slogan: *1984*)

INTRODUCTION

In a review of publication trends in Health Psychology, Krampen and Montada (1998) noted the relatively low rate of professional criticisms and professional criticism replies in the literature database. The figure they found (around 1%) is substantially lower than in other sub-disciplines of psychology, and though it is possible that this may reflect the youthful nature of the discipline, the relatively high proportion of literature overviews and introductory texts compared with empirical research provide no grounds for complacency. Rather they hint at a fervour to publicise and market the discipline ahead of developing a genuine knowledge base in it. We are of the view that the self-congratulatory tone present in much of the literature is unhelpful – for the discipline, for health sciences in general, for the academics employed in what could be regarded as ostensibly a marketing exercise, to the detriment of doing research and ultimately for recipients of health care who deserve better. There is nothing inevitable to how the discipline will unfold, nor that its development will necessarily be successful. Here we seek to deconstruct the subject matter from a number of critical perspectives which are active in the social sciences and to warn against the forces which could potentially lead to its stagnation and corruption. In the intoxicating international scramble to promote and expand the professional presence of health psychologists, a number of issues which warrant wider critical discussion have largely been left on the sidelines. The extent to which the discipline rises to this challenge for critical debate may be a litmus test for how its future will unfold. In this part of the book we will review the foremost of these concerns and attempt to draw the various strands into a coherent and alternative vision for examining psychological issues in health care. This critique will revolve around the following questions;

- Does health psychology form a coherent body of knowledge?
- What is the methodological and theoretical basis of health psychology?
- What motives underpin the current development of health psychology?
- What is the role of health psychology in society?

HEALTH PSYCHOLOGY: A COHERENT BODY OF KNOWLEDGE?

The rapid emergence of health psychology has been attributed to several factors. These include the increased recognition of the role of behavioural and psychosocial factors in disease (chiefly HIV infection and AIDS), the need to audit healthcare interventions, dissatisfaction with the depersonalisation endemic to the traditional medical approach to care, and the changing concepts of health which have arisen in the last forty to fifty years. Strictly speaking only the first of these is a demand to emerge from within the scientific community. The need for audit, though it encompasses a scientific dimension, is a response to the increasing demands and hence costs to health providers arising from the burdens of an increasingly ageing population with chronic diseases. The changing conceptions of health and well-being have their origins in the call by the World Health Organisation (WHO, 1948) to widen and humanise the scope of modern medicine following the calamity of the Second World War – a period which, it must not be forgotten, witnessed frightful collaboration by medical personnel with one of the most inhuman political regimes in history. Thus powerful forces have been at work shaping the emergence of several closely related disciplines – of which health psychology is but one. It could be argued that these are compelling enough to provide the rationale for a discipline of health psychology. Alternatively it could be said that the foundations for a new field of science should rest more on the nature of the current and likely future scientific problems faced by the research community and less on political and professional grounds. It is seldom considered what the minimum requirements to be met are in order to lay claim to being a distinct branch of knowledge.

Though numerous scientific disciplines are related, each can be characterised by being focused within a broadly unique if somewhat fuzzy epistemological range of convenience (Kelly, 1955) (see Chapter 1). Within this area, the agreed conventions of scientific method (publicly reproducible knowledge using reliable and valid forms of measurement) are followed which lead to the development of distinct methodologies and testable theories, the success of which in turn lead to lasting knowledge, distinct to that produced in related disciplines. So – the first question to ask of health psychology is whether the domain of knowledge it lays claim to is distinct. What exactly does health psychology offer which is all its own? Usually it is looked upon as concerning the role of behavioural and cognitive factors in producing, maintaining and responding to varying health or physiological processes. This includes attitudes and beliefs about health and illness and the evaluation of health care interventions and health states. There is, however, confusion about what distinguishes health psychology from the related fields of behavioural medicine and epidemiology. Gatchel, Baum and Krantz (1989), for example, defined health psychology in contrast to behavioural medicine, a field which they admit has itself engendered debate amongst professionals as to its precise nature. So while behavioural medicine is deemed to be

> the broad interdisciplinary field of scientific education and practice which concerns itself with health, illness and related physiological dysfunction (Krantz, 1989, p. 10)

health psychology, following Matarazzo (1980, p. 4),

> is the aggregate of the specific educational, scientific and professional contributions of the discipline of psychology to the promotion and maintenance of health, the prevention and treatment of illness and the identification of etiological and diagnostic correlates of health, illness and related dysfunction.

Sheridan and Radmacher (1992) adhere to this definition, but make no attempt to distinguish health psychology from other disciplines. Instead they offer a contrast between the medical model and the bio-psychosocial model which they argue incorporates psychological and social influences on health which do not fit the narrow framework of the biomedical model. While the strict biomedical model is clearly deficient – a point stressed throughout this text – contemporary medicine has itself moved beyond it, particularly in the fields of public health and epidemiology where such influences have been well recognised, indeed they were recognised and researched before health psychology came into being. Wilkinson (1996) has articulated this succinctly in describing the study of health as having now developed into a broad social science. Kaplan, Sallis and Patterson (1993), meanwhile, describe behavioural medicine as a collaboration of behavioural and medical scientists to improve health, whereas health psychology is the contribution of psychologists to this process. This comes perilously close to defining health psychology by who does it rather than what it is that they do. This is obviously contentious, although there are strong echoes of this reasoning in the current plans to professionalise the discipline ahead of general agreement on what constitute core practical skills and knowledge within it and confusion regarding the supposed recipients of such skills.

Ogden (1996) has offered the more pragmatic view that the new discipline emphasises the role of psychological factors in the cause, progression and consequences of health and illness. Its aims are fundamentally scientific – to understand, explain, develop and test theory and to put this theory into practice – and the agenda which will promote this is clearly based on research. But even if one unquestionably accepts the definitions of health psychology as a purely scientific activity rather than an attempt to promote professionalism in another branch of health, the question is whether psychologists or a distinct breed of psychologists have to do it. The major evidence for the role of psychological and psychosocial processes in health come predominantly from epidemiological studies such as the Alameda County Study (Belloc and Breslow, 1972), the Framingham study (Haynes, Levine and Scotch, 1978), the Multiple Risk Factor Intervention Trial (Multiple Risk Factor Intervention Trial Research Group, 1982), the Western Collaborative Group Study (Rosenman Brand, Sholz and Friedman, 1976) and the Whitehall studies (Marmot *et al.*, 1991). It can be argued that although the intent of these investigations is to relate psychological variables to health outcomes – even if psychologists might be better placed to interpret any such relationships – neither the theory nor the methodology requires the constitution of a new discipline. It is therefore erroneous to conclude as some have done (Philips, 1998; Graham, 1998,) that the plethora of research on health inequalities points intrinsically to a vibrant role for health psychology.

The question of what theoretical developments and methodologies have been developed from within health psychology will be taken up in the next section. One example which highlights the evident confusion regarding what is and what is not health psychology concerns the republication of a book which first appeared in the 1980s entitled *Stress and Health: Issues in Research Methodology* (Kasl and Cooper, 1987). This text reappeared in the 1990s with its amended title (*Research Methods in Stress and Health Psychology*) reflecting the appropriation of its contents by the new discipline of health psychology (Kasl and Cooper, 1995).

THE METHODOLOGICAL AND THEORETICAL BASIS OF HEALTH PSYCHOLOGY

As moves within some countries to standardise the curriculum of health psychology move full steam ahead, a prominent place in the theoretical core of the new discipline is devoted to models of health behaviours. We have reviewed several of these in this book – notably the Health Belief Model and the Theory of Planned Behaviour (see Chapter 7). Without doubt these models have merit as attempts to build bridges between thought and behaviour – long regarded as a problematic area by social psychologists. However, they also have serious shortcomings which include difficulties in operationalising the constructs, low predictive validity, and a failure to appreciate the historical and complex social context in which behaviour is situated. In their present form the models have not yet lived up to their promise. However, no-one has yet proposed any operational criteria for deciding whether these are meeting the aspirations of the scientific community. These aims must in the final calling pertain to explaining the behaviour and utilising the knowledge to bring about change, rather than adhering to any particular theory or model which is advanced, however it performs. The relatively poor ability of these models to predict behaviour could be interpreted as indicating that motivations and cognitions do not play a major role in explaining variations in the take-up or maintenance of healthy behaviours. The refusal to countenance abandoning the models in question – or relegating them in importance – seems to stem more from the role they occupy in promoting health psychology, than in their ability at the moment to explain phenomena. There is nothing inherent in this problem that it requires a psychological explanation. The way health psychology is currently being presented prevents appreciation of this. A major part of the problem is that the rationale for health psychology has been built on the premise of the individual's personal responsibility for their own health (Pitts, 1996). Whilst this may appear to be common sense to many and is certainly evident in lay perceptions of health (Blaxter, 1993, 1997), the validity of the premise is not self-evident and is far more restricted than many would like. The dangers in this perspective – chiefly of blaming people for their own poor well being and absolving social agencies of responsibility – cannot be overstated.

What if models of health behaviour do not provide a sufficiently strong basis for grounding the discipline? Are there any other suitable candidates around? Here the signs are more encouraging. Could quality of life for example act as a unifying concept around which a viable discipline could emerge? Defining and measuring what is meant by the idea is obviously crucial, we have reviewed several alternative schemes in Chapter 2, all of which have strengths and weaknesses. Development of the various instruments (for example the Nottingham Health Profile, SF-36, SEIQoL) has been predicated to a greater or lesser extent upon psychometric issues. This has enabled useful data to be generated on the impact of medical and psychosocial interventions, life events and social inequalities. However, to step away from the narrow concerns of psychometrics and address the quality and the detailed contents of the lives shared by people belonging to particular social groups (men, women, children, ethnic minorities, people with disabilities, members of different social classes, health service users – physical and mental) gives psychology an opportunity to avoid an excessive preoccupation with individualism. There are, for example, already indications that aspects of personality such as locus of control, neuroticism and coping style may be rooted in childhood social class (Bosma, van de Mheen and Mackenbach, 1999). Knowledge of how the psychological as well as the physical dimensions of people's lives have been structured in ways which burden their health deserves to be much better understood than is currently the case and warrants a serious role in theory and in health policy-making. Factors affecting interpersonal perceptions of quality of life in others is one area we have signposted as having extremely important ethical implications. Wider notions of quality of life – which pertain to the quality of the social, physical and economic environment – could usefully be married to the more traditional measures and, allied to the social dimensions listed, could be used to build more valid ecological models of human health. Work on the relationships between social cohesion and health have already proved a valuable source of new hypotheses in this direction (Kawachi *et al.*, 1997; Wilkinson, 1996b). Radley's (1995) contention that a *psychology of health* rather than health psychology offers a better route forward is not inconsistent with this, and work conducted under this auspice has demonstrated how people's accounts of their lives with illness can inform wider debates in social science discourse (Radley and Billig, 1996).

In recent years psychology and other social sciences have been witness to a fierce debate about what are the most appropriate methods of investigation. Rather than supplanting quantitative techniques, the growing respect afforded to qualitative methods offers a unique route for exploring questions of meaning in both quality-of-life research and that concerning the nature and role of social relationships (see Chapter 17). A particular area where this strategy will aid our understanding lies in the domain of social inequalities/differences in health. Epidemiologists are already positing that how people perceive the meaning of their social situation occupies a pivotal position in the pathways leading from environmental stressors to biological precursors of disease processes (Tarloff, 1996). These bottom-up data-gathering techniques serve two particular functions. Firstly, they can put flesh onto the bones of existing models so that they give concrete meaning to abstract statistical models. Secondly, they can serve as a source for generating more rigorous testable hypotheses (Burt and Oaksford, 1999). It might not always provide a *de rigour* objective account of verifiable processes in the material world, but on occasion it is the only and therefore the best available form of data for empirical investigations of meaning and self-determination in human affairs. Where this is the case – and it is precisely here that debate is called for – it should be considered that human testimony possesses intrinsic validity. This has long been recognised in other areas of psychology, notably in studies of memory and sleep which are recognised as areas of hard scientific enterprise. The application of qualitative methods to the emerging field of psychoneuroimmunology could, by addressing the meanings derived from important life events and their relationship to states of health, both enrich our understanding of the relationship between 'mind and body' and answer the criticism that there has been too little psychology in PNI research.

The dangers in using the new methodologies lie in rejecting out of hand notions of reliability, validity, logical rigour and scientific method, and accepting postmodernist philosophies uncritically. Following Hume and Kant we can subscribe to the view that an objective reality is unknowable in principle – but this certainly does not imply that all competing points of view have equal validity for our understanding of the world. The scientific method has a greater degree of validity because in its methodology it is in principle self-correcting. This form of self-reference does not paint an absolutely true picture of the world, but it permits ones which are clearly inaccurate to be rejected. Unless we allow at least some such basis for a natural selection of ideas, there seems little point in advocating any for a useful place in the world of ideas in the first place. Nor must the methodologies replace theory, as has some-

Structural equation models
Sometimes misleadingly referred to as causal modelling. A popular multivariate analytic technique in which a hypothetical model comprising a set of structured (linear) relationships between variables is tested against alternative models where the specified structure of relationships is different (e.g. it may be tested against a null model where there are no significant relationships between the specified variables).

times occurred with the use of focus groups and the method known as grounded theory.

Some of these dangers also exist with quantitative data analysis, where the elegance and apparent utility of complex multivariate or structural equation models may seem to override the need to explain how and why these relationships have arisen or indeed to validate them by testing them with new data. The unquestioned use of regression techniques, including path analysis and structural equation modelling, can also easily lead researchers into assuming that the only relationships of interest are those amenable to analyses using linear forms of modelling. Unless all the variance in a dependent variable has been statistically explained – and this is highly unusual outside of the physical sciences – then the demonstrated incompleteness of the model ought to lead researchers to ask whether other linear components, including inter-action terms, should be added to the model. And then if this does not work – that is, the model has been inadequately specified – additional consideration should be given as to whether the variables included in the model may have non-linear relationships with the outcome measure. Assessing the linearity of relationship is a matter of applying suitable diagnostic techniques (Fox, 1991). Questionable assumptions of linearity have without doubt held back our understanding of health behaviours which have strong situational determinants – sexual behaviour being an obvious example – and which probably require more complex mathematical models.

With all the uncertainty surrounding the theories, models and methods available in the health psychology armoury, it might seem a little surprising that in a number of countries moves are well underway to standardise the curriculum for future students and practitioners. But what exactly does it mean to practise health psychology? We will take this up in the next section.

WHAT MOTIVES UNDERPIN THE CURRENT DEVELOPMENT OF HEALTH PSYCHOLOGY?

The development of quality-of-life measures occupies a key theoretical niche in the emergence of health psychology. Though the theoretical rationale for psychological research in health is strong, whether this provides sufficient justification for a sub-discipline of health psychology distinct from other branches of health science is a question for readers. But what of the application of psychological knowledge? Much of the literature has laid emphasis on the importance of delivering psychological care particularly for those with chronic diseases. Without a doubt the needs for im-proved care and management here require the greater availability of psychological skills in medical personnel than currently exist. Although psychologists and coun-sellors may be the people best-placed to provide this training, this does not by itself provide a justification for health psychology as a scientific discipline. The provision of particular skills training is not a distinct scientific sub-speciality. Furthermore, the evaluation of counselling and psychotherapeutic interventions themselves are already accepted and integral parts of their own disciplines – no special claim can be made by psychologists practising in the health arena. Is counselling an individual, with let us say, motor neurone disease really any different in principle or in practice from counselling someone on their situation at work?

It could be argued that psychologists should be concentrating less on providing justification for their professional role in health care settings and more on working with client groups so that they empower themselves. Nowhere is this more evident that in the 'psychology of disability' where psychologists appear to be clinging to an outmoded and discredited model of disability, one moreover which is fiercely opposed by people with disabilities themselves. The desire to be experts on other people's situations is one which we must think long and hard about. In defence it could be said that health psychologists' emphasis on self-justification does owe something to the nature of medical politics and to the system of hierarchical structuring of personnel who deliver health care resources. We must ask, however, whether the use of psychologists' knowledge and skills would be better served by imitating the medical model or challenging it, an argument which in recent years has been gaining momentum in clinical psychology (Pilgrim, 2000).

The medical model has been subject to repeated critiques (Illich, 1977) over the years, though few have actually sought to examine the model of personal relationships which lie within it. Feminist psychologists have provided a valuable critical tool here (for example Nicolson and Ussher, 1992; Nicolson, 1998) by relating the practice of medicine both theoretically and practically to the power imbalance between males and females, whilst psychiatric practise has also been scrutinised in terms of the ethnocentric values implicit in the methods of diagnosis and treatment (Littlewood and Lipsedge, 1997; Fernando, Ndegwa and Wilson, 1998). These arguments need to be extended beyond gender and race to view the divisions in social status and control in medicine as expressions of class relations (that is hierarchically-structured power relations). With few exceptions, psychologists have been slow to realise the insidious nature of internalised lower self-esteem and how this permeates much of social life. From this vantage point the desire of psychologists – indeed of all health care professionals – who argue that the needs of patients are best served by positioning themselves for equal status with physicians does nothing to challenge the privileged status enjoyed by medical practitioners and ultimately leads to an aligning of professional interests with the medical profession. A useful avenue of research, indeed, would be to examine the development of attitudes and behaviours towards medical practitioners in terms of a wider social psychology of class relations, and to ascertain under what conditions these are subject to change. Some useful ideas may be gleaned from the current literature on doctor–patient communications and from studies of lay perceptions of health care although the suggestions being made here have a much wider remit.

What is being argued here is that the call for the professionalisation of health psychology as distinct from the existing sub-speciality of clinical health psychology or the development of psychological science in the area of health and health care is premature and difficult to rationalise on purely scientific grounds. It is disingenuous to claim otherwise. Rather, it forms part of a wider trend towards cementing power in the hands of ever smaller groups of professionals. In this context the moves in the UK in recent years to restrict formal postgraduate training in health psychology to those with undergraduate degrees in psychology and thereby to exclude many with nursing qualifications hardly helps to infuse psychological knowledge and skills into the working lives of other health professionals where it is most definitely needed. It is difficult to see how this can aid returning power to health service users. There are no inherent reasons why this process should not be the subject of investigation itself. Armed with these questions we can no longer avoid asking what role the current model of health psychology plays in the wider society?

HEALTH PSYCHOLOGY IN SOCIETY

The practice of psychology in health care settings involves research, education and the provision of psychological skills – either directly in a clinical or counselling capacity or through the medium of consultancy (Wren, 1998; Wallace, 1998). At the time of writing, this model effectively operates (with some variations) in the United States and Europe. The focus of these activities has largely been confined to health issues (chiefly chronic diseases) in richer countries, and in this sense it looks as if health psychology is to follow the practise of western medicine in devoting insufficient attention to health in poorer countries. So far Chesney's (1996) call for a shift of emphasis in health psychology towards global public health perspectives does not seem to have been heartily endorsed by a majority of psychologists. Globally infectious and parasitic diseases claim significantly more lives than circulatory diseases (WHO, 1999b), though with few exceptions have received scant attention in the literature. For example, a MEDLINE search indexed on the keywords *psychology* and *infectious disease* produced only 86 references over the period 1990–98, compared with 562 for a comparable search using *psychology* and *cardiovascular disease*. The specific health concerns in poor countries have likewise been neglected. Malaria, a major health risk for over half of the world's population, is but one example (Ager, Carr, Maclachlan and Kaneka-Chilongo, 1996). The threat posed by HIV infection and AIDS has been noted, but attempts at behavioural control have not been as successful as hoped and the role of global economic factors in destabilising traditional economies and patterns of behaviour which have led to greater spread of the virus has received too little mention from behavioural scientists. Greater awareness of how economic and social change relate to behavioural change in individuals is needed. Psychologists need to be making more explicit the links between the dimensions of personal behaviour and activities in the wider social context. The global threat to health from tobacco is also felt acutely in poor countries and comes from the political and economic freedom enjoyed by tobacco companies to peddle their products in an unrestrained global market. Future efforts to reign-in this threat will hopefully not include exhortations to the world's poor to realise the benefits of nicotine patches and enrolment in behaviour-modification programmes.

All this does not mean that psychology does not have a role to play in addressing global health issues. Indeed, drawing attention to the psychological damage inflicted on the people of the world starved of material resources would be a worthy endeavour. This role, however, must be seen as secondary in importance to interventions which are geared to reducing economic and material inequality. Research-based knowledge is likely to be more useful in addressing global health issues than clinically (psychologically) based practice. As an example, utilising psychological knowledge to design safer and healthier environments for people could theoretically help to reduce accidents in the home and outside. Road traffic accidents currently stand as the ninth leading cause of disease burden (WHO, 1999b), and with predicted increases in traffic the numbers of fatalities are predicted to increase alongside it. Research on the behaviour of pedestrians, drivers and passengers in a variety of physical settings could lead to important knowledge about the optimal means to engineer road traffic systems. Also, restructuring and redesigning the organisation of work whether to reduce stress, combat inappropriate drinking or improve the efficiency and enjoyment of work is likely to see better results than programmes tailored to individuals needs. Prevention here is most definitely better than cure.

Overall, the message we wish to convey here is that the future of health psychology may be short-lived if the individual and the social realms do not stand in closer relation (Eiser, 1996). This is true both theoretically in understanding the behavioural and cognitive phenomena related to health, and practically for designing interventions. A precursor to appropriate and effective interventions are appropriate and effective levels of analysis. In the context of socioeconomic inequalities, Carroll, Bennett and Davey Smith (1993) warn that

> Psychological interventions are unlikely to yield much in the way of dividends and indeed could inadvertently lead to victim blaming. (p. 295)

And

> programmes of behaviour modification will almost certainly make only the most modest contribution to countering the health inequalities attendant on socioeconomic position. (p. 310)

Bosma *et al.* (1999) add that increasing beliefs of control in those without real control in their lives will do little to the structural determinants which generate these beliefs. Health psychologists should ask themselves why other scientists feel it necessary to issue these warnings.

When we pose the question of what the role of health psychology in society is, we need to specify from whose perspective the answer should be delivered. Much of the history of the discipline is characterised by psychologists' incessant calls to have a unique role for themselves, but very little of how this will benefit or indeed harm anyone else – the general public, citizens, health consumers, other health scientists or policy-makers. More debate is needed regarding the costs and putative benefits to various peoples of the increasing professionalisation of knowledge and practice. It could even be said that rather than leading to greater diffusion of relevant psychological knowledge to others, professionalisation may lead to less – if so then we should not look elsewhere to throw the blame. In conclusion, we think three issues are key. Firstly, that the consequences of specialisation require greater debate. Secondly, that the matter of whether there are unique core skills and knowledge to practice health psychology be seriously questioned and not simply assumed. When Salmon (1994) examined the issue of whether health psychology met the criteria for being a profession, four central criteria were proposed. The possession of a distinct body of knowledge, discrete professional structures (which would for example distinguish it from clinical psychology), identifiable professional skills and autonomous practice with an identifiable client group. He concluded that nowhere was it close to fulfilling any of these criteria. As the twenty-first century lies before us, the most fundamental of these, a special repertory of skills and knowledge and an identifiable group on whose behalf these should be practised, is no nearer. Finally, can health psychology move in a direction in which individual and social issues are merged to form a more integrated body of knowledge which will excite the interests of workers in other fields? The danger is that health psychology will move closer to becoming the ultimate post-modern discipline – one possessing all the organisation and professional trappings but lacking a viable subject matter. It need not be that way.

Summary and conclusions

In this chapter we have sought to identify a number of issues pertinent to the past and potential future development of health psychology. How one sees the future of the discipline probably depends in part on how strongly one ties one's flag to the mast of health psychology. Several issues, though, will be crucial to how events unfold. These concern whether a coherent discipline with an appropriate knowledge and skills base can be identified distinct from the related disciplines of clinical psychology and epidemiology, and whether a profession possessing sufficient political might can impose itself in the wider arena of health science. As such it is probably less relevant whether psychologists agree amongst themselves whether or not to officially sanctify health psychology as a living breathing entity, than it is that other practitioners and researchers in health care and health science feel it to be necessary. There are always likely to be psychologists working in tandem with others in related health fields – though it can be argued whether this justifies a discipline of health psychology distinct to others. It is an interesting matter to ponder whether this attempt to widen the scope of psychology represents an attempt to break out of *its heartlands at a time* when the traditional boundaries of psychology itself are being eroded by the encroachment of the technologically-driven disciplines of neuroscience, artificial intelligence and behavioural genetics. Nevertheless, irrespective of any interdisciplinary 'turf wars' we believe the constellation of ideas which have been embraced by health psychology (and we would single out for consideration here, psychometrics, quality of life research, lay perspectives on health and psychoimmunology) will continue to expand their influence in health research.

Discussion points

A What does health psychology have to offer distinct from the related disciplines of behavioural medicine, epidemiology and clinical psychology?

B What value do qualitative research methods have in health psychology?

C What position should health psychologists adopt with regard to the origins of global health problems?

Suggested reading

Krampen, G. and Montada, L. (1998) 'Health Psychology: Bibliographic Results on the Emergence and Rapid Consolidation of a New Field of Research and Application', *Psychology and Health*, **13**(6): 1027–36.

Matarazzo, J.D. (1980) 'Behavioural Health and Behavioural Medicine: Frontiers for a New Health Psychology', *American Psychologist*, **35**: 807–17.

Salmon, P. (1994) 'Is Health Psychology a Profession or Can it Become One? First Ask The Right Questions', *The Psychologist*, **7**: 542–4.

World Health Organisation (1999) *World Health Report 1999.* (Geneva: WHO). Available from http://www.who.int/whr/1999/en/report.htm

Glossary

Agnosia A defect in recognition caused by neurological disease – can occur in any perceptual or cognitive system. Auditory agnosia, for example, refers to an inability to recognise or interpret the meanings of speech.

AIDS Acquired Immune Deficiency Syndrome. Occurs when the immune system is weakened beyond a certain point. Follows infection by the HIV virus that progressively disables the immune system.

Alzheimer's disease A chronic degenerative neurological disease characterised by a profound deterioration in intellectual and linguistic functions with accompanying personality change.

Anorexia nervosa A disorder of eating characterised by a drive for thinness, a refusal to maintain a normal body weight and loss of menses.

Aphasia The partial (sometimes referred to as dysphasia) or complete loss of linguistic ability.

Apraxia Disorder of movement, usually due to neurological disease or trauma.

Bulimia nervosa A disorder of eating characterised by a cycle of bingeing or purging, the latter often including laxative and diuretic abuse, self-induced vomiting, voluntary starvation and excessive exercise.

Comorbidity The prevalence of a given (medical) condition with other conditions.

Diabetes A disease characterised by chronically elevated blood sugar levels, of which two types are recognised. In Type 1 (insulin-dependent diabetes) the pancreas ceases to produce insulin, and in Type 2 (non-insulin-dependent diabetes) the body can still produce insulin though not in sufficient quantities.

Discourse analysis Analysis of the systematic and coherent nature of images, language and metaphors which embody a particular way of seeing the world.

DSM The Diagnostic and Statistical Manual of Mental Disorders. The guide to categorising and diagnosing mental disorders produced by the American Psychiatric Association.

Effect size An indication of the strength of relationship between independent and dependent variables. The effect size may be described as small, medium or large.

Epidemiology A branch of medicine investigating the distribution of disease in human populations through the use of quantitative methods. Several key methods are used to infer causal relationships including the presence of dose–response relationships, biological plausibility and repeatability of a given association at different times, in different places and in different populations.

Grounded theory A method of qualitative research in which theory is generated on the ground from the repeated inspection and collection of raw data.

HDL lipoprotein A protein involved in transporting cholesterol away from the walls of blood vessels.

Heritability The proportion of the variance in a dependent variable within a population which is accounted for by environmental or genetic factors. It is estimated from a regression equation (see Regression).

Immunocompetence The extent to which the immune system is functioning effectively. Thus immunosuppression refers to reduced functionality in some or all of the immune system. May be caused by many factors, for example HIV infection or stress.

Incidence Refers to the number of new cases (of a condition) which occur in a specific time period divided by the total number in the population who are potentially at risk. It may be expressed as a percentage or as the number of cases per 1000 or 100 000 of the population.

Jenkins Activity Survey A means of measuring the Type A behaviour pattern.

LDL lipoprotein A protein involved in transporting cholesterol to the walls of blood vessels.

Magnetic resonance imaging (MRI) An imaging technique based on the principles of nuclear magnetic resonance (NMR). Computerised images of internal body tissues are produced based on the resonance of hydrogen atoms within the body induced by the application of a powerful magnetic field and radio energy of a specific frequency. Images are monitored by the MRI computer, which processes them and displays them on a video monitor for interpretation or photographing for later interpretation. Contrast agents in MRI work by altering the local magnetic field in the tissue being examined. Normal and abnormal tissue responds differently to this alteration, giving different signals. These signals are translated into images, allowing the visualisation of different tissue abnormalities and disease processes.

Meta analysis A system of analysis in which the results from different studies investigating a particular hypothesis are pooled to examine the consistency of effect sizes reported and whether the pooled results (treated as if from a single study) are statistically significant. Studies to be pooled must be critically selected.

Multiple sclerosis A degenerative neurological disease involving the progressive demyelination of nerve fibres affecting both sensory and motor systems. Cognitive impairment is often present.

Myocardial infarction A heart attack. Occurs following severe blockage of arteries supplying the heart resulting in loss of oxygen supply and death of heart muscle.

Neuroleptics Another term for the group of drugs more usually used to treat psychoses.

Neurotransmitters The chemical messengers released from the pre-synaptic terminal of a nerve cell to convey excitatory or inhibitory information to another. Examples include acetylcholine, serotonin and dopamine.

Passive smoking Inhalation of the products of other people's smoking

Positivism A branch of philosophy which holds that only knowledge which can be empirically verified is of value.

Positron Emission Tomography (PET) A non-invasive means of measuring activity in different regions of the brain. A radioactivity-labelled isotope of a metabolite (usually glucose) used by the brain is injected into the bloodstream. This is incorporated into neurons in proportion to their metabolic rate. Collisions between particles emitted by the labelled substance and electrons in the neurons results in the emission of high-energy light particles (photons) which computer analysis converts into a pictorial representation of the level of activity in different regions of the brain.

Postmodernism A critical cultural movement contending that we have gone beyond the world view of modernism (associated with increasing certainty of knowledge, social progress and progression towards truth in science). Post-modern critiques contend that no set of values, morals and judgements can lay claim to special status compared to others. In relation to the practice of science this has led to arguments that no system of knowledge has a privileged position for describing and characterising the world.

Power Analysis Power analysis is conducted prior to running a study and is concerned with determining appropriate sample sizes so that there is a reasonably good chance that the effects of interest will be detected when the appropriate statistical analysis is performed.

Prevalence Refers to the number of existing cases (of a condition) divided by the total number in the population who are potentially at risk. Hence, point prevalence refers to the cases at a certain point in time, period prevalence refers to the number of cases over a specific period, and lifetime prevalence to the number of people who have had the condition at least once during their life.

Psychoneuroimmunology The field of study focusing on relationships between psychological events such as stress and nervous, endocrine and immune functioning responses.

Quality of Life The appraisal of those components of life (e.g. physical, financial, psychological, social, occupational) which constitute well-being. A variety of disease-specific and generic measures are used to measure it.

Regression A statistical technique which enables the simultaneous effect of several variables on a dependent variable to be estimated. The magnitude of the effects of individual variables are given by beta values (which can vary between zero and 1). The combined effects of all the variables are expressed in terms of the total percentage variation in the dependent variable which they (statistically) explain.

Reliability Refers to the consistency of findings. Is usually measured by means of a correlation coefficient.

Retinopathy Disease of the retina. May occur in diabetes.

Risk factor A variable with a statistically-significant association with some specified (health) outcome. A causal relationship is not assumed.

Stages of change A model of behavioural change which describes five stages: pre-contemplation, contemplation, preparation, action and maintenance.

Standardised mortality ratio (SMR) A measure of how likely a person is to die in a particular population compared to other people of the same age and sex. The SMR is the ratio of the actual number of deaths in a group to the expected number of deaths in the group. It is multiplied by 100 for ease of interpretation

Stress This is where the demands of a situation exceed the personal and situational resources to cope with it.

Structural equation models Sometimes misleadingly referred to as causal modelling. A popular multivariate analytic technique in which a hypothetical model comprising a set of structured (linear) relationships between variables is tested against alternative models where the specified structure of relationships is different (e.g. it may be tested against a null model where there are no significant relationships between the specified variables).

Type A behaviour pattern A pattern of behaviour characterised by hostility, impatience, competitive drive and vigorous speech. In contrast, the so-called Type B pattern comprises a relative absence of these characteristics. Has been investigated for its possible connection with coronary heart disease.

Type C personality The putative cancer-prone personality, otherwise known as the Type C personality, involves the suppression of negative emotions – notably anger and anxiety, as well as hopelessness or helplessness in the face of stress, and passivity.

U-shaped curve Describes the observed relationship between the level of alcohol consumption and coronary heart disease. So called because moderate drinkers have less risk than abstainers.

Validity Broadly speaking, validity is concerned with the ability of a model (or construct) to represent reality. Various types of validity exist; discriminant validity refers to the extent to which a scale discriminates between people who differ in their degree of a particular attribute; construct validity refers to the degree to which a new measure agrees with existing measures of the same construct.

Bibliography

Aaronson, N.K., Acquadro, C., Alonso, J., Apolone, G., Bucquet, D., Bullinger, M., Bungay, K., Fukuhara, S., Gandek, B., Keller, S., Razavi, D., Sanson-Fisher, R., Sullivan, M., Wood-Dauphinee, S., Wagner, A. and Ware, J.E. Jr. (1992) 'International Quality of Life Assessment (IQOLA) Project', *Quality of Life Research*, **1**: 349–51.

Abraham, C. and Sheeran, P. (1994) 'Modelling and Modifying Young Heterosexuals' HIV-Preventive Behaviour; A Review of Theories, Findings and Educational Implications', *Patient Education and Counselling*, **23**: 173–86.

Abraham, C., Sheeran, P. and Johnston, M. (1998) 'From Health Beliefs to Self-Regulation: Theoretical Advances in the Psychology of Action Control', *Psychology and Health*, **13**(4): 569–91.

Adam, B.D. (1989) 'The State, Public Policy, and AIDS Discourse', *Contemporary Crises*, **13**: 1–14.

Adams, W.L. and Cox, N.S. (1995) 'Epidemiology of Problem Drinking Among Elderly People', *International Journal of Addictions*, **30**(13–14): 1693–1716.

Addolorato, G., Taranto, C., Capristo, E. and Gasbarrini, G. (1998) 'A Case of Marked Cerebellar Atrophy in a Woman with Anorexia Nervosa and Cerebral Atrophy and a Review of the Literature', *International Journal of Eating Disorders*, **24**(4): 443–7.

Ader, R. and Cohen, N. (1982) 'Behaviourally Conditioned Immunosuppression and Murie Systemic Lupus Erythematosus', *Science*, **215**: 1534–6.

Ader, R. and Cohen, N. (1985) 'CNS-Immune System Interactions Conditioning Phenomenon', *Behavioural and Brain Sciences*, **8**: 379–95.

Agble, Y.M. (1998) 'Management of Sickle Cell Disease', Non-Addictive Analgesics can be as Effective as Morphine and Pethidine. *British Medical Journal*, **316**(7135): 935

Ager, A., Carr, S., Maclachlan, M. and Kaneka-Chilongo, B. (1996) 'Perceptions of Tropical Health Risks in Mponda, Malawi: Attributions of Cause, Suggested Means of Risk Reduction and Preferred Treatment', *Psychology and Health*, **12**(1): 23–31.

Aggleton, P. and Homans, H. (1987*) Educating about AIDS*. (London: National Health Service Training Authority).

Ahmedzai, S. and Brooks, D. (1997) 'Transdermal Fentanyl versus Sustained-Release Oral Morphine in Cancer Pain: Preference, Efficacy, and Quality of Life', *Journal of Pain Symptom Management*, **13**(5): 254–61.

Aiach, P. and Curtis, S. (1990) 'Social Inequalities in Self-Reported Morbidity: Interpretation and Comparison of Data from Britain and France', *Social Science and Medicine*, **31**: 267–74.

Ajzen, I. (1991) 'The Theory of Planned Behaviour', *Organisational Behaviour and Human Decision Processes*, **50**: 179–211.

American Heart Association (1999) *Cardiovascular Diseases* http://www/amhrt.org/statistics/03cardio.html

American Psychiatric Association (1994) *Diagnostic and Statistical Manual For Mental Disorders*, 4th Edn. (Washington, D.C.: American Psychiatric Association).

Amick, B.C. 3rd, Kawachi, I., Coakley, E.H., Lerner, D., Levine, S. and Colditz, G.A. (1998) 'Relationship of Job Strain and Iso-Strain to Health Status in a Cohort of Women in the United States', *Scandinavian Journal of Work, Environment and Health*, **24**(1): 54–61.

Anderson, H.R., Freeling, P. and Patel, S.P. (1983) 'Decision Making in Acute Asthma', *Journal of the Royal College of General Practitioners*, **33**: 105–8.

Anderson, J. St C., Sullivan, F. and Usherwood, T.P. (1990) 'The Medical Outcomes Study Instrument (MOSI) – Use of a New Health Status Measure in Britain', *Family Practice*, **7**(3): 205–18.

Angermeyer, M.C. (1982) 'The Association Between Family Atmosphere and Hospital Career of Schizophrenic Patients', *British Journal of Psychiatry*, **141**: 1–11.

Anionwu, E. (1995) 'Ethnic Minority Health. Fair Provision', *Nursing Standard*, **10**(12–14): 45.

Appleby, L. & Wessely, S. (1988). 'Public Attitudes to Mental Illness: The Influence of the Hungerford Massacre', *Medicine, Science and Law* **28**(4): 291–5.

Arber, S. (1997) 'Comparing Inequalities in Women's and Men's Health: Britain in the 1990s', *Social Science and Medicine*, **44**(6): 773–87.

Arens, D.A. (1993). 'What do the Neighbors Think Now? Community Residences on Long Island, New York', *Community Mental Health Journal* **29**(3): 235–45.

Argyle, M. (1987). *The Psychology of Happiness*. (London: Methuen).

Argyle, M. (1994) *Social Class*. (London: Routledge).

Aspinall, L.G., Kemeny, M.E., Taylor, S.E., Schneider, S.G. and Dudley, J.P. (1991) 'Psychosocial Predictors of Gay Men's AIDS Risk-Reduction Behaviour', *Health Psychology*, **3**: 113–27

Asthana, S. (1996) 'Women's Health and Women's Empowerment: A Locality Perspective', *Health and Place*, **2**(1): 1–13.

Austin, E.W. and Meili, H.K. (1994) 'Effects of Interpretation of Televised Alcohol Portrayals on Children's Alcohol Beliefs', *Journal of Broadcasting and Electronic Media*, 38(4): 417–35.

Available http://www.who.int/whr/1999/en/report.htm

Avis, M., Bond, M. and Arthur, A. (1997) 'Questioning Patient Satisfaction: An Empirical Investigation in Two Outpatient Clinics', *Social Science and Medicine*, 44(1): 85–92.

Axelsson, B. and Sjoden, P. (1998) 'Quality of Life of Cancer Patients and their Spouses in Palliative Home Care', *Palliative Medicine*, 12(1): 29–39.

Ayanian, J.Z., Udvarhelyi, I.S., Gatsonis, C.A., Pashos, C.L. and Epstein, A.M. (1993) 'Racial Differences in the Use of Revascularization Procedures after Coronary Angiography', *Journal of the American Medical Association*, 269(20): 2642–6.

Bachman, J.G., Johnson, L.D., O'Malley, P.M. and Humphrey, H. (1988) 'Explaining the Recent Decline in Marijuana Use: Differentiating the Effects of Perceived Risks, Disapproval and General Life-Style Factors', *Journal of Health and Social Behaviour*, 29: 92–112.

Bages, N., Warwick-Evans, L. and Falger, P.R.J. (1997) 'Differences Between Informants about Type A, Anger, and Social Support and the Relationship with Blood Pressure', *Psychology and Health*, 12: 453–65.

Bagley, C. (1971) 'The Social Aetiology of Schizophrenia in Immigrant Groups', *International Journal of Social Psychiatry*, 17: 292–304.

Bagnall, G. (1987) 'Alcohol Education and Its Evaluation – Some Key Issues', *Health Education Journal*, 46(4): 162–5.

Bailey, R. (1996) 'Prenatal Testing and the Prevention of Impairment: A Woman's Right to Choose', in J. Morris (Ed.) *Encounters with Strangers. Feminism and Disability.* (London: The Women's Press).

Baker, D., Roberts, R. and Towell, A. (2000) 'Factors Predictive of Bone Mineral Density in Eating Disordered Women: A Longitudinal Study', *International Journal of Eating Disorders*, 27: 29–35.

Baker, D., Sivyer, R., and Towell, A. (1998) 'Body Image Dissatisfaction and Eating Attitudes in Visually Impaired Women', *International Journal of Eating Disorders*. 24: 319–22.

Baker, P. (1990) 'I Hear Voices and I'm Glad To', *Critical Public Health*, 4: 21–7.

Baldwin, M.W., Fehr, B., Keedian, E., Seidel, M. & Thomson, D.W. (1993) 'An Exploration of the Relational Schemata Underlying Attachment Styles: Self-Report and Lexical Decision Approaches', *Personality and Social Psychology Bulletin*, 19: 746–54.

Ballard, C. and O'Brien, J. (1999) 'Treating Behavioural and Psychological Signs in Alzheimer's Disease', *British Medical Journal*, 319: 138–9.

Bandura, A. (1998) 'Health Promotion from the Perspective of Social Cognition Theory', *Psychology and Health*, 13(4): 623–50.

Bannister, D. and Fransella, F. (1971) *Inquiring Man.* (Penguin).

Banyard, P. (1996) *Applying Psychology to Health.* (Hodder and Stoughton).

Barham, P. and Hayward (Eds.) '(1991) 'Community Mental Patients', in P.Barham and R. Hayward (Eds.) *Relocating Madness: From the Mental Patient to the Person.* (London: Tavistock).

Barker, D.J.P., Bull, A.R., Osmond, C. and Simmonds, S.J. (1990) 'Fetal and Placental Size and Risk of Hypertension in Adult Life', *British Medical Journal*, 301: 259–63.

Barnard, M. and Mckeganey, N. (1996) 'Prostitution and Peer Education: Beyond HIV', in T. Rhodes and R. Hartnoll (Eds.) *AIDS, Drugs and Prevention.* (London: Routledge).

Barnes, C. (1991) *Disabled People in Britain: A Case For Anti-Discrimination Legislation.* (London: Hurst and Company).

Baron, R.S., Cutrona, C.E., Hicklin, D., Russell, D.W. and Lubaroff, D.M. (1990) 'Social Support and Immune Function Among Spouses of Cancer Patients', *Journal of Personality and Social Psychology*, 59(2): 344–52.

Barraclough, J., Pinder, P., Cruddas, M., Osmond, C., Taylor, I. and Perry, M. (1992) 'Life Events and Breast Cancer Prognosis', *British Medical Journal*, 304: 1078–81.

Barrow, J.D. (1992) 'Pi in the Sky: Counting, Thinking and Being'. (Oxford: Oxford University Press).

Bartley, M. (1985) 'Coronary Heart Disease and the Public Health, 1850–1983', *Sociology of Health and Illness*, 7: 289–313.

Bartley, M. and Owen, C. (1996) 'Relation Between Socioeconomic Status, Employment, and Health During Economic Change, 1973–93', *British Medical Journal*, 313: 445–9

Baxter, T., Milner, P., Wilson, K., Leaf, M., Nicholl, Freeman, Cooper, N. (1997) 'A Cost Effective, Community Based Heart Health Promotion Project in England: Prospective Comparative Study', *British Medical Journal*, 315: 582–5.

Beaglehole, R. and Bonita, R. (1997) *Public Health At the Crossroads.* (Cambridge University Press).

Beail, S. and Beail, N. (1982) 'Dependency and Personal Growth', New Forum: *Journal of the Psychology and Psychotherapy Association*, 8(3): 58–60.

Beck, A.T., Rial, W.Y. and Rickels, K. (1974) 'Short Form of Depression Inventory: Cross Validation', *Psychological Reports*, 34: 1184–6.

Belloc, N.B. and Breslow, L. (1972) 'Relationship Between Physical Health Status and Health Practices', *Preventive Medicine*, 1: 409–21.

Bemporad, J.R., Hoffman, D., & Herzog, D.B. (1989) 'Anorexia Nervosa in the Congenitally Blind: Theoretical Considerations', *Journal of the American Academy of Psychoanalysis*, 17: 89–101.

Benett, I.J. (1993) 'What do People with Diabetes Want to Talk about with their Doctors? *Diabetic Medicine*, 10(10): 968–971.

Bennett, P. and Murphy, S. (1997) *Psychology and Health Promotion.* (Open University).

Benschop, R.J., Jabaaij, L., Oostveen, F.G., Vingerhoets, A.J.J.M. and Ballieux, R.E. (1998) 'The Influence of Psychological Stress on Immunoregulation of Latent Epstein-Barr Virus', *Stress Medicine*, 1491): 21–9.

Ben-Shlomo, Y. and Davey Smith, G.(1991) 'Deprivation in Infancy Or in Adult Life: Which Is More Important For Mortality Risk?', *The Lancet* March 2nd, 337: 530–4.

Bentall, R. P. (1990) 'The Syndromes and Symptoms of Psychosis: Or Why You Can't Play 20 Questions with the Concept of Schizophrenia and Hope to Win', in R.P.Bentall (Ed) *Reconstructing Schizophrenia.* (London: Routledge).

Bentall, R. P. (2000) 'Hallucinations', in E. Cardena, S.J. Lynn and S. Krippner (Eds.) *Varieties of Anomolaus Experience.* (Washington: American Psychological Association).

Benzeval, M., Judge, K. and Whitehead, M. (1995) 'Unfinished Business', in M. Benzeval, K. Judge and M. Whitehead (Eds.) *Tackling Inequalities in Health.* (London: Kings Fund).

Benzeval, M., Judge, K. and Whitehead, M. (Eds.) (1995) *Tack-*

ling Inequalities in Health: An Agenda For Action. King's Fund. London.

Berke, J. (1979) *I Haven't Had to Go Mad Here.* (Harmondsworth: Pelican).

Berkman, L.F. and Syme, S.L. (1979) 'Social Networks, Host Resistance and Mortality: A Nine Year Follow-Up of Alameda County Residents', *American Journal of Epidemiology*, **109**: 186–204.

Bernard, J. (1972). *The Future of Marriage.* (New York: World).

Bernat, J. (1997) 'The Problem of Physician Assisted Suicide', *Seminal Neurology.* **17**(3): 271–9.

Berndt, T.J. (1996). 'Exploring the Effects of Friendship Quality on Social Development', in M. Bukowski, A.F. Newcomb and W.W. Hartup (Eds.) *The Company They Keep: Friendship in Childhood and Adolescence.* (Cambridge: Cambridge University Press).

Bernstein, B. (1971) *Class, Codes and Control.* (London: Routledge and Kegan Paul).

Berry, D., Michas, I.C., Gillie, T. and Forster, M. (1997) 'What do Patients Want to Know about their Medicines, and What do Doctors Want to Tell Them? A Comparative Study', *Psychology and Health*, **12**(4): 467–80.

Berscheid, E. Interpersonal Attraction. Chapter 21: P.413–84 Cited in L. Gardner and E. Aronson, (1985). *Handbook of Social Psychology: Special Fields and Application. Vol. II.* (3rd Ed) (USA: Newbery Award Records, Inc.).

Bhopal, R. (1997) 'Is Research into Ethnicity and Health Racist, Unsound, or Important Science?', *British Medical Journal*, **314**: 1751.

Bhopal, R. (1998) 'Spectre of Racism in Health and Health Care: Lessons from History and the United States', *British Medical Journal*, **316**: 1970–3.

Birchwood, , M., Hallett, S., Preston, M. (1988) *Schizophrenia.* (London: Longman).

Black, D. (1998) 'Coping with Loss; the Dying Child', *British Medical Journal* **316**: 1376–8.

Black, H.S. (1998) 'Influence of Dietary Factors on Actinically-Induced Skin Cancer', *Mutation Research*, **422**(1): 185–90

Blackburn, M. (1993) *Sexuality and Sex Education.* in M. Cross, R. Gordon, M. Kennedy and R. Marchant (1993) The ABCD Pack. Abuse and Children Who are Disabled. Department of Health.

Blair, A. (1995) 'Social Class and the Contextualization of Illness Experience', in A. Radley (Ed) *Worlds of Illness: Biographical and Cultural Perspectives on Health and Disease.* (London: Routledge).

Blair, S., Kohl, H., Gordon, N. and Paffenbarger, R. (1992) 'How Much Physical Exercise Is Good For Health?', in G. Omenn, J. Fielding and L. Lave Eds *Annual Review of Public Health (Vol 13)*: Palo Alto, CA: Annual Reviews.

Blanchard, E.B., Buckley, T.C., Hickling, E.J. and Taylor, A.E. (1998) 'Posttraumatic Stress Disorder and Comorbid Major Depression: Is the Correlation an Illusion?', *Journal of Anxiety Disorders*, **21**(1): 21–37.

Blane, D., Brunner, E. and Wilkinson, R. (Eds.) (1996) *Health and Social Organisation: Towards a Health Policy For the 21st Century.* (London: Routledge).

Blane, D., Davey Smith, G. and Bartley, M. (1993) 'Social Selection: What Does It Contribute to Social Class Differences in Health?', *Sociology of Health and Illness*, **15**(1): 1–15.

Blaxter, M. (1987) 'Alcohol Consumption', *Health and Lifestyles* Survey. *Health Promotion* Trust 109–19.

Blaxter, M. (1990a) 'Alcohol Consumption', *Health and Lifestyles.* (London: Routledge).

Blaxter, M. (1990b) *Health and Lifestyles.* (London: Tavistock/ Routledge).

Blaxter, M. (1993) 'Why do the Victims Blame Themselves?', in A. Radley (Ed) *Worlds of Illness: Biographical and Cultural Perspectives on Health and Disease.* (London: Routledge).

Blaxter, M. (1997) 'Whose Fault Is It? People's Own Conceptions of the Reasons For Health Inequalities', *Social Science and Medicine*, **44**(6): 747–56.

Blaxter, M. and Paterson, E. (1982) *Mothers and Daughters.* (London: Heinemann).

Bleich, A., Koslowsky, M., Dolev, A. and Lerer, B. (1997) 'Post-Traumatic Stress Disorder and Depression. An Analysis of Comorbidity', *British Medical Journal*, **170**: 479–82.

Bloch, M., Schmidt, P.J., Su, T.P., Tobin, M.B. and Rubinow, D.R. (1998) 'Pituitary-Adrenal Hormones and Testosterone Across the Menstrual Cycle in Women with Premenstrual Syndrome and Controls', *Biological Psychiatry*, **43**(12): 897–903.

Blondal, T., Gudmundsson, L.J., Olafsdottir, I., Gustavsson, G. and Westin, A. (1999) 'Nicotine Nasal Spray with Nicotine Patch For Smoking Cessation: Randomised Trial with Six Year Follow-Up', *British Medical Journal*; **318**: 285–8.

Blum, K., Noble, E.P., Sheridan, P.J., Montgomery, A., Ritchie, T., Jagadeeswaran, P., Nogami, H., Brigs, A.H. and Cohn, J.B. (1990) 'Allelic Association of Human Dopamine D2 Receptor Gene in Alcoholism', *Journal of the American Medical Association*, **263**: 2055–60.

Boccia, M.L., Scanlan, J.M., Laudenslager, M.L., Berger, C.L., Hijazi, A.S. and Reite, M.L. (1997) 'Juvenile Friends, Behavior, and Immune Responses to Separation in Bonnet Macaque Infants', *Physiology and Behavior*, **61**(2): 191–8.

Boivin, J. (1997) 'Is There Too Much Emphasis on Psychosocial Counselling For Infertile Patients?', *Journal of Assisted Reproduction and Genetics*, **14**(4): 184–6.

Bonn, D. (1998) 'Bringing Numbers to Bear in Breast-Cancer Therapy', *The Lancet*, **350**: 1304.

Boore, J. (1979) 'Prescription For Recovery'. (London: Royal College of Nursing).

Booth, M., Bauman, A., Owen, N. and Gore, C. (1997) 'Physical Activity Preferences, Preferred Sources of Assistance, and Perceived Barriers to Increased Activity among Physically Inactive Australians', *Preventative Medicine*, **26**(1): 113–17.

Bor, R. (1997) 'AIDS. in A.Baum, S.Newman, J. Weinman, R. West, C. Mcmanus (Eds.) *Cambridge Handbook of Psychology, Health, and Medicine.* (Cambridge University Press).

Borinstein, A.B. (1992). 'Public Attitudes Toward Persons with Mental Illness', *Health Affairs 3*: 186–96.

Bosma, H., Peter, R., Siegrist, J. and Marmot, M. (1998) 'Two Alternative Job Stress Models and the Risk of Coronary Heart Disease', *American Journal of Public Health*, **88**(1): 68–74.

Bosma, H., Van De Mheen, H.D. and Mackenbach, J.P. (1999) 'Social Class in Childhood and General Health in Adulthood: Questionnaire Study of Contribution of Psychological Attributes', *British Medical Journal*, 3 **18**: 18–22.

Botting, B. (1997) 'Mortality in Childhood', in M.Whitehead and F.Drever (Eds.) *Health Inequalities.* (London: Office of National Statistics).

Botting, D. and Cook, R. (1998) 'Therapy Evaluation. Evaluating the Effectiveness of Complimentary Therapies', *International Journal of Palliative Nursing*, **4**(1): 32–6.

Bovjberg, D.H., Redd, W.H., Maier, L.A., Holland, J.C., Lesko, L.M., Niedzwiecki, D., Rubin, S.E. and Hakes, T.B. (1990) 'Anticipatory Immune Suppression in Women Receiving Cyclic Chemotherapy For Ovarian Cancer', *Journal of Consulting and Clinical Psychology*, **58**: 153–7.

Bower, P., West, R., Tylee, A. and Hann, A. (1999) 'Patients' Perceptions of the Role of the General Practitioner in the Management of Emotional Problems', *British Journal of Health Psychology*, **4**(1): 41–52.

Bowlby, J and Parkes, C. (1970) 'Separation and Loss Within the Family', In: Anthony, E. (Ed) *The Child in His Family*. (New York: Wiley).

Bowlby, J. (1969). *Attachment and Loss, Vol. 1: Attachment*. (New York: Basic Books).

Bowlby, J. (1980). *Attachment and Loss, Vol. 3: Loss: Sadness and Depression* (New York: Basic Books).

Bowlin, S.J., Leske, M.C., Varma, A., Nasca, P., Wenstein, A. and Caplan, L. (1997) 'Breast Cancer Risk and Alcohol Consumption: Results from a Large Case-Control Study', *International Journal of Epidemiology*, **26**(5): 915–23.

Bowling, A. (1991) *Measuring Health: A Review of Quality of Life Measurement Scales*. (Buckingham: Open University Press).

Bowling, A. (1995) *Measuring Disease. A Review of Disease Specific Quality of Life Measurement Scales*. (Buckingham: Open University Press).

Boyle, C. M. (1970) 'Differences Between Patients' and Doctors' Interpretations of Common Medical Terms', *British Medical Journal*, **2**: 286–9.

Boyle, M. (1990a) *Schizophrenia: A Scientific Delusion*. (London: Routledge).

Boyle, M. (1990b) 'The Non-Discovery of Schizophrenia', in R.P.Bentall (Ed) *Reconstructing Schizophrenia*. (London: Routledge).

Boyle, M. (1996) *Schizophrenia*' Re-Evaluated. in T.Heller, J. Reynolds, R. Gomm, R. Muston and S.Pattison (Ed) *Mental Health Matters*. The Open University. (London: Macmillan Press).

Boyle, M.H., Offord, D.R., Racine, Y.A., Szatmari, P., Sanford, M. and Fleming, J.E. (1997) 'Adequacy of Interviews Vs Checklists For Classifying Childhood Psychiatric Disorder Based on Parent Reports', *Archives of General Psychiatry*, **54**(9): 793–9.

Bradley, C. (1994a) 'Contributions of Psychology to Diabetes Management', *British Journal of Clinical Psychology*, **33**: 11–21.

Bradley, C. (Ed.) (1994b) *Handbook of Psychology and Diabetes: A Guide to Psychological Measurement in Diabetes Research and Practice*. (Harwood).

Bradley, C. and Gamsu, D.S. (1994) 'Guidelines For Encouraging Psychological Well-Being', *Diabetic Medicine*, **11**: 510–16.

Bradlow, J., Coulter, A. and Brookes, P. (1992) *Patterns of Referral*. (Oxford: Health Services Research Unit).

Brannon, R.C. (1976) 'No "Sissy Stuff": The Stigma of Anything Vaguely Feminine', in D. David and R. Brannon (Eds.*) The Forty-Nine Percent Majority*. (Reading, MA: Addison-Welsey).

Brazier, J.E., Harper, R., Jones, N.M.B., O'Cathain, Thomas, K.J., Usherwood, T. and Westlake, L. (1992a) 'Validating the SF36', Letters. *British Medical Journal*, **305**: 646.

Brazier, J.E., Harper, R., Jones, N.M.B., O'Cathain, Thomas, K.J., Usherwood, T. and Westlake, L. (1992b) 'Validating the SF36 Health Survey Questionnaire: New Outcome Measures For Primary Care', *British Medical Journal*, **305**: 160–4.

Breggin, P. (1993) *Toxic Psychiatry*. (Fontana).

Bregman, S. (1984) 'Assertiveness Training For Mentally Retarded Adults', *Mental Retardation*, **22**(1): 12–16.

Brehm, S. (1992) *Intimate Relationships*. (London: McGraw Hill).

Breteler, M.H.M., Schotberg, E.J. and Schippers, G.M. (1996) 'The Effectiveness of Smoking Cessation Programs: Determinants and Outcomes', *Psychology and Health*, **11**: 133–53.

Breznitz, S., Ben Zur, H., Berzon, Y., Weiss, D.W., Levitan, G., Tarcic, N., Lischinsky, S., Greenberg, A., Levi, N. and Zinder, O. (1998) 'Experimental Induction and Termination of Acute Psychological Stress in Human Volunteers: Effects on Immunological, Neuroendocrine, Cardiovascular, and Psychological Parameters', *Brain Behaviour and Immunity*, **12**(1): 34–52.

British Medical Journal (1993) 'Environmental Smoke Causes Cancer, Says US Agency', *British Medical Journal*, **306**: 163.

British Medical Journal (1997) 'Passive Smoking Doubles Risk of Heart Disease', *British Medical Journal*, **314**: 1572.

British Psychological Society (1988) *Psychological Aspects of Alcohol*. (Leicester: British Psychological Society).

British Psychological Society (1993) *Code of Conduct, Ethical Principles and Guidelines*. (Leicester: British Psychological Society).

British Psychological Society (1996) *Attention Deficit Hyperactivity Disorder: A Psychological Response to an Evolving Concept*. Working Party Report.

Britten, N. (1998) 'Psychiatry, Stigma and Resistance', *British Medical Journal*, **317**: 763–4.

Britton, A., Thorogood, M., Coombes, Y. and Lewando-Hunt, G. (1998) 'Search For Evidence of Effective Health Promotion', *British Medical Journal*, **316**: 703.

Brockington, I.F., Hall, P., Levings, J. & Murphy, C. (1993). 'The Community's Tolerance of the Mentally Ill', *British Journal of Psychiatry* **162**: 93–9.

Brody, S. (1996) 'Incidence of HIV Infection Decreases Because of Nature of Epidemics', *British Medical Journal*, **312**: 125.

Brown, G. and Harris, T. (1989) *Life Events and Illness*. (New York: Guilford Press).

Brown, G.W. and Harris, T.O. (1978) *Social Origins of Depression. A Study of Psychiatric Disorder in Women*. Tavistock. London.

Brown, J.P., Mcgee, H.M. and O'Boyle, C. (1997) 'Conceptual Approaches to the Assessment of Quality of Life', *Psychology and Health*, **12**(6): 737–51.

Brown, J.P., O'Boyle, C., Mcgee, H.M. and Joyce, C.R.B. Et Al (1994) 'Individual Quality of Life in the Healthy Elderly', *Quality of Life Research*, **3**(4): 235–44.

Brunner, E. (1996) 'The Social and Biological Basis of Cardiovascular Disease in Office Workers', in D. Blane, E. Brunner and R. Wilkinson (Eds.) *Health and Social Organisation: Towards a Health Policy for the 21st Century*. (London: Routledge).

Brunner, E., White, I., Thorogood, M., Bristow, A., Curle, D. and Marmot, M. (1997) 'Can Dietary Interventions Change Diet and Cardiovascular Risk Factors? A Meta-Analysis of Randomised Controlled Trials', *American Journal of Public Health*, **87**(9): 1415–22.

Brunner, E.J., Marmot, M.G., White, I.R., Obrien, J.R., Etherington, M.D., Slavin, B.M., Kearney, E.M. and Davey Smith, G. (1993) 'Gender and Employment Grade Differences in Blood Cholesterol, Apolipoproteins and Haemostatic Factors in the Whitehall II Study', *Atherosclerosis* **102**: 195–207.

Buckshee, K. (1997) 'Impact of Roles of Women on Health in India', *International Journal of Gynaecology and Obstetrics*, **58**(1): 35–42.

Bullinger, M. (1997) 'The Challenge of Cross-Cultural Quality of Life Assessment', *Psychology and Health*, **12**(6): 815–25.

Bunker, J., Gomby, D.S. and Kehrer, B.H. (Eds.) (1989) 'Pathways to Health: The Role of Social Factors', Henry, J. Kaiser Family Foundation.

Bunker, J.P., Houghton, J. and Baum, M. (1998) 'Putting the Risk of Breast Cancer in Perspective', *British Medical Journal*, **317**: 1307–9.

Burack, J.H., Barrett, D.C., Stall, R.D., Chesney, M.A., Eksrtand, M.L., and Coates, T.J. (1993) 'Depressive Symptoms and CD4 Lymphocyte Decline Among HIV-Infected Men', *Journal of the American Medical Association*, **270**: 2568–73.

Burman, B and Margolin, G (1992). 'Analysis of the Association Between Material Relationships and Health Problems: An Interactional Perspective', *Psychological Bulletin*, **112**: 39–63.

Burston, D. (1996) *The Wing of Madness: The Life and Work of R.D. Laing*. Harvard University Press. Cambridge.

Burt, K. and Oaksford, M. (1999) 'Qualitative Methods: Beyond Beliefs and Desires', *The Psychologist*, **12**(7) 332–5.

Butler, C.C., Rollnick, S., Pill, R., Maggs-Rapport and Stott, F. (1999) 'Understanding the Culture of Prescribing: Qualitative Study of General Practitioners, and Patients Perceptions of Antibiotics For Sore Throats', *British Medical Journal*, **317**: 637–42.

Butler, R.W., Mueser, K.T., Sprock, J., and Braff, D.L. (1996) 'Positive Symptoms of Psychosis in Posttraumatic Stress Disorder', *Biological Psychiatry*, **39**(10): 839–44.

Caetano, R. and Tam, T.W. (1995) 'Prevalence and Correlates of DSM-IV and ICD-10 Alcohol Dependence: 1990 US National Alcohol Survey', *Alcohol* **30**(2): 177–86.

Calnan, M. (1987) *Health and Illness: The Lay Perspective*. (Tavistock).

Calnan, M. (1988) 'Images of General Practice: The Perceptions of the Doctor', *Social Science and Medicine*, **27**: 579–86.

Cameron, D. and Jones, I.G (1985) 'An Epidemiological and Sociological Analysis of the Use of Alcohol, Tobacco and Other Drugs of Solace', *Community Medicine*, **7**: 18–29.

Campbell, A., Converse, P.E. and Rodgers, W.L. (1976). *The Quality of American Life*. (New York: Sage).

Campbell, M.J., Julious, S.A. and Altman, D.G. (1995) 'Estimating Sample Sizes For Binary, Ordered Categorical, and Continuous Outcomes in Two Group Comparisons', *British Medical Journal*; **311**: 1145–8.

Campbell, P. (1996) 'The History of the User Movement in the United Kingdom', in T. Heller, J. Reynolds, R. Gomm, R. Muston and S.Pattison (Ed) *Mental Health Matters*. The Open University. (London: Macmillan Press).

Campling, J. (Ed.) (1985) *Images of Ourselves*. (London: Routledge and Kegan Paul).

Cancer Society of New Zealand (1995) 'Cigarette Advertising and Children', http://www.wce.Ac.nz/cancer/lifestyles_smokefree/childad.html

Cardenas, L., Vallbona, C., Baker, S. and Yusim, S. (1987) 'Late Onset DM: Glycemic Control and Family Function', *American Journal of Scientific Medicine*, **293**: 28–33.

Carney, B. (1986). 'A Preventive Curriculum For Anorexia Nervosa and Bulimia', BANA, Faculty of Human Kinetics, University of Windsor, Ontario, Canada.

Carpenter, C.C.J., Fischl, M.A., Hammer, S.M., Hirsch, M.S., Jacobsen, D.M., Katzenstetin, D.A., Montaner, J.S.G., Richman, D.D., Saag, M.S., Schooley, R.T., Thompson, M.A., Vella, S., Yeni, P.G. and Volberding, P.A. (1997) 'Antiretroviral Therapy For HIV Infection in 1997', *Journal of the American Medical Association*, **277**: 1962–9.

Carr-Hill, R. (1989) 'Assumption of the QUALY Procedure', *Social Science and Medicine*, **29**: 469–77.

Carroll, D., Bennett, P. and Davey Smith, G. (1993) 'Socio-Economic Health Inequalities: Their Origins and Implications', *Psychology and Health*, **8**: 295–316.

Carstairs, V. (1981) 'Multiple Deprivation and Health State', *Community Medicine*, **3**: 4–13.

Carstairs, V. and Morris, R. (1989) 'Deprivation: Explaining Differences in Mortality Between Scotland and England and Wales', *British Medical Journal*, October 7th **299**: 886–9.

Casparie, A. F. and Van Der Waal, M.A.E. (1995) 'Differenes in Preferences Between Diabetic Patients and Diabetologists Regarding Quality of Care', *Diabetic Medicine*, **12**: 828–32.

Casswell, S., Gilmour, L., Silva, P. and Brasch, P. (1993) 'Early Experiences with Alcohol: A Survey of an 8 and 9 Year Old Sample', *New Zealand Medical Journal*, **96**: 1001–3.

Catania, J.A., Kegeles, S.M. and Coates, T.J. (1990) 'Towards an Understanding of Risk Behaviour: An AIDS Risk Reduction Model', *Health Education Quarterly*, **17**: 53–72.

Cecil, D.W. and Killeen, I. (1997) 'Control, Compliance, and Satisfaction in the Family Practice Encounter', *Family Medicine*, **29**(9): 653–7

Cederlof, R., Friberg, L. and Lundman, T. (1977). 'The Interactions of Smoking, Environment and Heredity and their Implications For Disease Etiology. A Report of the Epidemiological Studies on the Swedish Twin Registries', *Acta Medica Scandinavia* (Suppl), 612.

Chamberlain, K., Stephens, C. and Lyons, A.C. (1997) 'Encompassing Experience: Meanings and Methods in Health Psychology', *Psychology and Health*, **12**(5): 691–709.

Chandalia, H.B., Bhargav, A. and Kataria, V. (1987) 'Dietary Pattern During Ramadam Fasting and Its Effect on the Metabolic Control of Diabetes', *Practical Diabetes*, **4**: 287–90.

Chapman S. (1993) 'The Role of Doctors in Promoting Smoking Cessation', *British Medical Journal*, **307**: 518–19.

Chapman, S. (1996) 'Smoking in Public Places', *British Medical Journal*, **312**: 1051–2.

Chapman, S. and Fitzgerald, B. (1982) 'Brand Preferences and Advertising Recall in Adolescent Smokers: Some Implications For Health Promotion', *American Journal of Public Health*, **72**: 491–4.

Charatan, F.B. (1998) 'Prostate Cancer Screening Reduces Deaths', *British Medical Journal*, **316**: 1625.

Charlton, B.G. (1990) 'A Critique of Biological Psychiatry', *Psychological Medicine*, **20**: 3–6.

Charnbess, M.E., Simon, R.P. and Greenberg, D.A. (1989) 'Medical Progress: Ethanol and the Nervous System', *New England Journal of Medicine*, **321**, 442–51.

Cherin, K. (1987). *Womansize: The Tyranny of Slenderness*. (Sydney: Allen & Unwin).

Chesney, M. (1996) 'AIDS and Health Psychology in the 21st Century', *Irish Journal of Psychology*.

Chichareon, S., Herrero, R., Muñoz, N., Bosch, F.X., Jacobs, M.V., Deacon, J., Santamaria, M., Chongsuvivatwong, V., Meijer, C.J, and Walboomers, J.M. (1998)Risk Factors For

Cervical Cancer in Thailand: A Case-Control Study. *Journal National Cancer Institute*, **90**(1): 50–57.

Chick, J., Lloyd, G. and Crombie, E (1985) 'Counselling Problem Drinkers in Medical Wards: A Controlled Study', *British Medical Journal*. 290. March 30th, 965–67.

Chikwem, J.O., Ola, T.O., Gashau, W., Chikwem, S.D., Bajami, M. and Mambula, S. (1988) 'Impact of Health Education on Attitudes to Acquired Immune Deficiency Syndrome (AIDS)', *Public Health*, **102**: 439–45.

Clafferty, R.A., Brown, K.W. and Mccabe, E. (1998) 'Under Half of Psychiatrists Tell their Patients their Diagnosis of Alzheimer's Disease', *British Medical Journal*, **317**: 603.

Clare, A. (1976) *Psychiatry in Dissent*. London: (London: Routledge).

Clare, N. (1998) 'Management of Sickle Cell Disease. Management Would Improve if Doctors Listened More to Patients', *British Medical Journal*, **316**(7135): 935.

Clark, J.A., Wray, N., Brody, B., Ashton, C., Giesler, B. and Watkins, H. (1997) 'Dimensions of Quality of Life Expressed By Men Treated For Metastatic Prostate Cancer', *Social Science and Medicine*, **45**(8): 1299–1309.

Clegg, F. (1988) 'Grief and Loss in Elderly People in a Psychiatric Setting', In: Chigier, E. (Ed.) *Grief and Mourning in Contemporary Society. Vol 1 Psychodynamics*. London: Freund, 191–8.

Coambs, R.B., Selina ,L. and Kozlowski, L.T. (1992) 'Age Interacts with Heaviness of Smoking in Predicting Success in Cessation of Smoking', *American Journal of Epidemiology*, **135**: 240–6.

Coates, T.J., McKusick, L., Kuno, R. and Stites, D.P. (1989) 'Stress Reduction Training Changed Number of Sexual Partners but not Immune Function in Men with HIV. *American Journal of Public Health*, **79**(7): 885–7.

Coates, T.J., McKusick, L., Kuno, R. and Stites, D.P. (1989) *Advances*, **6**(3): 7–8.

Cobb, S. (1976) 'Social Support as a Moderator of Life Stress', *Psychosomatic Medicine*, **38**: 300–13.

Coen, R., O'Mahoney, D., O'Boyle, C., and Joyce, C.R. *et al.* (1993) 'Measuring the Quality of Life of Dementia Patients Using the Schedule For the Evaluation of Individual Quality of Life. Special Issue: Psychological Aspects of Ageing: Well-Being and Vulnerability', **14**(1): 154–63.

Cohen, J. A Power Primer. *Psychological Bulletin* 1992: **112**: 155–9.

Cohen, J. and Stewart, I. (1994) *The Collapse of Chaos*. (Harmondsworth: Penguin).

Cohen, J.B. (1996) 'Smokers' Knowledge and Understanding of Advertised Tar Numbers: Health Policy Implications', *American Journal of Public Health*, **86**(1): 18–24.

Cohen, L., Ardjoen, R.C., and Sewpersad, K.S.M. (1997) 'Type A Behaviour Pattern as a Risk Factor After Myocardial Infarction: A Review', *Psychology and Health*, **12**(5): 619–32.

Cohen, R. and Hart, T. (1988) *Student Psychiatry Today: A Comprehensive Textbook*. (Oxford: Heinemann).

Cohen, S. and Herbert, T.B. (1996) Health Psychology: Psychological Factors and Physical Disease from the Perspective of Human Psychoneuroimmunology', *Annual Review of Psychology*, **47**: 113–42.

Cohen, S. and Wills,T.A. (1985) 'Stress, Social Support, and the Buffering Hypothesis', *Psychological Bulletin*, **98**: 310–57.

Cohen, Y.A. (1966) 'Patterns of Friendship. in Y.A. Cohen (Ed.).

Social Structure and Personality. (New York: Holt, Rinehart and Winston).

Coleman, A. (1995) *Controversies in Psychology*. (London: Longman).

Coleman, J., Butcher, J. and Carson, R. (1980) *Abnormal Psychology and Modern Life*. (London: Scott, Foresman).

Colhoun, H., Ben-Shlomo, Y., Dong, W., Bost, L. and Marmot, M. (1997) 'Ecological Analysis of Collectivity of Alcohol Consumption in England: Importance of Average Drinker', *British Medical Journal*, **314**(7088): 1164–8.

Colker, R. and Widom, C. (1980) 'Correlates of Female Athletic Participation: Masculinity, Femininity, Self-Esteem and Attitudes Towards Women', *Sex Roles*, **6**(1): 47–58.

Collins, G.B. (1993) 'Contemporary Issues in the Treatment of Alcohol Dependence', *Psychiatric Clinic North America*, **16**(1): 33–48.

Comings, D.E., Gade, R., Wu, S., Chiu, C., Dietz, G., Muhleman, D., Saucier, G., Ferry, L., Rossenthal, R.J., Lesieur, H.R., Rugle, L.J. and Macmurray, P. (1997) 'Studies of the Potential Role of the Dopamine D1 Receptor Gene in Addictive Behaviours', *Molecular Psychiatry*, **2**(1): 44–56.

Communicable Disease Surveillance Centre and Scottish Centre For Infection and Environmental Health (2000) 'AIDS/HIV Quarterly Surveillance Tables, 46:00/1. *Public Health* Laboratory Service AIDS and STD Centre.

Compliance with a Self-Care Manual For Bulimia Nervosa: Predictors and Outcome', *British Journal of Clinical Psychology*, **35**: 435–8.

Conill, C., Verger, E., Henriquez, I, Saiz, N., Espier, M., Lugo, F. and Garrigos, A. (1997) 'Symptom Prevalence in the Last Week of Life', *Journal of Pain Symptom Management*. **14**(6): 328–31.

Connell, C.M., Storandt, M. and Lichty, W. (1990) 'Impact of Health Belief and Diabetes-Specific Psychosocial Context Variables on Self-Care Behaviour, Metabolic Control, and Depression of Older Adults with Diabetes', *Behaviour Health and Aging*, **1**(3): 181–96.

Conner, M. and Norman, P. (1995) (Eds.) *Predicting Health Behaviour*. (Buckingham: Open University Press).

Conner, M. and Sparks, P. (1995) 'The Theory of Planned Behaviour and Health Behaviours', in M. Conner and P. Norman (Eds.) *Predicting Health Behaviour*. (Buckingham: Open University Press).

Connor, S. (1995) 'Research Shows How HIV Exhausts the Body', News. *British Medical Journal*, **310**: 145.

Conrad, B., Weidmann, E., Trucco, G., Rudert, W. A., Behboo, R., Ricordi, C., Rodriguez-Rilo, H., Finegold, D. and Trucco, M. (1994) 'Evidence For Super-Antigen Involvement in Insulin Dependent Diabetes Mellitus Aetiology', *Nature*, **371**: 351–5.

Constant, F., Guillemin, F., Collin, J.F. and Boulange, M. (1998). 'Use of Spa Therapy to Improve the Quality of Life of Chronic Low Back Pain Patients', *Medical Care*, **36**: 1309–14.

Constant, J. (1997) 'Alcohol, Ischemic Heart Disease and the French Paradox', *Clinical Cardiology*, **20**(5). 420–4.

Cook, D.G., Whincup, P.H., Papacosta, O., Strachan, D.P., Jarvis, M.J. and Bryant, A. (1993). 'Relation of Passive Smoking as Assessed By Salivary Cotinine Concentration and Questionnaire to Spirometric Indices in Children', *Thorax* 1993: **48**: 14–20.

Cooklin, R., Sturgeon, D., and Leff, J.P. (1983) 'The Relationship Between Auditory Hallucinations and Spontaneous Fluctuations of Skin Conductance in Schizophrenia', *British Journal of Psychiatry*, **142**: 47–52.

Cooper, C., Cooper, R.D. and Farragher, E.B. (1986) 'Psychosocial Stress as a Precursor to Breast Cancer: A Review', *Current Psychological Research and Reviews*, **5**(3) 268–80.

Cooper, D. (1974) *The Grammar of Living*. (London: Allen Lane).

Cooper, N. and Stevenson, C. (1998) 'New Science and Psychology', *The Psychologist*, **11**(10) 484–5.

Cooper, P.J., Taylor, M.J., Cooper, Z., & Fairburn, C.G. (1987). 'The Development and Validation of the Body Shape Questionnaire', *International Journal of Eating Disorders*, **6**: 485–94.

Copeland, J.R.M. (1990) 'Suitable Instruments For Detecting Dementia in Community Samples', *Age and Ageing*, **19**: 81–3.

Coupland, N. (1984) 'Accommodation At Work: Some Phonological Data and their Implications', *International Journal of the Sociology of Language*, **46**: 49–70.

Courneya, K.S., Nigg, C.R. and Estabrooks, P.A. (1998) 'Relationships Among the Theory of Planned Behaviour, Stages of Change, and Exercise Behaviour in Older Persons Over a Three Year Period', *Psychology and Health*, **13**(2): 355–68.

Cox, B., Blaxter, M., Buckle, A., Fenner, N.P., Golding, J.F., Gore, M., Huppert, F., Nickson, J., Roth, M., Stark, J., Wadsworth, M., Whichelow, M. (1987) 'The Health and Lifestyle Survey', London, *Health Promotion* Research Trust.

Cox, T. (1995) 'Stress, Coping and Physical Health', in A. Broome and S. Llewelyn. *Health Psychology: Process and Applications*. (New York: Chapman and Hall).

Cramer, D. (1998). *Close Relationships: The Study of Love and Friendship*. (London: Arnold).

Crary, W.G. and Crary, G.C. (1974) 'Emotional Crises and Cancer', *Cancer*, **24**: 36–9.

Crawford, C. and Unger, R.K. (1995) 'Gender Issues in Psychology', in A. M. Coleman (Ed) *Controversies in Psychology*. Longman.

Crisp, A. & Burns, T. (1983) 'Outcome of Anorexia in Males', *British Journal of Psychiatry*, **145**: 319–25.

Crombie, I.K., Smith, W.C.S., Tavendale, R. and Tunstall-Pedoe, H. (1990). 'Geographical Clustering of Risk Factors and Lifestyle For Coronary Heart Disease in the Scottish Heart Health Study', *British Heart Journal*, **64**: 199–203.

Croog, S.H. (1983) 'Recovery and Rehabilitation of Cardiac Patients: Psychological Aspects', in D.S.Krantz, A. Baum and J.E. Singer (Eds.) *Handbook of Psychology and Health (Vol 3)*. (New Jersey: Erlbaum).

Cross, M. (1981) 'The Psychology of Physical Disability – Helpful Or Harmful?', *Bulletin of the British Psychological Society*, **34**: 456–8.

Cross, M. (1998) *Proud Child, Safer Child*. (London: The Women's Press).

Cross, M., Gordon, R., Kennedy, M. and Marchant, R. (1993) 'The ABCD Pack. Abuse and Children Who are Disabled', Department of Health.

Crossley, N. (1998) 'R.D.Laing and the British Anti-Psychiatry Movement: A Socio-Historical Analysis', *Social Science and Medicine*, **47**(7): 877–99.

Crossmaker, M. (1991) 'Behind Locked Doors – Institutional Sexual Abuse', *Sexuality and Disability*, **9**(3): 201–19.

Crum, R.M., Muntaner, C., Eaton, W.W. and Anthony, J.C. (1995) 'Occupational Stress and the Risk of Alcohol Abuse and Dependence', *Alcohol Clinical and Experimental Research*, **19**(3): 647–55.

Cupach, W.P. and Spitzberg, B.H. (1994) 'The *Dark Side of Interpersonal Communication*. (Hillsdale N.J.: Erlbaum)

Cutrona, C.E. (1986) 'Behavioural Manifestations of Social Support: A Microanalytic Investigation', *Journal of Personality and Social Psychology*, **51**: 201–8.

Cyster, R. (1987) 'Alcohol Problems At the Workplace: The Search For an Effective Response', in R.Clarke (Ed) *Perspectives on Occupational Health*. British Health and Safety Society/Institute of Health Education.

Cyster, R. and Mcewen, J. (1988) 'Alcohol Problems At Work: A New Approach?', *Public Health*, **102**: 373–9.

Da Silva, F.C., Fossa, S.D., Aaronson, N.K., Serbouti, S., Denis, L., Casselman, J., Whelan, P., Hetherington, J., Fava, C., Richards, B. and Robinson, M.R. (1996) 'The Quality of Life of Patients with Newly Diagnosed M1 Prostate Cancer: Experience with EORTC Clinical Trial 30853', *European Journal of Cancer*, **32**(A:1): 72–7.

Dahl, E. (1996) 'Social Mobility and Health: Cause Or Effect?', *British Medical Journal*, **313**: 435–6.

Daneman, D., Olmsted, M., Rydall, A., Maharaj, S. and Rodin, G. (1998) 'Eating Disorders in Young Women with Type 1 Diabetes. Prevalence Problems and Prevention', *Hormone Research*, 50 Suppl **1**: 79–86.

Danziger, R. (1996) 'An Epidemic Like Any Other? Rights and Responsibilities in HIV Prevention', *British Medical Journal*, **312**: 1083–4.

Dattore, P.J., Shontz, F.C., Franklin, C. and Coyne, L. (1980) 'Premorbid Personality Differentiation of Cancer and Noncancer Groups: A Test of the Hypothesis of Cancer Proneness', *Journal of Consulting and Clinical Psychology*, **48**(3): 388–94.

Davey Smith, G. and Ebrahim, S. (1998) 'Author's Conclusions are Unjustified and Misleading', *British Medical Journal*, **316**: 705.

Davey Smith, G. and Egger, M. (1994) 'Who Benefits from Medical Intervention', *British Medical Journal*, **308**: 367–72.

Davey Smith, G. and Phillips, A.N. (1992) 'Confounding in Epidemiological Studies: Why "Independent" Effects May Not be All They Seem', *British Medical Journal*, **305**: 757–9.

Davey Smith, G., Blane, D. and Bartley, M.(1991) *Explanations For Socio-Economic Differentials in Mortality*. Community For the European Communities. Lisbon.

Davey Smith, G., Hart, C., Blane, D., Gillis, C., Hawthorne, V. (1997) 'Lifetime Socioeconomic Position and Mortality: Prospective Observational Study', *British Medical Journal*, **314**: 547–542.

Davey Smith, G., Phillips, A.N. and Neaton, J.D. (1992) 'Smoking as "Independent" Risk Factor For Suicide: Illustration of an Artefact from Observational Epidemiology?', *The Lancet*, **340**: 709–11.

Davidson, F.W.K., Woodill, G. and Bredberg, B. (1994) 'Images of Disability in 19th Century British Children's Literature', *Disability and Society*, **9**(1): 33–47.

Davidson, K., Hall, P. and MacGregor, M. (1996) 'Gender Differences in the Relation Between Interview-Derived Hostility Scores and Resting Blood Pressure', *Journal of Behavioural Medicine*, **19**(2): 185–201.

Davies, A.R. and Ware, J.E. (1991) 'GHAA's Consumer Satisfaction Survey and User's Manual', *Group Health Association of America*, Washington, DC.

Davies, D.L. (1962) 'Normal Drinking in Recovered Alcohol Addicts', *Quarterly Journal of Studies in Alcohol*, **23**: 94–104.

Davies, J.B. (1986) 'Unsolved Problems with Mass Media Drug Education Campaigns: Three Cautionary Tales', *Health Education Research*, 1(1): 69–74.

Davies, P.M. and Hickson, F.C.I. (1993) *Sex, Gay Men and AIDS*. (London: Falmer).

Davies, S.C. and Oni, L. (1997) 'Management of Patients with Sickle Cell Disease', *British Medical Journal* 1997; 315: 656–60.

Davis, M.A. (1981) 'Sex Differences in Reporting Osteoarthritic Symptoms: A Sociomedical Approach', *Journal of Health and Social Behaviour*, 22(3): 298–310.

Davis, M.S. (1968) 'Physiologic, Psychological and Demographic Factors in Patient Compliance with Doctor's Orders', *Medical Care*, 6: 115–22.

Davison, C., Frankel, S. and Davey Smith, G. (1992) 'The Limits of Lifestyle: Reassessing 'Fatalism' in the Popular Culture of Illness Prevention', *Social Science and Medicine*, 34(6): 675–85.

Day, S.J. and Graham, D.F. (1989) 'Sample Size and Power For Comparing Two Or More Treatment Groups in Clinical Trials', *British Medical Journal*; 299: 663–5.

De Boer, M.F., Van Den Borne, B., Pruyn, J.F., Ryckman, R.M., Volovics, L., Knegt, P.P., Meeuwis, C.A., Mesters, I. and Verwoerd, C.D. (1998) 'Psychosocial and Physical Correlates of Survival and Recurrence in Patients with Head and Neck Carcinoma: Results of a 6-Year Longitudinal Study', *Cancer*, 83(12): 2567–79.

De Ridder, D. (1997) 'Coping Assessment', *Psychology and Health*, 12(3): 417–31.

De Sanjosé, S., Bosch, F.X., Muñoz, N. and Shah, K. (1997) 'Social Differences in Sexual Behaviour and Cervical Cancer', *IARC Science Publications*, 138: 309–17.

De-Almeida, M.D., Graca, P., Lappalainen, R., Giachetti, I., Kaftos, A., Remaut De Winter, A. and Kearney, J.M. (1997) 'Sources Used and Trusted By Nationally Representative Adults in the European Union For Information on Healthy Eating', *European Journal of Clinical Nutrition*, 51: 16–22.

Dean, A. (1996) *Chaos and Intoxication: Complexity and Adaptation in the Structure of Human Nature*. (London: Routledge).

Dearnaley, D. and Melia, J. (1998) 'Early Prostate Cancer – to Treat Or Not to Treat?', *The Lancet*, 349: 692.

Deinzer, R. and Schueller, N. (1998) 'Dynamics of Stress-Related Decrease of Salivary Immunoglobulin A (Siga): Relationship to Symptoms of the Common Cold and Studying Behavior', *Behavioral Medicine*, 23(4): 161–9.

Dejong, W. (1996) 'When the Tobacco Industry Controls the News: KKR, RJR Nabisco, and the Weekly Reader Corporation', *Tobacco Control*, 5(2): 142–8.

Dennett, D.C. (1978) *Brainstorms: Philosophical Essays on Mind and Psychology*. (Sussex: Harvester Press).

Dennett, D.C. (1995) *Darwin's Dangerous Idea: Evolution and the Meanings of Life*. (Harmondsworth: Penguin).

Denollet, J. (1998) 'Personality and Risk of Cancer in Men with Coronary Heart Disease', *Psychological Medicine*, 28(4): 991–5.

Denzin, N.K. and Lincoln, Y.S. (Eds.) (1994) *Handbook of Qualitative Research*. Thousand Oaks. Sage. California.

Department of Education (1994) *Code of Practice on the Identification and Assessment of Special Educational Needs*. (London: HMSO)..

Department of Health (1992) *The Health of the Nation: A Summary of the Government's Proposal*. (London: HMSO).

Devins, G.M. and Seland, T.P. (1987) 'Emotional Impact on Multiple Sclerosis: Recent Findings and Suggestions For Further Research', *Psychology Bulletin*, 101(3): 363–75.

Dhabhar, F.S. (1998) 'Stress-Induced Enhancement of Cell-Mediated Immunity', *Annals of the New York Academy of Science*, 840: 359–72

Diamond, G.W. and Jaudes, P.K. (1983) 'Child Abuse in a Cerebral Palsied Population', *Developmental Medicine and Child Neurology*, 25: 169–74.

Dibble, S.L., Padilla, G.V., Dodd, M.J. and Miaskowski, C. (1998) 'Gender Differences in the Dimensions of Quality of Life', *Oncology Nursing Forum*, 25(3): 577–83.

Diclemente, C.C. (1993) 'Changing Addictive Behaviours: A Process Perspective', *Current Directions in Psychological Science*, 2: 101–6.

Diener, E., Sandvik, E., Seidlitz, L. and Diener, M. (1993) 'The Relationship Between Income and Subjective Well-Being: Relative Or Absolute?', *Social Indicators Research*, 28: 195–223.

Di-Fabio, R. P., Choi, T., Solderberg, J. and Hansen, C. (1997) 'Health-Related Quality of Life For Patients with Progressive Multiple Sclerosis: Influences of Rehabilitation', *Physical Therapy* 77(12) 1704–16.

Dignan, M.B. (1986) *Measurement and Evaluation of Health Education*. (Illinois: Charles. C. Thomas).

Dimatteo, M.R. (1985) 'Physician-Patient Communication: Promoting a Positve Healthcare Setting', in J.C.Rosen and L.J. Solomon (Eds.) *Prevention in Health Psychology*. (Hanover: University Press of New England).

Dimatteo, M.R. and DiNicola, D.D. (1982) *Achieving Patient Compliance: The Psychology of the Medical Practitioner's Role*. (New York: Pergamon Press).

Dinant, G.J. (1997) 'Medicine Based Evidence, a Prerequisite For Evidence Based Medicine', *British Medical Journal*, 315: 1109–10.

Dohmen K., Baraona E., Ishibashi H., Pozzato G., Moretti M., Matsunaga C., Fujimoto K., and Lieber, C.S. (1996) 'Ethnic Differences in Gastric Sigma-Alcohol Dehydrogenase Activity and Ethanol First-Pass Metabolism', *Alcohol Clinical and Experimental Research*, 20(9) 1569–76.

Donovan, M. and Heather, N. (1997) 'Acceptability of the Controlled-Drinking Goal Among Treatment Agencies in New South Wales', *Journal of Studies on Alcohol*, 58(3): 253–6.

Dorsey, T.L. and Dawitz, M.W. 1997 *Drugs and Crime Facts*. Bureau of Justice Statistics. US Department of Justice.

Downie, R.S., Fyfe, C. and Tannahill, A. (1991) 'Health Promotion: Models and Values', *Oxford Medical Productions*.

Doyal, L. (1995) *What Makes Women Sick: Gender and the Political Economy of Health*. (London: Macmillan).

Drever, F. and Whitehead, M. (Eds) *Health Inequalities*, Office of National Statistics (London: HMSO).

Drever, F., Whitehead, M. and Roden, M. (1996) 'Current Patterns and Trends in Male Mortality By Social Class', *Population Trends*, 86: 15–20.

Duff, R.S. and Campbell, A.G.M. (1973) 'Moral and Ethical Dilemmas in the Special Care Nursery', *The New England Journal of Medicine*, 289(17): 890–4.

Dunbar, G.C. and Morgan, D.D.V. (1987) 'The Changing Pattern of Alcohol Consumption in England and Wales 1978–85', *British Medical Journal* October 3rd 295: 807–8.

Dunbar, R. (1995) *The Trouble with Science*. (Faber and Faber).

Duncan, J.S. and Sander, J.W.A.S. (1991) 'The Chalfont Seizure Severity Scale', *Journal of Neurology, Neurosurgery and Psychiatry*, **54**: 873–6.

Dupont, S. (1997) 'Multiple Sclerosis', in A. Baum, S. Newman, J. Weinman, R. West and C. Mcmanus (Eds) *Cambridge Handbook of Psychology, Health and Medicine* (pp 538–40) (Cambridge: Cambridge University Press).

Durant, R.H., Rome, E.S., Rich, M., Allred, E., Emans, S.J. and Woods, E.R. (1997) 'Tobacco and Alcohol Use Behaviours Portrayed in Music Videos: A Content Analysis', *American Journal of Public Health*, **87**(7): 1131–5.

Ebrahim, S. and Davy Smith, G. (1997) 'Systematic Review of Randomised Controlled Trials Multiple Risk Factor Interventions For Preventing Coronary Heart Disease', *British Medical Journal*, **314**: 1666–74.

Edelstein, J. and Linn, M.W. (1985) 'The Influence of the Family on Control of Diabetes', *Social Science and Medicine*, **21**(5): 541–4.

Edwards, G. (1996) 'Sensible Drinking', *British Medical Journal*, **312**: 1.

Edwards, G. and Gross, M. (1976) 'Alcohol Dependence: Provisional Description of a Clinical Syndrome', *British Medical Journal*, **1**: 1058–61.

Eimers, J.M., Omtzigt, A.M., Vogelzang, E.T., Van Ommen, R., Habbema, J.D. and Te Velde, E.R. (1997) 'Physical Complaints and Emotional Stress Related to Routine Diagnostic Procedures of the Fertility Investigation', *Journal of Psychosomatics, Obstetrics and Gynaecology*, **18**(1): 31–5.

Eiser, J.R. (1996) 'Reconnecting the Individual and the Social in Health Psychology', *Psychology and Health*, **11**(5): 605–18.

Ellenson, G.S. (1986) 'Disturbances of Perception in Adult Female Incest Survivors', *Journal of Contemporary Social Work*. March. 149–59.

Ellgring, H., Seiler, Perleth, B., Frings, W., Gasser, T. and Oertel, W. (1993). 'Psychosocial Aspects of Parkinson's Disease', *Neurology*, Vol. **43**(12): Suppl. **6**: S41–4.

Elmer, E. (1977) 'A Follow-Up Study of Traumatized Children', *Pediatrics*, **59**: 273–9.

Elstada, J.I. (1996) 'Inequalities in Health Related to Women's Marital, Parental, and Employment Status – A Comparison Between the Early 70s and the Late 80s, Norway', *Social Science and Medicine*, **42**(1): 75–89.

European Centre For the Epidemiological Monitoring of AIDS (1997) 'HIV/AIDS Surveillance in Europe. Second Quarterly Report. No.54.

Evans, C. L. and Hughes, I.A. (1987) 'The Relationship Between Diabetes Control and Individual and Family Characteristics', *Journal of Psychosomatic Research*, **31**: 367–74.

Evans, D.L., Leserman, J., Perkins, D.O., Stern, R.A., Murphy, C., Zheng, B., Gettes, D., Longmate, J.A., Silva, S.G., Van Der Horst, C.M., Hall, C.D., Folds, J.D., Golden, R.N., Petitto, J.M. (1997) 'Severe Life Stress as a Predictor of Early Disease Progression in HIV Progression', *American Journal of Psychiatry*, **154**(5): 630–4.

Evans, P. (1998) 'Coronary Heart Disease', in M. Pitts, and K. Phillips (Eds.) *The Psychology of Health*. (2nd Edition). (London: Routledge).

Evans, P., Bristow, M., Hucklebridge, F. Clow, A. and Walters, N. (1993) 'The Relationship Between Secretory Immunity, Mood and Life Events', *British Journal of Clinical Psychology*, **32**: 227–36.

Evans, P., Clow, A. and Hucklebridge, F. (1997) 'Stress and the Immune System', *The Psychologist*, **10**(7): 303–7.

Eysenck, H.J. (1994) 'Cancer, Personality and Stress: Prediction and Prevention', *Advances in Behaviour Research and Therapy*, **16**(3): 167–215.

Fagerstrom, K.O., Schneider, N.G. and Lunell, E. (1993) 'Effectiveness of Nicotine Patch and Nicotine Gum as Individual Versus Combined Treatments For Tobacco Withdrawal Symptoms', *Psychopharmacology*, **111**: 271–7.

Faggiano, F., Partanen, T., Kogevinas, M. and Boffetta, P. (1997) 'Socioeconomic Differences in Cancer Incidence and Mortality', *IARC Science Publications*, **138**: 65–76

Faller, H., Lang, H., and Schilling, S. (1996) 'Causal "Cancer Personality" Attribution – An Expression of Maladaptive Coping with Illness?' (Trans). *Zeitschrift Klinical Psychologie Psychiatrie Und Psychotherapie*, **44**(1): 104–16.

Fallowfield, L. (1991) 'Counselling Patients with Cancer', in H. Davis and L. Fallowfield (Eds.) *Counselling and Communication in Health Care*. (London: John Wiley).

Fallowfield, L. (1995a) 'Quality of Life in Breast Cancer', *Acta Oncologica*, **34**(5): 689–94.

Fallowfield, L. (1995b) 'Improving the Quality of Communication and Quality of Life in Cancer Care', *Cancer Forum*, **19**(2): 129–31.

Fallowfield, L. (1995c) 'Questionnaire Design', *Archives of Diseases in Childhood*, **72**: 76–9.

Fallowfield, L. (1995d) 'Psychosocial Interventions in Cancer', *British Medical Journal*, **311**: 1316–17.

Fallowfield, L. (1995e) 'Can We Improve the Professional and Personal Fulfilment of Doctors in Cancer Medicine? *British Journal of Cancer*, **71**: 1132–3.

Fallowfield, L., Hall, A., Maguire, P., Baum, M. and A'Hern, R.P. (1994) 'Psychological Effects of Being Offered Choice of Surgery For Breast Cancer', *British Medical Journal*, **309**: 448.

Fallowfield, L.J. and Clark, A.W. (1994) 'Delivering Bad News in Gastroenterology', *The American Journal of Gastroenterology*, **89**(4): 473–9.

Fallowfield, L.J. and Roberts, R. (1992) 'Cancer Counselling in the United Kingdom', *Psychology and Health*, **6**: 107–17.

Fallowfield, L.J., Ford, S. and Lewis, S. (1995) 'No News Is Not Good News: Information Preferences of Patients with Cancer', *Psycho-Oncology*, **4**: 197–202.

Falvo, D. and Tippy, P. (1988) 'Communication Information to Patients – Patients Satisfaction and Adherence as Associated with Resident Skill', *Journal of Family Practice*, **26**: 643–7.

Faulkner, G. and Sparkes, A. (1999) 'Exercise Therapy For Schizophrenia: An Ethnographic Study', *Journal of Sport and Exercise Psychology*, **21**(1): 52–69.

Fawzy, I.F., Fawzy, N.W., Arndt, L.A. and Pasnau, R.O. (1995) 'A Critical Review of Psychosocial Interventions in Cancer Care', *Archives of General Psychiatry*, **52**: 100–113.

Feinstein, A., Feinstein, K., Gray, T. and O'Connor, P. (1997) 'Prevalence and Neurobehavioral Correlates of Pathological Laughing and Crying in Multiple Sclerosis', *Archives of Neurology*, **54**(9): 1116–121.

Fellows, B. and Jones, D. (1994) 'Popular Methods of Relaxation: A Survey with Implications For Therapy', *Contemporary Hypnosis*, **11**(3): 99–109.

Ferguson, E. and Cox, T. (1997) 'The Functional Dimensions of Coping Scale: Theory, Reliability and Validity', *British Journal of Health Psychology*, **2**(2): 109–30.

Fernandez-Ballesteros, R., Ruiz, M.A. and Garde, S. (1998) 'Emotional Expression in Healthy Women and Those with Breast Cancer', *British Journal of Health Psychology*, **3**: 41–50.

Fernando, S. Ndegwa, D. and Wilson, M. (1998) *Forensic Psychiatry, Race and Culture*. (London: Routledge).

Ferrans, C.E. and Powers, M.J. (1985) 'Quality of Life Index: Development and Psychometric Properties', *Advances in Nursing Science*, **8**: 15–24.

Fichter, M.M., & Noegelm, R. (1990). 'Concordance For Bulimia Nervosa in Twins', *International Journal of Eating Disorders*, **9**: 255–64.

Fielding, J. (1982) 'Effectiveness of Employee Health Improvement Programs', *Journal of Occupational Medicine*, **24**: 907–16.

Fillmore, K.M., Golding, J.M., Graves, K.L. Kneip, S., Leino, E.V., Romelsjo, A., Shoemaker, C., Ager, C.R., Allebeck, P. and Ferrer, H.P. (1998) 'Alcohol Consumption and Mortality. II. Studies of Male Populations', *Addiction*, **93**: 205–18.

Finkel, S., Silva, J., Cohen, G., Miller, S. and Sartorious, N. (1997) 'Behavioural and Psychological Signs and Symptoms of Dementia', *International Journal of Geriatric Psychiatry* **12**: 1060–61.

Finkelhor, D. (1994) 'The International Epidemiology of Child Sexual Abuse', *Child Abuse and Neglect*, **15**: 409–17.

Fishbein, M. and Ajzen, I. (1975) *Belief, Attitude, Intention and Behaviour: An Introduction to Theory and Research*. (Addison-Wesley).

Fitzgerald, J.T., Anderson, R.M. and Davis, W.K. (1995) 'Gender Differences in Diabetes Attitudes and Adherence', *The Diabetes Educator*, **21**(6): 523–9.

Fitzpatrick, R., Fletcher, A., Gore, S., Jones, D., Spiegelhalter, and Cox, D. (1992) 'Quality of Life Measures in Health Care. I: Applications and Issues in Assessment', *British Medical Journal*, **305**: 1074–7.

Fitzpatrick, R.M. and Hopkins, A. (1981) 'Patient's Satisfaction with Communication in Neurological Outpatient Clinics', *Journal of Psychosomatic Research*, Vol. **25**(5): 329–34.

Flowers, P., Sheeran, P., Beail, N. and Smith, J.A. (1997) 'The Role of Psychosocial Factors in HIV Risk-Reduction Among Gay and Bisexual Men: A Quantitative Review', *Psychology and Health*, **12**: 197–230.

Folkman, S. and Lazarus, R.S. (1985) 'If It Changes, It Must be a Process: A Study of Emotion and Coping During Three Stages of College Examination', *Journal of Personality and Social Psychology*, **48**: 150–70.

Folsom, J.C. (1968). 'Reality Orientation For the Elderly Patient', *Journal of Geriatric Psychiatry*, **1**: 1291–307.

Fonagy, P. (1996) 'Patterns of Attachment, Interpersonal Relationships and Health', in D. Blane, E. Brunner and R. Wilkinson (Eds.) *Health and Social Organisation: Towards a Health Policy For the 21st Century*. (London: Routledge).

Ford, S., Fallowfield, L. and Lewis, S. (1994) 'Can Oncologists Detect Distress in their Out-Patients and How Satisfied are They with their Performance During Bad News Consultations', *British Journal of Cancer*, **70**: 767: 770.

Forster, P. (1992) 'Nature and Treatment of Acute Stress Reactions', in L. Auston (Ed.) *Responding to Disaster: A Guide for Mental Health Professionals*. (Washington: American Psychiatric Press).

Foucault, M. (1965) *Madness and Civilisation*. (New York: Random House).

Fox, A.J., Goldblatt, P.O. and Jones, D.R. (1985) 'Social Class Mortality Differentials: Artefact, Selection Or Life Circumstances?', *Journal of Epidemiology and Community Health*, **39**: 1–8.

Fox, A.J., Goldblatt, P.O., and Jones, D.R. (1986) 'Social Class Mortality Differentials: Artifact, Selection Or Life Circumstances? in R.G. Wilkinson (Ed) *Class and Health*. (Tavistock).

Fox, J. (1991) 'Regression Diagnostics. Quantitative Applications in the Social Sciences', *Sage University Paper*, 79

Fox, J. (Ed) (1989) *Health Inequalities in European Countries*. (Aldershot: Gower).

Fox, J. and Benzeval, M. (1995) 'Perspectives on Social Variations in Health', in M.Benzeval, K.Judge and M.Whitehead (Eds.) *Tackling Inequalities in Health*. (London: Kings Fund).

Fox, J.W. (1990) 'Social Class, Mental Illness, and Social Mobility: The Social Selection-Drift Hypothesis for Serious Mental Illness', *Journal of Health and Social Behaviour*, **31**: 344–53.

Fox, J.W. (1993) 'The Conceptualisation and Measurement of Social Mobility Differences: A Brief Reply to Rodgers and Mann', *Journal of Health and Social Behaviour*, **34**(2): 173–7.

Foxx, R.M. and McMorrow, M.J. (1985) 'Teaching Social Skills to Mentally Retarded Adults: Follow-Up Results from Three Studies', *Behaviour Therapist*, **8**(4): 77–8.

Francis, R. (1999) *Ethics For Psychologists*. BPS Books. (Leicester: British Psychological Society).

Fraser, E. (1996) 'How Effective are Effectiveness Reviews?', *Health Education Journal*, **55**: 259–62.

Friedman, M. and Rosenman, R. (1959) 'Association of Specific Overt Behaviour Pattern with Blood and Cardiovascular Findings', *Journal of the American Psychiatric Association*, **12**: 1286–96.

Friedman, M., Thoresen, C.E., Gill, J.J., Ulmer, D., Powell, L.H., Proce, V.A., Brown, B., Thompson, L., Rabin, D., Breall, W.S., Bourg, E., Levy, R. and Dixon, T. (1986) 'Alteration of Type A Behaviour and Its Effect on Cardiac Recurrences in Post-Myocardial Infarction Patients: Summary of the Recurrent Coronary Prevention Project', *American Heart Journal*, **112**: 653–65.

Friedman, S.R., Des Jarlais, D.C., and Ward, T.C. (1994) 'Social Models For Changing Risk Behaviour', in J. Peterson and R. Diclemente (Eds.) 'Preventing AIDS: Theory and Practice of Behavioural Interventions', Plenum.

Frude, N. (1998) *Understanding Abnormal Psychology*. (Blackwell).

Fryer, G.E., Kraizer, S.K. and Miyoshi, T. (1987) 'Measuring the Actual Reduction of Risk For Child Abuse: A New Approach', *Child Abuse and Neglect*, **11**: 173–9.

Fulton. J.P., Buechner, J.S., Scott, H., Debuono, B.A., Feldman, J.P., Smith, R.A. and Kovenock, D. (1991) 'A Study Guided By the Health Belief Model of the Predictors of Breast Cancer Screening of Women Ages 40 and Older', *Public Health Reports*, **106**: 410–20.

Furnham, A. (1988) *Lay Theories*. (Oxford: Pergamon Press).

Furnham, A. and Rees, J. (1988). 'Lay Theories of Schizophrenia', *International Journal of Social Psychiatry* **34**(3): 212–20.

Futterman, D., Hein, K., Reuben, N., Dell, R. and Shaffer, N. (1993) 'Human Immunodeficiency Virus-Infected Adolescents: The First 50 Patients in a New York City Program', *Pediatrics*, **91**(4): 730–5.

Gabbard-Alley, A.S. (1995). 'Health Communication and Gender: A Review and Critique', *Health Communication*, **7**(1): 35–54.

Ganz, P.A., Rowland, J.H., Desmond, K., Meyerowitz, B.E. and Wyatt, G.E. (1998) 'Life After Breast Cancer: Understanding Women's Health-Related Quality of Life and Sexual Functioning', *Journal of Clinical Oncology*, **16**(2): 501–14.

Garcia S (1997) 'Ethical and Legal Issues Associated with Substance Abuse By Pregnant and Parenting Women', *Journal of Psychoactive Drugs*, **29**(1): 101–11.

Garner, D.M., & Garfinkel P.E. (1979). 'The Eating Attitudes Test: An Index of the Symptoms of Anorexia Nervosa', *Psychological Medicine*, **9**: 273–9.

Garratt, A.M., Ruta, D.A., Abdalla, M.I., Buckingham, J.K. and Rutter, I.T. (1993) 'The SF-36 Health Survey Questionnaire: An Outcome Measure Suitable For Routine Use Within the NHS?', *British Medical Journal*, **306**: 1440–4.

Gatchel, R.J., Baum, A. and Krantz, D.S. (1989) *An Introduction to Health Psychology* (2nd ed). (New York: Mcgraw Hill).

Gecas, V. and Seff, M.A. (1990) 'Social Class and Self Esteem: Psychological Centrality, Compensation, and the Relative Effects of Work and Home', *Social Psychology Quarterly*, **53**: 165–73.

Geersten, H.R., Gray, R.M. and Ward, J.R. (1973) 'Patient Non-Compliance Within the Context of Seeking Medical Care For Arthritis', *Journal of Chronic Diseases*, **26**: 689–98.

Geiss, S.K. and O'Leary, K.D. (1981). 'Therapist Ratings of Frequency and Severity of Marital Problems: Implications For Research', *Journal of Marriage and Family Therapy*, **7**: 515–20.

General Household Survey (1997) Office of National Statistics. (London: HMSO).

Gerth, M.M. and Wright Mills, C. (1970) *From Max Weber: Essays in Sociology*. (London: Routledge).

Gilbar, O.(1997) 'Women with High Risk For Breast Cancer: Psychological Symptoms', *Psychological Reports*, **80**(3) Pt 1: 800–2.

Gillespie, C. (1991) 'Optimizing Blood Glucose Monitoring', in C.Bradley, P. Home and M. Christie (Eds.) *The Technology of Diabetes Care: Converging Medical and Psychosocial Perspectives*. (Harwood: Churchill).

Gillespie-Sells, K., Hill, M. and Robbins, B. (1998) *She Dances to Different Drums: Research Into Disabled Women's Sexuality*. (London: Kings Fund).

Gillet, G. (1996) 'The Philosophical Foundations of Qualitative Psychology', *The Psychologist*, **8**(3): 111–14.

Glanz, K., Lankenau, B., Foerster, S., Temple, S., Mulis, R. and Schmid, T. (1995) 'Environmental and Policy Approaches to Cardiovascular Disease Prevention Through Nutrition: Opportunities For State and Local Action', *Health Education Quarterly*, **22**: 512–27.

Glaser, B.G. and Strauss, A.L. (1967) *The Discovery of Grounded Theory: Strategies For Qualitative Research*. (Chicago: Aldine).

Glenn, N.D. & Weaver C.N. (1988). 'The Changing Relationship of Marital Status to Reported Happiness', *Journal of Marriage and the Family*, **50**: 317–24.

Glover, J., Dibble, S. L., Dodd, M. J. and Miaskowski, C. (1995). 'Mood States of Oncology Outpatients: Does Pain Make a Difference?', *Journal of Pain Symptom Management* **10**: 120–8.

Goffman, E. (1961) *Asylums: Essays on the Social Situations of Mental Patients and Other Inmates*. (Penguin).

Goffman, E. (1963) *Stigma. Notes on the Management of Spoiled Identity*. (New Jersey: Prentice Hall).

Goldberg, D., Williams, P. (1988) *A User's Guide to the General Health Questionnaire*. NFER-Nelson, Windsor UK.

Goldberg, D. and Huxley, P. (1980) *Mental Illness in the Community*. (London: Tavistock).

Goldberg, E.M. and Morrison, S.L. (1963) 'Schizophrenia and Social Class', *British Journal of Psychiatry*, **109**: 785.

Goldblum, R.M. (1990) 'The Role of Iga in Local Immune Protection', *Journal of Clinical Immunology*, **10**: 64S-70S.

Goldhagen, D. J. (1997) *Hitler's Willing Executioners*. (London: Abacus).

Golding, J.F. (1988) 'The Effects of Cigarette Smoking on Resting EEG, Evoked Potentials and Photic Driving', *Pharmacology Biochemistry Behaviour*, **29**: 23.

Golding, J.F. (1992) 'Cannabis', in A. Smith and D. Jones (Eds.) *Factors Affecting Human Performance* Vol.II., pp 169–95. (London: Academic Press).

Golding, J.F.. (1995) 'Smoking', Chapter 18. In: R.A.L. Brewis, B. Corrin, D.M. Geddes and G.J. Gibson (Eds.) *Respiratory Medicine*. Second Edition, pp 531–44. (London: WB Saunders Co Ltd).

Goldston, D.B., Kovacs, M. and Obrosky, D.S. (1995) 'A Longitudinal Study of Life Events and Metabolic Control Among Youths with Insulin Dependent Diabetes Mellitus', *Health Psychology*, **14**(5): 409–14.

Goldthorpe, J. H. and Payne, C. (1986a) 'Trends in Class Mobility 1972–83', in J. H. Goldthorpe. *Social Mobility and Class Structure in Modern Britain*. (Oxford: Clarendon Press).

Goldthorpe, J. H. and Payne, C. (1986b) 'The Class Mobility of Women', in J. H. Goldthorpe. *Social Mobility and Class Structure in Modern Britain*. (Oxford: Clarendon Press).

Gomm, R. (1996) 'Mental Health and Inequality', in T.Heller, J. Reynolds, R. Gomm, R. Muston and S.Pattison (Ed) *Mental Health Matters*. The Open University. (London: Macmillan Press).

Gorman, D.M. and Speer, P.W. (1996) 'Preventing Alcohol Abuse and Alcohol Related Problems Through Community Interventions: A Review of Evaluation Studies', *Psychology and Health*, **11**: 95–131.

Gove, W.R. (1984) 'Gender Differences in Mental and Physical Illness: The Effects of Fixed Roles and Nurturant Roles. *Social Science and Medicine*, **19**(2): 77–91.

Gove, W.R., Hughes, M. and Style, C.B. (1983). 'Does Marriage Have Positive Effects on the Psychological Well Being of the Individual?', *Journal of Health and Social Behaviour*, **24**: 122–31.

Graham, B.S. (1998) 'Infection with HIV-1', *British Medical Journal*, **317**: 1297–301.

Graham, H. (1998) *Health Inequalities*: The Challenge For Health Psychology. *Health Psychology Update*, **34**: 13–18.

Graham, P., Stevenson, J. and Flynn, D. (1997) 'A New Measure of Health-Related Quality of Life For Children: Preliminary Findings', *Psychology and Health*, **12**(5): 655–66.

Gray, A., Jackson, D.N., Howard, J.H. (1989) 'Validation of the Survey of Work Styles: A Profile Measure of the Type A Behaviour Pattern', *Journal of Clinical Epidemiology*, **42**(3) 209–16.

Green, A.H. (1989) Quoted in P.Breggin (1993) *Toxic Psychiatry*. (Fontana).

Green, B.L., Lindy, J. and Grace, M.C. (1985) 'Post-Traumatic Stress Disorder. Toward DSM-4', *Journal of Nervous and Mental Diseases*, **173**: 406–11.

Green, J. and Britten, N. (1998) 'Qualitative Research and Evidence Based Medicine', *British Medical Journal*, **316**: 1230–2.

Green, L. (1979) 'National Policy in the Promotion of Health', *International Journal of Health Education*, **2**(3): 161–8.

Green, M.A. (1999) 'Time to Put Cot Death to Bed', *British Medical Journal*, **319**: 697–700.

Greenland, P., Hildreth, N.G. and Maiman, L.A. (1992) 'Attendance Pattern and Characteristics of Participants in Public Cholesterol Screening', *American Journal of Preventive Medicine*, **8**(3): 159–64.

Greer, H.S. and Morris, T. (1975) 'Psychological Attributes of Women Who Develop Breast Cancer: A Controlled Study', *Journal of Psychosomatic Research*, **19**: 147–53.

Greer, S., Moorey, S., Baruch, J.D.R., Watson, M., Robertson, B.M., Mason, A., Rowden, L., Lawm, M.G. and Bliss, J.M. (1992) 'Adjuvant Psychological Therapy For Patients with Cancer: A Prospective Randomised Trial', *British Medical Journal*, **304**: 675–80.

Grégoire, I., Kalogeropoulos, D. and Corcos, J. (1997) 'The Effectiveness of a Professionally Led Support Group For Men with Prostate Cancer', *Urology Nursing*, **17**(2): 58–66.

Greil, A.L. (1997) 'Infertility and Psychological Distress: A Critical Review of the Literature', *Social Science and Medicine*, **45**(11): 1679–1704.

Grey, M., Lipman, T., Cameron, M.E. and Thurber, F.W. (1997) 'Coping Behaviours At Diagnosis and in Adjustment One Year Later in Children with Diabetes', *Nursing Research*, **46**(6): 312–17.

Griffiths, R., and Farnill, D. (1996). 'Primary Prevention of Dieting Disorders: An Update', *Journal of Family Studies*. **2**(2): 179–91.

Grochowitz, P.M., Schedlowski, M., Husband, A.J., King, M.G., Hibberd, A.D. and Bowen, K.M. (1991) 'Behavioural Conditioning Prolongs Heart Allograft Survival in Rats', *Brain, Behaviour and Immunity*, **5**: 349–56.

Grønbæk, M., Becker, U., Johansen, D., Tønneson, H., Jensen, G. and Sørensen, T.I.A. (1998) 'Population Based Cohort Study of the Association Between Alcohol Intake and Cancer of the Upper Digestive Tract', *British Medical Journal*, **317**: 844–8.

Gross, R.H., Cox, A., Taytrek, R., Polloway, M. and Barnes, W.A. (1983) 'Early Manage-ment and Decision Making For the Treatment of Myelomeningocele', *Pediatrics*, **72**(4): 450–8.

Grunberg, N.E., Brown, K.J., and Klein, L.C. (1997) 'Tobacco Smoking', in B. Baum Et Al (Eds.) *Cambridge Handbook of Psychology, Health and Medicine*. (Cambridge: Cambridge University Press).

Gual, A. and Colom, J. (1997) 'Why Has Alcohol Consumption Declined in Countries of Southern Europe?', *Addiction*, **92**(Supp 1): S21–S31.

Gull, W.W. (1874). 'Anorexia Nervosa', (Apepsia Hysterica, Anorexia Hysterica). *Transactions of the Clinical Society of London*, **7**: 22–8.

Haan, M.N., Kaplan, G.A. and Syme, L. (1989) 'Some New Thoughts on Old Observations', in J. Bunker, D.S. Gomby and B.H. Kehrer (Eds.) *Pathways to Health: The Role of Social Factors*. Henry, J. Kaiser Family Foundation.

Haavio-Mannil, E. (1986) 'Inequalities in Health and Gender', *Social Science and Medicine*, **22**(2): 141–9.

Hagnell, O., Nyman, E. and Tunvirg, K. (1973) 'Dangerous Alcoholics', *Scandinavian Journal of Social Medicine*, **3**: 125–31.

Haines, A. and Smith, R. (1997) 'Working Together to Reduce Poverty's Damage', *British Medical Journal*, **314**: 529–30.

Hall, P., Brockington, I.F., Levings, J. & Murphy, C. (1993). 'A Comparison of Responses to the Mentally Ill in Two Communities', *British Journal of Psychiatry* 99–108.

Hall, S., Bobrow, M. and Marteau, T.M. (1997) 'Parents Attributions of Blame For the Birth of a Child with Down's Syndrome: A Pilot Study', *Psychology and Health*, **12**: 579–87.

Hamburg, P.H., Herzog, D.B., and Brotman, A. (1996). 'Treatment Resistance in Eating Disorders: Psychodynamic and Pharmalogic Perspectives', in M.H. Pollack, M.W. Otto, and J.F. Rosenbaum (Eds.) *Challenges in Clinical Practice: Pharmalogic and Psychosocial Strategies* (pp. 263–75). (New York: Guildford Press).

Hamburg, P.H., Herzog, D.B., Brotman, A., and Stasior, J.K. (1989). 'The Treatment of the Resistant Eating Disordered Patient', *Psychiatric Annals*, **19**: 494–9.

Hamilton, K., and Waller, G. (1993). 'Media Influences on Body Size Estimations in Bulimia and Anorexia', *British Journal of Psychiatry*, **162**: 837–40.

Hancock, L., Sanson-Siher, R.W., Redman, S., Burton, R., Burton, L., Butler, J., Girgis, A., Gibberd, R., Hensley, M., Mcclintock, A., Reid, A., Schofield, M., Tripodi, T. and Walsh, R. (1997) 'Community Action For Health Promotion: A Review of Methods and Outcomes 1990–5', *American Journal of Preventive Medicine*, **13**(4): 229–39.

Hannan, E.L., Kilburn, H. Jr, O'Donnell, J.F., Lukacik, G. and Shields, E.P. (1991) 'Interracial Access to Selected Cardiac Procedures for Patients Hospitalized with Coronary Artery Disease in New York State', *Medical Care*, **29**(5): 430–41.

Hanson, C.L., Henggeler, S.W., Harris, M.A., Burghen, G.A. and Moore, M. (1989) 'Family System Variables and the Health Status of Adolescents with IDDM', *Health Psychology*, **8**: 239–54.

Harburg, E., Erfurt, J.C., Chape, C., Hauenstein, L.S., Schull, W.J. and Schork, M.A. (1973) 'Socioecological Stressor Areas and Black-White Blood Pressure: Detroit', *Journal of Chronic Diseases*, **26**(9): 595–611.

Harding, Bethune, Maxwell and Brown (1997) 'Mortality Trends Using the Longitudinal Study', in M.Whitehead and F. Drever (Eds.) *Health Inequalities*. (London: Office of National Statistics).

Harding, S. (1985) 'Values and the Nature of Psychological Well-Being', in M. Abrams, D. Gerard and N. Timms (Eds.) *Values and Social Change in Britain*. (London: Macmillan).

Harding, S. and Maxwell, R. (1997) 'Differences in Mortality of Migrants', in M. Whitehead and F. Drever (Eds) *Health Inequalities*. (London: Office of National Statistics).

Hare, E.H. (1956) 'Mental Illness and Social Conditions in Bristol', *Journal of Mental Science*, **102**: 349–57.

Harlow, L.L., Prochaska, J.O., Redding, C.A., Rossi, J.S., Velicer, W.F., Snow, M.G., Schnell, D., Galavotti, C., O'Reilly, K., Rhodes, F. and the Aids Community Demonstration Research Group (1999) 'Stages of Condom Use in a High HIV-Risk Sample', *Psychology and Health*, **14**(1): 143–58.

Harre, R. and Gillet, G. (1994) *The Discursive Mind*. (California: Sage).

Harris, A., Parker, N. and Barker, C. (1998) 'Adults with Sickle Cell Disease: Psychological Impact and Experience of Hospital Services', *Psychology Health and Medicine*, **3**(2): 171–9.

Harris, R. and Linn, M.W. (1985) 'Health Beliefs, Compliance and Control of Diabetes Mellitus', *Southern Medical Journal*, **78**: 162–6.

Harrison, G., Owens, D., Holton, A., Neilson, D. and Boot, D.

(1988) 'A Prospective Study of Severe Mental Disorder in Afro-Caribbean Patients', *Psychological Medicine*, **18**(3), 643–57.

Harrison, J.A., Mullen, P.D. and Green, L.W. (1992) 'A Meta-Analysis of Studies of the Health Belief Model', *Health Education Research*, **7**: 107–16.

Harrison, L., Sutton, M. and Gardiner, E. (1997) 'Ethnic Differences in Substance Use and Alcohol-Use-Related Mortality Among First Generation Migrants to England and Wales', *Substance Use and Misuse*, **32**(7–8): 849–76.

Harrison, R.F., O'Moore, A.M., O'Moore, R.R., and Robb, D. (1984) 'Stress in Infertile Couples', in R.F. Harrison, J.Bunnar and W. Thomson (Eds.) *Fertility and Sterility*. (Lancaster: MTP Press).

Harrison, S. D., Glover, L., Feinmann, C., Pearce, S. A. and Harris, M. (1998). 'A Comparison of Antidepressant Medication Alone and in Conjunction with Cognitive Behavioral Therapy For Chronic Idiopathic Facial Pain', in: T. S. Jensen, J. A. Turner and Z. Wiesenfeld-Hallin (Eds), Proceedings of the 8th World Congress on Pain, International Association For the Study of Pain, Seattle, WA: pp. 663–72.

Hart, C.L., Davy Smith, G., Hole, D.J. and Hawthorne, V.M. (1999) 'Alcohol Consumption and mortality from All Causes, Coronary Heart Disease, and Stroke: Results from a Prospective Cohort Study of Scottish Men with 21 Years of Follow Up', *British Medical Journal*, **318**: 1725–9.

Hart, E.L., Lahey, B.B., Loeber, R., Hanson, K.S. (1994) 'Criterion Validity of Informants in the Diagnosis of Disruptive Behaviour Disorders in Children: A Preliminary Study', *Journal of Consulting and Clinical Psychology*, **62**(2): 410–14.

Hart, G. (1996) 'Gay Community Oriented Approaches to Safer Sex', in T. Rhodes and R. Hartnoll (Eds.) *AIDS, Drugs and Prevention*. (London: Routledge).

Hattersley, L. (1997) 'Expectation of Life By Social Class', in Drever, F. and Whitehead, M. (Eds.) *Health Inequalities*. Decennial Supplement. Series DS No.15: pp 73–82. Office of National Statistics. (London: HMSO).

Hauerwas, S. (1986) 'Suffering the Retarded: Should We Prevent Mental Retardation?', in P.R. Dokecki and R.M. Zaner (Eds.) *Ethics of Dealing with Persons with Severe Disabilities: Toward a Research Agenda*. (P.H.Brookes: Baltimore).

Havik, O.E. and Maelands, J.G. (1990) 'Patterns of Emotional Reactions After a Myocardial Infarction', *Journal of Psychosomatic Research*, **34**: 271–85.

Hawthorne, K. (1994) 'Accessibility and Use of Health Care Services in the British Asian Community', *Family Practice*, **11**(4): 453–59.

Haynes, S.G., Levine, S. and Scotch, N. (1978) 'The Relationship of Psychosocial Factors to Coronary Heart Disease', *American Journal of Epidemiology*, **111**: 37–58.

Haynes, S.G., Levine, S., Scotch, N., Feinleib, M. and Kannel, W.B. (1978) 'The Relationship of Psychosocial Factors to Coronary Heart Disease in the Framingham Study: 1. Methods and Risk Factors', *American Journal of Epidemiology*, **107**: 362–83.

Hays, R.D. and Shapiro, M.F. (1992) 'An Overview of Generic Health-Related Quality of Life Measures For HIV Research', *Quality of Life Research*, **1**: 91–7.

Hazan, C. and Shaver, P. (1987) 'Romantic Love Conceptualised as an Attachment Process', *Journal of Personality and Social Psychology*, **52**: 511–24.

He, J., Klag, M.J., Appel, L.J., Charleston, J. and Whelton, P.K. (1998) 'Seven-Year Incidence of Hypertension in a Cohort of Middle-Aged African Americans and Whites', *Hypertension*, **31**(5): 1130–5.

Health Education Authority (1999) www.hea.org.uk.

Heather, N. and Robinson, D. (1985) *Problem Drinking: The New Approach*. (Harmondsworth: Penguin).

Hebert, J.R., Harris, D.R., Sorensen, G., Stoddard, A.M., Hunt, M.K., and Morris, D.H. (1993) 'A Work-Site Nutrition Intervention: Its Effects on the Consumption of Cancer-Related Nutrients', *American Journal of Public Health*, **83**: 391–3.

Heller, K and Swindle, R.W. (1983). 'Social Networks, Perceived Social Support, and Coping with Stress', in R.D. Felner, L.A Jason, J. Moritsuga and S.S Faber (Eds.). *Preventive Psychology: Theory, Research, and Practice in Community Intervention*. (New York: Pergamon).

Heller, K. (1979). 'The Effects of Social Support: Prevention and Treatment Implications', in A.P Goldstein and F.H. Kanfer (Eds.). *Maximising Treatment Gains: Transfer Enhancement in Psychotherapy*. (London: Academic Press).

Heller, K. and Rook, K.S.(1997). 'Distinguishing the Theoretical Functions of Social Ties: Implications For Support Interventions', in S. Duck (Ed.). *Handbook of Personal Relationships: Theory, Research and Interventions*. (Chichester: John Wiley and Sons).

Hemingway, H. and Marmot, M. (1999) 'Psychosocial Factors in the Aetiology and Prognosis of Coronary Heart Disease: Systematic Review of Prospective Cohort Studies', *British Medical Journal*, **318**: 1460–7.

Hemingway, H., Nicholson, A., Stafford, M., Roberts, R. and Marmot, M. (1997) 'The Impact of Socioeconomic Status on Health Functioning as Assessed By the SF-36 Questionnaire: The Whitehall II Study', *American Journal of Public Health*, **87**(9): 1484–9.

Herbert, T.B. and Cohen, S. (1993) 'Stress and Immunity in Humans: A Meta-Analytic Review', *Psychosomatic Medicine*, **55**: 364–79.

Herrnstein, R.J. and Murray, C. (1994*) The Bell Curve: Intelligence and Class Structure in American Life*. (London: Free Press).

Hickey, A.M., Bury, G., O'Boyle, C.A., Bradley, F., O'Kelly, F.D. and Shannon, W. (1996) 'A New Short Form Individual Quality of Life Measure (Seiqol-DW): Application in a Cohort of Individuals with HIV/AIDS', *British Medical Journal*, **313**: 29–33.

Hickey, A.M., O'Boyle, C.A., Mcgee, H.M. and Mcdonald, N.J. (1997) 'The Relationship Between Post-Trauma Reporting and Carer Quality of Life After Severe Head Injury', *Psychology and Health*, **12**(6) 839–8.

Hill, A.B. (1965) 'The Environment Or the Disease: Association Or Causation?', *Proceedings of the Royal Society of Medicine*, **58**: 25–32.

Hill, S. and Harries, U. (1994) 'Assessing the Outcome of Health Care For the Older Person in Community Settings: Should We Use the SF-36? Outcomes Briefing, UK Clearing House For the Assessment of Health Outcomes', **4**: 26–7.

Hills, P. and Argyle, M. (1998) 'Positive Moods Derived from Leisure and their Relationship to Happiness and Personality', *Personality and Individual Differences* **25**(3): 523–35.

Hixenbaugh, P. and Warren, L. (1998) 'Diabetes', in M. Pitts, and K. Phillips (Eds.) *The Psychology of Health*. (2nd Ed). (London: Routledge).

Hixenbaugh, P., Roberts, R. and Castle, B. (2000) 'Predictors of Attendance At Diabetes Clinics'. (Submitted).

Ho, D.D., Neumann, A.U., Perelson, A.S., Chen, W., Leonard, J.M. and Markowitz, M. (1995) 'Rapid Turnover of Plasma Virions and CD4 Lymphicytes in HIV-1 Infection', *Nature*, 373: 123–6.

Hobcraft, J. (1993) 'Women's Education, Child Welfare and Child Survival: A Review of the Evidence', *Health Transition Review* 3(2): 159–75.

Hoch, T., Babbitt, R.L., Coe, D.A., Krell, D.M. and Hackbert, L. (1994) 'Contingency Contacting. Combining Positive Reinforcement and Escape Extinction Procedures to Treat Persistent Food Refusal', *Behaviour Modification*, 18(1): 106–28.

Hodgkins, S. and Orbell, S. (1998) 'Can Protection Motivation Theory Predict Behaviour? A Longitudinal Test Exploring the Role of Previous Behaviour', *Psychology and Health*, 13(2): 2327–250.

Hodiamont, P., Peer, N. and Syben, N. (1987) 'Epidemiological Aspects of Psychiatric Disorder in a Dutch Health Area', *Psychological Medicine*, 17: 495–505.

Holahan, C.J., Holahan, C.K., Moos, R.H. and Brennan, P.L. (1997) 'Psychosocial Adjustment in Patients Reporting Cardiac Illness', *Psychology and Health*, 12(3): 345–59.

Holden, U. and Woods, R. T. (1995) *Positive Approaches to Dementia Care.* Edinburgh: Churchill Livingstone.

Holland, A., Sicotte, N., & Treasure, J. (1988). 'Anorexia Nervosa-Evidence For a Genetic Basis', *Journal of Psychosomatic Research*, 32: 561–71.

Hollingshead, A. and Redlich, R.C. (1958) *Social Class and Mental Illness.* (New York: John Wiley).

Holman, C.D.J. and English, D.R. (1996) 'Ought Low Alcohol Intake to be Promoted For Health Reasons?', *Journal of the Royal Society of Medicine*, 89: 123–9.

Homedes, N. (1991) 'Do We Know How to Influence Patients' Behaviour?', *Family Practice*, 8(4): 412–23.

Hoover, D.R., Doherty, M.C., Vlahov, D. and Miotti, P. (1996) 'Incidence and Risk Factors For HIV-1 Infection – A Summary of What Is Known and the Psychiatric Relevance', *International Review of Psychiatry*, 8(2–3): 137–48.

Hore, B.D. (1987) 'Alcohol and Alcoholism: Their Effect on Work and the Industrial Response', in B.D. Hore and M.A. Plant (Eds) *Alcohol Problems in Employment.* (London: Croon Helm).

Horowitz, M. (1986) *Stress Response Syndromes.* (Nothvale, NJ: Aronson).

Howard, J. (1929) *The State of Prisons.* (New York: E.P.Dutton).

Howell, D.C. (1992) *Statistical Methods For Psychology.* (3rd Edition). Duxbury Press (Wadsworth Publishing Co.) Belmont, California.

Hshieh, S.Y. and Srebalus, D.J. (1997) 'Alcohol Treatment Issues: Professional Differences', *Alcoholism Treatment Quarterly*, 15(4): 63–73.

Hsu, L.K.G., Chesler, B.E., & Santhouse, R. (1990). 'Bulimia Nervosa in Eleven Sets of Twins: A Clinical Report', *International Journal of Eating Disorders*, 9: 275–82.

Hughes, K., Mackintosh, A.M., Hastings, G., Wheeler, C., Watson, J. and Inglis, J. (1997) 'Young People, Alcohol, and Designer Drinks: Quantitative and Qualitative Study', *British Medical Journal*, 314: 414–414

Humphries, S.E., Galton, D. and Nicholls, P. (1997) 'Genetic Testing For Familial Hypercholesterolaemia: Practical and Ethical Issues', *Quarterly Journal of Medicine*, 90(3): 169–81.

Hunt, S. and Mckenna, S.P. (1992) 'Validating the SF-36', Letters, *British Medical Journal*, 305: 645.

Hunt, S., McEwen, J. and McKenna, S.P. (1985a) 'Measuring Health Status: A New Tool For Clinicians and Epidemiologists. *Journal of the Royal College of Practitioners*, 35: 185–8.

Hunt, S., McEwen, J. and McKenna, S.P. (1985b) 'Social Inequalities in Perceived Health', *Effective Health Care*, 2: 151–60.

Hunt, S.M. and Macleod, M. (1987) 'Health and Behavioural Change: Some Lay Perspectives', *Community Medicine*, 9(1): 68–76.

Hutton, W. (1995) *The State We're In.* Vintage.

ICD-10 (1992) 'Classification of Mental and Behavioural Disorders: Clinical Descriptions and Diagnostic Guidelines. *World Health Organization.*

Illich, I. (1977) *Limits to Medicine.* (Harmondsworth: Penguin).

Illsley, R. and Baker, D (1991) 'Contextual Variations in the Meaning of Health Inequality', *Social Science and Medicine*, 32(4): 359–65.

Illsley, R. and Svensson, P.G. (Eds.) (1990) *Health Inequalities* in Europe. *Social Science and Medicine*, 31(3): 223–420.

Ingham, P. (1994) 'Sexuality and Health in Young People: Perceptions and Behaviour Related to the Threat of HIV-Infection', in G.N. Penny, P. Bennett and M. Herbert (Eds.) *Health Psychology: a Lifespan Perspective.* (Harwood).

Jachuk, S.J., Brierly, H., Jachuk, S. and Wilcox, P.M. (1982) 'The Effect of Hypertensive Drugs on the Quality of Life', *Journal of the Royal College of General Practitioners*, 32: 103–5.

Jackins, H. (1985) *The Human Side of Human Beings: The Theory of Re-Evaluation Counselling.* (Rational Island: Seattle).

Jackson, R., Scragg, R. and Beaglehole, R. (1991) 'Alcohol Consumption and Risk of Coronary Disease', *British Medical Journal*, 303: 211.

Jacobs, S. (1993) *Pathologic Grief: Maladaption to Loss.* (Washington, DC: American Psychiatric Press).

Jacobson, A.M. and Leibovitch, F.B. (1984) 'Psychosocial Issues in Diabetes Mellitus', *Psychosomatics*, 25: 7–15.

Jacobson, A.M., Adler, A.G., Derby, L., Anderson, B.J. and Wolsdorf, J.I. (1991) 'Clinic Attendance and Glycaemic Control', *Diabetes Care*, 14: 599–601.

Jacobson, A.M., Hauser, S.T., Willett, J.B., Wolfsdorf, J.I., Dvorak, R., Herman, L., and De Groot, M. (1997) 'Psychological Adjustment to IDDM: 10-Year Follow-Up of an Onset Cohort of Child and Adolescent Patients', *Diabetes Care*, 20(5): 811–18.

James 1: King. A *Counter-Blaste to Tobacco.* (Published Under Pseudonym 'R.B.' with Royal Coat of Arms.), R.B., London: Bodleian Library Copy, Oxford. 1604.

James, S.A., LaCroix, A.Z., Kleinbaum, D.G. and Strogatz, D.S. (1984) 'John Henryism and Blood Pressure Differences Among Black Men. II. The Role of Occupational Stressors', *Journal of Behavioural Medicine*, 7(3): 259–75.

James, W.P.T., Nelson, M., Ralph, A. and Leather, S. (1996) 'The Contribution of Nutrition to Inequalities in Health', *British Medical Journal*, 314: 1545–9.

Jarman, B. (1983) 'Identification of Underprivileged Areas', *British Medical Journal*, 286: 1705–9.

Jarvis, M.J., Belcher, M., Vesey, C. and Hutchison, D.C.S. (1986). 'Low Cost Carbon Monoxide Monitors in Smoking Assessment', *Thorax*, 41: 886.

Jeffs, B.W. and Saunders, W.M. (1983) 'Minimising Alcohol Related Offences By Enforcement of the Existing Licensing Legislation', *British Journal of Addiction*, 78: 67–77.

Jellinek, E.M. (1960) *The Disease Concept of Alcoholism*, New Jersey: Hillhouse Press.

Jemmott, L.S. and Jemmott, J.B. (1991) 'Applying the Theory of Reasoned Action to AIDS-Risk Behaviour: Condom Use Among Young Black Women', *Nursing Research*, **40**: 228–34.

Jenkins, J.E. (1996) 'The Influence of Peer Affiliation and Student Activities on Adolescent Drug Involvement', *Adolescence*, **31**(122): 297–306.

Jenkins,C., Zynanski, S.J. and Rosenman, R.H. (1979) *The Jenkins Activity Survey For Health Prediction*. (New York: The Psychological Corporation).

Jenkinson, C., Peto, V. and Coulter, A. (1996) 'Making Sense of Ambiguity: Evaluation of Internal Reliability and Face Validity of the SF-36 Questionnaire in Women Presenting with Menorrhagia', *Quality in Health Care*, **5**: 9–12.

Johnson, C.L. (1996) 'Regaining Self-Esteem: Strategies and Interventions For the Infertile Woman', *Journal of Obstetrics, Gynaecology and Neonatal Nursing*, **25**(4): 291–5.

Johnson, J.V. and Hall, E.M. (1988) 'Job Strain, Work Place, Social Support, and Cardiovascular Disease: A Cross Sectional Study of a Random Sample of the Swedish Working Population', *American Journal of Public Health*, **78**: 1336–42.

Johnston, M. (1995) 'Models of Disability. British Psychological Society, Presidents' Award Lecture', *The Psychologist*, **9**(5): 205–10.

Jones, A. and Faulkner, A.)1996) 'What Does Palliative Mean? Contemporary Professional Opinion', *Journal of Cancer Care*, **5**(1): 39–43.

Jones, J.M., Lawson, M.L., Daneman, D., Olmstead, M.P. and Rodin, G. (2000) 'Eating Disorders in Adolescent Females with and Without Type 1 Diabetes: Cross Sectional Study', *British Medical Journal*, **320**: 1563–6.

Jones, P.B., Bebbington, P., Foerster, A., Lewis, Shon-W.; *et al.* (1993) 'Premorbid Social Underachievement in Schizophrenia: Results from the Camberwell Collaborative Psychosis Study', *British Journal of Psychiatry*, **162**: 65–71.

Jones-Webb, R.J. and Snowden, L.R. (1993) 'Symptoms of Depression Among Blacks and Whites', *American Journal of Public Health*, **83**(2): 240–4.

Jorm, A.F., Korten, A.E., Jacomb, P.A., Rodgers, B., Pollitt, P., Chrisrtensen, H. (1997) 'Helpfulness of Interventions For Mental Disorders: Beliefs of Health Professionals Compared with the General Public', *British Journal of Psychiatry*, **171**: 233–7.

Jorres, R. and Magnussen, H. (1992). 'Influence of Short-Term Passive Smoking on Symptoms, Lung Mechanics and Airway Responsiveness in Asthmatic Subjects and Healthy Controls', *European Respiratory Journal*, **5**: 936–44.

Jose, B., Friedman, S.R., Neaigus, A., Curtis, R., Sufian, M., Stephenson, A. and Des Jarlais, D.C. (1996) 'Collective Organisation of Injecting Drug Users and the Struggle Against AIDS', in T. Rhodes and R. Hartnoll (Eds.) *AIDS, Drugs and Prevention*. (London: Routledge).

Jubik, A., Plesko, I. and Reissigova, J.(1998) 'Prediction of Lung Cancer Mortality in Four Central European Countries, 1990–2009', *Neoplasma*, 4592): 60–7.

Julien, R. M. (1996) *A Primer of Drug Action* (7th Edition) (W.H. Freeman).

Kahn, A.S. and Jean, P.J. (1983) 'Integration and Elimination Or Separation and Redefinition: The Future of the Psychology of Women', *Signs: Journal of Women in Culture and Society*, **8**: 659–70.

Kalat, J.W.. (1995) *Biological Psychology*. (California: Brookes/Cole Publishing Co).

Kalichman, S.C., Rompa, D., and Muhammad, A. (1997) 'Psychological Predictors of Risk For Human Immunodeficiency Virus (HIV) Infection Among Low-Income Inner-City Men: A Community-Based Survey', *Psychology and Health*, **12**: 493–503.

Kamei, T., Kumano, H. and Masumura, S. (1997) 'Changes of Immunoregulatory Cells Associated with Psychological Stress and Humor', *Perceptual and Motor Skills*, **84**(3) Pt 2: 1296–8.

Kandel, E.R, Schwartz, J.H and Jessell, T.M. (1995) *Essentials of Neural Science and Behaviour*. (London: Prentice Hall International (UK) Ltd).

Kannel, W.B. and Ellison, R.C. (1996) 'Alcohol and Coronary Heart Disease: The Evidence For a Protective Effect', *Clin Chim Acta*, **246**(1–2): 59–76.

Kaplan, B.H. (1975) 'An Epilogue: Toward Further Research on Family and Health', in B.H. Kaplan and J.C. Cassel (Eds.) *Family and Health: An Epidemiological Approach*. University of North Carolina.

Kaplan, R.M., Sallis, J.F. and Patterson. T.L. (1993) *Health and Human Behaviour*. Mcgraw-Hill. New York.

Karasek, R. (1979) 'Job Demands, Job Decision Latitude, and Mental Strain: Implications For Job Redesign', *Administrative Science Quarterly*, **24**: 285–307.

Karasek, R. and Theorell, T. (1990) *Healthy Work: Stress, Productivity and the Reconstruction of Working Life*. Basic Books. New York.

Karper, W. and Hopewell, R. (1998) 'Exercise, Immunity, Acute Respiratory Infections, and Homebound Older Adults', *Home-Care-Provid.*, **3**(1): 41–6.

Kasl, S.V. and Cooper, C.L. (1987) *Stress and Health: Issues in Research Methodology*. (New York: John Wiley).

Kasl, S.V. and Cooper, C.L. (1995) *Research Methods in Stress and Health Psychology*. (New York: John Wiley).

Kavan, M.G., Engdahl, B.E. and Kay, S. (1995) 'Colon Cancer: Personality Factors Predictive of Onset and Stage of Presentation', *Journal of Psychosomatic Research*, **39**(8): 1031–9.

Kavanagh, D.J., Sitharthan, T. and Sayer, G.P. 91996) 'Prediction of Results from Correspondence Treatment For Controlled Drinking', *Addiction*, **91**(10): 1539–45.

Kawachi, I., Kennedy, B.P., Lochner, K. and Prothrow-Stith, D. (1997) 'Social Capital, Income Inequality and Mortality', *American Journal of Public Health*, **87**(9): 1491–9.

Keane, T.M., Taylor, K.L. and Penk, W.E. (1997) 'Differentiating Post-Traumatic Stress Disorder (PTSD) from Major Depression (MDD) and Generalised Anxiety Disorder (GAD)', *Journal of Anxiety Disorders*, **11**(3): 317–28.

Keefe, K. (1994) 'Perceptions of Normative Social Pressure and Attitudes Towards Alcohol Use: Changes During Adolescence', *Journal of Studies on Alcohol*, **55**: 46–54.

Kelly, G.W. (1995) *The Psychology of Personal Constructs*. (New York: W.W. Norton).

Kelly, M.P. (1996) 'Health Education, the Health Promotion Movement, and Communication', *Journal of Biocommunication*, **23**(1): 13–17.

Kendell, R., De Roumanie, M. and Ritson, B. (1983) 'Effect of Economic Changes on Scottish Drinking Habits 1978–82', *British Journal of Addiction*, **75**: 365–80.

Kendell, R.E. (1975) *The Role of Diagnosis in Psychiatry*. (Oxford: Blackwell).

Kennedy, B.P., Kawachi, I., Glass, R. and Prothrow-Stith, D. (1998) 'Income Distribution, Socioeconomic Status, and Self Rated Health in the United States: Multilevel Analysis', *British Medical Journal*, 317: 917–21.

Kertzner, R.M., Goetz, R., Todak, G., Cooper, T., Lin, S., Reddy, M., M., Novacenko, H., Williams, J.B.W., Ehrhardt, A.A. and Gorman, J.M. (1993) 'Cortisol Levels, Immune Status, and Mood in Homosexual Men with and Without HIV Infection', *American Journal of Psychiatry*, 150(11): 1674–86.

Kessler, R., Foster, C., Joseph, J., Ostrow, D., Wortman, C., Phair, J. and Chmiel, J. (1991) 'Stressful Life Events and Symptom Onset in HIV Infection', *American Journal of Psychiatry*, 148(6): 733–7.

Kessler, R.C. (1982) 'A Disaggregation of the Relationship Between Socioeconomic Status and Psychological Distress', *American Sociological Review*, 47: 752–64.

Kewley, G.D. and Orford, E. (1998) 'Attention Deficit Hyperactivity Disorder is Underdiagnosed and Undertreated in Britain. Commentary: Diagnosis Needs Tightening', *British Medical Journal*, 316: 1594–6.

Kewley, G.D. (1998) 'Attention Deficit Hyperactivity Disorder Is Underdiagnosed and Undertreated in Britain', *British Medical Journal*, 316: 1594–6.

Keynon, W.M. (1979) 'Company Policies and Programmes', 16th Annual Report of the Meryside, Lancashire and Cheshire Council on Alcohol.

Kiecolt-Glaser, J.K., Glaser, R., Cacioopo, J.T. Maccallum, R.C., Syndersmith, M., Kim, C. and Malarkey, W.B., (1997) 'Marital Conflict in Older Adults: Endocrinological and Immunological Correlates', *Psychosomatic Medicine*, 59: 339–49.

Kiecolt-Glaser, J.K., Malarkey, W.B., Chee, M., Newton, T., Cacioopo, J.T., Mao, H. and Glaser, R. (1993) 'Negative Behaviour During Marital Conflict Is Associated with Immunological Down Regulation', *Psychosomatic Medicine*, 55: 395–409.

Kihara, H., Teshima, H., Sogawa, H. and Nakagawa, T. (1992) 'Stress and Superoxide Production By Human Neutrophils', *New York Academy of Sciences*, 550: 307–10.

Kinder, B.A., Pape, N.E., and Walfish, B.A. (1980) 'Drug and Alcohol Education Programs: A Review of Outcome Studies', *International Journal of the Addictions*, 15: 1035–1–54.

King, A., Haskell, W., Taylor, C., Kraemer, H. and Debusk, R. (1991) 'Group- Vs Home-Based Exercise Training in Healthy Older Men and Women: A Community-Based Clinical Trial', *Journal of the American Medical Association*, 266: 1532–42.

King, H. and Rewers, M. (1993) 'Global Estimates For Prevalence of Diabetes Mellitus and Impaired Glucose Tolerance in Adults', WHO Ad Hoc Diabetes Reporting Group. *Diabetes Care*, 16(1): 157–77.

Kinsbourne, M., & Lempert, H. (1980). 'Human Figure Representation By Blind Children', *Journal of General Psychology*, 102: 201–9.

Kirschbaum, C., Wust, S. and Hellhammer, D. (1992) 'Consistent Sex Differences in Cortisol Responses to Psychological Stress', *Psychosomatic Medicine*, 54: 648–58.

Kitwood, T. (1990) 'The Dialectics of Dementia: with Particular Reference to Alzheimers Disease', *Ageing and Society*, 10: 177–96.

Kitwood, T. (1996) 'A Dialectical Framework For Dementia', in R.T. Woods (Ed.) *Handbook of the Clinical Psychology of Ageing*. Chapter 14: pp. 267–82. (New York: John Wiley and Sons).

Klag, M.J., Whelton, P.K., Coresh, C.E. and Kuller, L.H. (1991) 'The Association of Skin Colour with Blood Pressure in US Blacks with Low Socioeconomic Status', *Journal of the American Medical Association*, 265(5): 599–602.

Klasky, A.L. (1996) 'Alcohol, Coronary Disease, and Hypertension', *Annual Review of Medicine*, 47: 149–60.

Klesges, R.C., Cigrang, J. and Glasgow, R.E. (1989) 'A Work-Site Smoking Modification Competition: Potential For Public Health Impact', *American Journal of Public Health*, 76: 198–200.

Knight, R G., Devereux, R.C.And Godfrey, H.P. (1997) 'Psychosocial Consequences of Caring For a Spouse with Multiple Sclerosis', *Journal of Clinical and Experimental Neuropsychology*, 19(1): 7–19.

Knight, R.G (1992) *The Neuropsychology of Degenerative Brain Diseases*. (New Jersey: Lawrence Erlbaum Associates).

Knight, R.G. and Godfrey, H.P. (1993) 'The Role of Alcohol-Related Expectancies in the Prediction of Drinking Behaviour in a Simulated Social Interaction', *Addiction*, 88(8): 1111–18.

Knox, S.S. and Follman, D. (1996) 'Gender Differences in the Psychosocial Variance of Framingham and Bortner Type A Measures', *Journal of Psychosomatic Research*, 37(7): 709–16.

Kobak, P.R. and Sceery, A. (1988). 'Attachment in Late Adolescence: Working Models , Affect Regulation, and Perception of Self and Others', *Child Development*, 59: 135–46.

Koester, S. (1996) 'The Process of Drug Injection. Applying Ethnography to the Study of HIV Risk Among Idus', in T. Rhodes and R. Hartnoll (Eds.) *AIDS, Drugs and Prevention*. (London: Routledge).

Konen, J.C., Summerson, J.H. and Dignan, M.B. (1993) 'Family Function, Stress and Locus of Control', Relationship to Glycemia in Adults with Diabetes Mellitus. *Archives of Family Medicine*, 2: 393–402.

Kono, S., Ikeda, M., Tokudome, S., Nishizumi, M. and Kuratsune, M. (1986) 'Alcohol and Mortality: A Cohort Study of Male Japanese Physicians', *International Journal of Epidemiology*, 15(4): 527–32.

Kraemer, R., Dzewaltowski, D., Blair, M., Rinehardt, K. and Castracane, V. (1990) 'Mood Alteration from Treadmill Running and Its Relationship to Beta-Endorphin, Corticotrophin, and Growth Hormone', *Journal of Sports Medicine and Physical Fitness*, 30(3): 241–6.

Krampen, G. and Montada, L. (1998) *Health Psychology*: Bibliographic Results on the Emergence and Rapid Consolidation of a New Field of Research and Application. *Psychology and Health*, 13(6): 1027–36.

Kranczer, S. (1997) 'Statistics Bulletin Metropolitan Insurance Company', 78(4): 2–8.

Krappmann, L. (1996). 'Amicitia, Drujba, Shin-Yu, Philia, Freundschaft, Friendship: on the Cultural Diversity of Human Relationship', in W.M Bukowski, A.F. Newcomb and W.W. Hartup (Eds.), the *Company They Keep: Friendship in Childhood and Adolescence*. (Cambridge: Cambridge University Press).

Kreitman, N. (1982) 'The Perils of Abstention?', *British Medical Journal*, February 13th 284: 444–5.

Krieger, N. (1994) 'Epidemiology and the Web of Causation: Has Anyone See the Spider?', *Social Science and Medicine*, 39: 887–902.

Kristensen, T.S. (1989) 'Cardiovascular Diseases and the Work Environment: A Critical Review of the Epidemiological Literature on Non-Chemical Factors', *Scandinavian Journal of Work, Environment and Health*, **15**: 165–79.

Krupinski, J. (1980) 'Health and Quality of Life', *Social Science and Medicine*, 14A, 203–11.

Kubik, A. and Plesko, I. (1998) 'Trends in Cigarette Sales and Lung Cancer Mortality in Four Central European Countries', *Central European Journal of Public Health*, **6**(1): 37–41.

Kübler-Ross, E. (1970) on *Death and Dying*. (London: Tavistock).

Kübler-Ross, E. (1991) *On Life After Death*. (Berkeley, CA: Celestial Arts).

Kunst, A.E., Groenhof, F., Mackenbach, J.P., and EU Working Group on Socioeconomic Inequalities in Health. (1998) 'Occupational Class and Cause Specific Mortality in Middle Aged Men in 11 European Countries: Comparison of Population Based Studies', *British Medical Journal*, **316**: 1636–42.

Kværner, K.J., Aasland, O.G., and Botten, G.S. (1999) 'Female Medical Leadership: Cross Sectional Study', *British Medical Journal*, **318**: 91–4.

La Vecchia, C., Tavani, A., Franceschi, S., Levi, F., Corrao, G. and Negri, E. (1997) 'Epidemiology and Prevention of Oral Cancer', *Oral Oncology*, 33(5): 302–12.

La Vecchia, C. and Boyle, P. (1993) 'Trends in the Tobacco-Related Cancer Epidemic in Europe', *Cancer Detection and Prevention*, 17(4–5): 495–506.

Labott, S.M., Ahleman, S., Wolever, M.E. and Martin, R.B. (1990) 'The Physiological and Psychological Effects of the Expression and Inhibition of Emotion', *Behavioural Medicine*, **16**(4): 182–9.

Lahelma, E., Manderbacka, K., Rahkonen, O. and Karisto, A. (1994) 'Comparisons of Inequalities in Health: Evidence from National Surveys in Finland, Norway and Sweden', *Social Science and Medicine*, **38**: 517–24.

Laing, R.D. And, Esterson, A. (1964) *Sanity, Madness and the Family*. (London: Tavistock).

Lamb, K.L., Brodie, D.A. and Roberts, K. (1988) 'Physical Fitness and Health Related Fitness as Indicators of a Positive Health State', *Health Promotion*, 3: 171–82.

Lampe, A., Sollner, W., Krismer, M., Rumpold, G., Kantner-Rumplmair, W., Ogon, M., Rathner, G., (1998) 'The Impact of Stressful Life Events on Exacerbation of Chronic Low Back Pain, *Journal of Psychosomatic Research* 44: 555–63

Landgraf, J.M. and Aberz, L.N. (1997) 'Functional Status and Well-Being of Children Representing Three Cultural Groups: Initial Self-Reports Using the CHQ-CF87', *Psychology and Health*, 12(6): 839–54.

Landrine, H., Klonoff, E.A. and Alcaraz, R. (1996) 'Asking Age and Identification May Decrease Minors' Access to Tobacco', *Preventive Medicine*, 25(3): 301–6.

Lask, B., & Bryant-Waugh, R. (1992). 'Early-Onset Anorexia Nervosa and Related Eating Disorders', *Journal of Child Psychiatry*, 33(1): 281–300.

Laugesen, M. and Meads, C. (1991) 'Tobacco Advertising Restrictions, Price, Consumption in OECD Countries, 1960–86', *British Journal of Addictions*, 86: 1343–54.

Lauterbach, D., Vrana, S., King, D.W. and King, L.A. (1997) 'Psychometric Properties of the Civilian Version of the Mississippi PTSD Scale', *Journal of Trauma Stress*, 10(3): 499–513.

Lazarus, R.S. and Folkman, S. (1984) *Stress, Appraisal and Coping*. (New York: Springer).

Leahey, T.H. (1991) *A History of Modern Psychology*. (London: Prentice Hall).

Lee, C. (1997) 'Social Context, Depression and the Transition to Motherhood', *British Journal of Health Psychology*, 2(2): 93–108.

Lee, K. (1979) 'Alcoholism and Cerebrovascular Thrombosis in the Young', *Acta Neurologica Scandinavica*, **59**: 270–4.

Leete, R. and Fox, J. (1977) 'Registrar General's Social Classes: Origins and Uses', *Population Trends*, **8**: 1–7.

Leff, J., Kuipers, L., Berkowitz, R., Eberlein-Vries, R. and Sturgeon, D. (1982) 'A Controlled Trial of Social Intervention in the Families of Schizophrenic Patients', *British Journal of Psychiatry*, **141**: 121–34.

Lefort, S. M., Gray, D. K., Rowat, K. M. and Jeans, M. E. (1998) 'Randomised Controlled Trial of Community-Based Psychoeducation Program For the Self-Management of Pain', *Pain*, **74**: 297–306.

Legrange, D. and Eisler, I. (1993) 'The Link Between Anorexia Nervosa and Excessive Exercise: A Review', *European Eating Disorders Review*, 1(2): 100–119.

Leon. D.A., Chenet,L., Shkolnikov, V.M., Zakharov, S., Shapiro, J., Rakhmanova, G., Vassin, S. and Mckee, M. (1997) 'Huge Variations in Russian Mortality Rates 1984–94: Artefact, Alcohol, Or What?', *The Lancet*, **350**: 9075: 383–8.

Lester, R.J. (1997) 'The (Dis)Embodied Self in Anorexia Nervosa', *Social Science and Medicine*. 44(4): 479–89.

Leventhal, H. (1970) 'Findings and Theory in the Study of Fear Communications', *Advances in Experimental Social Psychology*, 5: 119–86.

Leventhal, H., Diefenbach, M. and Leventhal, E.A. (1992) 'Illness Cognition: Using Common Sense to Understand Treatment Adherence and Affect Cognition Interactions', *Cognitive Therapy and Research*, 16: 143–63.

Levey, S. and Howells, K. (1994). 'Accounting For the Fear of Schizophrenia', *Journal of Community & Applied Social Psychology* 4: 313–28.

Levey, S. and Howells, K. (1995). 'Dangerousness, Unpredictability and the Fear of People with Schizophrenia', *Journal of Forensic Psychiatry* 6(1): 19–39.

Levi, P. (1989) *The Drowned and the Saved*. (London: Abacus).

Lewis-Beck, M.S. (1980) 'Applied Regression: An Introduction', Quantitative Applications in the Social Sciences. Sage University paper: 22.

Lewit, E., Coates, D. and Grossman, M. (1981) 'The Effects of Governmental Regulation on Teenage Smoking', *Journal of Law and Economics*, **24**: 545–69.

Ley, P. (1982) 'Satisfaction, Compliance and Communication', *British Journal of Clinical Psychology*, 21: 241–54.

Ley, P. (1988) *Communicating with Patients*. (London: Croon Helm).

Lieberman, E., Ryan, K.J., Monson, R.R. and Schoenbaum, S.C. (1987) 'Risk Factors Accounting for Racial Differences in the Rate of Premature Birth', *New England Journal of Medicine*, **317**(12): 743–8.

Liebermen, D.A. (1991) *Learning, Behaviour and Cognition*. (2nd Edition). (California: Brookes Cole).

Liebert, R.M. and Liebert, L.L. (1995) *Science and Behaviour* (4th Edition). (Prentice Hall).

Liebow, E. (1967). *Tally's Corner*. Boston: Little, Brown.

Lillie-Blanton, M. and Laveist, T. (1996) 'Race/Ethnicity, the Social Environment, and Health', *Social Science and Medicine*, **43**(1): 83–91.

Lim, H.C., Tan, C.B., Goh, L.G. and Ling, S.L. (1998) 'Why do Patients Complain? A Primary Health Care Study', *Singapore Medical Journal*, **39**(9): 390–5.

Lindblade. K., Foxman, B. and Koopman, J.S. (1994) 'Heterosexual Partnership Characteristics of University Women', *International Journal of Sexually Transmitted Diseases and AIDS*, **5**(1): 37–40.

Link, P.W. and Darling, C.A. (1986) 'Couples Undergoing Treatment For Infertility. Dimensions of Life Satisfaction', *Journal of Sex and Marital Therapy*, **12**: 46–59.

Littlewood, R. and Lipsedge, M. (1988) 'Psychiatric Illness Among British Afro-Caribbeans', *British Medical Journal*, **296**: 950–1.

Littlewood, R. and Lipsedge, M. (1989) *Aliens and Alienists: Ethnic Minorities and Psychiatry* (2nd Edition). Unwin.

Littlewood, R. and Lipsedge, M. (1997) *Aliens and Alienists: Ethnic Minorities and Psychiatry* (3rd Edition). (London: Routledge).

Lockhart, S.P., Carter, Y.H., Straffen, A.M., Pang, K.K., McLoughlin, J. and Baron, J.H. (1986) 'Detecting Alcohol Consumption as a Cause of Emergency General Medical Admissions', *Journal of the Royal Society of Medicine*, **79**(3): 132–6.

Logie, D. (1997) 'Cancellation of Debt of Poorest People Would be Worthy Memorial to Millennium', *British Medical Journal*. Letters, **314**: 1556.

Lowe, C.S. and Radius, S.M. (1982) 'Young Adults Contraceptive Practices: An Investigation of Influences', *Adolescence*, **22**: 291–304.

Lowe, G. (1996) 'Drinking Behaviour and Links with Humour and Laughter', *London Conference of the British Psychological Society*.

Lucas, E.G (1987) 'Alcohol in Industry', *British Medical Journal* February 21st **294**: 460–1.

Lumey, L.H., Pittman, B. and Wynder, E.L. (1998) 'Alcohol Use and Prostate Cancer in U.S. Whites: No Association in a Confirmatory Study', *Prostate*, **36**(4): 250–5.

Lu-Yao, G.L. and Yao,S.L. (1998) 'Population-Based Study of Long Term Survival in Patients with Clinically Localised Prostate Cancer', *The Lancet*, **349**: 906–10.

Lynch, J.W., Smith, G.D., Kaplan, G.A. and House, J.S. (2000) 'Income Inequality and Mortality: Importance to Health of Individual, Psychosocial Environment, Or Material Conditions', *British Medical Journal*, **320**: 1200–4.

Macdonald, K.G., Doan, B., Kelner, M. and Taylor, K.M. (1996). 'A Sociobehavioural Perspective on Genetic Testing and Counselling For Heritable Breast, Ovarian and Colon Cancer', CMAJ, **154**(4): 457–64

Macintyre, S. (1997) 'The Black Report and Beyond: What are the Issues?', *Social Science and Medicine*, **44**(6) 723–46.

Mackay, J. and Crofton, J. (1996) 'Tobacco and the Developing World', *British Medical Bulletin*, **52**(1): 206–21.

Mackenbach, J.P. (1992) 'Socio-Economic Health Differences in the Netherlands: A Review of Recent Empirical Findings', *Social Science and Medicine*, **34**: 213–26.

Mackenzie, A., Funderburk, F.R. and Allen, R.P. (1994) 'Controlled Drinking in Alcoholic Men: Beliefs Influence Actions', *International Journal of the Addictions*, **29**(11): 1377–92.

Mackinnon, L.T. (1998) 'Future Directions in Exercise and Immunology: Regulation and Integration', *International Journal of Sports Medicine*, Suppl 3: S205–9; Discussion S209–11.

Madakasira, S. and O'Brien, K. (1987) 'Acute Post-Traumatic Stress Disorder in Victims of a Natural Disaster', *Journal of Nervous and Mental Disease*, **175**: 286–90.

Magaziner, J., Hebel, R. and Warren, J.W. (1987) 'The Use of Proxy Responses For Aged Patients in Long-Term Care Settings', *Comprehensive Gerontology*, Section B, 118–21.

Magruder-Habib, K., Stevens, H.A. and Alling, W.A. (1993) 'Relative Performance of the MAST, VAST, and CAGE Versus DSM-III-R Criteria For Alcohol Dependence', *Journal of Clinical Epidemiology*, **46**(5): 435–41.

Maguire, C.P., Kirby, M., Coen, R., Coakley, Lawlor, B.A. and O'Neill, D. (1996) 'Family Members' Attitudes Toward Telling the Patient with Alzheimer's Disease their Diagnosis', *British Medical Journal*, **313**: 529–30.

Maier, S.F. and Watkins, L.R. (1999) 'Bidirectional Communication Between the Brain and the Immune System: Implications For Behaviour', *Animal Behaviour*, S7: 741–51.

Maier, S.F., Watkins, L.R. and Fleshner, M. (1994) 'Psychoneuroimmunology: The Interface Between Behaviour, Brain and Immunity', *American Psychologist*, **49**(12) 1004–17.

Mäkelä, K. (1997) 'Drinking, the Majority Fallacy, Cognitive Dissonance, and Social Pressure', *British Journal of Addictions*. in Press.

Mangan, G.L. and Golding, J.F. (1984) *The Psychopharmacology of Smoking*. (Cambridge: Cambridge University Press).

Mann, C. C. (1995) 'Epidemiology Faces Its Limits', *Science*, **269**: 164–69.

Manstead, A.S.R. (1992) 'Gender Differences in Emotion', in M.W. Eysenck and A. Gale (Eds.) *Handbook of Individual Differences*. (New York: John Wiley).

Maras, P. (1995) 'Whats 'E Doing 'Ere Then?', *The Psychologist*, **8**: 410–11.

Marcenes, W.S. and Sheiham, A.(1992) 'The Relationship Between Work Stress and Oral Health Status', *Social Science and Medicine*, **35**(12): 1511–20.

Marmot, M. (1996) 'The Social Pattern of Health and Disease', in D. Blane, E. Brunner and R. Wilkinson (Eds.) *Health and Social Organisation: Towards a Health Policy For the 21st Century*. (London: Routledge).

Marmot, M. (1997) 'Inequality, Deprivation and Alcohol Use', *Addiction*, **92**: Supp 1; S13–20.

Marmot, M. and Brunner, E. (1991) 'Alcohol and Cardiovascular Disease: The Status of the U-Shaped Curve', *British Medical Journal*, **303**: 565–8.

Marmot, M. and Feeney, A. (1996) 'Work and Health', in D. Blane, E. Brunner and R. Wilkinson (Eds.) *Health and Social Organisation: Towards a Health Policy For the 21st Century*. (London: Routledge).

Marmot, M. and Madge, N. (1987) 'An Epidemiological Perspective on Stress and Health', in S.V. Kasl and C.L. Cooper (Eds.) *Stress and Health: Issues in Research Methodology*. (Chichester: John Wiley).

Marmot, M., Ryff, C.D., Bumpass, L.L., Shipley, M. and Marks, N.F. (1997a) 'Social Inequalities in Health: Next Questions and Converging Evidence', *Social Science and Medicine*, **44**(6): 901–10.

Marmot, M.G., Adelstein, A.M. and Bulusu, L. (1984) 'Lessons from the Study of Immigrant Mortality', *The Lancet*, **1**(8392): 1455–7.

Marmot, M.G., Bosma, H., Hemingway, H., Brunner, E. and Stansfeld, S. (1997b) 'Contribution of Job Control and Other

Risk Factors to Social Variations in Coronary Heart Disease Incidence', *The Lancet*, 350: 235–9.

Marmot, M.G., Davey Smith, G.D., Stansfield, S., Patel, C., North, F., Head, J., White, I., Brunner, E. and Feeney, A. (1991) *Health Inequalities* Among British Civil Servants: The Whitehall II Study. *The Lancet*. June 8th, 1387–93.

Marmot, M.G., Shipley, M.J., and Rose, G. (1984) 'Inequalities in Death – Specific Explanations of a General Pattern?', *Lancet*, I, 1003–6.

Marsh, C. (1986) 'Medicine and the Media', *British Medical Journal*, 292: 953.

Marshall, G., Rose, D., Newby, H. and Vogler, C. (1989) *Social Class in Modern Britain*. (London: Unwin Hyman).

Marshall, J.R. and Funch, D.P. (1986) 'Gender and Illness Behaviour Among Colorectal Patients', *Women Health*, 11(3–4): 67–82.

Martin, R.A. and Lefcourt, H.M. (1983) 'Sense of Humour as a Moderator of the Relation Between Stressors and Moods', *Journal of Personality and Social Psychology*, 45: 1313–24.

Matarazzo, J.D. (1980) 'Behavioural Health and Behavioural Medicine: Frontiers For a New Health Psychology', *American Psychologist*, 35: 807–17.

Maxwell, K. and Streetly, A. (1998) 'Living with Sickle Cell Pain', *Nursing Standard*, 13(9): 33.

Mayfield, D., McLeod, G. and Hall, P. (1974) 'The CAGE Questionnaire: Validation of a New Alcoholism Screening Instrument', *American Journal of Psychiatry*, 131: 1121–3.

Maynard, A. (1986) 'Economic Aspects of Addiction Policy', *Health Promotion*, 1(1): 61–71.

Mayne, T.J., O'Leary, A., Mcgrady, B., Contrada, R. and La- bouvie, E. (1997) 'The Differential Effects of Acute Marital Distress on Emotional Physiological and Immune Functions in Maritally Distressed Men and Women', *Psychology and Health*, 12: 277–88.

Mayne, T.J., O'Leary, A.O., Mccrady, B., Contrada, R. and Labouvie, E. (1997) 'The Differential Effects of Acute Marital Distress on Emotional, Physiological and Immune Functions in Maritally Distressed Men and Women', *Psychology and Health*, 12(2): 277–88.

Mayor, S. (1999) 'Swedish Study Questions Mammography Screening Programmes', *British Medical Journal*, 318: 621.

Maza, G., G. (1996) 'Structuring Effective User Involvement. in T. Heller, J. Reynolds, R. Gomm, R. Muston and S. Pattison (Ed) *Mental Health Matters*. The Open University. (London: Macmillan).

McCarthy, M. (1989) 'The Benefit of Seat Belt Legislation in the United Kingdom', *Journal of Epidemiology and Public Health*, 43(3): 218–22.

McCarthy, M., Addington-Hall, J. and Altmann, D. (1997) 'The Experience of Dying with Dementia: A Retrospective Study', *International Journal of Geriatric Psychiatry*, 12(3): 404–9.

McCauley, M., Mintz, L. and Glenn, A. (1988) 'Body Image, Self Esteem, and Depression Proneness: Closing the Gender Gap', *Sex Roles*, 15(3/4): 185–95.

McClelland, D.C. and Cheriff, A.D. (1997) 'The Immuno- enhancing Effects of Humour on Secretory Iga and Resistance to Respiratory Infections', *Psychology and Health*, 12(3): 329– 44.

McDowell, I. and Newell, C. (1987) *Measuring Health: A Guide to Rating Scales and Questionnaires*. (Oxford: Oxford University Press).

McDowell, I. and Newell, C. (1996) *Measuring Health: A Guide to Rating Scales and Questionnaires*. (2nd Edition) (Oxford: Oxford University Press).

McElduff, P. and Dobson, A.J. (1997) 'How Much Alcohol and How Often? Population Based Case-Control Study of Alcohol Consumption and Risk of a Major Coronary Event', *British Medical Journal*, 314: 1159–64.

McEwan, R. and Bhopal, R. (1991) 'HIV/AIDS Health Promo- tion For Young People: A Review of Theory, Principles and Practice', *Health Education Authority*. London.

McFarlane, A.C. (1989). 'Blindness and Anorexia Nervosa', *Canadian Journal of Psychiatry*, 34: 431–3.

McGee, H.M., O'Boyle, C.A., Hickey, A., O'Malley, K. and Joyce, C.R.B. (1991) 'Assessing the Quality of Life of the Individual: The Seiqol in a Healthy and a Gastroenterology Unit Popula- tion', *Psychological Medicine*, 21: 749–59.

McGhee, R., Williams, S. and Elwood, M. (1994) 'Depression and the Development of Cancer – A Meta-Analysis', *Social Science and Medicine*, 26(3): 441–7.

McGovern, D. and Cope, R. (1987a) 'First Psychiatric Admission Rates of First and Second Generation Afro Caribbeans', *Social Psychiatry*, 22(3): 139–49.

McGovern, D. and Cope, R. (1987b) 'The Compulsory Detention of Males of Different Ethnic Groups, with Special Reference to Offender Patients', *British Journal of Psychiatry*, 150: 505–12.

McGrath, T. (1991) 'Overcoming Institutionalized Child Abuse: Creating a Positive Climate', *Journal of Child and Youth Care*, 6(4): 61–8.

McHorney, C.A., Ware, J.E., Rogers, W., Raczek, A.E. and Rachel, J.F. (1992) 'The Validity and Relative Precision of MOS Short and Long- Form Health Status Scales and Dart- mouth COOP Charts', *Medical Care*, 30(Suppl): 235–65.

McIntyre, S. (1993) 'Gender Differences in the Perceptions of Common Cold Symptoms', *Social Science and Medicine*, 36(1): 15–20.

McIntyre, S. and Pritchard, C. (1989) 'Comparisons Between Self-Assessed and Observer Assessed Presence and Severity of Colds', *Social Science and Medicine*, 29(11): 1243–8.

McIntyre, S., Hunt, K. and Sweeting, H. (1996) 'Gender Differ- ences in Health. Are Things Really as Simple as They Seem?', *Social Science and Medicine*, 42(4): 617–24.

McKeigue, P.M., Shah, B. and Marmot, M.G. (1991) 'The Rela- tion of Central Obesity and Insulin Resistance with High Dia- betes Prevalence and Cardiovascular Risk in South Asians', *The Lancet*, 337: 382–6.

McKenna, M.C., Zevon, M.A., Corn, B. and Rounds, J. (1999) 'Psychosocial Factors and the Development of Breast Cancer: A Meta-analysis', *Health Psychology*, 18(5): 520–31.

McManus, M. (1997) 'Factors Affecting Likelihood of Applicants Being Offered a Place in Medical Schools in the United King- dom in 1996 and 1997: Retrospective Study', *British Medical Journal*, 317: 1111–15.

McManus, M.,Richards, P. and Winder, B.C. (1998) 'Clinical Experience of UK Medical Students', *The Lancet*, 351: 9105: 802.

McNair, D.M., Lorr, M. and Droppleman, L.F. (1992) 'Edits Manual For the Profile of Mood States (POMS)', San Diego, California; Edits/Educational and Industrial Testing Service.

Meadows, S.H. (1961) 'Social Class Migration and Chronic Bronchitis', *Journal of Preventative and Social Medicine*, 15: 171–6.

Meenan, R.F. (1982) 'The AIMS Approach to Health Status Measurement: Conceptual Background and Measurement Properties', *Journal of Rheumatology*, 9: 785–8.

Mel'nikova, T.S. (1993). 'Thresholds of Pain Responses to Electric Stimuli in Patients with Endogenous Depression', Patol Fiziol Eksp Ter 4: 19–21.

Menezes, P.R., Johnson, S., Thornicroft, G., Marshall, J., Prosser, D., Bebbington, P. and Kuipers, E. (1996) 'Drug and Alcohol Problems Among Individuals with Severe Mental Illness in South London', *British Journal of Psychiatry*, 168(5): 612–19.

Merrill, J. and Owens, J. (1988) 'Psychiatric Illness among British Afro-Caribbeans', *British Medical Journal*, (Clin Res Ed), 296(6631): 1260.

Michels, T. and Kugler, J. (1998) 'Predicting Exercise in Older Americans: Using the Theory of Planned Behaviour', *Military Medicine*, 163(8): 524–9.

Middleton, L. (1992) *Children First: Working with Children and Disability*. Birmingham: Venture Press.

Midence, K., Fuggle, P. and Davies, S.C. (1993) 'Psychosocial Aspects of Sickle Cell Disease (SCD) in Childhood and Adolescence: A Review', *British Journal of Clinical Psychology*, 32(Pt 3): 271–80.

Miles, M.B. and Huberman, A.M. (1994) *Qualitative Data Analysis* (2nd Edition). (London: Sage).

Miller, G.E., Kemeny, M.E., Taylor, S.E., Cole, S.W. and Visscher, B.R. (1997) 'Social Relationships and Immune Processes in HIV Seropositive Gay and Bisexual Men', *Annals of Behavioural Medicine*, 19(2): 139–51.

Miller, J.B. (1986) *Toward a New Psychology of Women*. (Boston, MA: Beacon).

Miller, N.S. (1995) 'History and Review of Contemporary Addiction Treatment', *Alcoholism Treatment Quarterly*, 12(2): 1–22.

Miller, P.M., Smith, G.T. and Goldman, M.S. (1990) 'Emergence of Alcohol Expectancies in Childhood: a Possible Critical Period', *Journal of Studies on Alcohol*, 51(4): 343–9.

Miller, T.Q., Smith, T.W., Turner, C.W., Guijarro, M.L. and Hallet, A.J. (1996) 'A Meta-Analytic Review on Hostility and Physical Health', *Psychological Bulletin*, 119: 322–48.

Miller, W.R., and Rollnick, S. (1991). *Motivational Interviewing: Preparing People to Change Addictive Behaviour*. New York: Guildford.

Minchin, M. (1998) 'ADHD: Prevention as Well as Treatment?', *Electronic British Medical Journal* (2 June).

Minden, S.L. and Schiffer, R.B. (1990) 'Affective Disorders in Multiple Sclerosis. Review and Recommendations for Clinical Research', *Archives of Neurology*, 47(1): 98–104.

Mitchell, J.E., Fletcher, L., Gibean, L., Pyle, R.L., & Eckert, E. (1992). 'Shoplifting in Bulimia Nervosa', *Comprehensive Psychiatry*, 33: 342–5.

Mittwoch-Jaffe, T., Shalit F., Srendi, B. and Yehuda, S. (1995). 'Modification of Cytokine Secretion Following Mild Emotional Stimuli', *Neuroreport* 6: 789–92.

Molvaer, J., Hantzi, A. and Papadatos, Y. (1992) 'Psychotic Patients' Attributions For Mental Illness', *British Journal of Clinical Psychology* 31: 210–12.

Moncrieff, J., Drummond, D.C., Candy, B., Checinski, K. and Farmer, R. (1996) 'Sexual Abuse in People with Alcohol Problems. A Study of the Prevalence of Sexual Abuse and Its Relationship to Drinking Behaviour', *British Journal of Psychiatry*, 169(3): 255–360.

Montazeri, A. (1997) 'Social Marketing: a Tool Not a Solution', *Journal of the Royal Society of Health*, 117(2): 115–18.

Mookherjee HN (1997) 'Marital Status, Gender, and Perception of Well-Being', *Journal of Social Psychology*, 137(1): 95–105.

Moore, M., Beazley, S. and Maelzer, J. (1998) *Researching Disabilty Issues*. (Buckingham: Open University Press).

Morgan, M. (1998) 'Qualitative Research. Science Or Pseudo-Science? *The Psychologist*, 1(10): 481–3 & Postscript, 488.

Morgan, M., Rapkin, A..J., Delia, L., Reading, A. and Goldman, L. (1996) 'Cognitive Functioning in Premenstrual Syndrome', *Obstetrics and Gynecology*, 88(6): 961–6.

Morgan, S.R. (1987) *Abuse and Neglect of Handicapped Children*. (San Diego: Little-Brown).

Morgan, W., Costill, D., Flynn, M., Raglin, J. and O'Conner, P. (1988) 'Mood Disturbance Followed Increased Training in Swimmers', *Medicine and Science in Sports and Exercise*, 20: 408–14.

Morris, J. (1991) *Pride Against Prejudice*. (London: The Women's Press).

Morris, J. (1995) *Gone Missing? A Research and Policy Review of Disabled Children Living Away from their Families*. (London: The Who Cares Trust).

Morris, J. (Ed.) (1996) *Encounters with Strangers. Feminism and Disability*. (London: The Women's Press).

Morris, J.N. and Hardman, A.E. (1997) 'Walking to Health', *Sports Medicine*, 23: 306–32.

Morris, K. (1998) 'UK Experts Advise Against Prostate Cancer Screening', *The Lancet*, 349: 477.

Moynihan, C., Horwich, A. and Bliss, J. (1999) 'Counselling Is Not Appropriate For All Patients with Cancer', *British Medical Journal*, 318: 128.

Mueller, N. and Ackenheil, M. (1998) 'Psychoneuroimmunology and the Cytokine Action in the CNS: Implications For Psychiatric Disorders', *Progress in Neuro-Psychopharmacology and Biological Psychiatry*, 22(1): 1–33.

Mukherjee, S., Shukla, S., Woodle, J., Rosen, A.M. and Olarte, S. (1983) 'Misdiagnosis of Schizophrenia in Bipolar Patients: A Multiethnic Comparison', *American Journal of Psychiatry*, 140(12): 1571–4.

Muldoon, M.F., Barger, S.D., Flory, J.D. and Manuck, S.B. (1998) 'What are Quality of Life Measurements Measuring? *British Medical Journal*, 316: 542–5.

Mulhall, B.P. (1996) 'Sex and Travel: Studies of Sexual Behaviour, Disease and Health Promotion in International Travellers – A Global Review', (Editorial). *International Journal of Sexually Transmitted Diseases and AIDS*, 7(7): 455–65.

Multiple Risk Factor Intervention Trial Research Group (1982) 'The Multiple Risk Factor Intervention Trial – Risk Factor Changes and Mortality Results', *Journal of the American Medical Association*, 248: 1465–76.

Murray, M. and Mcmillan, C. (1993) 'Health Beliefs, Locus of Control, Emotional Control and Women's Cancer Screening Behaviour', *British Journal of Clinical Psychology*, 32: 87–100.

Murrell, R.C., Kenealy, P.M., Beaumont, J.G. and Lintern, T. (1999) 'Assessing Quality of Life in Persons with Severe Neurological Disability Associated with Multiple Sclerosis: The Psychometric Evaluation of Two Quality of Life Meaures', *British Journal of Health Psychology*, 4: 349–62.

Myers, D.G. (1992). *The Pursuit of Happiness: Who Is Happy and Why?* (New York: Morrow).

Nair, M.P., Saravolatz, L.D. and Scwartz, S.A. (1995) 'Selective

Inhibitory Effects of Stress Hormones on Natural Killer (NK) Cell Activity of Lymphocytes from AIDS Patients', *Immunological Investigations*, **24**(5): 6689–99.

Nanchahal, K. (1994) 'A Possible Mechanism Underlying the Relationship Between Socioeconomic Status and Cardiovascular Disease', M.Sc Thesis. (London: University College).

Nasrallah, H.A., Schroeder, D. and Petty, F. (1982) 'Alcoholism Secondary to Essential Tremor', *Journal of Clinical Psychiatry*, **43**: 163–4.

National Institutes of Health (1998) 'Economic Costs of Alcohol and Drug Abuse Estimated At $246 Billion in the United States. NIH News Release.

Nattiv, A., Puffer, J. and Green, G. (1997) 'Lifestyles and Health Risks of Collegiate Athletes: A Multi-Centre Study', *Clinical Journal of Sport Medicine*, **7**(4): 262–72.

Neugarten, B.L. and Datan, N. (1974) 'The Middle Years', in Arieti, S. (Ed.) *American Handbook of Psychiatry, Vol.1*. New York: Basic Books.

Neumarker, K.J. (1997) 'Mortality and Sudden Death in Anorexia Nervosa', *International Journal of Eating Disorders*. **21**(3): 205–12.

Neumark-Sztainer, D. (1996) 'School-Based Programs For Preventing Eating Disturbances', *Journal of School Health*. **66**(2): 64–71.

Newcomb, M.D. (1990) 'Social Support and Personal Characteristics: A Developmental and Interactional Perspective', *Journal of Social and Clinical Psychology*, **9**: 54–68.

Newcombe, R., Measham, F. and Parker, H. (1995) 'A Survey of Drinking and Deviant Behaviour among 14/15 Year-Olds in North West England', *Addiction Research*, **2**(3): 19–41.

Newlands, M. and Emery, J.S. (1991) 'Child Abuse and Cot Deaths', *Child Abuse and Neglect*, 1593): 275–8.

Newman, M. G. and Stone, A. A. (1996) 'Does Humor Moderate the Effects of Experimentally-Induced Stress?', *Annals of Behavioural Medicine* **18**: 101–9.

Nguyen, M., Potvin, L. and Otis, J. (1997) 'Regular Exercise in 30- to 60-Year Old Men: Combining Stages-of-Change Model and the Theory of Planned Behaviour to Identify Determinants For Targeting Heart Health Interventions', *Journal of Community Health*, **22**(4): 233–46.

Nicolson, P. (1986) 'Developing a Feminist Approach to Depression Following Childbirth', in S. Wilkinson (Ed.) *Feminist Social Psychology*. (Buckingham: Open University).

Nicolson, P. (1989) 'Counselling Women with Post Natal Depression', *Counselling Psychology Quarterly*, **2**(2): 123–32.

Nicolson, P. (1998) *Post-Natal Depression: Psychology, Science and the Transition to Motherhood*. (London: Routledge).

Nicolson, P. and Ussher, J. (Eds.) (1992*) The Psychology of Women's Health and Health Care*. (London: Macmillan).

Norman, R.M.G. and Malla, A.K. (1983) 'Adolescents' Attitudes Towards Mental Illness: Relationship Between Components and Sex Differences', *Social Psychiatry* **18**: 45–50.

Norman, R.M.G. and Malla, A.K. (1993a) 'Stressful Life Events and Schizophrenia I. A Review of the Research', *British Journal of Psychiatry*, **162**: 161–6.

Norman, R.M.G. and Malla, A.K. (1993b) 'Stressful Life Events and Schizophrenia II. Conceptual and Methodological Issues', *British Journal of Psychiatry*, **162**: 166–74.

Notzer, N., Eldad, N. and Donchin, Y. (1995) 'Assessment of Physician Competence in Prehospital Trauma Care', *Injury*, **26**(7): 471–4.

Nouri, F.M. and Lincoln, N.B. (1987) 'An Extended Activities of Daily Living Scale For Stroke Patients', *Clinical Rehabilitation*, **1**: 301–5.

Nunnally, J.C. (1961) *'Popular Conceptions of Mental Health*. (New York: Holt, Rinehart & Winston).

Nutbeam, D., Macaskill, P., Smith, C., Simpson, J.M. and Catford, J. (1993) 'Evaluation of Two School Smoking Education Programmes Under Normal Classroom Conditions', *British Medical Journal*, **306**: 102–7.

O'Boyle, C. (1994) 'The Schedule For the Evaluation of Individual Quality of Life (Seiqol). *International Journal of Mental Health*, **23**(3): 3–23.

O'Boyle, C. (1997) 'Quality of Life Assessment: A Paradigm Shift', *The Irish Journal of Psychology*, **18**(1): 51–66.

O'Boyle, C. and Waldron, D. (1997) 'Quality of Life Issues in Palliative Medicine', *Journal of Neurology*. **244**: Suppl 4: S18–25.

O'Brien, L.,S. (1998) *Traumatic Events and Mental Health*. (Cambridge: Cambridge University Press).

O'Callaghan, A. and Mead, G.M. (1997) 'Testicular Carcinoma', *Postgraduate Medical Journal*, **73**(862): 481–6.

O'Leary, A., Goodhart, F., Jemmott, L.S., Boccher-Latimore, D. (1992) 'Predictors of Safer Sexual Behaviour on the College Campus: A Social Cognitive Theory Analysis', *Journal of the American College Health*, **40**: 254–63.

Oakley, A. (1980) *Women Confined: Towards Sociology of Childbirth*. (Oxford: Martin Robertson).

Oakley, A., Fullerton, D., Holland, J., Arnold, S., France-Dawson, M., Kelley, P. and Mcgrellis, S. (1995) 'Sexual Health Education Interventions For Young People: A Methodological Review', *British Medical Journal*, **310**: 158–62.

Office For National Statistics (1997) *Health Inequalities* Supplementary Dataset. Government Statistical Service.

Office of Population Censuses and Surveys (OPCS) (1978) *Occupational Mortality 1970–2*. (London: HMSO).

Office of Population Censuses and Surveys (OPCS) (1996) *Living in Britain: Results from the 1994 General Household Survey*. (London: HMSO).

Ogden, J. (1996) *Health Psychology: A Textbook*. (Buckingham: Open University Press).

Ojanen, M. (1992) 'Attitudes Towards Mental Patients', *International Journal of Social Psychiatry* **38**(2): 120–30.

Olivardia, R., Harrison, G.P., Mangweth, B., & Hudson, J.I. (1995) 'Eating Disorders in College Men', *American Journal of Psychiatry*. **152**: 9. 1279–85.

Oliver, M. (1996) *Understanding Disability. From Theory to Practice*. Macmillan Press. Basingstoke.

Oliver, M. (1998) 'Theories of Disability in Health Practice and Research', *British Medical Journal*, **317**: 1446–9.

Oliver, M. and Barnes, C. (1998) *Disabled People and Social Policy: From Exclusion to Inclusion*. Longman.

Olmsted, M.P., Kaplan, A.S., Rockert, W. and Jacobsen, M. (1996) 'Rapid Responders to Intensive Treatment of Bulimia Nervosa', *International Journal of Eating Disorders*, **19**(3): 279–85.

Olsen, R. and Sutton, J. (1998) 'More Hassle, More Alone: Adolescents with Diabetes and the Role of Formal and Informal Support', *Child Care Health and Development*, **24**(1): 31–9.

Ong, L.M., De Haes, J.C., Hoos, A.M. and Lammes, F.B. (1995) 'Doctor-Patient Communication: A Review of the Literature', *Social Science and Medicine*, **40**(7): 903–18.

Onwuanyi, A., Hodges, D., Avancha, A., Weiss, L., Rabinowitz, D., Shea, S. and Francis, C.K. (1998) 'Hypertensive Vascular Disease as a Cause of Death in Blacks versus Whites: Autopsy Findings in 587 Adults', *Hypertension*, **31**(5): 1070–6.

Orbell, S. and Sheeran, P. (1998) ''Inclined Abstainers': A Problem For Predicting Health-Related Behaviour', *British Journal of Social Psychology*, **37**(2): 151–65.

Orford, J. (1985) *Excessive Appetites*. (London: John Wiley).

Orford, J. and Velleman, R. (1991) 'The Environmental Intergenerational Transmission of Alcohol Problems: A Comparison of Two Hypotheses', *British Journal of Medical Psychology*, **64**: 189–200.

Ornstein, S.I. (1980) 'Control of Alcohol Consumption Through Price Increase', *Journal of Studies on Alcohol*, **41**(9): 807–18.

Ornstein, S.I. and Levy, D. (1983) 'Price and income elasticities of demand for alcoholic beverages' 'Recent Developments in Alcohol', **1**: 303–45.

Östergren, P-O. (1991) *Psychosocial Resources and Health*. University of Lund. Malmo. Sweden.

Otten, M.W., Teutsch, S.M., Williamson, D.F. and Marks, J.S. (1990) 'The Effect of Known Risk Factors on the Excess Mortality of Black Adults in the United States', *Journal of the American Medical Association*, **263**: 845–50.

Packard, V. (1972). *A Nation of Strangers*. (New York: David Mckay).

Paisley, C.M. and Sparks, P. (1998) 'Expectations of Reducing Fat Intake. The Role of Perceived Need Within the Theory of Planned Behaviour', *Psychology and Health*, **13**: 341–53.

Pallanti, S., Quercioli, L. and Pazzagli, A. (1997) 'Relapse in Young Paranoid Schizophrenic Patients: A Prospective Study of Stressful Life Events, P300 Measures and Coping', *American Journal of Psychiatry*, **154**: 792–8.

Pappas, G. (1994) 'Elucidating the Relationships Between Race, Socioeconomic Status, and Health', *American Journal of Public Health*, **84**(6): 892–3.

Parazzini, F., Chatenoud, L., La Vecchia, C., Negri, E., Franceschi, S. and Bolis, G. (1998) 'Determinants of Risk of Invasive Cervical Cancer in Young Women', *British Journal of Cancer*, **77**(5): 838–41.

Parker E.S., Parker D.A., and Harford T.C. (1991) 'Specifying the Relationship Between Alcohol Consumption and Cognitive Functioning', *Journal of Studies on Alcohol*, **52**(4): 366–73.

Parkes, C. (1998) 'Coping with Loss; the Dying Adult', *British Medical Journal*, **316**: 1313–15.

Parlee, M.B. (1979) 'The Friendship Bond', *Psychology Today*, **13**: 43–54.

Parsons, H. (1999) 'More Doctors Would Aid Communication', *British Medical Journal*, **319**: 717.

Patrick, D.L. and Deyo, R.A. (1989) 'Generic and Disease Specific Measures in Assessing Health Status and Quality of Life', *Medical Care*, **27**(3) Supplement, 217–32.

Pattison, J. (1997) 'Hypnotherapy: Complementary Support in Cancer Care', *Nursing Standard*, **11**(52): 44–6.

Patton, G.C., Johnson-Sabine, E., Wood, K., Mann, A.H. and Wakeling, A. (1990) 'Abnormal Eating Attitudes in London Schoolgirls – A Prospective Epidemiological Study: Outcome At 12 Month Follow-Up', *Psychological Medicine*, **20**: 383–94.

Pearce, W. and English, M. (1997) 'Childhood and Adolescent Anorexia Nervosa the Refusal of Food Or the Control of Experience?', *Paediatric Nursing Review*. **10**(1): 4–8.

Pearlman, R.A. and Uhlmann, R.F. (1988) 'Quality of Life in Chronic Diseases: Perceptions of Elderly Patients', *Journal of Gerontology*, **43**: M25–30.

Peate, I. (1997) 'Testicular Cancer: The Importance of Effective Health Education', *British Journal of Nursing*, **6**(6): 311–16.

Pekkanen, J., Tuomilehto, J., Uutela, A., Vartiainen and Nissinen, A. (1995) 'Social Class, Health Behaviour, and Mortality Among Men and Women in Eastern Finland', *British Medical Journal*, 311: 589–93.

Pekurinen, M. (1989) 'The Demand For Tobacco Products in Finland', *British Journal of Addiction*, **84**: 1183–92.

Perry, B.D., Poland, R.A., Blakely, T.L., Baker, W.L. and Vigilante, D. (1995) 'Childhood Trauma, the Neurobiology of Adaptation, Use-Dependent Development of the Brain, Flaw States Become Traits', *Infant Medical Health Journal*, **16**: 271–91.

Peterson, D. (Ed.) (1982) *A Mad People's History of Madness*. (University of Pittsburgh Press).

Peterson, D., Zeger, S., Remington, R. and Anderson, H. (1992) 'The Effect of State Cigarette Tax Increases on Cigarette Sales 1955 to 1988', *American Journal of Public Health*, **82**: 94–6.

Pettigrew, M., Fraser, J.M. and Regan, M.F. (1999) 'Adverse Life-events and Risk of Breast Cancer: A Meta analysis', *British Journal of Health Psychology*, **4**(1): 1–18.

Phillips, A.N. and Davey Smith, G.(1991) 'How Independent are "Independent" Effects? Relative Risk Estimation When Correlated Exposures are Measured Imprecisely', *Journal of Clinical Epidemiology*, **44**(11): 1223–31.

Phillips, D. (1996) 'Medical Professional Dominance and Client Dissatisfaction. A Study of Doctor-Patient Interaction and Reported Dissatisfaction with Medical Care Among Female Patients At Four Hospitals in Trinidad and Tobago', *Social Science and Medicine*, **42**(10): 1419–25.

Phillips, D.I.W. (1993) 'Twin Studies in Medical Research: Can They Tell Us Whether Diseases are Genetically Determined?', *The Lancet*, **341**: 1008–9.

Phillips, K. (1991) 'The Primary Prevention of AIDS', in Phillips, K. and Pitts. M. (Ed) *The Psychology of Health*. (London: Routledge).

Phipps, S. and Srivastava, D.K. (1997) 'Repressive Adaptation in Children with Cancer', *Health Psychology*, **16**(6): 521–8.

Piachaud, D. and Webb, J. (1996) *The Price of Food: Missing Out on Mass Consumption*. STICERD. London.

Pierce, E., Rohaly, K. and Fritchley, B. (1997) 'Sex Differences on Exercise Dependence For Men and Women in a Marathon Race', *Perceptual and Motor Skills*, **84**(3): 991–4.

Pike, J.L., Smith, T.L., Hauger, R.L., Nicassio, P.M.,Patterson, T.L., Mcclintock, J., Costlow, C. and Irwin, M.R. (1997) 'Chronic Life Stress Alters Sympathetic, Neuroendocrine and Immune Responsivity to an Acute Psychological Stressor in Humans', *Psychosomatic Medicine*, **59**(4): 447–57.

Pikó, B. (1998) 'Social Support and Health in Adolescence: A Factor Analytic Study', *British Journal of Health Psychology*, **3**: 333–44.

Pilgrim, D. (2000) 'Psychiatric Diagnosis: More Questions Than Answers', *The Psychologist*, **13**(6): 302–5.

Pilgrim, D. and Rogers, A. (1993) *A Sociology of Mental Health and Illness*. (Buckingham: Open University Press).

Pilgrim, D. and Rogers, A. (1996) 'Two Notions of Risk in Mental Health Debates', in T.Heller, J. Reynolds, R. Gomm, R. Muston and S.Pattison (Eds.) *Mental Health Matters*. The Open University. (London: Macmillan).

Pill, R. and Stott, N. (1981) 'Relationship Between Health Locus of Control and Belief in the Relevance of Lifestyle to Health', *Patient Counselling and Health Education*, **3**: 95–9.

Pinerua-Shuhaibar, L., Prieto-Rincon, D., Ferrer, A., Bonilla, E., and Maixner Suarez-Roca, H. (1999) 'Reduced Tolerance and Cardiovascular Responses to Ischemic Pain in Minor Depression', *Journal of Affective Disorders* **56**: 119–26.

Pitts, M. (1996) *The Psychology of Preventive Health*. (London: Routledge).

Pitts, M. (1998) 'Cancer', in M. Pitts, M. and K. Phillips (Eds.) (1998) *The Psychology of Health*. (2nd Edition). (London: Routledge).

Pitts, M. (1998b) 'The Medical Consultation', in M. Pitts, and K. Phillips (Eds.) *The Psychology of Health*. (2nd Edition). (London: Routledge).

Pitts, M. and Phillips, K. (Eds.) (1998) *The Psychology of Health*. (2nd Edition). (London: Routledge).

Plant, M.A. (1987) 'Risk Factors in Employment', in B.D. Hore and M.A. Plant (Eds.) *Alcohol Problems in Employment*. Croon Helm.

Plant, M.A., Peck, D.F. and Samuel, E. (1985) *Alcohol, Drugs and School Leavers*. (Tavistock).

Poikolainen, K., Karkkainen, P. and Pikkarainen, J. (1985) 'Correlations Between Biological Markers and Alcohol Intake as Measured By Diary and Questionnaire in Men', *Journal of Studies on Alcohol*, **46**(5): 383–7.

Popper, K. (1972) *Conjectures and Refutations* (4th Edition). (London: Routledge).

Porter, M., Alder, B. and Abraham, C. (1999) *Psychology and Sociology Applied to Medicine*. (London: Churchill Livingstone).

Potter, J. and Wetherell, M. (1987) *Discourse and Social Psychology*. (London: Sage).

Potts, M. (1990) 'Cross-Cultural Perspectives on AIDS: A Commentary', in B.Voeller, J. Reinisch Machover and M. Gottlieb (Eds.) *AIDS and Sex – An Integrated and Biobehavioural Approach*. (Oxford: Oxford University Press).

Poulsen, P., Vaag, A.A., Kyvik, K.O.,Müller Jensen, D., Beck Nielsen, H. (1997) 'Low Birth Weight Is Associated with NIDDM in Discordant Monozygotic and Dizygotic Twin Pairs', *Diabetologia*, **40**(4): 439–46

Povey, R., Conner, M., Sparks, P., James, R. and Shepherd, R., (2000) 'Application of the Theory of Planned Behaviour to Two Dietary Behaviours: Roles of Perceived Control and Self Efficacy', *British Journal of Health Psychology*, **5**: 121–39.

Powell, M. (1988) 'Alcohol and Tobacco Tax Harmonisation in the European Community', *British Journal of Addiction*, 83.

Power, C., Fogelman, K. and Fox, A.J. (1986) 'Health and Social Mobility During the Early Years of Life', *Quarterly Journal of Social Affairs*, **2**(4): 397–413.

Power, C., Matthews, S. and Manor, O. (1996) 'Inequalities in Self Rated Health in the 1958 Birth Cohort: Lifetime Social Circumstances Or Social Mobility', *British Medical Journal*, **313**: 449–53

Prochaska, J.O. and DiClemente, C.C. (1983) 'Stages and Processes of Self-Change of Smoking: Toward an Integrative Model of Change', *Journal of Consulting and Clinical Psychology*, **51**: 390–5.

Prochaska, J.O. and DiClemente, C.C. (1984) *The Transtheoretical Approach: Crossing Traditional Boundaries of Change*. (Homewood: Irwin).

Quigley, B. and Doane, B. (1981) 'Anorexia Nervosa and Visual Experience (Letter)', *Lancet*, **2**: 1113.

Quill, T., Lo, B. and Brock, D. (1997) 'Palliative Options of Last Resort: A Comparison of Voluntarily Stopping Eating and Drinking, Terminal Sedation, Physician-Assisted Suicide, and Voluntary Active Euthanasia', *Journal of the American Medical Association*, **278**(23): 2099–104.

Rabinow, P. (1984) *The Foucault Reader. An Introduction to Foucault's Thought*. (Harmondsworth: Penguin).

Rabkin, J.G. (1974) 'Public Attitudes Toward Mental Illness: A Review of the Literature', *Schizophrenia Bulletin* **10**: Fall: 9–33.

Rabkin, J.G., Williams, J.B.W., Remien, R.H., Goetz, R., Kertzner, R. and Gorman, J.M. (1991) 'Depression, Distress, Lymphocyte Subsets, and Human Immunodeficiency Virus Symptoms on Two Occasions in HIV-Positive Homosexual Men', *Archives of General Psychiatry*, **46**: 81–7.

Radley, A. (Ed.) (1995) *Worlds of Illness*. (London: Routledge).

Radley, A. and Billig, M. (1996) 'Accounts of Health and Illness: Dilemmas and Representations', *Sociology of Health and Illness*, **11**: 230–52.

Rao, S.M., Huber, S.J. and Bornstein, R.A. (1992) 'Emotional Changes with Multiple Sclerosis and Parkinson's Disease', *Journal of Consulting and Clinical Psychology*, **60**(3): 369–78.

Rathus, S.A. and Boughn, S. (1994) *AIDS – What Every Student Needs to Know*. Harcourt Brace (2nd Edition).

Rawlings, J.S. and Weir, M.R. (1992) 'Race- and Rank-Specific Infant Mortality in a US Military Population', *American Journal of Diseases in Childhood*, **146**(3): 313–16.

Read, J. and Reynolds, J. (Eds.) (1996) *Speaking Our Minds*. (London: Macmillan Press).

Reid, W.H. and Wise, M.G. (1989) *DSM III-R Training Guide*. (New York: Brunner/Mazel).

Reis, H.T. (1984) 'Social Interaction and Well Being', in S.W. Duck (Ed.) *Personal Relationships 5: Repairing Personal Relationships*. (London: Academic Press).

Reisman, J.M. (1979). *Anatomy of Friendship*. (New York: Irvington).

Reisman, J.M. (1981). Adult Friendships', in S. Duck and R. Gilmour (Eds.) *Personal Relationships 2: Developing Personal Relationships*. (London: Academic Press).

Resnick, H.S., Kilpatrick, D.G., Best, C.L. and Kramer, T.L. (1992) 'Vulnerability Stress Factors in Development of Post-traumatic Stress Disorder', *Journal of Nervous and Mental Disease*, **180**: 424–30.

Rhodes, T. (1996) 'Individual and Community Action in HIV Prevention', in T. Rhodes and R. Hartnoll (Eds.) *AIDS, Drugs and Prevention*. (London: Routledge).

Richards, M., Sainsbury, R. and Kerr, D. (1997) 'Inequalities in Breast Cancer Care and Outcome', *British Journal of Cancer*, **76**(5): 634–8.

Richman, J.A., Raskin, V.D. and Gaines, C. (1991) 'Gender Roles, Social Support, and Postpartum Depressive Symptomatology: The Benefits of Caring', *Journal of Nervous and Mental Disease*, **179**: 139–47.

Rimm, E.B., Klatsky, A., Grobbee, D. and Stampfer, M.J. (1996) 'Review of Moderate Alcohol Consumption and Reduced Risk of Coronary Heart Disease: Is the Effect Due to Beer, Wine, Or Spirits?', *British Medical Journal*, **312**: 731–6.

Roberts I., Ashton, T., Dunn, R. and Lee-Joe, T. (1994) 'Preventing Child Pedestrian Injury: Pedestrian Education Or Traffic Calming?', *Australian Journal of Public Health*, **18**(2): 209–12.

Roberts, R. (1988) 'Hiccups in Alcohol Education', *Health Education Journal*, 47(2/3): 73–6.

Roberts, R. (1990) 'Psychiatry, Science and Mental Health', *Critical Public Health*, 4: 15–21.

Roberts, R. and Brunner, E. (1996) 'Diabetes, Health Selection and Occupational Mobility', Paper Presented At the 10th European Health Psychology Conference. Dublin. Ireland.

Roberts, R. and Brunner, E. (1998) 'Validating and Interpreting Regression Models in Health Research: Explaining Social Mobility in the Whitehall II Study', Unpublished MS.

Roberts, R. and Fallowfield, L.J. (1990) 'The Goals of Cancer Counsellors', *Counselling*, 1(3) 88–91.

Roberts, R., Brunner, E. and Marmot, M. (1995) 'Psychological Factors in the Relationship Between Alcohol and Cardiovascular Morbidity', *Social Science and Medicine*, 41(11): 1513–16.

Roberts, R., Brunner, E., White, I. and Marmot, M.(1993) 'Gender Differences in Occupational Mobility and Structure of Employment in the British Civil Service', *Social Science and Medicine*, 37(12): 1415–25.

Roberts, R., Cyster, R. and Mcewen, J (1988) 'Alcohol Consumption and the Workplace: Prospects For Change? *Public Health*, 102: 463–9.

Roberts, R., Hemingway, H. and Marmot, M. (1997) 'Psychometric and Clinical Validity of the SF-36 in the Whitehall II Study', *British Journal of Health Psychology*, 2: 285–300.

Roberts, R., Mayer, A.M and Mcewen, J. (1988) *Alcohol Education At the Workplace*. Health Education Authority. London.

Roberts, R., Towell, A, Golding, J, Reid, S. and Woodford, S. (1998) 'Socioeconomic Differences in Perceived Life Expectancy: Implications For Social-Cognition Models of Health Behaviours', 12th European Health Psychology Conference. Vienna.

Roberts, R., Towell, A., Golding, J. and Weinreb, I. (1999) 'The Effects of Students' Economic Circumstances on British Students' Mental and Physical Health', *American Journal of College Health*. 48: 103–9.

Robertson, K.R., Wilkins, J.W., Handy, J. and Van Der Horst, C. (1993) 'Psychoimmunology and AIDS: Psychological Distress and Herpes Simplex Virus in Human Immunodeficiency Virus Infected Individuals' (1993) *Psychology and Health*, 8(5): 317–27.

Robinson, N., Yateman, N.A., Protopapa, L.E. and Bush, L. (1990) 'Employment Problems and Diabetes', *Diabetic Medicine*, 7(1): 16–22

Rodgers, B. and Mann, S.L. (1993) 'Rethinking the Analysis of Intergenerational Social Mobility: A Comment of John W. Fox's "Social Class, Mental Illness, and Social Mobility" ', *Journal of Health and Social Behaviour*, 34(2): 165–72.

Roe, J.M., Feldman, S.S. and Drivas, A. (1988) 'Interactions with Three-Month Old Infants: A Comparison Between Greek Mothers and Institutional Caregivers', *International Journal of Behavioural Development*, 11: 359–67.

Rogers, R.W. (1975) 'A Protection Motivation Theory of Fear Appeals and Attitude Change', *Journal of Psychology*, 91: 93–114.

Rogers, R.W. (1983) 'Cognitive and Physiological Processes in Fear Appeals and Attitude Change', A Revised Theory of Protection Motivation Theory. in B.I.Cacioppo and L.L. Petty (Eds.) *Social Psychophysiology: A Source Book*. (London: Guilford Press).

Rogot, E. and Murray, J.L. (1980) 'Smoking and Causes of Death Among US. Veterans: 16 Years of Observation', *Public Health Reports*, 95: 213.

Romme, M. and Escher, S. (1994) 'Hearing Voices', *British Medical Journal*, 309: 670

Rook, K.S. (1984) 'The Negative Side of Social Interaction: Impact, on Psychological Well Being', *Journal of Personality and Social Psychology*, 46: 1097–108.

Rook, K.S. and Pietromonaco, P. (1987) 'Close Relationships: Ties That Heal Or Ties That Bind?', *Personal Relationships*, 1: 1–35.

Root, M.M.P. (1990) 'Disordered Eating in Women of Color', *Sex Roles*, 22: 525–36.

Rose, G. (1992*) The Strategy of Preventive Medicine*. (Oxford: Oxford University Press).

Rose, G. and Day, S. (1990) 'The Population Mean Predicts the Number of Deviant Individuals', *British Medical Journal*, 301: 1031–4.

Rosenhan, D.L. and Seligman, M.E. (1989) *Abnormal Psychology* (2nd Edition). Norton.

Rosenhan, D.L. and Seligman, M.E.P. (1989) *Abnormal Psychology* (2nd Edition). Norton.

Rosenman, R. H. (1978) 'The Interview Method of Assessment of the Coronary-Prone Behaviour Pattern', in T.M. Dembroski, S.M. Weiss, J.L. Shields, S.G. Haynes and M. Feinleib (Eds.) *Coronary Prone Behaviour*. Springer-Verlag. New York.

Rosenman, R.H., Brand, R.J., Sholz, R.I. and Friedman, M. (1976) 'Multivariate Prediction of Coronary Heart Disease During 8.5 Year Follow-Up in the Western Collaborative Group Study', *American Journal of Cardiology*, 37: 903–10.

Rosenstock, I. (1974) 'Historical Origins of the Health Belief Model', Health Education Monographs, 2: 328–35.

Rosenthal, D., Fernbach, M. and Moore, S. (1997) 'The Singles Scene: Safe Sex Practices and Attitudes Among At-Risk Heterosexual Adults', *Psychology and Health*, 12: 171–82.

Rosenzweig, M.R., Leiman, A.L. and Breedlove, S.M. (1995) 'Biological Psychology', (2nd Edition) Sinauer Associates, MA.

Roter, D.L. and Hall, J.A. (1998) 'Why Physician Gender Matters in Shaping the Physician-Patient Relationship', *Journal of Women's Health*, 7(9): 1093–7.

Royal College of Physicians (1987) *A Great and Growing Evil: The Medical Consequences of Alcohol Abuse*. (London: Tavistock).

Royal College of Psychiatrists (1979) *Alcohol and Alcoholism*. (London: Tavistock).

Royal College of Psychiatrists (1986) *Alcohol: Our Favourite Drug*. (London: Tavistock).

Rubin, R.R. and Peyrot, M. (1992) 'Psychosocial Problems and Interventions in Diabetes', *Diabetes Care*, 15911): 1640–55.

Rusch, R.G., Hall, J.C. and Griffin, H.C. (1986) 'Abuse-Provoking Characteristics of Institutionalized Mentally Retarded Individuals', *American Journal of Mental Deficiency*, 90(6): 618–24.

Rush, K.L. (1997) 'Health Promotion Ideology and Nursing Education', *Journal of Advanced Nursing*, 25(6): 1292–8.

Russell, G.F.M. (1970) 'Anorexia Nervosa: Its Identity as an Illness and Its Treatment', in J.H. Price (Ed), *Modern Trends in Psychological Medicine*. pp. 131–64. London, Butterworth.

Russell, G.F.M. (1979) 'Bulimia Nervosa: an Ominous Variant of Anorexia Nervosa', *Psychological Medicine*, 9: 429–48.

Russell, G.F.M. (1981) 'Comment: The Current Treatment of Anorexia Nervosa', *British Journal of Pyschiatry*, 138: 164–6.

Russell, G.F.M. (1985) 'Premenarchal Anorexia Nervosa and Its Sequelae', *Journal of Psychiatric Research*, **119**: 363–9.

Russell, P. and Sander, R. (1998) 'Palliative Care: Promoting the Concept of a Healthy Death', *British Journal of Nursing*, **7**(5): 256–61.

Russo, C. and Brose, W. (1998) 'Chronic Pain', *Annual Review of Medicine*. **49**: 123–33.

Rutter, M. (1989) 'Intergenerational Continuities and Discontinuities in Serious Parenting Difficulties', in D.Crichetti and V. Carlson (Eds.) *Child Maltreatment: Theory and Research on Causes and Consequences of Child Abuse and Neglect*. (Cambridge: Cambridge University Press).

Ryan, J. and Sackrey, C. (1984) *Strangers in Paradise: Academics from the Working Class*. (Boston: South End Press).

Sacker, A., Firth, D., Fitzpatrick, R., Lynch, K. and Bartley, M. (2000) 'Comparing Health Inequality in Men and Women: Prospective Study of Mortality 1986–96', *British Medical Journal*, **320**: 1303–7.

Salmon, P. (1994) 'Is Health Psychology a Profession Or Can It Become One? First Ask the Right Questions', *The Psychologist*, **7**: 542–4.

Sanders, C., Egger, M., Donovan, J., Tallon, D. and Frankel, S. (1998) 'Reporting on Quality of Life in Randomised Controlled Trials: Bibliographic Study', *British Medical Journal*, **317**: 1191–4.

Sant, M., Capocaccia, R., Verdecchia, A., Estève, J., Gatta, G., Micheli, A., Coleman, M.P. and Berrino, F. (1998) 'Survival of Women with Breast Cancer in Europe: Variation with Age, of Diagnosis and Country', The EUROCARE Working Group. *International Journal of Cancer*, **77**(5): 679–83.

Sapolsky, R.M. and Mott, G.E. (1987) 'Social Subordinance in Wild Baboons Is Associated with Suppressed High Density Lipoprotein-Cholesterol Concentrations: The Possible Role of Chronic Social Stress', *Endocrinology*, **121**: 1605–10.

Sarafino, E.P. (1995) *Health Psychology: Biopsychosocial Interactions* (2nd Edition). (New York: John Wiley).

Sarafino, E.P. (1998) *Health Psychology: Biopsychosocial Interactions* (3rd Edition). (New York: John Wiley).

Sarason, B.R., Sarason, I.G. and Gurung, R.A.R. (1997) 'Close Personal Relationships and Health Outcomes: A Key to the Role of Social Support', in S. Duck, (Ed.) *Handbook of Personal Relationships: Theory, Research and Interventions*. (Chichester: John Wiley & Sons).

Savan, B. (1988) *Science Under Siege: The Myth of the Objectivity of Scientific Research*. (London: CBC Enterprises).

Saxton, M. and Howe, F. (Eds.) '(1988) with *Wings: An Anthology of Literature By Women with Disabilities*. (London: Virago).

Schag, C.A.C., Ganz, P.A., Kahn, B. and Peterson, L. (1992) 'Assessing the Needs and Quality of Life of Patients with HIV Infection: Development of the HIV Overview of Problem Situations Evaluation System (HOPES)', *Quality of Life Research*, **1**: 397–413. 15.

Schatzman, M. (1973) *Soul Murder*. (London: Allen Lane).

Schmidt, U., Tiller, J., Blanchard, M., Andrews,B. and Treasure, J. (1997) 'Is There a Specific Trauma Precipitating Anorexia Nervosa?', *Psychological Medicine* **27**(3): 523–30.

Schreiner-Engel, P., Schiavi, R.C., Vietorisz, D and Smith, H. (1987) 'The Differential Impact of Diabetes Type on Female Sexuality', *Journal of Psychosomatic Research*, **31**(1): 23–33.

Schröder, K.E.E. and Konertz, W. (1998) 'Coping as a Mediator in Recovery from Cardiac Surgery', *Psychology and Health*, **13**(1): 83–97.

Schubert, C. (1998) 'Psychoneuroimmunologische Forschung Im Kontext Biochemisher Erkenntnisfortschritte Und Ihre Paradigmatischen Grenzen', *Zeitschrift Fuer Psychosomatische Medizin Und Psychoanalyse*, **44**(1): 1–20.

Schwartz, M. and Schwartz, J. (1974) 'Evidence Against a Genetical Component to Performance on IQ Tests', *Nature*, March 1, **248**: 84–5.

Schwartz, M. and Schwartz, J. (1975) 'No Evidence For Heritability of Social Attitudes', *Nature*, May 29, **255**: 429.

Scott, D.W. (1986) 'Anorexia Nervosa: A Review of Possible Genetic Factors', *International Journal of Eating Disorders*, **5**: 1–20.

Seedhouse, D. (1995) 'The Way Around Health Economics' Dead End', *Health Care Analysis*, **3**: 205–20.

Seeman, M., Seeman, A.Z. and Budros, A.(1988) 'Powerlessness, Work, and Community: A Longitudinal Study of Alienation and Alcohol Use', *Journal of Health and Social Behaviour*, **29**: 185–98.

Seibt, R., Boucsein, W. and Sheuch, K. (1998) 'Effects of Different Stress Settings on Cardiovascular Parameters and their Relationship to Daily Life Blood Pressure in Normotensives, Borderline Hypertensives and Hypertensives', *Ergonomics*, **41**(5): 634–48.

Seitz, H.K., Poschl, G. and Simanowski, U.A. (1998) 'Alcohol and Cancer', *Recent Developments in Alcohol*, **14**: 67–95.

Selye, H. (1956) *Stress of Life*. (New York: McGraw-Hill).

Senior, K. (1997) 'How Can Components of Common Foods Affect Cancer Risk?', *Molecular Medicine Today*, **3**(3): 103–7

Sennett, R. and Cobb, J. (1972) *The Hidden Injuries of Class*. Vintage.

Sereny, G. (1974) *Into That Darkness: From Mercy Killing to Mass Murder*. (London: Pimlico).

Shacham, S. Dar, R. and Cleeland, C. S. (1984) 'The Relationship of Mood State to the Severity of Clinical Pain', *Pain* **18**: 187–97.

Shah, D. and Button, J.C. (1998) 'The Relationship Between Psychological Factors and Recurrent Genital Herpes Simplex Virus', *British Journal of Health Psychology*, **3**(3): 191–214.

Shakespeare, T. (1994) 'Cultural Representations of Disabled People: Dustbins For Disavowal', *Disability and Society*, **9**(3): 283–301.

Shalev, A.Y., Freedman, S., Peri, T., Brandes, D., Sahar, T., Orr, S.P. and Pitman, R.K. (1998) 'Prospective Study of Posttraumatic Stress Disorder and Depression Following Trauma', *American Journal of Psychiatry*, **155**(5): 630–7.

Shaper A.G., Wannamethee, G. and Walker, M.(1988) 'Alcohol and Mortality in British Men: Explaining the U-Shaped Curve', *The Lancet*, December 3rd 8623: 1267–73.

Shaper, A.G., Wannamethee, G. and Walker, M. (1989) 'Alcohol and the U-Shaped Curve', *The Lancet*, Feb 11th P.336.

Sharp, C.W. and Freeman, C.P.L. (1993) 'The Medical Complications of Anorexia Nervosa', *British Journal of Psychiatry*. **162**: 452–62.

Shaw, W. S., Patterson, T., Semple, S., Grant, I., Yu, E., Zhang, M., He, Y. and Wu, Y. (1997) 'A Cross-Cultural Validation of Coping Strategies and their Associations with Caregiving Distress', *Gerontologist* **37**(4) 490–504.

Shea, J., Clover, K. and Burton, R. (1991) 'Relationship Between Measures of Acute and Chronic Stress and Cellular Immunity', *Medical Science Research*, **19**: 221–2.

Sheeran, P. and Abraham, C. (1994) 'Modelling and Modifying Young Heterosexuals' HIV-Preventive Behaviour; a Review of Theories, Findings and Educational Implications', *Patient Education and Counselling*, **23**: 173–86.

Sheeran, P. and Abraham, C. (1995) 'The Health Belief Model', in M. Conner and P. Norman (Eds.) *Predicting Health Behaviour*. (Buckingham: Open University Press).

Sheridan, C.L. and Radmacher, S.A. (1992) *Health Psychology: Challenging the Biomedical Model*. (New York: John Wiley).

Sherman, A.C., Higgs, G.E. and Williams, R.L.(1997) 'Gender Differences in the Locus of Control Construct', *Psychology and Health*, **12**: 239–48.

Sherrard, C. (1998) 'Social Dimensions of Research', *The Psychologist*, **11**(10): 486–7.

Shillitoe, R.W. and Miles, D.W. (1989) 'Diabetes Mellitus', in A. Broome (Ed.) *Health Psychology: Processes and Applications*. New York: Chapman and Hall.

Shiloh, S., Vinter, M. and Barak, A. (1997) 'Correlates of Health Screening Utilization: The Roles of Health Beliefs and Self-Regulation Motivation', *Psychology and Health*, **12**: 301–17.

Shoham-Salomon, V. (1985) 'Are Schizophrenics' Behaviors Schizophrenic? What Medically Versus Psychosocially Oriented Therapists Attribute to Schizophrenic Persons', *Journal of Abnormal Psychology* **94**(4): 443–53.

Sieg, K.G., Hidler, M.S., Graham, M.A., Steele, R.L. and Kugler, L.R. (1997) 'Hyperintense Subcortical Brain Alterations in Anorexia Nervosa', *International Journal of Eating Disorders*, May; **21**(4): 391–4.

Siegel, K., Mesagno, F.P., Chen, J. and Christ, G. (1989) 'Factors Distinguishing Homosexual Males Practising Risky and Safer Sex', *Social Science and Medicine*, **28**: 561–169.

Siegrist, J., Peter, R., Junge, A., Cremer, P. and Siedel, D. (1990) 'Low Status Control, High Effort At Work and Ischaemic Heart Disease: Prospective Evidence from Blue Collar Men', *Social Science and Medicine*, **31**: 1127–34.

Simmons, D., Williams, D.R. and Powell, M.J. (1992) 'Prevalence of Diabetes in Different Regional and Religious South Asian Communities in Coventry', *Diabetic Medicine*, **9**(5): 428–31.

Simnett, I. (1996) *Managing Health Promotion*. (Wiley).

Singh, S.P., Croudace, T., Beck, A. and Harrison, G. (1998) 'Perceived Ethnicity and the Risk of Compulsory Admission', *Social Psychiatry and Psychiatric Epidemiology*, **33**(1): 39–44.

Sinicco, A., Fora, R., Raiteri, R., Sciandra, M., Bechis, G., Calvo, M.M. and Gioanni, P. (1997) 'Is the Clinical Course of HIV-1 Changing? Cohort Study', *British Medical Journal*, **314**: 1232–7.

Slade, P. (1995) 'Prospects for Prevention', in *Handbook of Eating Disorders; Theory, Treatment and Research* (pp. 385–98). (Chichester: John Wiley & Sons)

Slade, P.D. and Cooper, R. (1979) 'Some Conceptual Difficulties with the Term Schizophrenia: An Alternative Model', *British Journal of Social and Clinical Psychology*, **18**: 309–17.

Slattery, M.L., Boucher, K.M., Caan, B.J., Potter, J.D. and Ma, K.N. (1998) 'Eating Patterns and Risk of Colon Cancer', *American Journal of Epidemiology*, **148**(1): 4–16.

Sloggett, A. and Joshi, H. (1994) 'Higher Mortality in Deprived Areas: Community Or Personal Disadvantage?', *British Medical Journal*, **309**: 1470–4.

Small, G. W., Rabins, P. V., Barry, B. P., Buckholtz, N. S., Dekosky, S. T., Ferris, S. H., Finkel, S. I., Gwyther, L. P., Khachaturian, Z. S., Lebowitz, B. D., Mcrae, T. D., Morris, J.

C., Oakly, F., Schneider, L. S., Streim, J. E., Sunderland, T., Terri, L. A. and Tune, L. E. (1997) 'Diagnosis and Treatment of Alzheimer Disease and Related Disorders', *Journal of the American Medical Association*, October, **278**(16): 1363–71.

Smeenk, F., Dewitte, L., Vanhaastregt, J., Schipper, R., Biezemans, H. and Crebolder, H. (1998) 'Transmural Care of Terminal Cancer Patients: Effects on the Quality of Life of Direct Caregivers', *Nursing Research*, **47**(3): 129–36.

Smith, G.R. and Mcdaniels, S.M. (1983) 'Psychologically Mediated Effect on the Delayed Hypersensitivity Reaction to Tuberculin in Humans', *Psychosomatic Medicine*, **45**: 65–70.

Smith, R. (1987) 'A Poor Start For the Health Education Authority', *British Medical Journal*, **294**: 664.

Sobell, M.B. and Sobell, L.C. (1973) 'Individualised Behaviour Therapy For Alcoholics', *Behaviour Therapy*, **4**(1): 49–72.

Sobsey, D. (1994) *Violence and Abuse in the Lives of People with Disabilities*. (London: Paul H. Brookes).

Sobsey, D., Randall, W. and Parrila, R.K. (1997) 'Gender Differences in Abused Children with and Without Disabilities', *Child Abuse and Neglect*, **21**(8): 707–20.

Socall, D.W. and Holtgraves, T. (1992) 'Attitudes Toward the Mentally Ill: The Effects of Label and Beliefs', *Sociological Quarterly* **33**(3): 435–45.

Social Exclusion Unit (1998) 'Truancy and School Exclusion Report', www.open.gov.uk.

Sodroski, J.G., Rosen, C.A. and Haseltine, W.A. (1984) 'Trans-Acting Transcription of the Long Terminal Repeat of Human T Lymphocyte Viruses in Infected Cells', *Science*, **225**: 381–5.

Solomon, G.F. and Temoshok, L. (1987) 'A Psychoneuroimmunologic Perspective on AIDS Research; Questions, Preliminary Findings and Suggestions', *Journal of Applied Social Psychology*, **17**: 286–308.

Solomon, G.F. Temoshok, L. O'Leary, A. and Zich, J.A. (1987) 'An Intensive Psychoneuroimmunologic Study of Long Surviving Persons with AIDS: Pilot Work, Background Studies, Hypotheses and Methods', *Annals of the New York Academy of Sciences*, **46.**, 647–55.

Solvason, H.B., Ghanta, V.K. and Hiramoto, R.N. (1988) 'Conditioned Augmentation of Natural Killer Cell Activity: Independence from Nociceptive Effects and Dependence on Interferon-Beta', *Journal of Immunology*, **140**: 661–5.

Songer, T.J., Laporte, R.E., Dorman, J.S., Orchard, T.J., Becker, D.J. and Drash, A.L. (1989) 'Employment Spectrum of IDDM', *Diabetes Care*, **12**: 615–22.

Sontag, S. (1979) *Illness as a Metaphor*. Allen Lane. London.

Spicer, J., Jackson, R. and Scragg, R. (1997) 'Type A Behaviour, Social Contact and Coronary Death', *Psychology and Health*, **11**(5): 733–43.

Stainton-Rogers, W. (1999) 'Why We Need a Critical Health Psychology', 13th Conference of the European Health Psychology Society. Florence.

Stansfeld, S. (1999) 'Social Support and Social Cohesion', In. M.Marmot and R.G.Wilkinson (Eds.) *Social Determinants of Health*. (Oxford: Oxford University Press).

Stansfeld, S. and Marmot, M. (1992) 'Social Class and Minor Psychiatric Disorder in British Civil Servants: A Validated Screening Survey Using the General Health Questionnaire', *Psychological Medicine*, **22**: 739–49.

Stansfeld, S., Feeney, A., Head, J., Canner, R., North, F. and Marmot, M. (1995) 'Sickness Absence for Psychiatric Illness', *Social Science and Medicine*, **40**: 189–97.

Stansfeld, S., Roberts, R. and Foot, S. (1997) 'Assessing the Validity of the SF-36 General Health Survey', *Quality of Life Research*, **6**: 217–24

Steinberg, M.,Najman, J., Cartwright, C., Macdonald, S. and Williams, G. (1997) 'End of Life Decision Making: Community and Medical Practitioners' Perspectives', *Medical Journal of Australia*. **166**(3): 131–5.

Stenström, U., Wikby, A., Andersson, P-O. and Rydén, O. (1998) 'Relationship Between Locus of Control Beliefs and Metabolic Control in Insulin-Dependent Diabetes Mellitus', *British Journal of Health Psychology*, **3**: 15–25.

Stephens, R., Hopwood, P., Girling, D. and Manchin, D. (1997) 'Randomized Trials with Quality of Life Endpoints: Are Doctors' Ratings of Patients' Physical Symptoms Interchangeable with Patients' Self-Ratings?', *Quality of Life Research*. **6**(3): 225–36.

Steptoe, A. and Butler, N. (1996) 'Sports Participation and Emotional Well-Being in Adolescents', *Lancet*, **347**(9018): 1789– 92.

Stewart, A., Mills, K., Sepsis, P., King, A., Mclellan ,B., Roitz, K. and Ritter, P. (1997) 'Evaluation of CHAMPS, a Physical Activity Promotion Program For Older Adults', *Annals of Behavioral Medicine*, **19**(4): 353–61.

Stewart, A.L., Hays, R.D. and Ware, J.E. (1992) 'The MOS Short-Form General Health Survey', *Medical Care*, **26**(7): 724–35.

Stewart, I. (1997) *Does God Play Dice? the New Mathematics of Chaos* (2nd Edition). Penguin.

Stewart, M., Brown, J.B., Boon, H., Galajda, J., Meredith, L. and Sangster, M. (1999) 'Evidence on Patient-Doctor Communication', *Cancer Prevention and Control*, **3**(1): 25–30.

Strauss, A.L. and Corbin, J. (1990) *Basics of Qualitative Research: Grounded Theory Procedures and Techniques*. (California: Sage).

Streiner, D.L. and Norman, G.R. (1991) *Health Measurement Scales: A Practical Guide to their Development* and *Use*. (Oxford: Oxford University Press).

Striegel-Moore, R.H. (1993) 'Etiology of Binge Eating: A Developmental Perspective', in C. Fairburn and G.T. Wilson (Eds.) *Binge Eating*. (New York: Guilford).

Stroebe, W. and Stroebe, M.S. (1995) *Social Psychology and Health*. (Buckingham: Open University Press).

Stronks, K., Van De Mheen, H., Looman, C. W.N. and Mackenbach (1998) 'The Importance of Psychosocial Stressors For Socio-Economic Inequalities in Perceived Health', *Social Science and Medicine*, **46**(4–5): 611–23.

Stubbins, J,. (Ed.) (1977) *Social and Psychological Aspects of Disability*. (Baltimore: University Park Press).

Sullivan, A., Kelso, J., and Stewart, M.A. (1990) 'Mother's View on the Ages of Onset For Childhood Disorders', *Child Psychiatry and Human Development*, **20**(4): 269–78.

Sullivan, P.M. and Knutson, J.F. (1999) 'Maltreatment and Disabilities: A School Based Epidemiological Study', Unpublished MS.

Sussman, S., Dent, C.W., Simon, T.R., Stacy, A.W., Galaif, E.R., Moss, M.A., Craig, S. and Johnson, C.A. (1995) 'Immediate Impact of Social Influence-Oriented Substance Abuse Prevention Curricula in Traditional and Continuation High Schools', *Drugs and Society*, **8**: 65–81.

Sutherland, A. (1981) *Disabled We Stand*. (London: Souvenir Press).

Suttles, G.D. (1970) 'Friendship as a Social Institution', in G Mccall, M.M. Mccall, N.K. Mccall, G.D. Suttles and S.B Kurth (Eds.) *Social Relationships*. (Chicago: Aldine).

Sweeting, H. (1994) 'Reversals of Fortune? Sex Differences in Health in Childhood and Adolescence', *Social Science and Medicine*, **40**: 77.

Syme, S.L. (1996) 'To Prevent Disease: The Need For a New Approach', in D. Blane, E. Brunner and R. Wilkinson (Eds.) *Health and Social Organisation*. (London: Routledge).

Syme, L.S. (1990) 'Control and Health: A Personal Perspective', in A. Steptoe and A.Appels (Eds.) *Stress, Personal Control and Health*. (New York: John Wiley).

Szasz, T. (1961) *The Myth of Mental Illness*. (New York: Dell).

Szasz, T. (1991) 'Diagnoses are Not Diseases', *The Lancet*, **338**: 1574–6.

Szmukler, G. and Patton, G. (1995) 'Sociocultural Models of Eating Disorders', in G. Szmukler, C. Dare and J. Treasure (Eds.) *Handbook of Eating Disorders: Theory, Treatment and Research*. (Chichester: John Wiley and Sons).

Szmukler, G., Dare, C. and Treasure, J. (1995). *Handbook of Eating Disorders: Theory, Treatment and Research*. (Chichester: John Wiley).

Tabachnick, B.G. and Fidell, L.S. (1989) *Using Multivariate Statistics*. (London: Harper Collins).

Tarlov, A. (1996) 'Social Determinants of Health: The Sociobiological Translation', in D. Blane, E. Brunner and R. Wilkinson (Eds.) *Health and Social Organisation: Towards a Health Policy For the 21st Century*. (London: Routledge).

Tarlov, A.R., Ware, J.E., Greenfield, S., Nelson, E.C., Perrin, E. and Zubkoff, M. (1989) 'The Medical Outcomes Study. An Application of Methods For Monitoring the Results of Medical Care', *Journal of the American Medical Association*, **262**(7): 925–30.

Tarter, R.E., Hegedus, A.M., Goldstein, G. and Shelly, C. and Alterman, A.I. (1984) 'Adolescent Sons of Alcoholics: Neuropsychological and Personality Characteristics', *Journal of Studies on Alcohol*ism, **46**: 329–56.

Tattersall, R.B. and Lowe, J. (1981) 'Diabetes in Adolescence', *Diabetologia*, **26**: 517–23.

Taylor, A., Doust, J. and Webborn, N. (1998) 'Randomised Controlled Trial to Examine the Effects of GP Exercise Referral Programme in Hailsham, East Sussex, on Modifiable Coronary Heart Disease Risk Factors', *Journal of Epidemiology and Community Health*, **52**(9): 595–601.

Taylor, S.E. (1995) *Health Psychology*. (New York: McGraw Hill).

Terry, D.A. Galligan, R.F. and Conway, V.J. (1993) 'The Prediction of Safe Sex Behaviour: The Role of Intentions, Attitudes, Norms and Control Beliefs', *Psychology and Health*, **8**: 355–68.

Terry, D.J. and O'Leary, J.E. (1995) 'The Theory of Planned Behaviour: The Effects of Perceived Behavioural Control and Self-Efficacy', *British Journal of Social Psychology*, **345**: 199–220.

Thambirajah, M.S. (1998) 'Danger Is One of Overdiagnosis', Letters. *British Medical Journal*, **317**: 1250.

The Lancet (1998) 'The Prostate Question, Unanswered Still. (Editorial), **349**: 443.

Thornley, B. and Adams, C. (1998) 'Content and Quality of 2000 Controlled Trials in Schizophrenia Over 50 Years', *British Medical Journal*, **317**: 1181–4.

Touyz, S.W., O'Sullivan, B.T. and Gertier, R. (1988) 'Anorexia Nervosa in a Woman Totally Blind Since Birth', *British Journal of Psychiatry*, **153**: 248–50.

Toves, C., Schill, T. and Ramanaiah, N. (1991) 'Sex-Differences, Internal-External Control and Vulnerability to Life Stress', *Psychological Reports*, **49**: 508.

Townsend, P. and Davidson, N., (1982) *The Black Report*. (Harmondsworth: Pelican).

Townsend, P., Phillimore, P. and Beattie, A. (1988) *Health and Deprivation: Inequality and the North*. (London: Croom Helm).

Tran, P.B. and Miller, R.J. (1999) 'Aggregates in Neurodegenerative Disease: Crowds and Power?', *Trends in Neuroscience*, 22(5): 194–7.

Treasure, J., Schmidt, U. and Keilen M. (1992) 'How do Eating Disorders Affect the Quality of Life? A Comparison Between Eating Disorder Sufferers and Controls', Poster Presented At the Annual Meeting of the Royal College of Psychiatrists. Dublin.

Treasure, J.L., Katzman, M., Schmidt, U., Troop, N., Todd, G. and De Silva, P. (1999) 'Engagement and Outcome in the Treatment of Bulimia Nervosa: First Phase of a Sequential Design Comparing Motivation Enhancement Therapy and Cognitive Behavioural Therapy', *Behaviour Research and Therapy*, 37: 405–18.

Treede, R.D., Kenshalo, D.R., Gracely, R.H and Jones, A.K.P. (1999) 'The Cortical Representation of Pain', *Pain*, 79: 105–111.

Trief, P.M., Elbert, K., Grant, W. and Weinstock, R.S. (1998) 'Family Environment, Glycemic Control, and the Psychosocial Adaptation of Adults with Diabetes', *Diabetes Care*, 21(2): 241–5.

Trouton, D.S. and Maxwell, A.E. (1956) 'The Relation Between Neurosis and Psychosis: An Analysis of Symptoms and Past History of 819 Psychotics and Neurotics', *Journal of Mental Science*, 102: 1–21.

Trovato, F. and Lalu, N.M. (1996) 'Narrowing Sex Differences in Life Expectancy in the Industrialised World: Early 1970s to Early 1990s', *Social Biology*, 43(1–2): 20–37.

Trudeau, E. Kristal, A.R., Li, S. and Patterson, R.E. (1998) 'Demographic and Psychosocial Predictors of Fruit and Vegetable Intakes Differ: Implications For Dietary Interventions', *Journal of the American Dietary Association*, 12: 1412–17.

Tuinstra, J., Groothoff, J., Van-Den, H., Wim, J. and Post, D. (1998) 'Socio-Economic Differences in Health Risk Behaviour in Adolescence. Do They Exist?', *Social Science and Medicine*, 47(1): 67–74.

Tunstall-Pedoe, H., Woodward, M., Tavendale, R., Brook, R.A. and Mccluskey, M.K. (1997) 'Comparison of the Prediction By 27 Different Risk Factors of Coronary Heart Disease and Death in Men and Women of the Scottish Heart Health Study: Cohort Study', *British Medical Journal*, 315: 722–9.

Turkington, D. and Drummond, D.C. (1988) 'How Should Opiate Withdrawal be Measured?', *Drug and Alcohol Dependence*, 24(2): 151–3.

Tursky, B., Jammer, J.D. and Friedman, R. (1982) 'The Pain Perception Profile: A Psychophysical Approach to the Assessment of Pain Report', *Behaviour Therapy*, 13: 376–94.

Tweedie, R.L. and Mengerson, K.L. (1992) 'Lung Cancer and Passive Smoking: Reconciling the Biochemical and Epidemiological Approaches', *British Journal of Cancer*, 66: 700–5.

Twisk, J.W., Kemper H.C., Mechelen, W. and Post, G.B. (1997) 'Which Lifestyle Parameters Discriminate High from Low-Risk Participants For Coronary Heart Disease Risk Factors. Longitudinal Analysis Covering Adolescence and Young Adulthood', *Journal of Cardiovascular Risk*, 4(5–6): 393–400.

Uchino, B.N., Cacioppo, J.T. and Kiecolt-Glaser, J.K. (1996) 'The Relationship Between Social Support and Psychological Processes: A Review with Emphasis on Underlying Mechanisms and Implications For Health', *Psychological Bulletin*, 119: 488–531.

Unschuld, P. (1986) 'The Conceptual Determination (Uberformung) of Individuals and Collective Experiences of Illness', in C. Currer and M. Stacey (Eds.) *Concepts of Health Illness and Disease*. (Leamington Spa: Berg).

Urba, S. G. (1996) 'Nonpharmacologic Pain Management in Terminal Care', *Clinical Geriatric Medicine* 12: 301–11.

US Department Health and Human Services (1979) 'Smoking and Health. A Report of the Surgeon General', US Government Printing Office, Washington, DC.

US Department Health and Human Services (1988) 'The Health Consequences of Smoking: Nicotine *Addiction*. A Report of the Surgeon General. US Department of Health and Human Services', Maryland.

US Department of Health and Human Services (1989) 'Reducing the Health Consequences of Smoking: 25 Years of Progress', US Government Printing Office. Washington DC.

Ussher, J. (1992) 'Reproductive Rhetoric and the Blaming of the Body', in P. Nicolson and J. Ussher (Eds.) *The Psychology of Women's Health and Health Care*. (London: Macmillan).

Vaidya, S.G., Naik, U.D. and Vaidya, J.S. (1996) 'Effects of Sports Sponsorship By Tobacco Companies on Children's Experimentation with Tobacco', *British Medical Journal*, 313: 400.

Vaillant, G.E. (1996) 'A Long Term Follow-Up of Male Alcohol Abuse', *Archives of General Psychiatry*, 53(3): 243–9.

Valdimarsdottir, H.B. and Bovbjerg, D.H. (1997) 'Positive and Negative Mood: Association with Natural Killer Cell Activity', *Psychology and Health*, 12(3): 319–27.

Van De Mheen, H., Stronks, K., Van Den Bos, J. and Mackenbach, J.P. (1997) 'The Contribution of Childhood Environment to the Explanation of Socioeconomic Inequalities in Health in Adult Life: A Retrospective Study', *Social Science and Medicine*, 44(1): 13–24.

Van Der Doef, M. and Maes, S. (1998) 'The Job Demand-Control (-Support) Model and Physical Health Outcomes: A Review of the Strain and Buffer Hypotheses', *Psychology and Health*, 13(5): 909–36.

Van Der Velde, F., Hookyaas, C. and Van Der Pligt, J. (1992) 'Risk Perception and Behaviour: Pessimism, Realism, and Optimism about AIDS-Related Behaviour', *Psychology and Health*, 6: 23–38.

Van Duijn, C.M. and Hofman, A. (1991) 'Relation Between Nicotine Intake and Alzheimer's Disease', *British Medical Journal*; 302: 1491–4.

Van Praag, E. and Perriens, J.H. (1996) 'Caring For Patients with HIV and AIDS in Middle Income Countries', *British Medical Journal*, 313: 440.

Van Rood, Y., Fgoulmy, E., Blokland, E., Pool, J., Van Rood, J. and Van Houwelingen (1995) 'Stress Related Changes in Immunological and Psychological Variables Induced By the Preparation and Defense of a Phd Thesis', *Psychology and Health*, 10: 229–44.

Vandereycken, W. (1986) 'Anorexia Nervosa and Visual Impairment', *Comprehensive Psychiatry*, 27: 545–8.

Varni, J.W., Rapoff, M.A., Waldron, S.A., Gragg, R.A., Bernstein, B.H., and Lindsley, A. (1996). *Journal of Behavioural Medicine*, 19: 515–28.

Vassend, O., Eskild, A. and Halvorsen, R. (1997) 'Negative Affectivity, Coping, Immune Status, and Disease Progression in

HIV Infected Individuals', *Psychology and Health*, **12**(3): 375–88.

Vassilas, C.A. and Donaldson, J. (1999) 'Few Gps Tell Patients of their Diagnosis of Alzheimer's Disease', *British Medical Journal*, **318**: 536.

Vázquez-Barquero, J.L., Diez-Manrique, F.J., Peña, C., Aldama, J., Samaniego Rodrigues, C., Menéndez Arango, J. and Mirapeix, C. (1987) 'A Community Mental Health Survey in Cantabria: A General Description of Morbidity', *Psychological Medicine*, **17**: 227–41.

Veiel, H.O.F. and Baumann, U. (1992) 'The Many Meanings of Social Support', in H.O.F Veiel and U. Baumann, (Eds.) *The Meaning and Measurement of Social Support*. (New York: Hemisphere).

Velten, E. (1968) 'A Laboratory Task For Induction of Mood States', *Behavioural Research and Therapy*. **6**: 473–82.

Verbrugge, L.M. (1988) 'Unveiling Higher Morbidity For Men', in M.W.Riley and B.J. Huber (Eds.) Social *Structures and Human Lives*. (London: Sage).

Verbrugge, L.M. (1989) 'The Twain Meet: Empirical Explanations of Sex Differences in Health and Mortality', *Journal of Health and Social Behaviour*, **30**: 282.

Verdugo, M.A., Bermejo, B.G. and Fuertes, J. (1995) 'The Maltreatment of Intellectually Handicapped Children and Adolescents', *Child Abuse and Neglect*, **19**: 205–15.

Veroff, J., Douvan, E. and Kulka, R. (1981). *The Inner American*. (New York: Basic).

Vertinsky, P. (1998) '"Run, Jane, Run": Central Tensions in the Current Debate about Enhancing Women's Health Through Exercise', *Women-Health*, **27**(4): 81–111.

Vilato, C., Marini, A., Toews, J., Lockyer, J. and Fidler, H. (1997) 'Feasibility and Psychometric Properties of Using Peers, Consulting Physicians, Co-Workers, and Patients to Assess Physicians', *Academic Medicine*, **72**(10: Suppl 1): S82–S84.

Wadsworth, M. (1986) 'Serious Illness in Childhood and Its Association with Later-Life Achievement', in Wilkinson, R. *Class and Health*. (Tavistock).

Waechter, E. (1971) 'Children's Awareness of Fatal Illness', *American Journal of Nursing*. **7**: 1168–72.

Wahl, O.F. (1987) 'Public vs. Professional Conceptions of Schizophrenia', *Journal of Community Psychology* **15**: 285–91.

Wahl, O.F. (1992) 'Mass Media Images of Mental Illness: A Review of the Literature', *Journal of Community Psychology* **20**: 343–52.

Wahl, O.F. (1993) 'Community Impact of Group Homes For Mentally Ill Adults', *Community Mental Health Journal* **29**(3): 247–59.

Wahl, O.F. and Kaye, A.L. (1991) 'The Impact of John Hinckley's Insanity Plea on Public and Professional Publication', *American Journal of Forensic Psychology* **9**(3): 31–9.

Wahl, O.F. and Kaye, A.L. (1992) 'Mental Illness Topics in Popular Periodicals', *Community Mental Health Journal* **28**(1): 21–8.

Wahl, O.F. and Lefkowits, J.Y. (1989) 'Impact of a Television Film on Attitudes Toward Mental Illness', *American Journal of Community Psychology* **17**(4): 521–8.

Walberg, P., Mckee, M., Shkolnikov, V., Chenet, L. and Leon, D.A. (1998) 'Economic Change, Crime, and Mortality Crisis in Russia: Regional Analysis', *British Medical Journal*, **317**: 312–18.

Wald N.J., Nanchahal K., Thompson, S.G. and Cuckle, H.S. (1986) 'Does Breathing Other People's Tobacco Smoke Cause Lung Cancer? *British Medical Journal*, **293**: 1217.

Waldron, I. (1976) 'Why do Women Live Longer Than Men? *Journal of Human Stress*, **2**: 1–13.

Walker, L.G. and Eremin, O. (1995) 'Psychoneuroimmunology: A New Fad Or the Fifth Cancer Treatment Modality', *The American Journal of Surgery*, **170**: 2–4.

Wall, S. (1997) 'The Development of Referrals and Diagnoses of Children and Adolescents with Attention Deficit Hyperactivity Disorder (ADHD) and Behavioural Problems During a Twenty Year Period (1977–97)', M.Sc Dissertation. University of Westminster, London.

Wallace, L.M. (1998) 'Consultancy in Health Psychology: An NHS CEO's Views', *Health Psychology Update*, **34**: 42–7.

Wallin, U., Roijen, S and Hansson, K. (1996) 'Too Close Or Too Separate: Family Function in Families with an Anorexia Nervosa Patient in Two Nordic Countries', *Journal of Family Therapy*. **18**(4) 397–414.

Wannamethee, G. and Shaper, A.G. (1988) 'Changes in Drinking Habits in Middle-Aged British Men', *Journal of the Royal College of General Practitioners*, **38**: 440–2.

Wannamethee, G. and Shaper, A.G. (1988) 'Men Who do Not Drink: A Report from the British Regional Heart Study', *International Journal of Epidemiology*, **17**(2): 307–16.

Wardhaugh, J. and Wilding, P. (1993) 'Towards an Explanation of the Corruption of Care', *Critical Social Policy*, **13**: 4–31.

Ware, J.E. (1990) 'Measuring Patient Function and Well-Being: Some Lessons from the Medical Outcomes Study', in K.A. Heithoff and K.N. Lohr (Eds) *Effectiveness and Outcomes in Health Care*. (Washington D.C.: National Academy Press).

Ware, J.E. and Sherbourne, C.D. (1992) 'The SF-36 Short Form Health Status Survey: 1. Conceptual Framework and Item Selection', *Medical Care*, **30**(6) 473–83.

Ware, J.E. Jnr and Gandek, B. (1994) 'The SF-36 Health Survey: Development and Use in Mental Health Research and the IQOLA Project', *International Journal of Mental Health*, **23**(2): 49–73.

Ware, J.E. Jr and Snyder, M.K. (1975) 'Dimensions of Patient Attitudes Regarding Doctors and Medical Care Services', *Medical Care*, **13**(8), 669–82.

Ware, J.E., Snow, K.K., Kosinski, M. and Gandek, B. (1993) *SF-36 Health Survey: Manual and Interpretation Guide*. (Boston, MA: The Health Institute, New England Medical Center).

Warren, L. and Hixenbaugh, P. (1996) 'The Role of Knowledge and Health Professional Support in Adaptation and Adherence', paper presented at the 10th European Health Psychology Conference, Dublin, Ireland.

Waters, J. and Thomas, V. (1995) 'Pain from Sickle-Cell Crisis', *Nursing Times*, **91**(16): 29–31.

Watten, R.G. (1997) 'Gender and Consumption of Alcohol: The Impact of Body Composition, Sensation Seeking and Coping Styles', *British Journal of Health Psychology*, **2**: 15–25.

Wearden, A., Morriss, R., Mullis, R., Strickland, P., Pearson, D., Appleby, L., Campbell, I.And Morris, J. (1998) 'Randomised, Double-Blind, Placebo-Controlled Treatment Trial of Fluoxetine and Graded Exercise For Chronic Fatigue Syndrome', *British Journal of Psychiatry*, **172**(6): 485–90.

Weathgerall, D.J. (1997) 'ABC of Clinical Haematology. The Hereditary Anaemias', *British Medical Journal*, **314**(7079): 492–6.

Wechsler, D. (1986) *Wechsler Adult Intelligence Scale: Revised UK Edition (WAIS-R UK)*. (Sidcup: Psychological Corporation).

Weidner, G. (1998) 'The Gender Gap: Why do Women Have Less Heart Disease Than Men?', 12th European *Health Psychology* Congress. Vienna.

Weil, C.M. (1988) 'Hassles, Social Supports, Symptoms and Alcohol Involvement. Their Interaction in Young Alcoholic and Non-Alcoholic Families', *Dissertation Abstracts International*, 49: 922–3.

Weinberger, M., Ferguson, J.A., Westmoreland, G., Mamlin, L.A., Segar, D.S., Eckert, G.J., Greene, J.Y., Martin, D.K. and Tierney, W.M. (1998) 'Can Raters Consistently Evaluate the Content of Focus Groups?', *Social Science and Medicine*, 46: 929–33.

Weinman, J. (1990) 'Providing Written Information For Patients: Psychological Consequences', *Journal of the Royal Society of Medicine*, 83: 303–5.

Weisenberg, M., Raz, T. and Hener, T. (1998) 'The Influence of Film-Induced Mood on Pain Perception', *Pain* 76: 365–75.

Weisenberg, M., Tepper, I. and Schwarzwald, J. (1995) 'Humor as a Cognitive Technique For Increasing Pain Tolerance', *Pain* 63: 207–12.

Welch, R., Boorman, S., Golding, J.F., Towell, T. and Roberts, R. (1999) 'Variations in Health By Occupational Grade in the British Post Office: The Q-Health Project', *Occupational Medicine*, 49(8): 491–7.

Wenneker, M.B. and Epstein, A.M. (1989) 'Racial Inequalities in the Use of Procedures for Patients with Ischemic Heart Disease in Massachusetts', *Journal of the American Medical Association*, 261(2), 253–7.

Wertheim. E.H., Paxton, S., Maude, D., Szmukler, G., Gibbons, K., and Hiller, L. (1992) 'Psychosocial Predictors of Weight Loss Behaviours and Binge Eating in Adolescent Girls and Boys', *International Journal of Eating Disorders.* 12: 2: 151–60.

West, P., Ford, G., Hunt, K., Mcintyre, S. and Ecob, R. (1994) 'How Sick Is the West of Scotland? Age Specific Comparisons with National Datasets on a Range of Health Measures', *Scottish Medical Journal*, 39: 101.

Westcott, H. (1993) Quoted in Cross, M., Gordon, R., Kennedy, M. and Marchant, R. (1993) 'The ABCD Pack. Abuse and Children Who are Disabled', Department of Health.

Westcott, H. and Cross, M. (1996) *This Far and No Further: Toward Ending the Abuse of Disabled Children*. Venture Press. Birmingham.

Westcott, H.L. and Jones, D.P.H (1999) 'The Abuse of Disabled Children', *Journal of Child Psychology and Psychiatry and Allied Disciplines*, 40(4): 497–506.

Whiffen, V.E. (1992) 'Is Postpartum Depression a Distinct Diagnosis?', *Clinical Psychology Review*, 12: 485–508.

While, D., Kelly, S., Huang, W. and Charlton, A. (1996) 'Cigarette Advertising and Onset of Smoking in Children: Questionnaire Survey', *British Medical Journal*, 313: 398–9.

White, C. (1997) 'BMA Urges Coordinated National Strategy For Care of Drug Misusers', *British Medical Journal*, 315: 7–12

Whitehead, M. (1987) *The Health Divide*. (London: Health Education Council).

Whitehead, M. (1995) 'Evidenced-Based Health Education', *Health Education Journal*, 55: 1–2.

Whitehead, M. and Diderichsen, F. (1997) 'International Evidence on Social Inequalities in Health', in M.Whitehead and F.Drever (Eds.) *Health Inequalities*. Office of National Statistics. London.

Wicklund, I., Sanne, H., Vendin, A. and Wilhelmsson, C. (1984) 'Psychosocial Outcome One Year After a First Myocardial Infarction', *Journal of Psychosomatic Research*, 28: 309–21.

Wilkinson, R. (1986) *Class and Health*. Tavistock.

Wilkinson, R. (1996a) 'How Can Secular Improvements in Life Expectancy be Explained?', in D. Blane, E. Brunner and R. Wilkinson (Eds.) *Health and Social Organisation: Towards a Health Policy For the 21st Century*. (London: Routledge).

Wilkinson, R. (1996b) *Unhealthy Societies*. (London: Routledge).

Wilkinson, R.G. (1992) 'Income Distribution and Life Expectancy', *British Medical Journal*, 304: 165–8.

Williams, C., Milton, J., Strickland, P., Ardagh-Walter, N., Knapp, J., Wilson, S., Trigwell, P., Feldman, E. and Sims, A.C.P. (1997) 'Impact of Medical School Teaching on Pre-registration House Officers' Confidence in Assessing and Managing Common Psychological Morbidity: Three Centre Study', *British Medical Journal*, 315: 917–18.

Williams, S. and Calnan, M. (1991) 'Convergence and Divergence: Assessing Criteria of Consumer Satisfaction across General Practice, Dental and Hospital Care Settings', *Social Science and Medicine*, 33, 707–16.

Wilson, E., Wardle, E.V., Chandel, P. and Walford, S. (1993) 'Diabetes Education: An Asian Perspective', *Diabetic Medicine*, 10(2): 177–80.

Wilson, M. (1995) 'Infectious Diseases', *British Medical Journal*, 311: 1681–4.

Wilson, P. (1980) 'Drinking Habits in the United Kingdom', *Population Trends*, 22: 14.

Wise, J. (1998) 'Very Low Fat Diets May Harm Some People', *British Medical Journal*, 316: 571.

Wolfson, M., Kaplan, Lynch, J., Ross, N. and Backlund, E. (1999) 'Relation Between Income Inequality and Mortality: Empirical Demonstration', *British Medical Journal*, 319: 953–7.

Wood, W., Rhodes, N., and Whelan, M. (1989) 'Sex Differences in Positive Well-Being: A Consideration of Emotional Style and Marital Status', *Psychological Bulletin*, 106: 249–164.

Woodrow, P. (1998) 'Interventions For Confusion and Dementia. 3: Reminiscence', *British Journal of Nursing*, 7(19): 1145–9.

Wooley, H., Stein, A., Forrest, G. and Baum, J. (1989) 'Imparting the Diagnosis of Life Threatening Illness in Children', *British Medical Journal*, 298: 1623–6.

World Health Organisation (1946) 'World Health Organisation Constitution'. (Geneva: WHO).

World Health Organisation (1980) 'International Classification of Impairments, Disabilities and Handicaps'. (Geneva: WHO).

World Health Organisation (1987) 'Measurement in *Health Promotion* and Protection', WHO. Regional Publications, European Series No.22.

World Health Organisation (1999a) 'Weekly Epidemiological Record (WER)', 74: 401–8.

World Health Organisation (1999b) 'World Health Report 1999'. (Geneva: WHO).

Wren, B. (1998) 'Consultancy in Health Psychology: An Introduction', *Health Psychology* Update, 34: 39–41.

Wright, D.B. (1997) *Understanding Statistics*. (London: Sage).

Wright, L., Harwood, D. and Coulter, A. (1992) 'Health and Lifestyles in the Oxford Region', *Oxford Health Services Research Unit*.

Wright, M. and Rodway, M. (1988) 'Sexually Transmitted Diseases: Psychosocial Parameters and Implications For Social

Work Practice', *Journal of Social Work and Human Sexuality*, **6**(2): 21–35.

Yardley, L. (1999) 'Advantages of a Material-Discursive Approach to Health', 13th Conference of the European *Health Psychology* Society. Florence.

Yarnold, P.R., Michelson, E.A., Thompson, D.A. and Adams, S.L. (1998) 'Predicting Patient Satisfaction: A Study of Two Emergency Departments', *Journal of Behavioural Medicine*, **21**(6): 545–63.

Yehuda, R. and McFarlane, A.C. (1995) 'Conflict Between Current Knowledge about Posttraumatic Stress Disorder and Its Original Conceptual Basis', *American Journal of Psychiatry*, **152**: 1705–13.

Yehuda, R., Schmeidler, J., Siever, L.J., Binder Brynes, K, and Elkin, A. (1997) 'Individual Differences in Posttraumatic Stress Disorder Symptom Profiles in Holocaust Survivors in Concentration Camps Or in Hiding', *Journal of Trauma Stress*, **10**(3): 453–63.

Ziebland, S., Fitzpatrick, R. and Jenkinson, C. (1993) 'Tacit Models of Disability Underlying Health Status Instruments', *Social Science and Medicine*, **37**: 69–75.

Zigmond, A.S. and Snaith, R.P. (1983) 'The Hospital Anxiety and Depression Scale', Acta Psychiatrica *Scandinavica*, **67**: 361–70.

Zimbardo, P.G., Ebbesen, E.B., and Maslach, C. (1977) *Influencing Attitudes and Changing Behavior* (2nd Edition) (Reading, MA: Addison-Wesley).

Zucker, K.J., Bradley, S.J. and Sanikhani, M. (1997) 'Sex Differences in Referral Rates of Children with Gender Identity Disorder: Some Hypotheses', *Journal of Abnormal Child Psychology*, **25**(3): 217–27.

Author Index

Subject Index